Anthony E. Henry · **Understanding Strategic Management**

Second Edition

Anthony E. Henry

Understanding Strategic Management

Second Edition

OXFORD
UNIVERSITY PRESS

OXFORD

UNIVERSITY PRESS

Great Clarendon Street, Oxford OX2 6DP

Oxford University Press is a department of the University of Oxford.
It furthers the University's objective of excellence in research, scholarship,
and education by publishing worldwide in

Oxford New York

Auckland Cape Town Dar es Salaam Hong Kong Karachi
Kuala Lumpur Madrid Melbourne Mexico City Nairobi
New Delhi Shanghai Taipei Toronto

With offices in

Argentina Austria Brazil Chile Czech Republic France Greece
Guatemala Hungary Italy Japan Poland Portugal Singapore
South Korea Switzerland Thailand Turkey Ukraine Vietnam

Oxford is a registered trade mark of Oxford University Press
in the UK and in certain other countries

Published in the United States
by Oxford University Press Inc., New York

British Library Cataloguing in Publication Data

Data available

Library of Congress Cataloging in Publication Data
Library of Congress Control Number: 2010941698

Typeset by Graphicraft Limited, Hong Kong
Printed in Great Britain on acid-free paper by Ashford Colour Press Ltd

ISBN 978–0–19–958161–0

9 10 8

To my wife Sue, Max and Isabel

'and you shall know the truth, and the truth shall set you free.'
John 8:32

Brief Contents

Detailed Contents

PART THREE Strategy Formulation

PART FOUR Strategy Implementation

List of Cases

PART FOUR **Strategy Implementation**

Acknowledgements

I owe a debt of thanks to all the contributors to the field of strategic management. At Oxford University Press, I would like to thank all those involved with the production of this book. I would like to extend a special thank you to Alexandra Lazarus-Priestley, also Hannah Brannon, Claire Brewer, Fiona Goodall, and Philippa Hendry. My foremost thanks go to my wife Sue, for her patience, encouragement, and support.

Every effort has been made to trace and contact copyright holders but this has not been possible in every case. If notified, the publisher will undertake to rectify any errors or omissions at the earliest opportunity.

About the Author

Anthony Henry is a former university Senior Lecturer in Strategic Management. In developing and teaching strategy modules over several years, he has gained a deep understanding of students' needs, as well as insights into how a textbook can be a powerful tool in aiding successful teaching.

Prior to joining the university sector Anthony worked as a Market Analyst for HSBC in central London. He has experience working in both public and private sector organizations including Arthur Andersen. He has also counted traffic for a firm of transport consultants, worked in a soap factory, and taught strategy in the UK and Germany to managers from around the globe working for a FTSE 250 organization. Anthony is a senior manager for a large medical centre.

About the Book

The aim of the first edition of *Understanding Strategic Management* was to help those on modular courses better understand strategic management by clearly explaining strategy concepts, then analysing and evaluating them to show how these are applied in the business world. This approach encouraged students to apply their own critical faculties because rather than simply describing strategic concepts, models, and frameworks, these were explained and also critiqued. Juxtaposing alternative concepts and frameworks with those being discussed enabled readers to see for themselves how the analytical process is undertaken when evaluating different strategic concepts. The separation of analysis, formulation, and implementation, referred to as the *strategic management process*, continues. However, as is constantly alluded to throughout the book, organizations seldom engage in analysis before graduating to formulation and implementation in a linear fashion.

We used the pursuit of *sustainable competitive advantage* as a key theme throughout the first edition. The second edition continues this tradition. This is not slavishly followed but rather tempered by experience which suggests that increasingly turbulent markets mean that any competitive advantage achieved by an organization may only ever be ephemeral. Since the first edition was written we have experienced a global financial crisis. The second edition covers the global financial crisis in detail. In Chapter 12 we explain why the global financial crisis occurred, the failure of financial institutions and regulatory frameworks to prevent it, and the solutions proposed which may alter the frequency of its occurrence. We also discuss the impact of globalization in greater detail in Chapter 9 using a new, larger case study to show the impact globalization can have on individuals.

In the second edition more than half of all the Case Studies have been completely changed to keep the cases relevant and up to date with changes in the business world. More questions have been added to these and every other Case Study to aid student learning and understanding. We have also extended the length of Case Studies to help students more clearly understand concepts covered in the main text. Where it was felt a new strategy focus would better help the reader's understanding of a particular strategic concept the strategy focus has been changed. At the end of each chapter all the Review Questions have been changed to further aid student learning and understanding. In addition, Research Topics and Discussion Questions have been updated.

To help readers grasp concepts more readily the Key Work icons contained in the text have been substantially increased. This allows students to expand on key concepts discussed in the text by accessing more material in the Online Resource Centre. The second edition introduces Tools and Techniques—where it is felt that certain concepts would benefit from a worked example and greater explanation. These are provided in the Online Resource Centre. As with Key Work, the Tools and Techniques are clearly signposted in the main text. Also new to the second edition are five Case Studies that have been included in the Online Resource Centre; this benefits student understanding without compromising the modular structure of the textbook.

Anthony E. Henry
August 2010

How to use this book

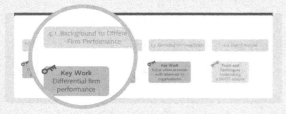

A 'Chapter Map' at the start of each chapter shows which topics are covered in the chapter and signposts additional material on the Online Resource Centre to aid navigation of the text.

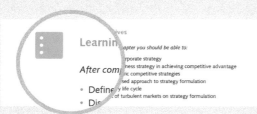

Learning Objectives display the learning outcomes that students are expected to achieve after completing each chapter. This helps students to focus their learning, and evaluate their knowledge and understanding of each chapter.

INTANGIBLE RESOURCES ...ngible resources comprise intellectual/technological resources and reputation. ...logical resources include an organization's ability to innovate and the speed may be embedded in routin... ...ich innovation occurs. Intellectual resources include patents and copyrights practices that have develope... ...emselves may derive from the organization's technological resources. For over time within the organiz... ...ovation of its founder, James Dyson, which competitors have been unable They include an organization... ...ssfully imitate. Organizations with valuable tacit knowledge built up through reputation, its culture, its ... ...ulture, processes, and employees possess an intangible resource which cannot knowledge, and its brand... ...ly be transferred.

The reputation or 'goodwill' of an organization is increasingly recognized as a valu-able intangible asset which can easily be damaged by ill-thought-out strategies and marketing campaigns. Some organizations, such as Benetton, have made a point of

Key Terms are highlighted and defined when they first appear in the text, and are also collated in a page referenced glossary at the end of the book to enable you to locate definitions quickly.

Strategy Focus are short illustrations taken from a range of sources, included throughout the book. These relate the concepts being discussed to actual situations in the business world so you can see theory in practice.

Case Studies apply the theory being discussed in each chapter to real life business situations. Each case study includes Questions that help you to assess your understanding of the material covered in the chapter.

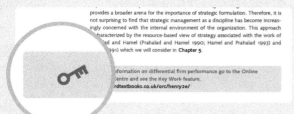

Key Work signposts where additional detail on a particular topic is provided on the book's Online Resource Centre.

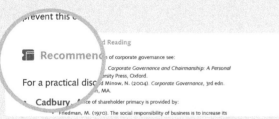

Tools and Techniques signposts where a worked example and explanation on a certain concept are provided on the Online Resource Centre, to help you delve deeper into the topic.

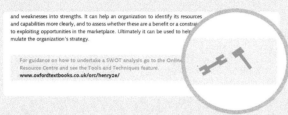

Recommended Readings have been provided as a guide to help you broaden your understanding of the topics covered in each chapter.

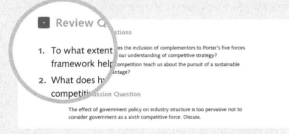

Review and Discussion Questions at the end of each chapter help you to assess what you have learned and provide you with the opportunity for discussion. **Research Topics** allow you to gain a deeper understanding of the concepts and frameworks covered in each chapter by undertaking focussed research of specific issues.

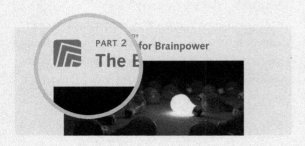

End of Part Case Studies and Questions are designed to reinforce your knowledge of concepts covered in each Part.

How to use the Online Resource Centre

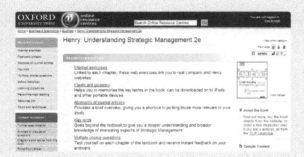

www.oxfordtextbooks.co.uk/orc/henry2e/

For students

Multiple Choice Questions

Each chapter is accompanied by multiple choice questions you can complete online. These self-marking questions include instant feedback on your answers and cross-references back to the textbook, to assist with independent study.

Key Work

In each chapter you will find a reference to Key Work on a particular topic with additional detail online. This coverage gives you a deeper understanding and broader knowledge of interesting aspects of Strategic Management.

Tools and Techniques

This feature offers additional coverage of quantitative or analytical tools and techniques to help you gain a deeper understanding of topics.

Flashcard Glossary

Glossary terms presented in an interactive flashcard format to help you revise key terms and concepts.

Resource Box

An ideal tool for starting research for an essay or project, this one-stop-shop provides a comprehensive list of resources, websites, and material you will find useful for further study in Strategic Management.

Internet Exercises

For each chapter, these web exercises link you to company and news websites where you can find the answers to the exercise questions. This is a fun and interesting way to broaden your knowledge and understanding of Strategic Management in the real world as well as sharpening your online research skills.

Abstracts of Journal Articles

Reading and using journals is an important skill for all students, but the vast array of articles can be daunting. These short précis of pertinent articles provide a brief overview, giving you a shortcut to picking those most relevant to your study.

For registered adopters of the textbook

Preparing your course

PowerPoint slides
A suite of fully customizable PowerPoint slides has been included for use in lecturer presentations to save preparation time. Downloadable by chapter and picking out the key points from each topic, these also make useful class handouts.

Diagrams and Tables
The diagrams and tables from the book are available to download to use as handouts or to customize your own presentations.

Revision and exams

Test Bank
A ready-made assessment tool with which to test your students' understanding of Strategic Management. Twenty questions per chapter are provided in a variety of question styles, with automated feedback and grading, and can be imported into your university's Virtual Learning Environment.

During your course

Answers to Discussion Questions
Each chapter ends with a question raised for class discussion, and these suggested answers highlight key points that students could consider in their debate.

Case Studies
A further collection of interesting and topical case studies are available to download for use in tutorials or assessments. Accompanied by questions, each highlights a key concept from the textbook and is drawn from a news article focussing on a well-known organization.

Business » Henry: Understanding Strategic Management » Lecturer resources » Additional case studies

Henry: Understanding Strategic Management

Additional case studies

A collection of interesting and topical case studies are available to download for use in tutorials or assessments. Accompanied by questions, each highlights a key concept from the textbook and is drawn from a news article focussing on a well-known organization. Click on the links below to access the cases studies.

Corporate Social Responsibility: Wal-mart and global warming [PDF, 33.4kB]

Questions to consider:

- How can Wal-mart manage the problem of global warming?
- Has the ability to dramatically reduce the carbon footprint become a threshold competence or can it be used as a basis of differentiation?

Managing strategic change: Boden and technological change [PDF, 29.8kB]

Questions to consider:

- Why did Boden seem to misjudge the need for better I.T systems?

1 What is Strategy?

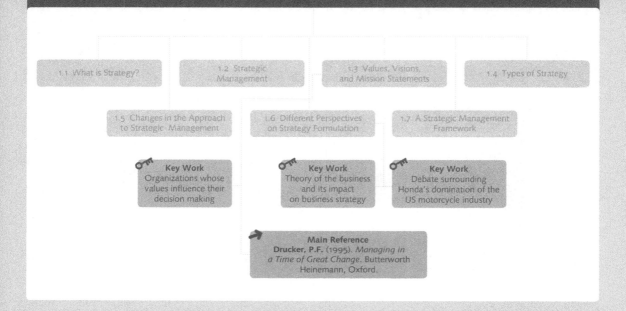

| 1.1 What is Strategy? | 1.2 Strategic Management | 1.3 Values, Visions, and Mission Statements | 1.4 Types of Strategy |

| 1.5 Changes in the Approach to Strategic Management | 1.6 Different Perspectives on Strategy Formulation | 1.7 A Strategic Management Framework |

Key Work
Organizations whose values influence their decision making

Key Work
Theory of the business and its impact on business strategy

Key Work
Debate surrounding Honda's domination of the US motorcycle industry

Main Reference
Drucker, P.F. (1995). *Managing in a Time of Great Change*. Butterworth Heinemann, Oxford.

 ## Learning Objectives

After completing this chapter you should be able to:

- Explain what is meant by strategy
- Describe a strategic management process
- Discuss the role of values, vision, and mission statements
- Explain what is meant by a theory of the business
- Evaluate different perspectives on strategy formulation
- Explain the linkages between an organization's strategy and its external and internal environment

 ## Introduction

What is strategy? How is strategy formulated and implemented? Are values important in determining which markets organizations seek to compete in? These are some of the questions that will be discussed in this first chapter. We start the chapter with a discussion of what strategy is. There is general agreement that the purpose of strategy is to help organizations achieve a sustainable competitive advantage. Where this consensus begins to break down is when we discuss *how* this should be achieved. We can identify two broad perspectives that we can call the *rationalist* or *positioning* approach, and the *resource-based view* of strategy. Each of these perspectives will be evaluated in greater detail in subsequent chapters. For now, we will simply introduce these perspectives and some of their chief protagonists when we address different approaches to strategy formulation.

This chapter also looks at a strategic management process which includes strategy analysis, formulation, and implementation. We note that this essentially linear framework is very useful for exposition but has limitations when seeking to explain strategy in practice. The role of an organization's values, vision, and mission is explained as we discuss their importance in setting strategic goals, and the role of strategy in achieving these goals. We address an organization's assumptions about its competitive environment or its theory of the business and discuss how they can lead to organizational failure. We end the chapter with a discussion of a strategic management framework which will be useful for navigating subsequent chapters.

- Section 1.1 explains what strategy is and discusses some of its military antecedents.
- Section 1.2 deals with the strategic management process which explains strategy analysis, strategy formulation, and strategy implementation.
- In Section 1.3 we discuss the impact of an organization's values, vision, and mission in guiding decision making and employees' behaviour. A theory of the business is also discussed.
- Section 1.4 briefly discusses different types of strategy. These include corporate strategy, business strategy, and functional strategy.
- In Section 1.5 we look at the different approaches to strategic management and the changes that have taken place.
- Section 1.6 evaluates two different perspectives on strategy formulation: the positioning or design school, and the learning school.
- The chapter concludes with a strategic management framework which explains the linkages between an organization's internal and external environment, its strategy, and its stakeholders.

1.1 What is Strategy?

The use of strategy has existed for many centuries although its use in management has a more recent history, dating back about forty years. Strategy was born out of military conflicts and the use of a superior strategy enabled one warring party to defeat another. Von Clausewitz, writing in the nineteenth century, states that the decision to wage war ought to be *rational*, that is, based on estimates of what can be gained and the costs incurred by the war (von Clausewitz 1982). War should also be *instrumental*, that is, waged to achieve some specific goal, never for its own sake, and that strategy should be directed to achieve one end, in this case, victory. While policy makers may be unsure about what they expect from modern military engagements, military personnel from commander down to foot soldier all know to ask one question: what is our objective in committing to a particular course of action? If the goal or objective is unclear they can expect the formulation of strategy to be disjointed and its implementation to be unsuccessful.

In *The Art of War*, the Chinese philosopher and insightful military strategist Sun Tzu wrote:

> the one who figures on victory at headquarters before even doing battle is the one who has the most strategic factors on his side. The one who figures on inability to prevail at headquarters before doing battle is the one with the least strategic factors on his side . . . Observing the matter in this way, I can see who will win and who will lose. (See Hawkins and Rajagopal 2005)

We need to exercise caution in drawing military analogies. Unlike military conflicts where might, power, and strength of numbers often determine the outcome, strategy is more subtle. As Sun Tzu notes, battles are often won in the mind long before enemy forces engage. In the modern business arena organizations are increasingly aware of the benefits of cooperation as well as competition.

There is agreement that the role of strategy is to achieve *competitive advantage* for an organization. Competitive advantage may usefully be thought of as that which allows an organization to meet consumers' needs better than its rivals. Its source may derive from a number of factors including its products or services, its culture, its technological know-how, and its processes. To be sustainable, however, the competitive advantage must be difficult for competitors to imitate. As Henderson (1989) astutely points out, 'Your most dangerous competitors are those that are most like you. The differences between you and your competitors are the basis of your advantage'.

The use of strategy in decision making is the primary way in which managers take account of a constantly changing external environment. An effective strategy allows them to use their organization's resources and capabilities to exploit opportunities and limit threats in the external environment. A debate arises when we try to pin down *what is strategy* and, importantly, *how is strategy formulated*? This discussion has continued unabated for decades and is rooted in a desire for managers to undertake better strategic thinking and therefore better strategic decisions.

Strategy can be defined in a number of different ways. We should be aware that any definition is likely to be rooted within the different perspectives adopted by its authors. For this reason a definition of strategy, which is accepted by everyone, is not as straightforward as might first appear. As individuals we all devise strategies to help us achieve certain goals or objectives. For instance, consider a couple on a long journey with two young children under five in the back of the car. Do they set off early because this will beat the traffic congestion and make sense because the toddlers rise early? Or do they leave in the evening at the children's bedtime when they will hopefully sleep for the entire journey, giving Mum and Dad a much-needed break? Do they take the main roads in the hope of cutting the journey time but with the downside of congestion, or take less travelled roads which avoid traffic jams but may take longer? What this emphasizes is that strategy is all about choice. At the organizational level the choices are far more complex.

In an article entitled 'What is strategy?', Porter (1996) asserts that 'competitive strategy is about being different. It means deliberately choosing a different set of activities to deliver a unique mix of value'. Markides (1999a) argues that the essence of strategy is for an organization to select one strategic position that it can claim as its own. A strategic position represents a company's answers to the following questions:

- *Who* should the company target as customers?
- *What* products or services should the company offer the targeted customers?
- *How* can the company do this efficiently?

In this way a company can achieve success by choosing a strategic position which differs from the competitors in its industry. Kay (1993) sees the strategy of an organization as 'the match between its internal capabilities and its external relationships', that is, the match between what an organization is particularly capable of doing and its relationships with its stakeholders: employees, customers, shareholders, and suppliers. Strategy is about the firm using analytical techniques to help it understand, and therefore influence, its position in the market.

The organization is faced with a constantly changing external environment and needs to ensure that its own internal resources and capabilities are more than sufficient to meet the needs of the external environment. Organizations do not exist simply to survive in the marketplace but want to grow and prosper in a competitive environment. In order to make sense of what is going on around them, firms must undertake an analysis of their external and internal environment.

An organization's external environment comprises the general environment and the competitive environment. The general or macro-environment consists of factors which may not have an immediate impact on the firm but have the capacity to change the industry in which the firm competes and even create new industries. The competitive environment deals with the industry in which the firm competes. For an organization to prosper it needs to achieve a competitive advantage over its competitors in the industry. Changes within an organization's competitive environment, such as an increase in the number of competitors, will have a far more immediate impact on the organization. The tools of analysis for analysing the external environments are considered in detail in **Chapters 2** and **3**. In contrast, the internal environment of the organization deals with the organization itself. It includes its values, goals, resources and capabilities, and internal structure. The values that the firm embodies will guide its choice and implementation of strategic goals, and how it deals with crises (see Strategy Focus on Johnson & Johnson). We will consider some tools of analysis for analysing the internal environment of the organization in **Chapters 4** and **5**.

1.2 Strategic Management

If a strategy allows an organization to match its resources and capabilities to the needs of the external environment in order to achieve competitive advantage, the process of bringing about the strategy is strategic management. All organizations set goals they want to achieve. Strategic management is about analysing the situation facing the firm, and on the basis of this analysis formulating a strategy and finally implementing that strategy. The end result is for the organization to achieve competitive advantage over its rivals in the industry. A point worth noting is that these elements are co-dependent, that is, in formulating a strategy an organization must also consider how that strategy will be implemented. Failure to consider these issues in tandem will decrease the likelihood of success. We might also note that this neat sequential pattern may not resemble how a given organization might undertake strategic management. Figure 1.1 illustrates that each part of the strategic management process is interdependent. Analysis, formulation, and implementation all need to be considered if the organization's strategy is to meet the needs of its environment effectively.

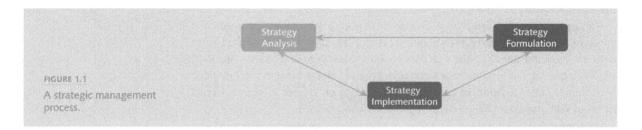

FIGURE 1.1

A strategic management process.

For example, some organizations might actually implement a strategy without fully analysing their current situation. This may be because events in their industry are changing so fast that they feel they simply do not have the luxury of undertaking detailed analysis. An organization's leader might take a series of decisions based on experience or intuition. In reality, without the use of some analysis the organization will never know if its strategy succeeds, and why it succeeds. It will not fully understand how it meets the industry's key success factors. Key success factors are those elements in the industry that keep customers loyal and allow the organization to compete successfully. By analysing what consumers want and the basis of competition in the industry, an organization is able to ascertain the key success factors for its

KEY SUCCESS FACTORS

elements in the industry which keep customers loyal and allow the organization to compete successfully industry. For instance, it might ask: Which elements of its resources and capabilities brought it success? What was the role played by its internal structure and organizational culture? What factors drive competition in this industry? In short, without analysis its success will likely be short-lived and difficult to repeat.

1.2.1 Strategy Analysis

This is also referred to as situation analysis. Whilst bearing in mind that the strategic management process is co-dependent, the undertaking of strategy analysis by the organization is a useful starting point. As we shall see in **Chapters 2** and **3**, this involves an analysis of the general environment and the competitive environment. Strategy analysis also deals with the organization's internal environment. It allows the organization to evaluate how well it is positioned to exploit the opportunities in its external environment.

1.2.2 Strategy Formulation

A careful analysis of the firm's internal environment and the needs of the external environment will allow the firm to assess where it can best achieve a strategic fit between the two. Without some form of analysis decisions can only be based on experience. Experience alone may have been fine in the stable industries of the 1960s, but in today's turbulent environments an organization cannot expect to follow today's patterns tomorrow. Mintzberg (1994) reminds us that strategy formulation also occurs as a creative and, at times, subconscious act which synthesizes experiences to form a novel strategy. Ohmae (1984) accepts that strategic thinking starts with analysis but stresses creative insight in the formulating of great strategies. Such insight does not form part of any conscious analysis.

Markides (1999b) argues that 'effective strategic design is a process of continuously asking questions . . . correctly formulating the questions is often more important than finding a solution'. Ohmae (1984) makes a similar point. He states that a vital part of strategic thinking is to formulate questions in a way that will help find a solution. A key part of strategy formulation is strategy evaluation which recognizes that an organization is seldom faced with one strategy but requires a criterion to judge competing strategies. We will return to some of these points later when we evaluate different perspectives on strategy formulation. Strategy formulation primarily takes place at two different levels within the organization: the *business level* and the *corporate level*. The different types of strategy are briefly discussed in **Chapter 5**, Introduction. Business- and corporate-level strategies are addressed in detail in **Chapters 7** and **8**. For now we can say that business-level strategy deals with *how* an organization competes in its chosen markets, whereas corporate strategy deals with the fundamental question of *what* business (or businesses) we want to be in.

1.2.3 Strategy Implementation

The best formulated strategy in the world will amount to nothing if it is poorly communicated throughout the organization and incorrectly implemented. Effective implementation of strategies requires the organization to be sufficiently flexible in its organizational structure and design. Strategies need to be communicated, understood, and properly coordinated with stakeholders inside and outside the organization. In an age of collaboration, this may involve discussions with suppliers and partners. Although the leader of an organization will ultimately be responsible for a strategy's success or failure, their role should be to encourage and create an organizational culture which empowers managers to respond to opportunities. In this way each employee will be confident to try out new ideas and innovate without fear of reprisals. The values of an organization will be important here.

At a fundamental level we can ask: What is the purpose of any organization? Why does it exist? These questions are relevant irrespective of whether an organization operates in the private or public sector since all organizations must have a clear sense of direction based upon agreed objectives if they are to understand what they are seeking to achieve. If, for example, organizations in the private sector seek to maximize returns to shareholders whilst taking account of stakeholder expectations, and likewise firms in the public sector seek to utilize their resources in an optimal manner, strategy is simply the way in which an organization bridges the gap between its stated goals and how it intends to achieve them. Often purpose and goals are used interchangeably, but this misses an important distinction between the two: the goals that an organization sets derive from its purpose. This will become clearer as we look at the purpose or *raison d'être* of organizations and how this has guided their strategy.

1.3 Values, Visions, and Mission Statements

VISION

is often associated with the founder of an organization and represents a desired state that the organization aspires to achieve in the future

A **vision** is often associated with the founder of an organization and represents a desired state that the organization aspires to achieve in the future. In contrast with goals and objectives, a vision does not change over time. A vision must tap into the personal goals and values of the organization's employees if it is to be internalized by them. When it bears little resemblance to reality, disregards the capabilities of the organization and the problems of the organization, it will be rejected by employees. Employees will also reject a vision where they see a credibility gap between managers' rhetoric and their actions. The prerequisite for producing a vision is not great intellect but imagination, intuition, and an ability to synthesize disparate information.

A vision may or may not find its expression in a *vision statement* (Lipton 1996). The length and complexity of vision statements differ between organizations, but clearly they must be easy to understand and remember.

An organization's mission seeks to answer the question why an organization exists. A *mission statement* can be defined as a way in which the organization communicates the business it is in to the outside world. Drucker (1995) argues that a mission statement is the same as asking the question: What business are we in? A mission statement needs to appeal to a broad spectrum of stakeholders if all these stakeholders are to accept it. In this respect, a mission statement which simply exhorts the need to maximize shareholder value will be unlikely to motivate employees. It is not unusual, particularly in the public sector, for organizations to have mission statements at different levels ranging from a department all the way down to individual teams. If these statements are to guide employee behaviour, then it would seem that two conditions are necessary: (1) such statements are communicated clearly to all employees; (2) those employees internalize these statements and use them to direct their behaviour. The use of these statements may constitute a necessary but not sufficient condition for organizational success. At some point we might ask what actually is being accomplished as a result of vision and mission statements.

Campbell *et al.* (1990) make a distinction between an organization's *mission* and its *sense of mission*. They see a mission as an intellectual concept that can be used to guide the policies of an organization. However, a sense of mission is an emotional commitment that employees feel towards the organization. It occurs when employees feel that there is a match between the values of an organization and those of the individual. The key point is that individuals with a sense of mission are emotionally committed to the organization, what it stands for, and what it is trying to achieve.

In their quest for what makes a visionary organization, Collins and Porras (1994) describe a core ideology which is made up of core values and purpose. The core values are an organization's essential and enduring tenets which will not be compromised for financial expediency and short-term gains. They do not shift as competitive conditions change but remain largely inviolate. It is what members are expected to endorse and internalize as part of working for such organizations. More than that, it is what attracts individuals to these types of organizations in the first place. IBM's former chief executive officer, Thomas J. Watson Jr, put it this way:

> *I firmly believe that any organization, in order to survive and achieve success, must have a sound set of beliefs on which it premises all its policies and actions . . . the most important single factor in corporate success is faithful adherence to those beliefs . . . Beliefs must always come before policies, practices, and goals. The latter must always be altered if they are seen to violate fundamental beliefs. (Collins and Porras 1994, p. 74)*

MISSION

seeks to answer the question why an organization exists

CORE IDEOLOGY

is made up of core values and purpose

CORE VALUES

are an organization's essential and enduring tenets which will not be compromised for financial expediency and short-term gains

STRATEGY FOCUS
Core Purpose at Tesco

Tesco is the UK's most profitable supermarket retailer. It continues to expand beyond its core business into new markets such as non-food, and services such as telecoms. It expects its employees to internalize the following core values:

Our Core Purpose is to create value for customers to earn their lifetime loyalty.

Surprisingly simple. Refreshingly honest. And yet incredibly powerful. Everything we do, every innovation we bring to market, every business decision we take, is driven by our customers.

We believe that we continually demonstrate that we're good at getting things done, good at 'what' we do, and we take pride in being good at the way in which we achieve it too, the 'how' we do it. We believe that by living by our Values, we will encourage and demonstrate behaviour that will help us achieve our Core Purpose and set us apart from our competitors.

Values enable us to build a common way of working. We want people in our business who feel comfortable with these Values and feel they can genuinely demonstrate them. They aren't about being soft and lovely, but about being rigorous and single minded about how we achieve our goals.

Some of the values which Tesco says make it what it is today and what it will be in the future are:

- Be energetic, be innovative, and be first for customers
- Look after our people so they can look after our customers
- Treat people how we like to be treated
- Ask more than tell, and share knowledge so that it can be used
- Trust and respect each other
- Strive to do our very best
- Enjoy work, celebrate success, and learn from experience

Source: From recruitment pages at www.tesco.com

A similar point was made by the founder of Johnson & Johnson, Robert Wood Johnson, when he wrote the organization's *credo* or set of beliefs in 1943. Unusually for this time Johnson explicitly recognized the importance of meeting stakeholder needs. Stakeholders are those individuals and groups upon whom the organization depends to achieve its goals. Stakeholders, in turn, have an interest in and can influence the success of the organization. They include customers, suppliers, shareholders, employees, and the local community, among others. Robert Wood Johnson codified that service to their customers should always come first, service to the organization's employees and management should be second, the local community third, and lastly service to shareholders. It is only when this chronology of events occurs that the shareholders will receive a *fair return*. See Strategy Focus: Organizational Values which illustrates how Johnson & Johnson's credo guided their executive management decisions some forty years later when they were faced with a crisis.

STRATEGY FOCUS

Organizational Values

Johnson & Johnson: How their Credo Guides their Strategy

General Robert Wood Johnson guided Johnson & Johnson from a small, family-owned business to a worldwide enterprise. In doing so he had an enlightened view of a corporation's responsibilities beyond the manufacturing and marketing of products. In 1935, in a pamphlet titled *Try Reality*, he urged his fellow industrialists to embrace 'a new industrial philosophy'. Johnson defined this as the corporation's responsibility to customers, employees, the community, and stockholders.

Eight years later, in 1943, Johnson wrote and first published the Johnson & Johnson *Credo*, a one-page document outlining these responsibilities in greater detail. Putting customers first and stockholders last was a refreshing approach to the management of a business. However, Johnson was a practical businessman. He believed that by putting the customer first the business would be well served, and it was. Johnson saw to it that his company embraced the Credo, and he urged his management to apply it as part of their everyday business philosophy.

In 1982 Johnson & Johnson faced a crisis when a drug from one of its operating companies, Tylenol, was altered and cyanide placed in the capsule form of the product, resulting in seven deaths. Johnson & Johnson's strategic response was inspired by the philosophy embodied in the Credo. The product was voluntarily recalled and destroyed, even though testing found the remaining capsules to be safe. Johnson & Johnson took a $100 million charge against earnings. In 1986, as a result of a second

Courtesy of Johnson & Johnson

General Robert Wood Johnson: the man who guided Johnson & Johnson from a small, family-owned business to a worldwide enterprise.

tampering incident and another fatality, Johnson & Johnson took the decision
to discontinue the sale of Tylenol in capsule form. The operating company
reintroduced Tylenol in tamper-proof packaging and regained its leading share
of the analgesic market. Faced with the loss of millions of dollars, the values
that are embodied in Johnson & Johnson's Credo guided its strategic response
and ensured its quick and honest handling of the crisis preserved the company's
reputation.

   When Robert Wood Johnson wrote and then institutionalized the Credo within
Johnson & Johnson, he never suggested that it guaranteed perfection. But its
principles have become a constant goal, as well as a source of inspiration, for all
who are part of the Johnson & Johnson Family of Companies.

Source: adapted from www.johnson&johnson.com

Johnson & Johnson provides a classic example of how an organization's values (credo)
guide its behaviour with its stakeholders. The example of Johnson & Johnson demonstrates the importance of values in guiding how an organization decides and imple-
ments its strategy. It is values that form and shape the corporate culture over time
and provide signposts for acceptable behaviour of internal and external stakeholders.
For example, as organizations continue to outsource activities overseas in search of
cheap production economies, they must ensure that employee conditions conform to
their own organizational values. The use of child labour in some countries has forced
organizations to face up to and bridge a credibility gap between their rhetoric and
their deeds. The more robust the values in an organization are, the greater the clarity
this provides for setting goals and therefore strategic direction and action. The more
ambiguous the values within an organization are, the greater the opportunity for
conflicting goals and for decisions to go unchallenged. A discussion of values is dealt
with in greater detail in **Chapter 10**.

   Purpose represents the reasons an organization exists beyond making a profit. The
purpose of an organization is distinct from its goals and strategies. Its primary function is to guide and inspire individuals. A purpose should be broad, fundamental, and
enduring in its composition. It should be capable of being stated succinctly. A purpose
is comparable to a vision in that organizations never achieve their purpose; it is an
ongoing journey. For example, Walt Disney stated, 'Disneyland will never be completed, as long as there is imagination in the world' (Collins and Porras 1994, p. 77).
The American pharmaceutical company Merck has its stated purpose as: 'We are
in the business of preserving and improving human life. All our actions must be
measured by our success in achieving this' (Collins and Porras 1991). In an address to
members of Hewlett-Packard, its co-founder, David Packard, outlined his company's
purpose as follows:

PURPOSE

the reasons an organization exists
beyond making a profit

I want to discuss why a company exists in the first place. In other words, why are we here? I think many people assume, wrongly, that a company exists simply to make money. While this is an important result of a company's existence, we have to go deeper and find the real reasons for our being . . . The real reason for our existence is that we provide something which is unique [that makes a contribution]. (Collins and Porras 1994, p. 56)

A purpose need not be unique, but it must be sincerely held. Other corporations might endorse a similar purpose to Merck and Hewlett-Packard, for example, but the key difference is the authenticity. How is that purpose worked out in the daily lives of corporate employees? This shows the difference between an organization's rhetoric and reality. An organization's core purpose does not prevent change; it simply provides a compass by which organizations can steer as they exploit new business opportunities.

The challenge for organizations is how to preserve what is their very essence but still respond to a changing competitive environment. Collins and Porras (1994) suggest the use of BHAGs to stimulate progress. BHAGs are Big Hairy Audacious Goals. A BHAG is clear and compelling, and it serves as a rallying cry to all employees as to where their energies should be focused. It has a finite time span so that everyone knows when it is achieved. Such goals include President John F. Kennedy's commitment in 1961 to landing a man on the moon and returning him safely to earth before the decade was out. BHAGs are easy to understand, and no matter how many different ways they may be put, they are still understood by everyone. In 1907, Henry Ford proclaimed that he wanted to democratize the automobile and 'build a car for the great multitude . . . so low in price that no man making a good salary will be unable to own one' (Collins and Porras 1994, p. 97). At that time Ford was one of over thirty car companies competing in this emerging market. It succeeded but its success was short-lived. This highlights a couple of important points to bear in mind with BHAGs. First, they must fit with an organization's core ideology; this was the case with Ford. Second, once achieved they need replacing. Ford achieved its BHAG but did not set another. This allowed General Motors to supplant its dominant position in the automobile industry.

For more information on organizations whose values influence their decision making go to the Online Resource Centre and see the Key Work feature.
www.oxfordtextbooks.co.uk/orc/henry2e/

Drucker (1995) argues that organizations encounter difficulties when the assumptions on which they are built and the basis on which they are being run no longer fit reality. These assumptions affect an organization's behaviour and its decisions about what and what not to do, and determine what an organization thinks are meaningful results. They include assumptions about markets, customers, competitors, and the

THEORY OF THE BUSINESS

the assumptions that affect an
organization's behaviour, its
decisions about what and what
not to do, and determine what
an organization thinks are
meaningful results

organization's strengths and weaknesses. Drucker refers to this as a company's **theory of the business**. Every organization has a theory of the business regardless of whether it operates in the public, private, or not-for-profit sector. The reason many large corporations are no longer successful is that their theory of the business no longer works. For example, when the computer was in its infancy IBM's theory of the business suggested that the future of computing was in mainframes. Around this time the first personal computer was developed by enthusiasts. At the same time as *serious* computer makers were *reminding* themselves that there was absolutely no reason for personal computers, the Apple and the Macintosh went on sale, starting the PC revolution.

An organization's theory of the business has four characteristics. First, the assumptions about the environment, mission, and core competencies must fit reality. Simon Marks, the co-founder of Marks & Spencer, realized that continued success in his business meant that he as merchant should develop new core competencies. He would design products based on his customer knowledge, and find manufacturers to make them to his costs. This went against the established practice of manufacturers producing products *they* thought the consumer might buy. Second, the assumptions in all three areas have to fit one another. Third, the theory of the business must be known and understood throughout the organization. This is relatively easy when an organization is founded, but as it grows it must be reinforced if the organization is not to pursue what is expedient rather than what is right. Fourth, the theory of the business has to be continually tested. In effect, the theory of the business has to have the ability to change to meet changing conditions. Intel's ability under the stewardship of CEO Andy Grove to move away from memory chips on which the company was founded and embrace microprocessors is a classic example of an organization willing to test its theory of the business. The rivalry from Japanese competitors willing to compete aggressively on price threatened its core memory chip business. Grove took the difficult decision to make microprocessors, which at the time were little more than a niche, the mainstay of the organization. This was no mean feat given that the founders of the organization and staff had considerable emotional capital invested in memory chips. See Case Study: Theory of the Business for the challenges facing the UK's Royal Mail as its current business model continues to be challenged.

CASE STUDY 1.1
Theory of the Business

'THE post office is a wonderful establishment!' exclaims Jane Fairfax in Jane Austen's *Emma*. 'The regularity and dispatch of it! If one thinks of all that it has to do, and all that it does so well, it is really astonishing!' She would be far less impressed by Britain's Royal Mail today, as it prepares for a second strike in protest against much-needed modernisation.

Royal Mail post box

© iStockphoto.com/Peter Austin

The root cause of the strike is the impact of new communications technology on the postal business. For ladies in distress and businesses all over the world, e-mail, websites, text messages and social-networking services have replaced paper; and recession has accelerated the trend. From India to Finland to America, postmen have fewer letters to deliver, meaning sharply lower profits or even losses for postal services. In the year to March 2008 India Post handled 6 billion pieces of ordinary post, down from over 15 billion at the start of the decade. First-class letters dropped by 9% in the first half of this year at Finland's Itella; junk mail fell by 16%. America's postal service is in crisis as volumes fall. It is expecting a third consecutive annual loss this year, after losing $2.8 billion in the year to September 2008.

With technology undermining the old monopolies that postal services used to enjoy, the obvious answer is to privatise them and let them sink or swim. But the post is not just another business knocked sideways by the internet. Post offices unite communities and the postal service connects remote regions to the centre, so voters are uncomfortable with radical change.

On October 28th Japan's new government replaced the leadership of Japan Post, as part of its reversal of the previous government's decision to privatise the group. The new government plans to reunite the financial services, delivery and post-office activities as a way to subsidise loss making outlets in rural areas. In France, where a popular left-wing politician, Olivier Besancenot, also happens to be a postman, an anti-privatisation group has successfully drummed up opposition to a proposed change to the legal status of La Poste that could open the door to privatisation. Even in Britain, home of privatisation, the government has abandoned its plan to bring in a private minority shareholder for the Royal Mail.

The cheque's in the post

Opponents of privatisation say that state ownership is essential to protecting postal services. Experience suggests otherwise. Governments have, for the most part, run their postal services shockingly badly, siphoning off cash, holding back modernisation and undermining sensible business strategies by blocking moves to increase flexibility. In the 1990s the Royal Mail was a model modern post office. French and German postal executives used to visit and learn, and it profited from selling its know-how around the world. Today, starved of the investment in automation it so badly needed, the Royal Mail is 40% less efficient than its local competitors. Government-owned La Poste, too, lags in profitability and speed of delivery, though France's size and population density plays a part too.

Private postal operators are, by and large, better positioned to cope with falling demand than state-owned operators are. Deutsche Post and the Netherlands' TNT Post, which have both been privatised, have diversified into parcels and express deliveries and are as efficient as postal services get. Belgian Post, in which CVC Capital Partners, a private-equity firm, took a large stake in 2006, has also sharpened up its performance. Until the British government's U-turn in July, CVC and TNT Post were competing to come in as the Royal Mail's private partner.

Opponents of selling off postal services say that private-sector owners will bleed them for profit rather than investing in their future. That's not what's happened at Deutsche Post, TNT Post and Belgian Post. They have invested for the long term—the first in acquisitions at home and abroad, the second in far-flung foreign expansion and the third in automation.

Politicians think that post offices need to be protected from change; but they need more of it, not less. When their business model is collapsing, they need the freedom to invent a new one. Government ownership will restrict their liberty, and lead to deepening losses and, in the end, taxpayer bail-outs. Pressure from private shareholders, in contrast, could push postal bosses to drop expensive services that carry comparatively little benefit for customers, such as next-day delivery for business. If voters want services such as delivery to remote regions, then governments can pay for them.

Jane Austen's Mr Knightley had the right idea about postal services: 'The public pays,' he told Miss Fairfax, 'and must be served well.' Privatisation is the best way to ensure that the public does not, instead, end up serving the post office.

Source: 'Why privatisation is the best way to protect postal services as letters die out' *The Economist* 29 October 2009

Questions

1. How would you describe the Royal Mail's theory of the business?

2. To what extent is this determined by political factors outside the control of Royal Mail's management?

3. How might managers try to influence this organization's theory of the business?

Drucker argues that every theory of the business will eventually become obsolete and no longer meet the needs of the organization. However, there are two preventive measures. The first is *abandonment*. Drucker suggests that every three years an organization might look at its markets, products, and policies and ask itself: If we were not already in it, would we still want to be in it now? This forces managers in organizations to question the assumptions on which their business is based—their theory of the business. The second is to study what is happening outside the business, especially with non-customers. This is because fundamental change rarely happens within your own industry or with your own customers. This type of change invariably first manifests itself with your non-customers. We will say much more on detecting changes that might impact one's competitive environment in **Chapter 2**.

A theory of the business becomes obsolete when an organization has achieved its original objectives. As with the example earlier of Ford democratizing the automobile, the achievement of the objective may point to the need for new thinking rather than be a cause for celebration. As Sam Walton, the founder of the American retailer Wal-Mart noted:

> *You can't just keep doing what works one time, because everything around you is always changing. To succeed you have to stay out in front of that change. (Collins and Porras 1994, p. 81)*

Thomas J. Watson Jr argued that an organization's basic beliefs should remain inviolate:

> *If an organization is to meet the challenges of a changing world, it must be prepared to change everything about itself except its basic beliefs . . . The only sacred cow in an organization should be its basic philosophy of doing business. (Collins and Porras 1994, p. 81)*

For a wider discussion of the theory of the business and its impact on business strategy go to the Online Resource Centre and see the Key Work feature. www.oxfordtextbooks.co.uk/orc/henry2e/

1.4 Types of Strategy

There are three basic forms of strategy that interest organizations. These are corporate strategy, business strategy, and functional strategy. In reality, most organizations are concerned with business-level strategy and corporate strategy. These are described below.

Corporate Strategy

Corporate strategy is concerned with the broader issues of what industries the organization wants to compete in. It deals with mergers and acquisitions, and allocates resources between the organization's strategic business units (SBUs). The Royal Bank of Scotland's takeover of National Westminster Bank was part of their corporate strategy, as was Intel's move away from memory chips and towards microprocessors. Corporate strategy is often seen as the preserve of the most senior management within an organization.

Business Strategy

Business strategy, sometimes called competitive strategy, deals with how an organization is going to compete within a particular industry or market. It is concerned with how the organization will achieve a competitive advantage over its rivals. In contrast with corporate strategies, managers of SBUs, who are usually given substantial autonomy, formulate business strategies. Business strategy is dealt with in **Chapter 3**, when we assess the competitive environment.

Functional Strategy

We might note that there is a third category, functional strategy. This deals with decisions according to functional lines such as R&D, marketing, and finance. These functions will be involved in the support of the business strategy. Therefore we will subsume this within business strategy in our discussions.

1.5 Changes in the Approach to Strategic Management

We have seen that strategic management is concerned with how firms achieve and sustain competitive advantage. However, a major disagreement arises when we look at *how* competitive advantage is achieved by the firm. The true test of how organizations achieve and sustain competitive advantage is ultimately decided in the marketplace. Therefore one might expect research to help provide an answer. Again, there is controversy here as research findings are both accepted and contested.

The changes in strategic management as a discipline reflect the changing dynamics of modern economies. For example, during the 1950s and 1960s firms could rely on stable and expanding market conditions with a customer emphasis on price. Under such conditions it was natural that organizations would engage in corporate planning. It was not unusual for major corporations to have a corporate planning function or department which annually developed long-term plans for the next five years, and even longer in some instances. These were primarily finance-based budgetary control systems, giving the assurance that there was some scientific basis to this kind of planning. In times of relative stability, which in turn provides for some degree of predictability, this type of corporate planning was the norm.

In the 1960s and 1970s the corporate landscape was beating to the drum of diversification, in particular how to increase market share by capturing new markets. Ansoff's growth vector matrix explains how organizations can engage in related and unrelated diversification to increase their market shares (Ansoff 1965). Diversification works well as long as synergies ensue resulting in increased profitability and an increase in the capital value of the firm. It also presupposes that management has sufficient skills and capabilities to run businesses operating in markets of which they may have little or no knowledge.

In the 1980s, the work of Porter (1980, 1985) on industry analysis shifted the emphasis to firms analysing the competitive forces inherent within their industry as a means of gaining competitive advantage. Porter argued that firms should position themselves favourably against adversarial forces within their industry and adopt a strategy that would enable them to compete effectively. In the 1980s corporations had also begun to focus on the core elements of their businesses. This was a period in corporate history in which managers sought to *stick to the knitting*, as exemplified in the best-selling book *In Search of Excellence* (Peters and Waterman 1982).

This continued throughout the 1990s as new management techniques taught corporate leaders about downsizing, outsourcing, delayering, total quality management, economic value analysis, benchmarking, and re-engineering. Organizations were outsourcing all but the essential elements or the core competencies of the organization. In contrast with Porter's work the resource-based view (RBV) of the firm, exemplified by the work of Grant (1991), Kay (1993), and Prahalad and Hamel (Prahalad and Hamel 1990; Hamel and Prahalad 1994), exhorts the organization to look within itself at its own resources and core competencies, and use these as a basis for competitive advantage. Amit and Schoemaker (1993) see the resource-based view of the firm as a complement to the industry analysis framework of Porter since industry analysis views the sources of profitability to be the characteristics of the industry and the firm's position within the industry, while the resource view sees the determinants of profitability as the firm's resources and capabilities.

D'Aveni (1994) coined the term *hypercompetition* to describe the new competitive situation where firms must continually innovate, developing new products or services for the customer. For D'Aveni, sustainable competitive advantage now requires firms to constantly develop new products to provide customers with increased functionality and performance. Microsoft is a classic example of a hypercompetitive firm (see **Chapter 3** for a discussion of hypercompetition). However, not everyone is convinced that hypercompetition represents a new framework for understanding competition. For example, Porter (1996) argues that hypercompetition can be seen as an excuse for a lack of managerial ability and poor strategic thinking. Mintzberg (1994) argues that turbulence, inasmuch as it exists at all, is an opportunity for organizations to learn from a changing environment, as the Japanese have done. Mintzberg is not denying turbulence *per se*; he is simply pointing out that there is a tendency in strategic management to characterize the previous decades as stable, and our current decade as turbulent. Research by McNamara *et al.* (2003) seems to support Mintzberg, as they suggest that 'hypercompetition perspectives are important but no more so now than they were in recent years'.

In the 1990s organizations began to see the benefits of collaboration, cooperation, and joint alliances. 'Networking' between corporations became the new buzzword. Supplier relationships were seen as a source of competitive advantage and not as one of competition. Brandenburger and Nalebuff (1996) refer to this détente as *co-opetition*, that is, a blend of competition and cooperation existing simultaneously, in effect a non-zero-sum game. This is discussed in detail in **Chapter 3**.

1.6 Different Perspectives on Strategy Formulation

The issue of how strategy is actually formulated has led to claims and counter-claims about the merits of different schools of thought within strategic management. This ongoing debate has been largely implicit in strategic management books, but waged more explicitly in the various strategic management journals (Mintzberg 1990; Ansoff 1991). There are numerous perspectives on strategy formulation which in many respects overlap and branch off from each other (see Mintzberg and Lampel (1999) for an identification of ten different schools of strategic thought and whether these are fundamentally different ways of making strategy or different parts of the same process). We can identify two broad perspectives of strategy management which at first reading may appear to be polar opposites: the *design school* and the *learning school*.

1.6.1 The Design School

The design school is associated with the work of Andrews (1971) and Ansoff (1965). According to Andrews, an organization needs to match its strengths and weaknesses (which are internal to the firm, and derive from its resources and competencies) with the needs of its competitive environment. The competitive environment comprises both threats and opportunities. This provides the familiar SWOT analysis of strengths, weaknesses, opportunities, and threats. An external analysis is used to identify the opportunities and threats facing the firm, while an internal analysis of the organization identifies its strengths and weaknesses.

For the design school, the match between these elements will lead to the creation of a number of different strategies, each of which can be evaluated and the best strategy then implemented. In the 1960s organizations had planning departments which created strategies for managers to implement. The role of top management was to choose the most appropriate strategy. Ansoff's product matrix was an attempt to help organizations understand the relationship between their existing products and new products, and how these fitted with the organization's competencies. An awareness of this relationship allows the organization to assess more clearly its strategy, and therefore reduce its risks. For the past quarter of a century Porter, more than any other, has exemplified this rationalist approach to strategy formulation using *generic* strategies.

1.6.2 The Learning School

In contrast with the design school, Mintzberg (1990) argues that a rational approach to strategy fails to take account of how strategy making occurs in reality. Mintzberg and Waters (1985) suggest three approaches to strategy making: intended, realized, and emergent strategies. An intended strategy is one that the organization has deliberately chosen to pursue and will therefore have been worked out in detail. A realized strategy is the strategy that the organization actually carries out. For a variety of reasons, for example a change in consumer preferences, the intended strategy may no longer be relevant to market conditions and therefore is not implemented. Mintzberg and Waters refer to this as an unrealized strategy. In such a case managers will use their experience and learning to develop an emergent strategy which meets the needs of the external environment. When this emergent strategy is implemented it becomes the realized strategy. They argue that strategy formulation is far more likely to be a result of emergent strategies rather than based on any detailed intentions. This process is shown in Figure 1.2.

INTENDED STRATEGY

the strategy that the organization has deliberately chosen to pursue

REALIZED STRATEGY

the strategy that the organization actually carries out

EMERGENT STRATEGY

where managers use their experience and learning to develop a strategy that meets the needs of the external environment

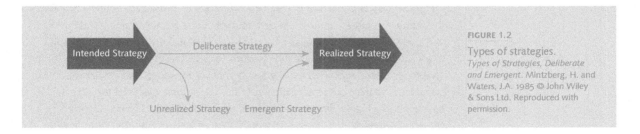

FIGURE 1.2

Types of strategies.
Types of Strategies, Deliberate and Emergent. Mintzberg, H. and Waters, J.A. 1985 © John Wiley & Sons Ltd. Reproduced with permission.

Mintzberg (1994) points out that 'strategy is an immensely complex process, which involves the most sophisticated, subtle, and, at times subconscious elements of human thinking . . . strategies can develop inadvertently, without the conscious intention of senior management, often through a process of learning'. However, Mintzberg does allow 'that all viable strategies have emergent and deliberate qualities, since all must combine some degree of flexible learning with some degree of cerebral control'. See Case Study: Deliberate and Emergent Strategies, which shows competing perspectives on Honda's success and ultimate domination of the US motorcycle industry. The design school or rationalists see Honda's success as part of a deliberate strategy. Mintzberg, in contrast, argues that it results from an emergent strategy.

For a greater understanding of the debate surrounding Honda's domination of the US motorcycle industry go to the Online Resource Centre and see the Key Work feature.
www.oxfordtextbooks.co.uk/orc/henry2e/

CASE STUDY 1.2
Deliberate and Emergent Strategies

Honda and the Super Cub is probably the best known and most debated case in business strategy. In the 1950s, motorcycles were sold through specialist outlets welcoming only testosterone-loaded young men. Bikes were powerful and noisy, and the riders' leather clothes smelt of leaking oil. Honda entered the US market in 1959 and changed everything. Five years later the company made one in two bikes sold in the US. Their best-selling machine was the 50cc Super Cub. The company's advertising slogan was 'You meet the nicest people on a Honda'.

The story benefits from deconstruction. One school of explanation derives from the original Harvard Business School case study. That case is based on a 1975 report by the Boston Consulting Group for the British government that described these events as the archetype of an orchestrated attack on Western markets by Japanese manufacturers of consumer goods. Having established large economies of scale in the domestic market, Honda was able to exploit its cost advantage globally.

A quite different history was given by Richard Pascale, who went to Tokyo to interview the elderly Japanese who had managed Honda's first steps in the US. These executives explained that Honda had never imagined that small bikes, popular in Japan, would find a market in the wide-open spaces of the US. They had focused on large machines, planning to compete with US manufacturers. Mr Honda, they said, was especially confident of success with these products because the shape of the handlebars looked like the eyebrows of Buddha.

But the eyebrows of Buddha were not appealing in the world of Marlon Brando and James Dean. The Japanese hawked their wares around the western US, to dealers 'who treated us discourteously and gave the impression of being motorcycle enthusiasts who, secondarily, were in business'. The few machines they sold, ridden more aggressively than was possible in Japan, leaked even more oil than their US counterparts.

Dispirited and short of foreign currency, the Honda executives imported some Super Cubs to ease their own progress around the asphalt jungle of Los Angeles. Passers-by expressed interest, and eventually a Sears buyer approached them. And the 'nicest people' slogan? That was invented by a University of California undergraduate on summer assignment. Only the naive will believe either account.

Successful business strategy is a mixture of luck and judgment, opportunism and design, and even with hindsight the relative contributions of each cannot be disentangled. Mr Honda was an irascible genius who made inspired intuitive decisions—with assistance from the meticulous market analysis of his colleagues and the intense discipline of Honda's production line operations. It is a mistake to believe the ultimate truth about Honda can be established through diligent research and debate. The Harvard account, although paranoid, is right to emphasize Honda's operational capabilities. Mr Pascale correctly stresses the human factors but his interviewees must have laughed as he wrote down the story of the eyebrows of Buddha.

The Boston Consulting Group naturally saw the experience curve at work and later, when peddling a different panacea, realized it was an example of time-based competition. Gary Hamel and C.K. Prahalad perceived the development of Honda's 'core competence' in engine manufacture. Henry Mintzberg seized on Mr Pascale's account as an instance of emergent strategy. But there is no true story and no point in debating what it might be.

The lesson of Honda is that a business with a distinctive capability that develops innovative products to exploit that capability and recognizes the appropriate distribution channels for such innovations can take the world by storm. And that lesson is valid whether Honda's achievement was the result of careful planning or serendipity.

Source: 'Driving through the spin on Honda's big success' *Financial Times* 16 November 2004

Questions

1. What factors determine whether Honda's strategy was deliberate or emergent?
2. Explain why it is possible for an organization's success to be a result of deliberate and emergent strategies.
3. If Honda's success is put down to serendipity, how would you account for Honda's success today?

We argued at the start of this section on different perspectives that the truth often lies somewhere between competing positions and drawn battle lines. The question is not whether some approaches to strategic management are overly rational and analytical, failing to take account of more complex processes within strategy making. Perhaps the real question is how strategic management as a discipline moves forward and ultimately benefits the performance of organizations, and in so doing increases society's net benefit. There is a danger that emanates from having battle lines and positions too clearly demarcated, which is that common ground can often be overlooked. However, as is often the case, the truth lies somewhere between these two perspectives. Successful strategy formulation will inevitably involve both analytical techniques and a creative process: 'it's a complicated world out there. We all know we shall get nowhere without emergent learning alongside deliberate planning' (Mintzberg 1996).

1.7 A Strategic Management Framework

A framework is useful to help us to structure our thoughts and navigate around the different aspects of strategic management. If the purpose of strategy is to enable an organization to achieve a sustainable competitive advantage, then any framework needs to address the process necessary for this. In Figure 1.3 we outline a framework which includes an analysis of the organization's external environment and its internal resources and capabilities. However, as we saw in the Strategy Focus on Johnson & Johnson, all organizations need a clear sense of direction and this is provided by their values (or credo), which in turn will direct the goals they set and, therefore, the strategy necessary to achieve them. It is in this respect that strategy can be seen as a means to an end. It is the lynchpin between an organization's internal and external environment.

Figure 1.3 shows the importance of values in the strategy-making process. Hence the arrow emanating from *values* which determine the *goals* the organization sets, the *resources and capabilities* it requires, and the *structures and processes* necessary to achieve those goals. Goals need to be clearly defined throughout the organization as they provide the direction and motivation for individuals within the firm. The more clearly the goals are stated and imbued within the organization, the greater the understanding by the organization's participants of their role in achieving these goals. An organization's goals will reflect its internal *strengths and weaknesses* and the *opportunities and threats* within its external environment. Values and goals will also determine the types of resources the organization accumulates. How the organization is structured and the processes it utilizes will again reflect the organization's goals and what it sees as important—its values. An organization's values will also determine the relationship with its stakeholders.

Stakeholders are those individuals and groups who are impacted by the behaviour of the organization, and whose own behaviour can, in turn, have an impact on the

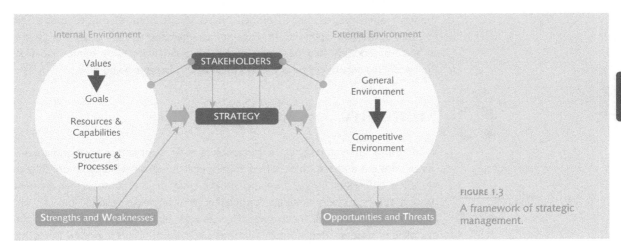

FIGURE 1.3

A framework of strategic management.

organization's strategy. This is shown in the framework by arrows which emanate from stakeholders to strategy, and strategy to stakeholders. Stakeholders occur within the internal and external environment, as shown by the linkages in the diagram. For example, managers and employees are internal stakeholders, while suppliers, share-holders, and the local community are external stakeholders. The dichotomy between internal and external stakeholders is not always this simple, since a shareholder may also be an employee of the firm.

Figure 1.3 links strategy and the internal environment since each new strategy adopted must meet the organization's values and goals. Similarly there is a link between the firm and its external environment since its values will determine the types of markets it will and will not operate within. This is perhaps most clearly seen in the strategies being pursued by ethical investment fund managers. The two-way arrows positioned between an organization's strategy and its internal and external environments provide feedback on the appropriateness of the intended strategy. As we have seen, the intended strategy may not be implemented, perhaps because of a change in market conditions, and an emergent strategy then becomes the realized strategy. The arrow emanating from the general environment to the competitive environment draws our attention to the fact that changes in the general environment may have their greatest impact on the competitive environment. For example, a change in technology in the general environment resulted in the destruction of the typewriter industry.

Do organizations analyse their internal and external environments and then develop a strategy based upon this analysis and in line with their values? Or do they develop a strategy based upon experience and resources contained within the firm and then seek to exploit or leverage this within their external environment? This is an inter-esting question that has provoked much debate within strategic management. On the one hand is the positioning school (Henderson 1989), which is characterized by the work of Harvard professor Michael Porter. This is often referred to as strategic fit or an 'outside-in' approach to strategic management. On the other hand is the resource-based view that has come to be associated with Gary Hamel and C.K. Prahalad. This debate will be addressed in detail in **Chapters 3** and **5**.

 ## Summary

In addressing what strategy is, we have looked at different perspectives and a number of different authors. These different perspectives will be evaluated more fully as we assess differential firm performance in later chapters. The strategic management process covers strategy analysis, formulation, and implementation. However, we might reiterate that this linear approach, although highly useful in explaining the discipline of strategy, may not fully capture how strategy occurs in reality. This is not to demean its usefulness since all organizations need to undertake analysis before they are ready to take decisions. It is more to open up thinking about the different ways in which strategy formulation occurs, whether deliberately or emerging.

A vision is often associated with the leader of an organization and represents a desired state that the organization aspires to achieve in the future. In contrast with goals and objectives, a vision does not change over time. To be effective, a vision should tap into the personal values of employees. A mission seeks to answer the question why an organization exits. A mission statement is a way in which the organization communicates the business it is in to the outside world. A mission statement needs to appeal to a broad spectrum of stakeholders if all these stakeholders are to accept it. The research of Collins and Porras into visionary organizations shows the importance of an organization's core ideology. This comprises core values and purpose. Core values are an organization's essential and enduring tenets which will not be compromised for financial expediency and short-term gains. Purpose represents the reasons an organization exists beyond making a profit. The purpose of organizations will be more fully evaluated in **Chapter 12** on corporate governance. Organizations encounter difficulties when the assumptions on which they are built and the basis on which they are being run no longer fit reality. Drucker refers to this as a company's *theory of the business*. The reason many large corporations are no longer successful is that their theory of the business no longer works.

This chapter has introduced the reader to some of the complexities that emanate from a study of strategic management. There are conflicting and competing definitions. There is disagreement over how strategy is formulated, which gives rise to competing perspectives. This should not be seen as an insurmountable issue since any discipline as young as strategic management will inevitably be concerned with the exactitude of its terminology and the rigour of its modus operandi. What we have tried to show is that, in and amongst all this ambiguity, there is common ground and clarity of thought and expression. The fact that different perspectives exist at all is simply part of the dynamic nature of strategic management.

Review Questions

1. What is strategy?
2. Explain the difference between the learning and design school in strategy formulation.

Discussion Question

To understand which companies will survive and prosper and which will fail, one has only to look at the management in each company and evaluate their theory of the business. Discuss.

Research Topic

1. Identify organizations in which clearly communicated values correlate with organizational success.
2. Select a combination of private and public sector organizations and evaluate the extent to which their mission statement signposts to stakeholders what business they are in.

Recommended Reading

- **Porter, M.E.** (1996). What is strategy? *Harvard Business Review*, **74**(6), 61–78.

For an insight into the debate on deliberate and emergent strategies see:

- **Pascale, R.T.** (1984). Perspectives on strategy: the real story behind Honda's success. *California Management Review*, **26**(3), 47–72.
- **Mintzberg, H.** (1990). The design school: reconsidering the basic premises of strategic management. *Strategic Management Journal*, **11**(3), 171–95.
- **Ansoff, H.I.** (1991). Critique of Henry Mintzberg's 'The design school: reconsidering the basic premises of strategic management. *Strategic Management Journal*, **12**(6), 449–61.
- **Pascale, R.T.** (1996). Reflections on Honda. *California Management Review*, **38**(4), 112–17.
- **Mintzberg, H.** (1996). Learning 1, Planning 0. *California Management Review*, **38**(4), 92–3.

For a discussion of the importance of core ideology to visionary organizations and the place of BHAGs in stimulating progress see:

- **Collins**, J. and **Porras**, J.I. (1994). *Built to Last: Successful Habit of Visionary Companies*. Harper, New York.

online resource centre

www.oxfordtextbooks.co.uk/orc/henry2e/
Visit the Online Resource Centre that accompanies this book for activities and more information on strategy.

References

Amit, R. and **Schoemaker, P.J.H.** (1993). Strategic assets and organisational rents. *Strategic Management Journal*, **14**(1), 33–46.

Andrews, K.R. (1971). *The Concept of Corporate Strategy*. Irwin, New York.

Ansoff, H.I. (1991). Critique of Henry Mintzberg's 'The design school: reconsidering the basic premises of strategic management. *Strategic Management Journal*, **12**(6), 449–61.

Ansoff, I. (1965). *Corporate Strategy*, Chapter 6. McGraw-Hill, New York.

Brandenburger, A. and **Nalebuff, B.J.** (1996). *Co-opetition*. Currency Doubleday, New York.

Campbell, A., Devine, M., and **Young, D.** (1990). *A Sense of Mission*. Economist Publications/Hutchinson, London.

Collins, J.C. and **Porras, J.I.** (1991). Organizational vision and visionary organizations. *California Management Review*, **34**(1), 38.

Collins, J.C. and **Porras, J.I.** (1994). *Built to Last: Successful Habit of Visionary Companies*. Harper, New York.

D'Aveni, R.A. (1994). *Hypercompetition: Managing the Dynamics of Strategic Manoeuvring*. Free Press, New York.

Drucker, P.F. (1995). *Managing in a Time of Great Change*. Butterworth Heinemann, Oxford.

Grant, R.M. (1991). The resource-based theory of competitive advantage: implications for strategy formulation. *California Management Review*, **33**(Spring), 114–35.

Grove, A.S. (1996). *Only the Paranoid Survive*. Random House, New York.

Hamel, G. and **Prahalad, C.K.** (1994). *Competing for the Future*. Harvard Business School Press, Boston MA.

Hawkins, D.E. and **Rajagopal, S.** (2005). *Sun Tzu and the Project Battleground*. Basingstoke, Palgrave Macmillan.

Henderson, B.D. (1989). The origin of strategy. *Harvard Business Review*, **67**(6), 139–43.

Kay, J. (1993). *Foundations of Corporate Success*. Oxford University Press, Oxford.

Lipton, M. (1996). Demystifying the development of an organizational vision. *Sloan Management Review*, **37**(4), 83–92.

McNamara, G., Vaaler, P.M., and **Devers, C.** (2003). Same as it ever was: the search for evidence of increasing hypercompetition. *Strategic Management Journal*, **24**(3), 261–78.

Markides, C.C. (1999a). A dynamic view of strategy. *Sloan Management Review*. **40**(3), 55–63.

Markides, C.C. (1999b). In search of strategy. *Sloan Management Review*, **40**(3), 6–7.

Mintzberg, H. (1990). The design school: reconsidering the basic premises of strategic management. *Strategic Management Journal*, **11**(3), 171–95.

Mintzberg, H. (1994). The fall and rise of strategic planning. *Harvard Business Review*, **72**(1), 107–14.

Mintzberg, H. (1996). Learning 1, Planning 0. *California Management Review*, **38**(4), 92–3.

Mintzberg, H. and **Lampel, J.** (1999). Reflecting on the strategy process. *Sloan Management Review*, **40**(3), 21–30.

Mintzberg, H. and **Waters, J.A.** (1985). Of strategies, deliberate and emergent. *Strategic Management Journal*, **6**(3), 257–72.

Ohmae, K. (1984). *The Mind of the Strategist: The Art of Japanese Business*. McGraw-Hill, New York.

Peters, T.J. and **Waterman, R.H.** (1982). *In Search of Excellence*. Harper & Row, New York.

Porter, M.E. (1980). *Competitive Strategy: Techniques for Analysing Industries and Competitors*. Free Press, New York.

Porter, M.E. (1985). *Competitive Advantage*. Free Press, New York.

Porter, M.E. (1996). What is strategy? *Harvard Business Review*, **74**(6), 61–78.

Prahalad, C.K. and **Hamel, G.** (1990). The core competence of the organization. *Harvard Business Review*, **68**(3), 79–91.

von Clausewitz, K. (1982). *On War* (ed. A. Rapaport). Penguin, Harmondsworth.

PART 1 CASE STUDY
Laura Ashley

© iStockphoto.com/Kateryna Govorushchenko

Laura Ashley's folksy, flowery patterns sum up 1970s English fashion.

Last week, Laura Ashley, the retailer whose folksy, flowery patterns sum up 1970s English fashion, reported one of the strongest Christmas trading performances in the retail sector. At a time when traditional retailers are supposed to be suffering at the hands of supermarkets and internet retailers, Laura Ashley is a rare success story. It really shouldn't be like this. The quintessentially British company has been through 11 chief executives in the last 14 years, it is majority-owned by a Malaysian conglomerate, and the billowy iconic style it is best known for went out of favour decades ago.

However, somehow Laura Ashley has transformed itself. Shares have doubled since early 2006, and profits for the year to the end of this month are expected to be double the £6 million reported last year. Last week the company paid its first interim dividend since 1996. Like-for-like sales for the year to date are up 8.7 per cent. It is boom time at Laura Ashley. Analysts think its success is here to stay. 'I don't think it is a flash in the pan. The strategy they are employing is a good one,' says Rob Brent, an analyst at Peel Hunt.

It has been a long and rocky journey for Laura Ashley, whose eponymous founder was a mixture between Beatrix Potter and Marjorie Scardino, the chief executive of Pearson. The company was a British success story for decades, until tragedy, management arrogance, and changing trends nearly wiped it out completely. 'It was, up until the 1980s, a family-run niche retailer with a good culture, it was iconic and pretty focused. It was really very effective, but then success went to its head and it tried to play on a bigger stage than it should,' says a former board member. For the first half of its existence, Laura Ashley was the ultimate cottage industry made good.

In the 1950s, Laura Ashley and husband Bernard started to produce headscarves, tablemats, and napkins on the kitchen table of their flat in Pimlico. The breakthrough came in 1966, when Laura Ashley produced its first dress for social occasions rather than for work around the house. Between 1970 and 1975 annual sales grew from £300,000 to £5 million and the company opened stores across the UK. It also opened concessions in department stores in Australia, Canada, and Japan, and outlets in Paris and San Francisco. By 1979 sales were £25 million.

In the early 1980s, Laura Ashley peaked as the epitome of cosy Britishness. 'Laura Ashley started from such an honest beginning and remained true for a long time. It was English kitchen table. In the 1980s it tapped right into that Sloane Ranger scene, where the whole British scene was about pretty prints and soft romance, on the back of the Lady Diana wave. It just hit it right with fashion,' says Tamasin Doe, fashion director of *In Style*, the fashion magazine. But just as the business was about to make a major step change in its growth, disaster struck. While staying at the Cotswolds home of one of her children on her 60th birthday in 1985, Laura fell down the stairs. She fell into a coma and died 10 days later in a Coventry hospital.

Despite the tragedy Bernard ploughed on. Two months after Laura's death the company floated in London with a value of around £200 million. But it was shortly after this that problems set in—problems that would beset the company for the best part of 20 years. Fashions were changing; the formality of the previous decade was replaced by a new casualness. 'Laura Ashley was completely left behind. It didn't adapt. It did what many companies do in those circumstances and seized up. It became more and more classic until it was so classic that it became an octogenarian style,' says Doe. Hopes that Laura Ashley's woes could be fixed were given a boost in 1995 by the appointment of Ann Iverson, a feisty American with a reputation for shooting from the hip, as chief executive.

Iverson should have retrenched Laura Ashley and returned it to its roots. But she did the exact opposite. She expanded Laura Ashley overseas and tried to appeal to younger customers in the UK. The most ambitious part of her strategy was launching 30 huge flagship stores in the US. The trouble was, there was not enough product to fill them. 'The US was Ann's big folly. She rolled out a bunch of 25,000 sq ft stores with high rents. The stores themselves were five times too big for the product catalogue,' says a former senior director. Iverson was sacked in 1997 and a rescue team put in. This team, which included a finance director called Richard Pennycook, now FD of the supermarket William Morrison, had the tricky brief of sorting the chain out. 'It was a mess. When Ann left this was a business with £350 million of turnover but was operating in 30 countries. It was manufacturing, retailing, franchising, licensing. A total mess,' says a former executive.

It was at this time that Laura Ashley was thrown a lifeline by its current largest shareholder, Malayan United Industries (MUI), the Malaysian conglomerate chaired by Dr Khoo Kay Peng. The company bought 40 per cent of the chain. Dr Khoo also bought a large stake personally through a company called Bonham Industries. As part of its purchase MUI appointed four new board directors. The following year Laura Ashley sold its 100 US stores to their management for $1. MUI gave the company the stability that it desperately needed. It also started to implement a sensible long-term strategy for the chain. However, there has been a revolving door of management along the way.

David Cook, Laura Ashley's finance director, declines to comment on the 11 CEOs over the last 14 years. 'I'd really rather focus on driving the business forward,' he says. Executives talk of an inevitable clash of cultures when a Far Eastern conglomerate takes over a slightly twee English chain. However, Laura Ashley is now firing on all cylinders. The biggest move over recent years has been the huge growth of the homewares and furniture business, and the relative shrinking of the clothing side. In the UK, where Laura Ashley has 180 stores, home-related products now account for 80 per cent of sales, while clothing accounts for just 20 per cent. Just five years ago, clothing accounted for more than 50 per cent of the sales. This move has been applauded. 'The demand for Laura Ashley home furnishings is there. It is good-quality middle-market product, and that area of the market is devoid of good-quality household goods. Marks & Spencer largely pulled out of it, so where do you go? Big department stores are the only option,' says Peel Hunt's Brent.

Interiors experts say that Laura Ashley has the 'shabby chic' appeal that is fashionable now. Its chandeliers are one of this season's must-have items among London's media fashionistas. Cook says that elements of the market do not appreciate that the company is now much more of a homeware retailer than a fashion one. 'The perception is that Laura Ashley is very much a fashion brand and within that we focus very much on florals. It is very hard to change those perceptions that people have,' says Cook.

Laura Ashley has also relocated its poorer-performing stores from prime sites on high streets to larger off-pitch stores. The move is part of a deliberate strategy to save money and make Laura Ashley a 'destination' store. It seems to be working. 'We have a very loyal customer base who are well aware of what we do. The challenge is building on it,' says Cook, who promises an 'aggressive' store opening programme. The company also has a strong overseas following through 200 franchised stores. Blogs from foreign customers view the chain as a nostalgic slice of England. Some bloggers talk about 'the smell from long-ago Europe' that apparently infuses every store. It is no surprise that 70 per cent of sales overseas come from the fashion, rather than the homeware, ranges.

In Style's Doe says that the retailer's current fashion ranges have plundered its rich heritage. 'They are absolutely straight back to the 1960s and 1970s. It is back to the kitchen table with Laura Ashley, which taps into the current fashion. It is very on trend,' she says. The retro English print look is also evident by the success of upmarket designers such as Cath Kidston. Through folksy beginnings, tragedy, failed attempts at global domination, and incongruous owners, Laura Ashley has become one of the most unlikely business success stories of 2007.

Source: 'Not just a pretty dress' *Sunday Telegraph* 21 January 2007

Questions

1. What were the reasons for Laura Ashley's initial success?
2. To what extent has Laura Ashley's theory of the business failed to keep pace with changes in its environment?
3. How would you characterize Laura Ashley's current strategy?

PART 2

Strategic Analysis

2 The General Environment

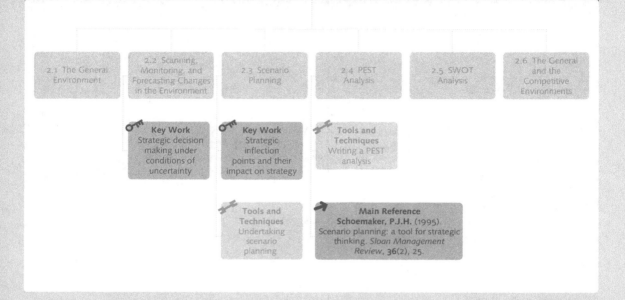

| 2.1 The General Environment | 2.2 Scanning, Monitoring, and Forecasting Changes in the Environment | 2.3 Scenario Planning | 2.4 PEST Analysis | 2.5 SWOT Analysis | 2.6 The General and the Competitive Environments |

Key Work
Strategic decision making under conditions of uncertainty

Key Work
Strategic inflection points and their impact on strategy

Tools and Techniques
Writing a PEST analysis

Tools and Techniques
Undertaking scenario planning

Main Reference
Schoemaker, P.J.H. (1995). Scenario planning: a tool for strategic thinking. *Sloan Management Review*, **36**(2), 25.

Learning Objectives

After completing this chapter you should be able to:

- Define what constitutes the general environment
- Evaluate the role of scanning and monitoring in detecting environmental trends
- Apply scenario planning to decision making in uncertain environments
- Evaluate PEST as a framework for analysing the macro-environment
- Explain the use of SWOT analysis
- Evaluate the relationship between the general and the competitive environment

Introduction

In the previous chapter we looked at what strategy is and introduced a number of different perspectives on strategy formulation. We addressed the importance of values in determining why an organization exists, and looked at how an organization's values, its vision, and its mission guide individuals' behaviour by signposting what is important to the organization. We explained the importance of an organization being willing to change the assumptions that underpin its theory of the business if it is to adapt to changes in its environment. We also introduced a strategic management process which involves strategy analysis, strategy formulation, and strategy implementation. We noted that this essentially linear approach is useful for exposition but may not always accurately replicate decisions in the business world. With this caveat in mind we can start to evaluate some tools of analysis that can be used for strategy analysis.

What happens in the general environment is important to an organization. This is because changes that take place in the general environment may point to trends that can substantially impact upon an organization's competitive environment. These changes, sometimes called *discontinuities*, *fractures*, or *tipping points*, that fundamentally impact on the competitive environment will be considered in this chapter. The tools of analysis an organization can use to discern changes in its general environment will also be considered. This includes scenario planning, which will be assessed as an aid to organizational decision making in uncertain environments. The benefits and limitations of a PEST framework, which includes political, economic, social, and technological factors, will be addressed. A SWOT analysis and its links with scenario planning and PEST analysis will be briefly discussed before being taken up in detail in a later chapter. The aim of the chapter is not simply to apply these techniques but, importantly, to understand their limitations. The chapter ends with a discussion of the links between the general and competitive environment.

- Section 2.1 defines the general environment and explains its importance to the competitive environment.

- Section 2.2 evaluates the role of scanning and monitoring the general environment to try to discern *discontinuities* that have the potential to disrupt an organization's competitive environment.

- In Section 2.3 we assess the role of scenario planning in helping organizations to deal with uncertainty in their environment. This section also includes how to undertake scenario planning.

- Section 2.4 evaluates PEST analysis as a tool for analysing the macro-environment. It shows how an organization can detect and monitor *weak signals* in the hope of recognizing the discontinuities or trends that shape the environment.

- In Section 2.5 we explain the use of SWOT analysis with reference to the general and competitive environment.

- The chapter concludes in Section 2.6 with an evaluation of the relationship between the general and competitive environments.

2.1 The General Environment

The external environment facing the organization consists of both a general environment and a competitive environment. The competitive environment consists of the industry and markets in which an organization competes. The competitive environment is analysed in detail in **Chapter 3**. The general environment, in contrast, is often referred to as the macro-environment. This is because changes that occur here will have an effect that transcends firms and specific industries. Figure 2.1 shows the relationship between the general environment, the competitive environment, and the organization. It should be noted that, other things being equal, it is the competitive environment that has the most direct and immediate impact on the organization.

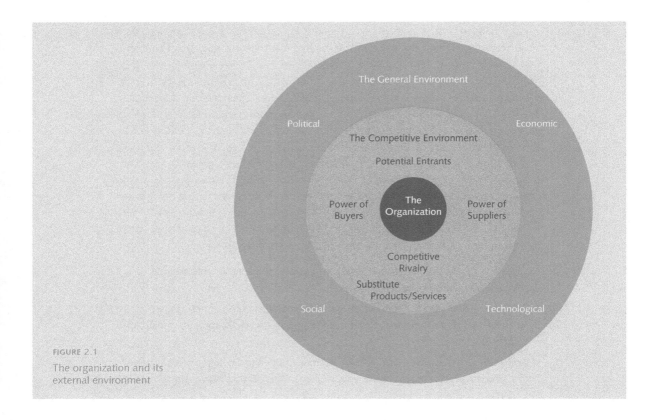

FIGURE 2.1

The organization and its external environment

That said, organizations must continually scan and monitor their general environment for signals, often weak or barely perceptible, which might indicate a change in their competitive environment. For example, firms in the industry that produced typewriters would have been unwise not to scan the general environment for signs of change, in this case technological change. The advent of micro-technologies was a clear threat to the typewriter industry, ushering in as it did the era of the word processor. It is easy to forget that individuals who relied upon the use of the typewriter were initially sceptical about learning how to use the new technology. Nowadays one is hard pushed to see typewriters in use.

In order to scan and monitor their environment, firms require tools of analysis or models that will allow them to factor in the changes in the general environment and evaluate their impact. One such approach involves *scanning* the environment to detect signals that will act as a signpost for future changes in the organization's industry. In addition, an organization must *monitor* its environment to discern patterns and trends that are beginning to form and try to *forecast* the future direction of these trends. Ginter and Duncan (1990) argue that macro-environmental analysis can act as an early-warning system by giving organizations time to anticipate opportunities and threats and develop appropriate responses.

Therefore, the aim of macro-environmental analysis is to aid the organization in discerning trends in the general environment which might impact upon its industry and markets. The organization is then able to formulate a strategy and use its internal resources and capabilities to position itself to exploit opportunities as they arise. At the same time the strategy will be acting to mitigate the effects of any threats. However, as we shall see in **Chapter 3**, there is a belief that the pace of change in the macro-environment is increasing, and is becoming more turbulent and unpredictable. This uncertainty effectively shortens the lead time an organization has to anticipate and respond to changes in its environment.

2.2 Scanning, Monitoring, and Forecasting Changes in the Environment

The purpose of scanning and monitoring the general environment is to try to discern changes, however small, that have the potential to disrupt an organization's competitive environment. Once these changes are discerned, it is up to the organization to monitor them and see if they might become a trend that can affect its industry. Clearly, experience and intuition will be involved in trying to forecast where these changes will eventually manifest themselves, or indeed if they will have any impact at all. We look at scanning, monitoring, and forecasting changes in the general environment below.

2.2.1 Scanning the Environment

It is often said that there are two certainties in life: *death and taxes*. However, a third certainty can be added: *change*. If the external environment facing organizations was stable and simple to understand, then firms would be faced with an enviable situation of having relatively little change or, if change occurs, it would be easy to forecast based on historic trends. Some commodity markets exhibit a relative degree of stability, making predictions or extrapolations based on past data quite reliable. However, most environmental conditions facing organizations are complex, uncertain, and prone to change. They are complex because of the sheer volume of data that exists in the environment. Therefore any analytical tool or framework can only extract and simplify a tiny proportion of this data. At the same time, any given source of data, for example economic data on the well-being of the economy, is ambiguous as it can be interpreted in a number of different ways.

If past performance is no guarantee of what will occur in the future because of uneven changes and discontinuities then attempts at forecasting the future are fraught with uncertainty. Discontinuities refer to the threats faced by organizations and industries that have the potential to undermine the way they do business. We have already mentioned the typewriter industry; other examples include Amazon.com and Dell, which have both taken advantage of the Internet to change the way established products are customized and delivered to end consumers.

Fahey and Narayanan (1986, quoted by Mercer 1998) suggest three goals for an analysis of the general environment. First, the analysis should provide an understanding of current and potential changes taking place in the environment. Second, it should provide important intelligence for strategic decision makers. Third, environmental analysis should facilitate and foster strategic thinking in organizations. For Fahey and Narayanan, scanning may reveal 'actual or imminent environmental change because it explicitly focuses on areas that the organization may have previously neglected' (see Mercer 1998). Scanning the environment as a general activity has been made far more cost effective with the advent of the Internet. Prior to the Internet, the view was that scanning was a costly activity which could only take account of a fraction of the information that existed in an organization's environment. By redefining search costs, the Internet has changed the economics of undertaking scanning. At the same time it has provided an opportunity to access a wealth of data which requires time and effort to structure properly.

Scanning, therefore, is an opportunity for the organization to detect weak signals in the general environment before these have coalesced into a discernible pattern which might affect its competitive environment. Weak signals refer to minor changes in the external environment that an organization's scanning of the environment may barely register. This is because their impact has yet to be felt. The key for organizations is to be able to read these signals correctly and monitor them until they coalesce into a more clearly discernible pattern. However, there are errors that can follow when looking for patterns. The first is that the organization may fail to identify these signals. The second is that the organization may discern a pattern that is not there but is based on the assumptions and mental models that managers carry in their heads. We saw in **Chapter 1** how senior management's reliance on its existing theory of the business can affect the success of the organization by blindsiding them to changes taking place in the environment. Ansoff (1984) makes the point that the detection of weak signals requires senior management commitment and sensitivity on the part of the observers. This means that the organization must be diligent in continually scanning its macro-environment for weak signals. When it believes that it has discerned something significant occurring in its general environment, this broad scanning can turn into a more focused monitoring.

2.2.2 Monitoring the Environment

While scanning the environment may make organizations aware of weak signals, unless these are carefully monitored the resulting patterns will be missed. Monitoring can be seen as the activity that follows these initially disparate signals and tracks them as they grow into more clearly discernible patterns. Monitoring allows an organization to see how these general environment trends will impact on its competitive environment. Whereas scanning is a more broad-brush approach, monitoring uses a finer brush stroke. However, the two are inseparable, since without an identification of weak signals in the general environment there is no focus for an organization's monitoring activities. One way in which an organization might monitor weak signals is to set thresholds such that any activity which occurs above the threshold will be monitored. This might include, for example, when an interest is shown by a major competitor in a particular social or technological change. This interest then becomes the threshold at which the organization itself starts to take an interest.

2.2.3 Forecasting Changes in the Environment

The purpose of scanning and monitoring the general environment is to aid the organization in developing viable forecasts of future trends before they become an unmitigated threat. This is particularly useful when dealing with discontinuities which themselves will usually evolve from weak signals that exist in the environment. The objective is to use this information to develop robust strategies that ensure a degree of competitive advantage.

Van der Heijden (1996) identifies three main types of uncertainty.

1. **Risks.** This is where past performance of similar events allows us to estimate the probabilities of future outcomes.
2. **Structural uncertainties.** This is where an event is unique enough not to offer evidence of such probabilities.
3. **Unknowables.** This is where we cannot even imagine the event.

Most managers are capable of dealing with the type of uncertainty that appears in the form of *risks*. Also, what is *unknowable* cannot, by definition, be forecast and

STRUCTURAL UNCERTAINTIES

where no probable pattern of
outcomes can be derived from
previous experience

therefore the organization must wait for the event to occur before it can react to it. This leaves structural uncertainties where no probable pattern of outcomes can be derived from previous experience. In such a situation, van der Heijden suggests scenario planning as a useful tool of analysis to help the organization make sense of an uncertain and dynamic environment that has little in the way of clear road maps.

For information on strategic decision making under conditions of uncertainty go to the Online Resource Centre and see the Key Work feature. **www.oxfordtextbooks.co.uk/orc/henry2e/**

2.3 Scenario Planning

Schoemaker (1995) states that 'scenario planning is a disciplined method for imagining possible futures'. It is 'an internally consistent view of what the future might turn out to be' (Porter 1985, p. 446). The oil multinational Royal Dutch Shell has used scenario planning since the 1970s to help it generate and evaluate its strategic options. Scenario planning has given Shell a better success rate in its oil forecasts than its competitors, and it was the first oil company to see overcapacity in the tanker business and Europe's petrochemicals (Schoemaker 1995). Kahane (1992) reminds us that:

> In the oil industry, experts have sometimes been able to suggest, but rarely to predict, the key turning points in crude oil prices... The Shell approach to strategic planning is, instead of forecasts, to use scenarios, a set of stories about alternative futures.

SCENARIO

a challenging, plausible, and
internally consistent view of what
the future might turn out to be

These *stories* promote a discussion of possibilities beyond the most likely one and encourage the organization to consider 'what if' questions. Therefore, a scenario can be seen as a challenging, plausible, and internally consistent view of what the future might turn out to be. They are not forecasts in the sense that one is able to extrapolate using past data. However, they do deal with the future and provide a tool of analysis for the organization to structure the surfeit of information that is contained in the present. In particular, scenarios help organizations recognize the weak signals that signpost changes in its environment. It is these weak signals which precede environmental discontinuities, fractures, or *strategic inflection points* that help shape the competitive environment (Morgan 1988; Grove 1996). If an organization is to remain proactive in its competitive environment it must not allow the rules of the game to be

TIPPING POINT

an unexpected and unpredictable
event that has a major impact on
an organization's environment

changed to its detriment, that is, it must be capable of dealing with a tipping point (Gladwell 2000), an unexpected and unpredictable event that has a major impact on an organization's environment.

For a discussion of strategic inflection points and their impact on strategy go to the Online Resource Centre and see the Key Work feature. www.oxfordtextbooks.co.uk/orc/henry2e/

2

Strategic decisions are almost always fraught with ambiguity and uncertainty which create complexity for decision makers. As human beings we are subject to biases and imperfect reasoning about uncertainty, that is, as individuals we will tend to misread events that are unlikely and either ignore or overemphasize unlikely but significant events. In an attempt to resolve these shortcomings, most companies will use some form of discounted cash flow coupled with sensitivity analysis when analysing risky strategic decisions (Gertner 2000). The problem with these quantitative approaches is that they imbue the decision making with a false sense of objectivity and can be misleading. For example, sensitivity analysis is seen as overly simplistic in that by varying one parameter at a time it fails to incorporate any links or correlations between them. Scenario planning is an approach to decision making under conditions of uncertainty that helps to overcome many of the shortcomings of traditional decision-making methods; that is, scenario planning allows organizations to change several variables at the same time without keeping other variables constant. Crucially, scenario planning helps to overcome some of the *biases* and *imperfect reasoning* that human beings make under conditions of uncertainty.

Scenarios are a tool of analysis to help improve the decision-making process set against the background of a number of possible future environments. They benefit the organization by readily helping managers think in a more systematic way. This allows individuals to more readily recognize change in their business environment instead of ignoring or rejecting it. Van der Heijden (1996), a former head of scenario planning at Shell, states that the benefits of scenario planning for Shell have been:

- More robust strategic decisions.
- Better thinking about the future by a 'stretching mental model'.
- Enhancing corporate perception and recognizing events as a pattern (the recognition and monitoring of weak signals until they coalesce into a pattern is clearly important here).
- Improving communication throughout the company by providing a context for decisions.
- A means to provide leadership to the organization.

The process of scenario planning should have the objective of positively influencing the strategy of the organization. This requires that the scenarios devised should stretch the imagination of management while also remaining plausible. In order to achieve this, organizations must be prepared to invest resources in educating managers to help them make the best use of scenarios. They need to recognize that developing scenarios takes time and is most effective when managers from different parts of the business interact. By constructing multiple scenarios, an organization can explore the consequences of uncertainty for its choice of strategies. Furthermore, an organization can formulate strategies knowing that the assumptions on which it competes, what Drucker (1995) refers to as its theory of the business, are surfaced and adequately assessed. (See Case Study: Novacroft which highlights some of the difficulties of taking account of a changing environment).

CASE STUDY 2.1

Novacroft—Dealing with change

Over the past five years Novacroft, which designs, develops and manages smartcards for travel and leisure-service providers, such as Transport for London, has enjoyed strong demand thanks to policies promoting public transport and Oyster-style integrated ticketing systems.

But proposed public spending cuts and tough trading conditions in the travel industry make future investments more doubtful, according to Novacroft's managing director Debra Charles.

'Our market should be both emerging and growing, but there are economic barriers,' she admits. 'Organisations, especially in the public sector, have to make savings. Our competitors are financially stretched so they are selling cheap. We must innovate to find new clients as well as saving our existing customers money.'

Charles, who has a background in both technology and marketing, launched Novacroft in 1998 with money inherited from her parents. As the company's name suggests, she was inspired to start a firm that would use the web to develop new ways of working.

'I thought it would be great to create a transparent online database so that organisations could see what was happening with their money and their clients,' she remembers.

Now, the Northampton-based firm manages more than 1m customer records for clients that issue pre-paid travel tickets and other smart cards. Staff verify and process paper or online applications before loading the information onto a chip, producing plastic cards, processing payments and providing a help centre that answers cardholders' queries. Novacroft can also analyse records ranging from call notes to scanned documents to help clients understand their customers' habits.

One of Novacroft's highest profile contracts is to manage the concessionary Oyster cards for students, children and 16- and 17-year olds on behalf of Transport for London.

As well as checking that applicants have given correct information about their age, address and place of education, the company's helpline deals with questions such as how to replace lost or stolen cards. The company also manages concessionary travel cards on behalf of the Scottish government and handles online applications for Young Persons, Family and Senior Railcards for the Association of Train Operating Companies.

'In the past, clients might have used several different firms to produce cards, provide databases and integrate systems, but we have all that under one roof,' explains Charles, whose chief rivals are major systems integrators such as Accenture and Logica.

'We have been successful in getting big companies on board through the tender process because we have invested in hiring and training the right people and really thinking about what the customer needs. We even self-impose penalty clauses.'

As a result, Novacroft made a substantial profit last year on a turnover of £6m, up from £4.9m in 2007. The company has 96 employees, which rises to approximately 200 when extra staff are brought in to the call centre during the busy start to the academic year.

Finding new clients by maximizing the range and quality of service is a key challenge for Novacroft. As Charles points out, in the aftermath of the bank bail-outs, pledges such as transport secretary Lord Adonis's promise to consider incentives for train operating companies that introduce smart ticketing look far from secure.

'Can we really assume that these statements are facts or that money is ring-fenced?' she says. 'The real certainty is that the government and train operating companies have to save money.'

In recent months Novacroft has worked on scenario planning to consider how the company might react to changing demand. The company prides itself on a 'foxy' approach to market conditions, moving nimbly and using all its available tools to tackle future trends. 'We spent 14 hours in a hotel room thinking about what we know, what we don't know and studying the rules of the game and our competition.'

Understandably, Charles is reluctant to reveal her conclusions, but she is very confident that the exercise was worthwhile. 'We have created a massive opportunity that's totally outside what our competitors are thinking about.' Some diversification into products such as money cards is likely, while building databases that clients can outsource to India is another possibility.

Improving efficiency to keep prices competitive for cash-strapped public sector organisations is another priority. Since March, Charles has introduced a series of lean management techniques that have cut costs by more than £80,000 while maintaining service standards. For example, a study of customer service queries revealed that the number of calls processed by the help centre could be cut by improving online information.

The company is also reaping the benefits of investing around £40,000 in staff leadership training over the past three months, she says.

Charles believes that, despite the slowdown, Novacroft could achieve a turnover of up to £20m within the next five years. 'We stand for innovation, service delivery and value for money—and that's always attractive.'

Source: 'Smart ticketing business Novacroft is looking to play its cards right' *Daily Telegraph*, 14 August 2009

▪ Questions

1. In what ways might scenario planning help Novacroft to remain competitive?
2. What remedies might Novacroft pursue to reduce its reliance on public sector finance?
3. Comment on Debra Charles's confidence in Novacroft's business model.

2.3.1 Undertaking Scenario Planning[1]

Scenario planning is relevant to almost any situation in which a decision maker needs to understand how the future of his or her industry or strategic business unit might develop. It divides our knowledge into two areas: (1) things we think we know something about, and (2) things we consider uncertain or unknowable. The first area is based on the past and continuity. For example, an organization can make fairly safe assumptions about the direction of a country's demographic profile. The uncertain elements include such things as future oil prices, interest rates, and the outcomes of political elections. Even here it is not necessary to account for every possible outcome, since simplifying the outcome is fine for scenario planning. Therefore, an organization might simply categorize future interest rates as high, medium, or low, rather than trying to work out every possible permutation. Also, as scenarios highlight possible futures but not specific strategy formulations, outside opinions such as those of consultants can be included in the process.

A process for developing scenarios is as follows.

1. **Define the scope.** This involves setting the time frame and the scope of analysis. The time frame can be determined by factors such as product life cycles and rate of technological change. The scope of analysis may include products, markets, and geographical areas. Once the time frame is set, the question becomes: What knowledge would the organization benefit most from in that timescale?

2. **Identify the major stakeholders.** Those who can affect and are affected by the organization's decisions. The organization needs to know their current levels of interests and power, and how these have changed over time.

3. **Identify basic trends.** Which political, economic, social, technological, and industry factors will have the most impact on the issues identified in Step 1? The impact of these trends on current strategy can be listed as positive, negative, or uncertain.

4. **Identify key uncertainties.** Which events that have an uncertain outcome will most affect the issues the organization is concerned with? Here again the

organization might consider political, economic, social, and technological factors, in addition to industry factors. For example, what will characterize future consumer trends? An organization should develop possible outcomes for each of these uncertainties. These should be limited to keep the analysis simple.

5. **Construct initial scenario themes.** Once trends and uncertainties are developed, the organization has the basic building blocks for scenario planning. It can then identify extreme world views by juxtaposing all positive elements in one scenario and the negative elements in another broad scenario.

6. **Check for consistency and plausibility.** This involves checking to see if the trends identified are compatible with the chosen time frame. If they are not, then remove all the trends that do not fit the time frame. Do the scenarios combine outcomes of uncertainty that actually go together? In other words, ensure that inconsistent outcomes are not put in a scenario, such as having full employment and zero inflation together. Lastly, have major stakeholders been placed in a position they will not tolerate or cannot change? In this case, the scenario described will probably change into another one. The key then is to identify this ultimate scenario.

7. **Develop learning scenarios.** Here the role is to develop relevant themes for the organization around which possible outcomes and trends can be organized. The scenarios can be given a name or title to reflect that they tell a story. This also helps individuals to remember the scenarios. At this stage the scenarios are useful for research and further learning within the organization rather than decision making.

8. **Identify research needs.** At this stage, further research may be required to understand uncertainties and trends more fully. This is because organizations are knowledgeable about their own competitive environment but less knowledgeable about other industries. Therefore, the organization may need to study changes, in technology for instance, which have yet to impact its industry but may ultimately do so.

9. **Develop quantitative models.** Once further research has been gained, the organization may wish to revisit the internal consistency of the scenarios and decide whether it might benefit from formalizing some interactions in a quantitative model.

10. **Evolve towards decision scenarios.** The ultimate aim of this process is to move the organization towards scenarios that can be used to test its strategy formulation and help it generate new ideas. At this point it is helpful to double check Steps 1–8 to see if the scenarios take account of the issues facing the organization.

If the scenarios are useful to the organization, they might have the following characteristics: (1) they address the concerns of individuals in the organization; (2) the scenarios are internally consistent; (3) they describe fundamentally different futures

2

as opposed to being variations on a particular theme; and (4) each scenario describes an equilibrium state that can exist for a considerable period of time as opposed to being merely short-lived. In summary:

> *scenario planning attempts to capture the richness and range of possibilities, stimulating decision makers to consider changes they would otherwise ignore . . . organizing . . . into narratives that are easier to grasp and use than great volumes of data. Above all . . . scenarios are aimed at challenging the prevailing mind-set. (Schoemaker 1995, p. 27)*

It is perhaps worth reiterating that scenarios are not intended to predict the future. They are designed to help managers deal with a highly uncertain and dynamic environment. They may be aimed at the general or competitive environment (for a discussion of why scenario analysis should be applied at the industry level see Porter (1985)). Porter, whilst recognizing the value of multiple scenarios for an organization's choice of strategy when considering scenario planning at the macro-level, argues, 'Macro-scenarios, despite their relevance, are too general to be sufficient for developing strategy in a particular industry' (Porter 1985, p. 447). Whether this statement is accepted may depend more on the industry being addressed rather than scenario planning *per se*. Scenarios encourage management to 'think the unthinkable', to question and surface assumptions they hold about the environment, and to be prepared to view events from a radically different perspective. Scenarios are a tool of analysis that examines the impact of uncertainty on organizations and industries by explicitly identifying some of the key uncertainties—the scenario variables. For scenarios to be effective, they must encourage the creation of robust strategies that match the organization's limited resources with the endless challenges in the external environment. To do this, scenario planning must ensure that as many as possible of the long-term opportunities and threats facing the organization are identified and addressed.

For more information on how to undertake scenario planning go to the Online Resource Centre and see the Tools and Techniques feature.
www.oxfordtextbooks.co.uk/orc/henry2e/

2.4 PEST Analysis

A useful tool when scanning the general environment is PEST analysis. This refers to political, economic, social, and technological factors. It is worth noting that some commentators include legal and environmental factors separately, preferring to extend the acronym to PESTLE. However, the legal element of the acronym can be subsumed within the political factor. In addition, the use of the last E (which refers to environmental factors) is often meant to signify the effects of our lifestyles on our environment, such as the use of fossil fuels and their impact upon climate change. In this respect it can be captured within the 'social' factor, or indeed within all four factors in one form or another. Therefore, it is not important whether we use PEST (or STEP) or PESTLE, but to understand how this framework can be used and to be aware of its limitations. As long as the choice of acronym is clearly defined we have a consistent approach.

What will PEST do for the organization? PEST analysis is simply another tool to help the organization detect and monitor those weak signals in the hope of recognizing the discontinuities or fractures shaping the environment. PEST analysis can be used to help detect trends in the external environment that will ultimately find their way into the competitive environment. It provides a link between the general and competitive environments in that weak signals in the general environment can become key forces for change in the competitive environment.

Although we will deal with each factor in turn, it should be noted that interrelationships between the factors exist. For example, a social trend of healthier eating and consumers' increasing distaste for factory farming (the crowding of animals and fowl in confined spaces prior to their sale for human consumption) may signal to supermarkets a change in consumer behaviour and spending patterns.

2.4.1 Political Factors

The political factor of PEST deals with the effects of government policy. Inasmuch as government policy is worked out through legislation, it encompasses all legal elements of this analysis. This includes items such as government stability, taxation policy, and government regulation. Government stability is not a major issue in Western economies. However, where multinational corporations operate across international borders, the stability of governments and political systems in those countries needs to be taken into account. These corporations need to be assured that there will not be any sudden and detrimental changes that might jeopardize the substantial investments they will have made. The safety of their personnel operating in these countries will be paramount, as will the existence of an infrastructure which allows the efficient transfer of goods and services as well as financial assets.

For instance, a government policy of deregulation or privatization has the effect of opening up markets to competition. Previously comfortable industries feel the chill wind of change, and organizations within the industry are forced to innovate and cut costs to remain competitive. This is because new entrants will often enter a market with lower cost curves and more innovative products and services owing to a better use of technology and a clearer understanding of consumer needs. To avoid being surprised, companies need to be scanning their environment for signs of change in government policy which might impact on their industry.

An air or sea disaster which costs human lives may prompt tighter government regulations in the areas of health and safety, particularly where an investigation shows that the disaster could have been avoided. Companies operating within these industries should not be waiting to react to the outcome but should have worked out the ramifications of government involvement and be positioning themselves to take advantage of government regulation. The reduction in carbon dioxide emissions and new fuel consumption standards for cars came about as a result of intergovernmental regulations. This, in turn, was a result of widespread concern by consumers and environmental groups about climate change due to increased levels of 'greenhouse gases' in the atmosphere. This highlights the links between social trends and political change.

Government regulation need not be something for companies to fear. Porter and van der Linde (1995) point out that environmental regulations, such as reducing pollution, may act to spur competitive companies on to innovate and reduce costs to counter the increased costs of regulation. While the US car makers fought new fuel consumption standards in the vain hope that they would go away, the Japanese and German car makers developed lighter and more fuel-efficient cars. The companies that reap the competitive benefits will be the early movers: 'the companies that see the opportunity first and embrace innovation-based solutions' (Porter and van der Linde 1995). To do this, managers need to develop a new mindset which recognizes environmental improvement as a competitive opportunity rather than a threat.

CORPORATE SOCIAL RESPONSIBILITY

recognition that organizations need to take account of the social and ethical impact of their business decisions on the wider environment in which they compete

There is evidence across the Anglo-American economies of the UK and the US that some organizations are beginning to recognize that good business can involve **corporate social responsibility** (CSR). For example, the world's leading media company, Time Warner, produced its first comprehensive report on its corporate social responsibility activities in 2006. It states:

> *Corporate social responsibility is not an afterthought at our company. It is central to what we do. That's because Time Warner cannot be a great company unless we are a good company . . . It's simply good business to do so. (Time Warner 2006)*

In the US the Sarbanes–Oxley Act 2002 resulted from the corporate collapse of Enron, WorldCom, and Tyco. There was widespread concern that boardroom executives (including non-executives) and the accountancy profession had failed to safeguard shareholders' interest, and in the case of Enron had actively operated to pervert that interest. Internal auditors were seen as ineffectual and often completely unaware of what powerful executives were doing. This legislation can work to the advantage of companies that are proactive in their response to it. For example, shareholders will be more confident in investing in a company which can show that it already has stringent ethical guidelines in place and that any breach of those guidelines will be taken seriously.

The Building Society Act 1986 allowed building societies in the UK to offer current accounts and financial services that were previously the preserve of banks. This had far-reaching effects on the financial services sector, intensifying competition for customers and leading to consolidation within the industry. A player within the industry would have been wise to conduct some form of PEST analysis in order to determine the effects of these politically driven changes within the industry and on their organization.

2.4.2 Economic Factors

Key economic indicators include interest rates, disposable income, unemployment rates, retail price index (inflation), gross domestic product (GDP), and exchange rates. However, economic data can be notoriously fickle and ambiguous. In addition, an economic indicator can never provide a complete picture (even of the subset of data it purports to track), but rather provides a snapshot and simplification of complex economic phenomena. This makes scanning and monitoring the general environment for signs of economic shifts which might impact an organization's industry a little difficult.

The strengthening of an economy will generally benefit industries, but the extent of its effect will vary according to which economic factors are most affected. For example, the construction industry and manufacturing are most susceptible to increases in the rate of interest. Manufacturing organizations which export goods abroad will be scanning the general environment for signs of an appreciation in exchange rates, the effect of which will be to make it harder for them to sell their goods abroad but relatively easier for importers to sell their goods in the domestic market. In order to remain competitive, manufacturers exporting abroad will need to make efficiency gains and innovate so that they can offset the unfavourable exchange rate with a reduction in price or increase in quality.

STRATEGY FOCUS
PEST Analysis—
The Construction Industry

The construction industry worldwide is renowned for operating on narrow profit margins. Any sudden and prolonged rises in interest rates can have a profound effect on industry profitability. The key for players in this industry is to borrow funds at an interest rate which allows building projects to be completed successfully, on budget, and on time. Where there is slippage of large-scale construction projects, as was seen with the Channel Tunnel, this immediately brings into doubt their financial viability. Any delay inevitably increases the final project cost. Investors will be acutely aware that their investment in a project has an opportunity cost, that is, their money might be better invested elsewhere. If interest rates begin to climb this

2

Construction firms already scanning and monitoring their environment can anticipate economic trends and prepare for them.

© iStockphoto.com/David Newton

exacerbates the situation, as investors will demand a greater return. The consortium of banks financing loans will want to rearrange the interest rates on offer to reflect the increased risk and changing economic conditions.

UK and US banks are known for their preference for short-term financing and unwillingness to invest in the equity of construction projects, in contrast with their Japanese counterparts. This makes the monitoring of data and detecting any changes in the environment of great importance. Investment banks will readily pick up any adverse change in the economic fundamentals of a project. Therefore, the organization must not only be aware of these changes but also have contingent plans in place for dealing with them. It also helps if the organization is aware of the interrelationships between economic variables—that a rise in inflation will probably cause the monetary authorities to consider increasing interest rates. They can then work through the ramifications of such changes on their projects. If one of the government's political priorities is to manage the economy, we can see a relationship between economic and political factors. Construction firms already scanning and monitoring their environment will be expecting these trends and therefore be prepared.

Central bankers, such as the chairman of the US Federal Reserve Bank and the Governor of the Bank of England, are faced with a number of dilemmas. For instance, the economic data they will be tracking and monitoring will contain conflicting views. This forces them to use their judgement to look for similar patterns that have occurred in the past as a basis on which they can make decisions. This is not all that they have to contend with. The balance of economic data being monitored may lead them to believe that the economy is overheating. Their response may be a quarter-point increase in interest rates. However, the time it takes to implement the interest rate rise and for this to impact on the economy may take a further six months. In that time it is conceivable that more recent economic data will point to the economy actually slowing down. Therefore, the effect of the rise in interest rates will be to accelerate the likelihood of an economic downturn. This reinforces the need for sombre and intelligent judgement when using PEST analysis.

2.4.3 Social Factors

Social factors include cultural changes within the environment and are often referred to as socio-cultural. In the UK, increasing consumer concern with genetically modified food (GMF) and lobbying from consumer groups forced the government to scale down its introduction of genetically modified crops. Clearly, such social trends are of great importance to companies which research and produce genetically modified products. Many have been caught unawares by the strength of consumer response and find that they must first allay consumer fears if their products are to be fully accepted. Indeed, the frozen food retailer Iceland was one of the first retailers to state emphatically that none of the food products it stocks contains genetically modified ingredients. In doing so Iceland had accurately read a change in social trends and recognized that it would influence consumer spending patterns. Other supermarkets were quick to follow.

STRATEGY FOCUS
Demographic Changes

The US and Western Europe face an ageing population with attendant problems for pension fund provisions. As the base of the working population continues to shrink, while advances in medical science and healthier eating ensure that people continue to live longer, companies are faced with shortfalls in the pension fund provisions they make for employee retirement. One solution is to encourage employees to take out personal pension plans that will supplement any state provision. Another solution being considered by governments is for employees to consider working for longer. In this way they can build up their pension fund to an acceptable level and avoid any shortfall.

In response to a falling birth rate, companies like Johnson & Johnson, involved with the provision of baby-care products, have effectively targeted these products at an adult female

Courtesy of Johnson & Johnson

In response to a falling birth rate, companies like Johnson & Johnson have targeted their baby products at an adult female audience.

2

audience. For example, their baby lotion is now marketed as being kind and gentle to women's skin, as well as that of babies. This represents a response to changes in the general environment that directly affect their industry. Retail organizations in the US and Europe are increasingly responding to the changing demographics of an ageing population by employing older personnel. They recognize that retired employees possess a wealth of experience and respect for others that can be used to add value when serving customers.

2.4.4 Technological Factors

Without doubt some of the major changes taking place in the general environment that are impacting the competitive environment are technological. One merely has to think about how Amazon and Dell have used the Internet to change traditional retailing within their respective industries. For instance, for a small retailer operating in a remote location, the financial outlay of marketing its product to customers nationwide would prove prohibitive. However, with the advent of the Internet, a retailer can access these consumers with a basic web page advertising its wares worldwide. It is interesting to note that small family businesses find their goods being demanded far outside their national borders because of awareness of their products through the Internet.

Technological factors include the rates of obsolescence, that is, the speed with which new technological discoveries supersede established technologies. The rate of change in technology and innovations has the effect of causing new industries to emerge and also changes the ways in which existing industries compete. Technological advances include the Internet, the use of sophisticated software (increasingly being used in the design and testing of automobiles), genetic engineering (see Section 2.4.3), and nanotechnology.

The rapid rate of change of technology has changed the dynamics of industries such as newspaper publishing, banking, financial services, and insurance. This has allowed new entrants to enter the market at a lower cost base than incumbents, thereby offering more competitively priced products and services and gaining market share in the process. Direct Line insurance in the UK cuts out the insurance broker (intermediate) by providing insurance quotations direct to the consumer over the telephone. This allowed it to gain rapid market share and eventually become the marker leader. It changed the rules of the insurance industry, forcing incumbent players to follow suit or face a loss in market share. As the insurance industry becomes increasingly commoditized, differentiation becomes harder to achieve as organizations compete on price. Direct Line's first-mover advantage is being eroded, as competing firms such as Norwich Union prove capable of competing on a price basis.

First Direct, a subsidiary of HSBC, pioneered the use of telephone banking in the UK. At the time competitors were slow to follow suit, but, once it was established, all players offered a telephone banking option. The same is true of Internet banking. Telephone and Internet banking provide obvious consumer benefits as the financial cost of undertaking transactions within a bank branch is far in excess of the same transaction undertaken by telephone or online. In fact, when the transaction is undertaken online the cost falls substantially. Therefore, organizations must be prepared to innovate and adopt new technologies if they wish to remain competitive.

The Internet has been compared to the Industrial Revolution in terms of the changes it has brought about. The pace of change of technology is increasing. Its unpredictability is increasing. Markets are becoming increasingly turbulent. This makes it important to try to detect the weak signals which grow into discernible patterns that have the potential to change how industries operate. Moreover, if tipping points are unexpected, we need to change our thinking via the use of scenario planning to expect the unexpected. Organizations may not be able to predict these events but they will be in a stronger competitive position to respond to them once they have occurred. While the impact of technological change and changing consumer preferences continues to challenge the business model of traditional high street retailers such as the UK's WH Smith, such changes are not exclusively the preserve of the private sector. Organizations in the public sector also face changes, often socio-political in nature, and here too an understanding of PEST analysis can benefit the organization. (See Case Study: Radical Change in the NHS, which highlights some of the important factors driving change within the National Health Service).

CASE STUDY 2.2
Radical Change in the NHS

Senior officials have set 'aggressive' targets to reduce the number of patients referred to specialists, or treated in Accident and Emergency departments, while GPs will be asked to cut down on the amount of time spent in consultations. The plans are being issued as senior managers warned that the NHS is about to face the greatest financial pressures since its inception. They fear that when the current spending round ends in 2011, the impact of an anticipated real-terms freeze or cuts—coming as the demands on the NHS of an ageing population increase—will be devastating.

The NHS Confederation, which represents NHS managers, will tell this week's Labour Party conference that the impending challenge is so great that hospital closures and job cuts must be enforced across the country.

The National Health Service

It comes as two leading think tanks predict a future funding gap of between £20bn and £40bn within six years of 2011.

Regional health authorities have ordered hospitals and primary care trusts to draw up plans for cuts worth billions.

In London, NHS trusts have been told to divert more than half of A&E patients, and those seeing specialists, to cheaper 'polyclinics' run by groups of GPs. Meanwhile, family doctors will be asked to speed up their consultations, reducing the average time per patient from 12 minutes to eight. The instructions drawn up by NHS London, and seen by *The Sunday Telegraph*, order trusts to demonstrate that they can deliver an 'aggressive scenario' in response to funding pressures.

Under its 'affordability assumptions', already-controversial plans to reduce the number of patients treated in hospital are given more demanding targets in an attempt to cut costs.

Sixty per cent of activity which now takes place in A&E departments should happen in community clinics within five years, the document says, along with 55 per cent of outpatient treatment. Thirty per cent of outpatient appointments will be stopped altogether. Managers say not all appointments are necessary, though many doctors argue it is impossible to know in advance which patients do not need to be seen. The number of diagnostic tests carried out will be cut by 15 per cent, while the amount of surgery will be reduced by seven per cent.

Although the 'polyclinic' model, to reduce demand on hospitals, is supposed to shift more treatment into the community, GPs will be told to reduce their average appointment time by one third, from 12 minutes to eight.

Senior managers in other regions, who will draw up their own plans later this year, said rural communities faced particular pressures, with small maternity and district general hospitals likely to struggle in the funding crisis.

In a speech tonight to the Labour Party conference in Brighton, the NHS Confederation will warn that the service across the country faces unprecedented difficulties, which require 'bold and decisive measures'.

Its policy director Nigel Edwards told *The Sunday Telegraph*: 'The NHS has never experienced a financial challenge of this magnitude or duration in its history.'

He said improving the operation of the NHS, and treating more patients earlier in primary care, would not be enough to balance the books.

Delegates will be told: 'Savings only start to become available when we can shut entire buildings, sites and reduce staffing numbers.'

The organisation, which represents NHS managers, will also call for 'uncomfortable decisions' to be made to limit staff pay.

Under a three-year deal already agreed, nurses will receive a rise of 2.25 per cent in April.

Sir Robert Naylor, chief executive of University College Hospital in London, said pay should be frozen for NHS staff after that point. If it was not, every one per cent pay rise could cost 10,000 job cuts, he said.

The chief executive said that while he supported plans to treat more patients in the community, he was concerned that PCTs were planning to cut back on hospital services before alternatives were put in place.

'The investment in those services has to come first or where do the patients go?' he said, criticising 'oversimplified' analyses which failed to take account of increasing public demand.

Dr Laurence Buckman, chairman of the British Medical Association's GP committee, described the plans as 'desperate and inadequately thought through'.

Dr Buckman, who works as a GP in London, said targets to reduce outpatient appointments by 30 per cent would put patients at particular risk.

He said: 'All this means is that those people who are refused a referral to a specialist will be forced to go privately, or go nowhere. This will be difficult for doctors, but patients will be the real victims.'

While some specialist referrals turn out to be unnecessary, GPs only asked for a specialist opinion when they needed it, Dr Buckman said.

A study by the King's Fund and the Institute for Fiscal Studies forecasts a funding gap of between £20bn and £40bn by 2017, if funding for the NHS receives no increase, or gets a real-terms freeze which only keeps pace with inflation.

Sue Slipman, director of the Foundation Trust Network, which represents the best hospitals, warned of an 'Armageddon scenario' which could unfold without decisive action on pay, and terms and conditions.

She said: 'There is a trade-off between saving jobs, and pay increases, and in the current climate, protecting jobs needs to be a priority.'

Katherine Murphy, from the Patients Association, accused NHS managers of wasting billions on management and repeated organisational restructuring during the boom years of record investment. She said there was no evidence that plans to shift patients into the community would provide safe care.

'Elderly patients often require intensive support which often means lots of staff, in hospitals. The need is only going to get greater—these plans look like madness,' she said.

A spokesman for NHS London said its documents provided planning scenarios, rather than forecasts, to cope with a changing economic environment. He said the NHS was investing heavily to ensure care was provided in the most appropriate setting.

Source: 'Plans for swingeing hospital cuts as NHS on brink of Armageddon' *Sunday Telegraph*, 26 Sep 2009

Questions

1. Outline the PEST factors driving change within the NHS.

2. Which PEST factors do you consider to be the most important, and why?

3. How can an analysis of PEST factors help the government and NHS chief executives to resolve the crisis in the health service?

2.4.5 Limitations of PEST Analysis

The economic example illustrates some of the limitations of dealing with macro-environmental analysis. First, PEST analysis is not simply writing a 'shopping list'—the use of disparate bullet points without any consideration of their wider ramifications. In listing the economic factors, for example, one must clearly draw out the implications of each factor on the organization's environment. In addition, the rate of change of PEST factors in the general environment and their increasing unpredictability act to limit the use of PEST analysis. Some have argued that the competitive environment is the only true arena for the organization to analyse since it is the competitive environment that has the greatest impact on a firm's markets and products (Porter 1985, particularly Chapter 13). Whilst there is agreement that the competitive environment has the greatest effect on an organization's ability to achieve competitive advantage, it would be unwise to refrain from analysing the general environment.

For information on how to write a PEST analysis go to the Online Resource Centre and see the Tools and Techniques feature.
www.oxfordtextbooks.co.uk/orc/henry2e/

2.5 SWOT Analysis

SWOT analysis refers to strengths, weaknesses, opportunities, and threats. Strengths and weaknesses refer to the organization's internal environment over which the firm has control. Strengths are areas where the organization excels in comparison with its competitors, while weaknesses are areas where the organization may be at a comparative disadvantage. Opportunities and threats refer to the organization's external environment, over which it has much less control. SWOT may arise in both the general and the competitive environment. However, the unpredictable nature of events in the general environment tends to make the use of SWOT analysis more problematic.

Taken together, scenario planning and PEST analysis can help to identify the external opportunities and threats (OT) facing an organization. The firm's internal strengths and weaknesses (SW) can best be determined following an appraisal of its resources and capabilities. SWOT analysis allows an organization to assess its current strategy in light of its changing environment (and its competitors), and to help turn potential threats into opportunities and weaknesses into strengths. A key point to keep in mind is that it is the external analysis that precedes the internal analysis of a firm's resources and capabilities. SWOT analysis can usefully be conducted once an audit of the external environment and the firm's own internal environment has been completed. With this in mind we will revisit SWOT analysis in **Chapter 4**.

2.6 The General and the Competitive Environments

By making the links between the general environment and the competitive environment explicit, an organization can conduct its analyses in more depth by assessing its ability to deal with the impact of these trends on its industries and markets. To be of benefit, these general environment factors require constant and structured monitoring. They should be seen as an additional framework in which to detect the important weak signals that coalesce into discernible patterns and foretell structural changes in an industry. In this respect, both scenario planning and PEST have an important role to play in identifying the discontinuities that will have the greatest impact on an organization's competitive environment. Although the general and competitive environments are discussed in separate chapters, it may be helpful to think of them as part of the same continuum. Seen in this way the analysis undertaken simply moves an organization further along this continuum.

 ## Summary

All organizations need to be aware of the events taking place in their general environment and understand what impact these might have on their industry and markets. Changes in the general environment can affect the way existing industries compete and cause new industries to emerge. Therefore, it becomes important for organizations to scan and monitor their general environment in order to detect signs of change. We have seen that weak signals, which are often difficult to detect, may act as a precursor of discontinuities. These discontinuities may arise as a result of step changes in technology, for example, and represent structural changes that will have an impact on an organization's industry. If the organization is to be able to deal with tipping points that are unexpected and unpredictable, it must be willing to think outside its usual parameters and expect the unexpected. In that way, although the organization cannot predict when tipping points will occur, it can at least learn to expect them.

The use of scenario planning is relevant here to help the organization develop different ways of thinking about its environment. Scenario planning involves developing a challenging, plausible, and internally consistent view of what the future might turn out to be. The scenarios are not forecasts in the sense that one is able to extrapolate using past data. However, they do deal with the future and provide a tool of analysis for the firm to structure the abundant information that is contained in the present. A major benefit of scenarios is to help organizations recognize the weak signals that signpost change in the environment, and to enable managers to question the assumptions they hold about the nature of competition.

PEST analysis is also used for making sense of an organization's general environment. The political, economic, social, and technological factors are interrelated. By monitoring changes in these factors the organization is more able to position itself to take advantage of opportunities and mitigate any threats.

SWOT analysis deals with the strengths and weaknesses in the internal environment of the firm, and the opportunities and threats of its external environment. It can be applied when an organization has undertaken an analysis of its external environment, using a PEST analysis, to identify the opportunities and threats, and, when the organization has conducted an appraisal of its internal capabilities, to determine its strengths and weaknesses, and therefore its ability to handle external threats and opportunities.

We have seen that a relationship exists between the general environment and the competitive environment. Events taking place in the general environment will find their way into an organization's competitive environment. Therefore, scanning and monitoring the general environment, using analytical tools such as scenario planning and PEST, will actually benefit the organization in its competitive environment. It will allow the organization to expect the unexpected and thereby actively position itself to take advantage of structural changes likely to affect its industry. It also allows senior managers to periodically test the theory of the mental business models they hold. And all-important technological trends can be detected and acted upon before they rewrite the ways in which organizations compete in an industry.

Review Questions

1. Explain the role that *weak signals* play in helping managers to understand potential changes in their competitive environment.
2. Why might PEST analysis be more appropriate for an organization than scenario planning?

Discussion Question

Scenario planning is little more than an educated guess. Discuss.

Research Topics

1. Using information from a wide variety of sources, such as business and scientific magazines, academic journals, company reports, and the Internet, develop:

   (a) two plausible scenarios for the UK high street retailer WH Smith; and

   (b) two plausible scenarios for the Japanese car manufacturer Toyota.

   Note: You may want to go beyond a simple pessimistic and optimistic set of scenarios and develop more thought-provoking scenarios based upon a comprehensive reading of the literature.

2. Evaluate the impact of a discontinuity on two well-known organizations that compete in different markets. Explain how each organization dealt with the discontinuity.

Recommended Reading

Two books that deal with the use of scenario planning in the macro-environment and the competitive environment are:

- **Porter, M.E.** (1985). *Competitive Advantage*, Chapter 13. Free Press, New York.
- **Van der Heijden, K.** (1996). *Scenarios: The Art of Strategic Conversation*. Wiley, New York.

For a discussion of how to undertake scenario planning and its benefits, see:

- **Schoemaker, P.J.H.** (1995). Scenario planning: a tool for strategic thinking. *Sloan Management Review*, **36**(2), 25–40.

For an interesting read on the effects of weak signals, see:

- **Gladwell, M.** (2000). *The Tipping Point: How Little Things Can Make a Big Difference*. Little, Brown and Co., Boston, MA.

www.oxfordtextbooks.co.uk/orc/henry2e/
Visit the Online Resource Centre that accompanies this book for activities and more information on scenario planning.

Note

¹ Section 2.3.1 is based on Schoemaker (1995).

References

Ansoff, H.I. (1984). *Implementing Strategic Management*. Prentice Hall, Englewood Cliffs, NJ.

Drucker, P.F. (1995). *Managing in a Time of Great Change*. Butterworth Heinemann, Oxford.

Fahey, L. and **Narayanan, V.K.** (1986). *Macroenvironmental Analysis for Strategic Management*. Thomson Learning, Florence, KY.

Gertner, R. (2000). Scenario analysis: telling a good story. In *Mastering Strategy*. Prentice Hall, Harlow.

Ginter, P. and **Duncan, J.** (1990). Macroenvironmental analysis for strategic management. *Long Range Planning*, **23**(6), 91–100.

Gladwell, M. (2000). *The Tipping Point: How Little Things Can Make a Big Difference*. Little, Brown and Co., Boston, MA.

Grove, A.S. (1996) *Only the Paranoid Survive*. Random House, New York.

Kahane, A. (1992). Scenario for energy: sustainable world vs. global mercantilism. *Long Range Planning*, **25**(4), 38–46.

Mercer, D. (1998). *Marketing Strategy: The Challenge of the External Environment*. Open University, Milton Keynes.

Morgan, G. (1988). *Riding the Cutting Edge of Change*. Jossey Bass, San Francisco, CA.

Porter, M.E. (1985). *Competitive Advantage*. Free Press, New York.

Porter, M.E. and **van der Linde, C.** (1995). Green and competitive: ending the stalemate. *Harvard Business Review*, **73**(5), 120–33.

Schoemaker, P.J.H. (1995). Scenario planning: a tool for strategic thinking. *Sloan Management Review*, **36**(2), 25–40.

Time Warner (2006). *Corporate Social Responsibility Report*. Time Warner, New York.

Van der Heijden, K. (1996). *Scenarios: The Art of Strategic Conversation*. Wiley, New York.

3 The Competitive Environment

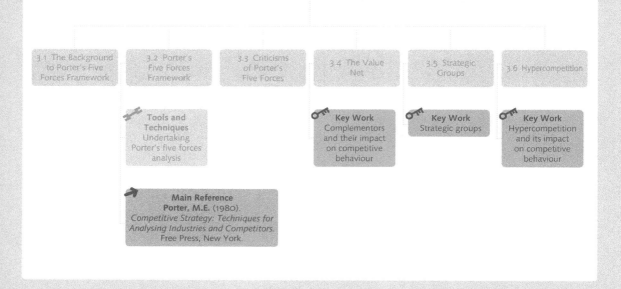

3.1 The Background to Porter's Five Forces Framework	3.2 Porter's Five Forces Framework	3.3 Criticisms of Porter's Five Forces	3.4 The Value Net	3.5 Strategic Groups	3.6 Hypercompetition
	Tools and Techniques Undertaking Porter's five forces analysis		**Key Work** Complementors and their impact on competitive behaviour	**Key Work** Strategic groups	**Key Work** Hypercompetition and its impact on competitive behaviour

Main Reference
Porter, M.E. (1980).
Competitive Strategy: Techniques for Analysing Industries and Competitors.
Free Press, New York.

Learning Objectives

After completing this chapter you should be able to:

- Discuss the background to Porter's five forces
- Evaluate Porter's five forces framework as a tool of competitor analysis
- Discuss the value net and the role of complementors in creating value
- Explain the benefits of co-opetition
- Undertake an analysis of strategic groups within an industry
- Assess the impact of hypercompetition on competitive behaviour

Introduction

The external environment facing an organization consists of a general environment and a competitive environment. Any changes that occur in the general environment have the potential to impact upon an organization's competitive environment. Therefore, it is important that organizations scan and monitor their general environment to discern *weak signal*s that have the ability to affect or fundamentally change the industry within which they compete. The general environment was discussed in **Chapter 2**. In this chapter we will assess the impact of the competitive environment and how an organization can achieve competitive advantage.

It is widely accepted that the nature of competition in an industry is more directly influenced by developments taking place in the competitive environment. This is not to suggest that the general environment is unimportant but that its impact is often less obvious than events taking place in the competitive environment. In this chapter we discuss Porter's approach to competitive strategy and focus on his structural analysis of industries: the *five forces framework*. The strategy formulations emanating from the five forces framework will be discussed in detail in **Chapter 7**, when we consider business-level strategy. These *generic strategies* are a response to the five forces discussed in this chapter.

We start the chapter with a brief discussion of the background to the five forces framework. By placing the five forces framework in context this helps us to understand what it is trying to achieve, how it should be used, and, as we shall see later, what its limitations are. We look at how an organization makes sense of its competitive environment using Porter's five forces framework. We consider some of the criticisms of the five forces framework and include Porter's reaction to these. We discuss the value net and the importance of complementors in their own right and in extending Porter's work. The chapter also includes a discussion of strategic groups within an industry. We end the chapter with an assessment of hypercompetition and its impact on competitor behaviour.

- In Section 3.1 we start the chapter with a discussion of the context within which Porter's five forces framework was developed.

- In Section 3.2 we evaluate the five forces framework as a tool of competitor analysis and discuss its impact on industry profitability.

- Section 3.3 assesses the criticisms of Porter's five forces and includes Porter's response to some of these criticisms.

- Section 3.4 discusses the value net and the importance of complementors in creating industry value. This section also explains co-opetition.

- In Section 3.5 we evaluate strategic groups within an industry and their impact on strategy formulation.

- The chapter ends in Section 3.6 with a discussion of hypercompetition and its effect on competitive behaviour.

3

3.1 The Background to Porter's Five Forces Framework

Michael Porter's ideas on competitive strategy include some of the most pervasive analytical tools used in strategic management. Arguably, there is not a single business school that would not include some elements of Porter's (1980) seminal analyses of industries, competitors, and strategic positioning in its repertoire. In the 1970s Michael Porter was working with two different disciplines—business policy (strategy) and industrial organization. Both disciplines involved evaluating industries and therefore had common issues, but they remained very much separate subject areas. Porter recognized that an opportunity existed to bring thinking about industrial organization into strategy, and thinking about strategy into industrial organization. Thus, he sought to synthesize these two different disciplines—strategy (business policy) and industrial organization, which is a branch of micro-economics.

Porter was faced with a dilemma. The Harvard Business School tradition used case studies to try to capture what was going on in an organization. This meant going out and collecting data from organizations, commonly referred to as field research. However, each organization is unique with different employees producing different products and operating in different markets. Thus, the data collected about one organization cannot be used to predict what might occur in another organization. Therefore, what was needed was to put all these individual case studies of firms together and see what common patterns emerged over time. In this way Porter hoped to make some generalizations that affect all organizations. Porter's early work on business economics used models to try to represent what was occurring in the business world. Such economic models are a simplification of reality, as they can never fully replicate the complexity that exists in the real world. The use of models is an attempt to try to represent what goes on in the real world and to predict or derive useful outcomes.

In the end Porter used neither case studies nor statistical modelling. Instead he opted to use what he calls *frameworks*. (For a discussion of the background to Porter's five forces see Argyres and McGahan (2002)). The benefit of using frameworks is that they can more readily capture the full richness of a phenomenon with a limited number of dimensions. In framework building, the skill is to use the smallest number of core elements that still capture the wide variation that takes place between organizations in competition. As Porter recognized, these dimensions have to be intuitive, that is, they must make sense to practitioners in the context of their own industry. Porter's contribution was to develop a framework for analysing industries that could be generalized from a few core elements, in this case five—hence the *five forces framework*. The five forces framework is an attempt to capture the variation of competition, while being pervasive and rigorous. Porter's insight is that organizations seeking above-average profits should not just react to their competitive environment but should actively seek to shape it. However, as we shall see, Porter's five forces framework is not without its critics.

3.2 Porter's Five Forces Framework

The **five forces framework** is undertaken from the perspective of an incumbent organization, that is, an organization already operating in the industry. The analysis is best used at the level of an organization's strategic business unit (SBU). Although each organization in an industry is unique, the forces within the industry which affect its performance, and hence its profitability, will be common to all organizations in the industry. It is in this sense that Porter's contribution is pervasive—the ability to generalize these five forces to all organizations within the industry. Although the five forces analysis is undertaken from the perspective of an incumbent firm, it can be used to determine whether a firm outside an industry should enter the industry. In this case the barriers to entry which may be protecting the incumbents is an additional cost that outsiders must factor into their analysis of whether to enter the industry. An organization thinking of entering an industry will need to know that it can successfully compete with incumbents in the industry. This will require it to adopt a distinctive **positioning**. For example, Amazon effectively entered book retailing by utilizing the Internet to create support activities which provide a sustainable competitive advantage.

FIVE FORCES FRAMEWORK
a tool of analysis to assess the attractiveness of an industry based on the strengths of five competitive forces

The five forces framework is an analytical tool for assessing the competitive environment (see Porter (1980, Chapter 1) for a discussion of the structural analysis of industries). It enables an organization to determine the attractiveness or profit potential of a particular industry by examining the interaction of five competitive forces. It is the combined strength of these five forces which will ultimately determine an organization's return on investment or the potential for profits within a given industry. The five forces are (1) *threat of new entrants*, (2) *bargaining power of buyers*, (3) *bargaining power of suppliers*, (4) *threat of substitute products or services*, and (5) *intensity of rivalry among firms in an industry*. By examining all five competitive forces an organization is able to assess its ability to compete effectively in an industry. The five forces framework is based on an economic theory known as the 'structure–conduct–performance' (SCP) model. This states that the structure of an industry determines an organization's competitive behaviour (*conduct*), which in turn determines its profitability (*performance*).

POSITIONING
a view that strategy is about how an organization positions itself to mitigate the prevailing industry structure (five forces) that exists

The five forces framework is a rigorous approach to looking at industries and where organizations stand in relation to their industry. In this respect it differs from SWOT analysis which was introduced in **Chapter 2**, and will be further expounded in **Chapter 4**. SWOT analysis is company specific, while Porter's five forces framework is industry specific. The five forces framework allows an organization to make informed decisions, given its resources, about whether competitive rivalry, bargaining power of suppliers, bargaining power of buyers, threat of new entrants, and threat of substitutes make this industry an attractive (profitable) one to compete in.

Using Porter's five forces, an incumbent organization can, for example, decide that industry conditions suggest that it would be more beneficial to use its resources and capabilities in an alternative industry, that is, it should exit the industry or at least decrease its resource commitment to that industry. The five forces framework also enables an organization to improve its competitive positive in relation to industry trends. For example, an awareness of a trend towards consolidation among suppliers (leading to an increase in supplier power) might lead an organization to strengthen its relationships with its existing supplier to avoid downward pressures on its profit margins. Therefore, accurately estimating future trends in the five forces should also provide an organization with an indication of future profits in the industry.

Clearly, if the five forces do not have the same impact upon different industries then we would expect different industries to exhibit different levels of profit. Similarly, within an industry each of these five competitive forces will have a different impact on the industry structure. For Porter, the aim of competitive strategy is to find a position within the industry that an organization can effectively defend against the impact of the five forces, or to try to influence the five forces in its favour. In evaluating the five forces, managers need to be aware that each competitive force will have a different effect on their industry. Therefore, managers need to understand the relative impact of each of the five forces on their industry structure. They can then ascertain their ability to influence the forces with the greatest impact on their industry structure through their strategy formulation. Their ability to change the industry structure will be in direct proportion to their influence over the five forces.

The five forces framework of industry competition is shown in Figure 3.1. We can discuss each of the constituent elements that make up the five forces and ascertain their impact on industry profitability.

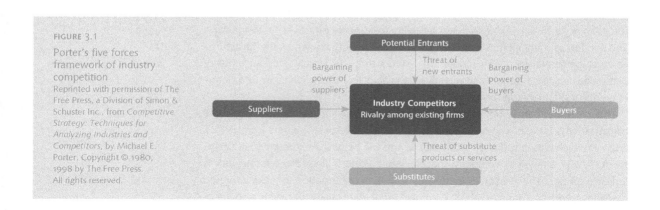

FIGURE 3.1

Porter's five forces framework of industry competition

Potential Entrants

Bargaining power of suppliers

Threat of new entrants

Bargaining power of buyers

Suppliers

Industry Competitors
Rivalry among existing firms

Buyers

Threat of substitute products or services

Substitutes

3.2.1 The Threat of New Entrants[1]

The threat of new entrants is the extent to which new competitors may decide to enter an industry and reduce the level of profits being earned by incumbent firms. Where organizations in an industry earn profits well in excess of their cost of capital, the more likely it is to attract new entrants. The problem for many industries is that they are too easy to enter—and the easier it is for new organizations to enter the industry, the greater the excess capacity and more intense the competition. The threat of entry will depend on the existence of *barriers to entry* and the reaction of existing competitors. If entry barriers are high the threat of entry to the industry by new organizations will be low. Similarly, if a new entrant expects that existing firms will retaliate, for example by lowering their price, this will act to deter the firm from entering the market.

The main barriers to entry include economies of scale, capital requirement, product differentiation, access to distribution channels, cost advantages independent of size, and switching costs.

Economies of scale

Economies of scale occur when the cost of each individual unit produced falls as the total number of units produced increases. Economies of scale tend to be associated with manufacturing organizations since the high capital costs of their plant need to be recovered over a high volume of output. In industries such as chemicals, automobiles, and aerospace large-scale production is imperative to achieve efficiency. The effect of economies of scale is to deter new entrants because it forces them to choose between two undesirable options: either they enter the industry at a high volume of output and risk a strong reaction (retaliation) from existing organizations, or they enter the industry at a small scale, avoiding a reaction from existing firms but operating at a cost disadvantage.

Capital requirements

If organizations need to invest substantial financial resources to compete in an industry, this creates a barrier to entry. For example, organizations wishing to enter the oil industry would face huge capital costs involved in exploration and in specialist plant and machinery. This entry barrier is further strengthened because the major oil companies are vertically integrated. They compete in different stages of production and distribution, that is, both *upstream* and *downstream* activities.

Product differentiation

Where an organization's products are already established in an industry, providing it with high brand awareness and generating customer loyalty, new entrants will have to spend disproportionately on advertising and promotion to establish their product.

Switching costs

Buyers from firms in the industry will be faced with one-off costs when switching from one supplier's product to another. Where switching costs are high, a new entrant must offer a product that is greatly improved or comes at a lower cost if the buyer is to switch.

Access to distribution channels

A new entrant will need to have access to distribution for its product in order to compete successfully in the industry. For example, Haagen-Dazs effectively prevented Ben & Jerry's from successfully competing in the luxury segment of the ice cream market by having sole agreements with distributors. Supermarket retailers are reticent to provide shelf space to new products from small producers who may lack the resources to advertise their products effectively. This can create a barrier to entry.

Cost advantages independent of size

Some competitors within an industry may possess advantages that are independent of size or economies of scale. They may benefit from early entry into the market and associated 'first-mover' advantages. The early experience that such firms acquire may make it difficult for new entrants to imitate their success. Other cost advantages include government policies which may favour incumbent firms, favourable low-cost access to raw materials, and the use of patents to protect proprietary knowledge. (See Porter (1980, Chapter 1) for a full discussion of cost advantages independent of size.)

3.2.2 The Bargaining Power of Buyers

Buyers can affect an industry through their ability to force down prices, bargain for higher quality or more services, and to play competitors off against each other. This power of buyers will reflect the extent to which their purchase represents a sizeable proportion of the organization's overall sales. The power of buyers is increased in the following circumstances.

There is a concentration of buyers and buying volumes are high

Where there is a concentration of buyers in relation to the number of suppliers, and the volume purchase of any one buyer is high, the importance of the buyer's business to the supplier increases. For example, Wal-Mart, the world's largest retailer, is able to exert massive pressure on its suppliers' margins because of the size of the purchases it makes and the importance of these huge purchases to the suppliers. This can be a source of conflict. For example, the Competition Commission, which assesses competition issues in the UK, was asked to look into the bargaining power of UK

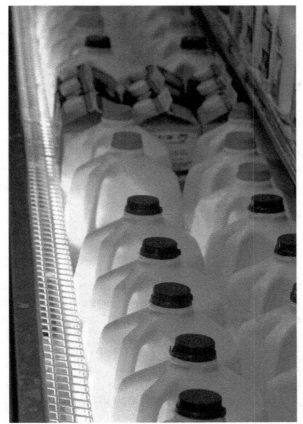

© iStockphoto.com/G.W. Mullis

Suppliers of farm produce
have long complained that
the concentration of
supermarkets' purchases
allows them to drive down
margins for their products,
such as milk.

supermarkets and their influence over suppliers' margins. Suppliers of farm produce
have long complained that the concentration of supermarkets' purchases allows them
to drive down margins for their products.

The products it purchases from the industry are standard or undifferentiated

When they are dealing with a standard or undifferentiated product, buyers are confident that they can always find alternative suppliers. Because the product is standard,
buyers exert pressure on price rather than product features as they play one competitor off against its rival.

Switching costs are low

Where the costs to the buyer of switching supplier is low or involves few risks, the
buyer's bargaining power is enhanced.

There is a threat of backward integration

When buyers have the ability to integrate backwards, that is, to supply the product or service themselves, they pose a threat to the supplier which will strengthen their bargaining position. An example is a shipbuilding company threatening to buy an iron and steel firm to ensure supply of its raw materials.

The industry's product is unimportant to the quality of the buyer's products or services

When the quality of the buyer's product is affected by the industry's product, the buyer will be less price sensitive. Where the quality of the buyer's product is not affected by the industry's product, the buyer will be more price sensitive and therefore in a better bargaining position.

The buyer earns low profits

A buyer's low profits will motivate him or her to lower the purchasing costs charged by suppliers in an effort to secure margins. Where buyers are highly profitable they will generally be less price sensitive.

The buyer has full information

Where buyers have full information on demand and cost they will be in a stronger position. The Internet has greatly reduced the expense of finding out the costs of comparative products.

3.2.3 The Bargaining Power of Suppliers

Suppliers can exert bargaining power over participants in an industry by raising prices or reducing the quality of purchased goods and services. The factors that increase supplier power are the mirror image of those that increase buyer power. In this case the buyer is the firm in the industry and the supplier is the producer of that firm's inputs. This can be confusing and lead to a misapplication of the five forces. Suppliers are powerful under the following circumstances.

The suppliers' industry is dominated by a few companies and is more concentrated than the industry it sells to

The larger the supplier and the more dominant it is, the more pressure it can place on firms in the industry it sells to. This is especially the case where a supplier is selling to many fragmented buyers.

Suppliers are faced with few substitutes

Where there are few or no substitute supplies available the supplier will be in a powerful position.

The industry is not an important customer of the supplier

When suppliers sell to several industries, and any given industry does not represent a significant proportion of its sales, suppliers will be in a more powerful position.

The supplier's products are an important input to the buyer's business

When the supplier's products are an important part of the buyer's manufacturing process or its product quality, such as specialist components for the aerospace industry, the bargaining power of suppliers will be high.

The supplier's products are differentiated or it has built up switching costs for the buyer

If switching to other suppliers will prove difficult and costly for buyers this prevents them playing one supplier off against another. This may arise because a buyer's product specifications tie it to a particular supplier.

There is a threat of forward integration

When suppliers have the ability to integrate forwards into the buyers' industry and compete with their buyers, this will act to reduce profitability in the buyers' industry. It also provides a means of stemming the industry's ability to improve the terms on which it buys.

3.2.4 The Threat of Substitute Products and Services

This is not competition from new entrants, but from products and services which can meet similar needs. By placing a ceiling on the prices organizations in the industry can profitably charge, substitutes limit the potential returns of an industry. The existence of substitutes means that customers can switch to these substitutes in response to a price increase. The more attractive is the *price–performance ratio* of substitute products, the greater the restraint on an industry's profits. An attractive price–performance ratio could be a substitute product that is of a lesser quality but comes at a cheaper price. Examples of substitutes include fax machines and emails for document delivery companies such as FedEx and UPS, and bottled water for carbonated drinks. In trying to determine a substitute product, the organization will need to identify products which can perform the same function as the industry product.

© iStockphoto.com/Brandon Laufenberg

Bottled water has developed as a substitute for carbonated drinks.

3.2.5 The Intensity of Rivalry among Competitors in an Industry

A determinant of the competitive state of most industries and their overall profitability is competition among the organizations within the industry. When organizations in an industry exhibit a high degree of rivalry, this causes industry profits to be reduced. Such rivalry may take the form of incumbents competing aggressively on price. Price cuts can easily be matched by rivals and ultimately lower profits for all organizations in the industry. In contrast, advertising, product innovations, and improved customer service may act to expand overall demand in the industry. Rivalry can increase when competitors in an industry see an opportunity to improve their market position. However, this will invariably be met by retaliatory moves from other organizations in the industry. The following factors affect competitive rivalry.

Numerous or equally balanced competitors

Where there are many competitors in an industry, some organizations may believe that they can make moves without attracting attention. Where there are few competitors in an industry and they are of a similar size, there is likely to be intense competition as each competitor fights for market dominance. Examples include supermarket retailers, investment banks and oil companies.

Slow industry growth

When an industry is characterized by slow growth an organization can only increase its market share at the expense of competitors in that industry.

High fixed costs

High fixed costs in an industry create pressure for organizations to increase their capacity to gain economies of scale. Where the demand conditions will allow only some firms in the industry to reach the volume of sales required to achieve scale economies, this will engender a fight for market share. The excess capacity in the industry usually results in a price war.

Lack of differentiation or switching costs

Where products are undifferentiated competition will be more intense, driven by customer choice based on price and service. Lack of switching costs implies that competitors are unable to prevent customers from going to their rivals.

Extra capacity in large increments

Where extra capacity is added in large increments, this may disrupt the industry's supply–demand balance and create periodic excess capacity leading to price competition.

High exit barriers

The existence of high exit barriers may hinder firms needing to exit the industry. For example, some plants are so specialized that they cannot easily be used to produce alternative goods and services. As demand conditions deteriorate, this creates excess capacity in the industry and acts to reduce profitability within the industry.

CASE STUDY 3.1
Tesco—UK Supermarket Retailer

Tesco is the UK's leading supermarket retailer and the world's third biggest retailer. It is the dominant supermarket in more than 70 per cent of Britain's 121 postcodes. Tesco's long-term strategy has consistently focused on four key objectives: (1) to grow its core UK business; (2) to be a successful international retailer; (3) to be as strong in non-food as in food; (4) to develop retailing services such as Tesco Personal Finance, Telecoms and Tesco.com. As part of their corporate social responsibility they would include a fifth strategic objective—to take account of community needs in all they do. The rationale for the strategy is to broaden the scope of the business to enable it to deliver strong, sustainable long-term growth by following the customer into large expanding markets at home—such as financial services, non-food and telecoms—and new markets abroad, initially in Central Europe and

Tesco, the UK's leading supermarket. Courtesy of Tesco plc

Asia, and more recently in the United States. The pursuit of this strategy has meant Tesco diversifying into growing emerging markets which bring opportunities and threats. Diversification reduces Tesco's reliance on a few business areas but also increases its risks since the industry life cycle is less well understood in emerging markets. In 2010 Tesco had yet to break even with its US Fresh & Easy venture.

Tesco's core UK grocery retail market remains significant within the group with 70 per cent of group sales—£41.5bn—coming from the UK albeit down from 80 per cent a few years ago. In the UK, Tesco employs 286,000 staff and has over 2,300 stores. In Europe and Asia, group sales are £10.1bn and £7.6bn respectively, with residual £0.2bn sales in the USA (see Figure 3.2). It acquired 36 hypermarkets in South Korea, its largest market outside the UK, and is seeking to develop a wholesale cash and carry business in India as part of its strategy of growth into new markets. Worldwide Tesco has over 4,300 stores operating in 14 countries employing 470,000 staff.

In 2006 Tesco reported a 16.7 per cent increase in group profits before tax of £2.2bn. Its group sales were a staggering £43.1bn, representing an increase of 16.5 per cent on the previous year. By 2009 group profits before tax had risen to almost £3bn: up 5.5 per cent on the previous year. Group sales had increased to £59.4bn: up 15 per cent on the previous year. It has grown its financial services business, Tesco Personal Finance (TPF), to 6 million customers showing that it is capable of successfully leveraging its brand. In 2008 it bought out the Royal Bank of Scotland's remaining 50 per cent in the TPF joint venture for £950m as part of its objective to become a full-service retail bank. This strategy of partnering with established businesses—the Royal Bank of Scotland in the UK, Samsung in South Korea, and Trent, the retail arm of the Tata Group, in India—has allowed Tesco to

£59.4bn
Group sales

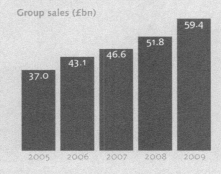

Group sales (£bn)

| 37.0 | 43.1 | 46.6 | 51.8 | 59.4 |
| 2005 | 2006 | 2007 | 2008 | 2009 |

Group sales by region

£0.2bn
£7.6bn
£10.1bn
£41.5bn

UK
EUROPE
ASIA
US

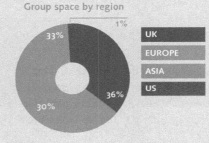

Group space by region

1%
33%
30%
36%

UK
EUROPE
ASIA
US

FIGURE 3.2
Tesco sales figures
©Tesco plc annual review and summary, financial statement 2009

gain access to their existing investment in systems and infrastructure and enabled Tesco to develop profitable business models quickly whilst limiting its own investment and risk in the early years.

Its share of the UK grocery market dropped to 31 per cent in the 12 weeks to 9 August 2009 from 31.2 per cent during the same period a year ago. The other 'big four' UK supermarket retailers all gained market share during this period with ASDA at 17.2 per cent up from 16.7 per cent , Sainsbury's at 15.9 per cent up from 15.6 per cent, and Morrisons at 11.4 per cent up from 11.0 per cent a year ago (see Figure 3.3). During 2009, amidst an economic downturn, Tesco also lost market share to German discount chain Aldi as consumers sought to economise on expenditure, as well as ASDA, Morrisons and Sainsbury's. Tesco's response in late 2009 was to double the number of points awarded by its Clubcard loyalty scheme backed up by a national TV and press campaign. A few months earlier Tesco had limited the double points to specific categories such as clothing and entertainment. Even so, it attracted almost half a million new Clubcard customers. As the recession begins to ease so consumers have begun to migrate back to their regular 'big four' supermarket in 2010.

In common with many larger supermarket chains in the UK (e.g. ASDA and Sainsbury's), Tesco's expanding range of electrical products competes with established non-food retailers such as Dixon's and Comet. Over the years

FIGURE 3.3
The market share of UK supermarket retailers, twelve weeks to 9 August 2009
Source: TNS Worldpanel

the industry has consolidated as firms have engaged in takeovers, as seen by the takeover of Safeway (UK) by Morrisons, a supermarket that is based primarily in the north of England. The US giant and number-one retailer in the world, Wal-Mart, gained an entry into the UK when it took over the UK supermarket ASDA.

The Market Share of Supermarkets in the UK

In 2009 the UK supermarkets had the market shares shown in Figure 3.3. Tesco is the market leader and the dominant player within the industry. However, to sustain this position it must carefully monitor trends in its external environment to provide product innovations and services that will build brand loyalty among its customers. It is also interesting to note that Tesco's arch-rival Sainsbury's continues to improve its competitive position under the leadership of chief executive Justin King, albeit still a long way behind Tesco. This emphasizes an important point that even where an industry may be experiencing constraints on average profitability, a market leader can achieve profits way above the average.

The range of Tesco's products and services highlights an interesting issue. We have placed Tesco within the retail industry and yet, given its product range, a case can be made for suggesting that it operates in different industries, including competing within the telecommunications industry. This point will be returned to later in the chapter when we consider industry boundaries.

The Threat of New Entrants

A new entrant must assess the risk that incumbent firms might retaliate if a newcomer enters the industry. Here relative cost advantages are crucially important and will determine the extent to which an established player can reduce prices and force a new entrant into a costly and damaging price war. Supermarkets in the UK have sought to differentiate their products using own-label brands and segmenting these according to price to reflect different consumer incomes. The question is: to what extent can differentiation within the industry be quickly imitated and therefore competed away? In analyzing the threat of entry we should not lose sight of the fact that firms are attracted to an industry by the profits that can be gained. If an organization can develop a competitive advantage in an industry, it can still be highly profitable even under difficult trading conditions.

In October 2009, the antitrust watchdog, the Competition Commission, formally recommended tighter planning rules to prevent dominant supermarket retailers squeezing out their rivals. The proposal was designed to favour retailers not operating in a town when permission for a new supermarket is sought. It would effectively ban those supermarkets that already have a strong local presence from adding further space. Peter Freeman, chairman of the Competition Commission, argued the planning test would 'stop individual retailers consolidating strong positions in local areas to the detriment of consumers'. Whilst its rivals J Sainsbury and ASDA gave the Competition Commission recommendation a cautious welcome, Tesco criticised the test as ill-conceived, lodging an appeal with the Competition Appeals Tribunal. This resulted in an exception for small extensions of 300 sq. m. (3,200 sq. ft.) to the groceries part of stores, provided those stores were not extended in the previous five years. Nonetheless as the competition test moves closer Tesco is faced with competing against rivals who may yet gain a helping hand from this proposed legislation: something that a careful analysis of its PEST environment might have shown.

The Bargaining Power of Buyers

The fact that customers have a choice of where to shop will act to keep profits down within the industry. In the UK customers can choose between relatively undifferentiated products on offer among rival supermarkets. Switching costs within the industry for buyers is determined by the ease with which consumers can replace their purchases at Tesco with a rival supermarket. As noted above, during 2009 some consumers sought to economise on their grocery bill expenditure by shopping at German discount chains. This highlights the fragility of undifferentiated product offerings. However, the bargaining power of buyers is also determined by their concentration. Although Tesco must be mindful that consumers can go to a competitor for a similar offering, the issue is the impact that this has on their customer base. Furthermore, the Competition Commission issue described above is a proactive attempt to engineer greater consumer choice and benefit for consumers by deliberately restricting dominant retailers from adding more local space and making it easier for rival grocers to open.

The Bargaining Power of Suppliers

Large food manufacturers such as Kellogg's and Heinz need the shelf space that Tesco and food retailers provide for their products to reach a wide customer base. At the same time, Tesco's customers expect to see these branded products in their stores. Tesco effectively hires out its shelf space to whichever manufacturer assures it of the highest profit per square inch. This explains the difficulty that new products from small firms have in competing for supermarket shelf space. However, in the case of farm produce, ranging from milk to poultry, Tesco faces relatively small suppliers producing similar products. The bargaining power of these suppliers is influenced by the extent to which Tesco is able to purchase a substantial volume of their output.

The Threat of Substitutes

These are products and services which can meet similar needs. Therefore the question becomes: If one chooses not to buy from the industry, what alternatives are available? Here the price–performance ratio comes into play. The more attractive is the price–performance ratio of substitute products, the greater is the restraint on an industry's profits. Therefore the price–performance ratio of supermarkets *vis-à-vis* their substitutes will determine profitability levels within the industry.

The Intensity of Rivalry

An industry can be characterized in terms of its concentration ratio. The four-firm concentration ratio is the market share of the four largest firms in the industry. In this industry, Tesco, ASDA Wal-Mart, Sainsbury's, and Morrisons comprise the four largest firms and between them dominate the food retail industry with a combined market share of around 75 per cent. For the industry as a whole, the four-firm concentration ratio will point to the extent of rivalry in the industry.

Sources: 'Christmas spoils go to Morrisons in 'big four' fight' *The Times*, 22 January 2010; 'Tesco wins a concession, but competition test for supermarkets moves a step closer' *The Times*, 3 October 2009; 'Tesco attacks 'senseless' Competition Commission planning test' *Telegraph.co.uk*, 2 October 2009; 'Supermarkets should face local 'competition test' says watchdog' *Guardian.co.uk*, 2 October 2009; 'Tesco to give shoppers double points on Clubcard' *Guardian.co.uk*, 14 August 2009; Tesco Annual Report & Financial Statements 2009; Tesco Annual Review & Summary Financial Statement 2009; 'Waitrose outperforms grocery market' *Retail Week*, 18 August 2009; 'Tesco achieves £3bn annual profit' www.bbc.co.uk/business, 21 April 2009.

Questions

1. Conduct a five forces analysis on two of Tesco's strategic business units: that is, supermarket retailing, personal financial services, mobile phones, or consumer electronics. You might label each competitive force as High, Medium, or Low depending on their relative strength and potential impact on Tesco's profitability.

2. If UK supermarket retailers are all producing similar products with low switching costs how do you account for Tesco's superior profitability?

3. Although not one of the five forces, what impact might the Competition Commission have on Tesco's ability to achieve superior returns? Why should the Competition Commission be taking a keen interest in Tesco?

For help when undertaking Porter's five forces analysis go to the Online
Resource Centre and see the Tools and Techniques feature.
www.oxfordtextbooks.co.uk/orc/henry2e/

3.2.6 A Summary of Porter's Five Forces Framework

Porter's five forces framework can help organizations to ascertain the attractiveness
or profit potential of their industry by analysing the relative impact of each of the
five forces on their industry structure. Organizations can benefit from an understanding of the drivers of industry structure by formulating a strategy which defends their
position in relation to the five forces. Furthermore, organizations might be able to
devise a strategy that will actively influence these five competitive forces in their
favour. It is important to remember that Porter's five forces framework works best
when used at the level of the strategic business unit. For example, Tesco competes in
many different industries, such as financial services, consumer electronics, household
goods, and food, among others. To try to aggregate Tesco's products and services
into a single industry for the purpose of analysis would lead to dubious results. In
theory, organizations need only to compete in industries which exhibit few competitors, have high bargaining power against buyers and suppliers, and where the
threat of new entrants or substitutes is minimal. Unfortunately for organizations
this is a tall order, particularly in today's global environment. In reality, organizations
need to compete in industries where their resources and capabilities allow them to
position themselves in relation to the five forces to achieve a sustainable competitive advantage.

   Porter's work on strategy formulation includes three *generic* strategies: overall
cost leadership, differentiation, and focus (Porter 1980, Chapter 2). These strategies
enable an organization to position itself in an industry in order to mitigate the impact
of the five forces and achieve competitive advantage. The generic strategies are discussed in detail in **Chapter 7**.

3.3 Criticisms of Porter's Five Forces

A number of criticisms of Porter's five forces framework exist. Some of these, such as
the concept of complements (Brandenburger and Nalebuff 1995), can be seen as an
attempt to expand and improve the framework. Some of these criticisms represent
different perspectives on how sustainable competitive advantage might be achieved.
For example, proponents of the resource-based view of strategy, which we consider
in the next chapter, argue that an organization's competitive advantage derives

from the resources and capabilities which reside inside that organization. Given that Porter's work has had an impact on strategy for the last quarter century, it is also interesting to consider Porter's response to his critics.

1. The five forces framework assumes a *zero-sum game*, that is, competitors can only succeed at the expense of other players in the industry. However, organizations are increasingly aware of the added value that other players, such as suppliers (and indeed competitors), can contribute. This has led to collaborative relationships which benefit both parties. For example, in the automobile industry Toyota and Honda work closely with their suppliers to ensure that parts are available at the right price, of the exact quality, and only when needed in order to reduce inventory and associated costs.

2. The five forces framework is a static analysis which assumes relatively stable markets. It tells us little about how players in the industry interact with each other and the effects of actual and anticipated competitor moves on an organization's decision making. It represents a traditional view of strategy that is less capable of dealing with today's rapidly changing environment. Prahalad (2000) states that organizations face significant and discontinuous change in the competitive environment, for example the impact of the Internet on the way in which organizations conduct their business (see also Hamel and Prahalad 1993, 1994 for a discussion of how industry players with relatively few resources but big ambitions can take on industry giants and win). Pralahad argues that the disruptive forces which have brought about this change are accelerating. For Prahalad, strategy is not about positioning the company in a given industry space but about influencing, shaping, and actually creating industry space. He argues there is a need for a new paradigm which embraces disruptive competitive changes. Similarly, D'Aveni (1994) refers to an aggressive type of competition known as *hypercompetition* in which organizations refuse to accept any competitors. Under conditions of hypercompetition organizations use all the tools at their disposal to effectively destabilize a competitor's competitive advantage by creating constant disequilibrium and change. Hypercompetition is briefly discussed at the end of this chapter, and addressed in much greater detail in **Chapter 7** when we look at strategy formulation in turbulent markets. Waterman (quoted in Argyres and McGahan 2002) also supports this criticism, contrasting Porter's view of positioning in existing industry space with a skills-based view. Using an analogy drawn from ice hockey, Waterman suggests that companies need to 'skate to where the puck will be' rather than 'to where the puck is now'.

3. Many strategies are not deliberate but are allowed to emerge. Mintzberg and Waters (1985) argue that organizations may develop an intended or deliberate strategy, but unexpected changes in the environment may force them to abandon that strategy. A subsequent strategy emerges as a result of *ad hoc* management decision making. In this respect the strategy being followed is not planned but is allowed to *emerge* in response to changes in the competitive environment.

Furthermore, in emerging industries you do not know who your rivals are, which makes the use of the five forces framework problematic.

4. Why are there only five forces? Some have argued that other forces, in addition to the five forces, are required. For example, the government has been put forward as one possible candidate. However, given the complexity of what constitutes government and the myriad ways in which it operates, it might be difficult to integrate this usefully into the five forces framework.

5. The five forces framework needs to be more dynamic. In addition to criticisms (see points 2 and 4 above), a revision of the five forces is required which brings us closer to a dynamic theory of strategy. Brandenburger and Nalebuff (1996) utilize game theory to show how organizations can collaborate as well as compete with their competitors to create a larger industry in which everyone gains. This is referred to as *co-opetition*, which we discuss below. In extending Porter's five forces framework they introduce the concept of the *value net*. This is a framework for analysing an organization's competitive environment that is similar to Porter's five forces framework. Where Brandenburger and Nalebuff differ from Porter is in introducing *complementors* into their framework. Complementors refer to organizations that produce products and services which complement (or support) those of another organization and, therefore, add value within the industry. For example, an organization producing DVD players requires the film industry to support this hardware by making films available in the DVD format. We return to the issue of complementors later in the chapter.

3.3.1 Porter's Response to the Critics[2]

Emerging industries and opportunistic strategies

Porter argues that there is a large body of research evidence suggesting that an industry can be understood in a textured way using five forces analysis. Good strategies involve the need to make choices that are all consistent. Companies cannot randomly make a lot of choices that all turn out to be consistent. Porter concedes there is an element of emergent strategy in every company. However, he points out that a company needs to see the design, see how the pieces fit together, and make interdependent choices consistent for strategy to be successful.

The five forces framework is a static analysis

Porter argues that the five forces framework is time invariant, that is, it applies at any point in time. Furthermore, the five forces framework helps to reveal whether changes in the industry are important. He does concede that there is room for more work to be done on how the elements of industry emerge and that more research would be useful to understand the links between organizational behaviour and industry structure.

'Skating to where the puck is'

In response to Waterman, Porter contends that skills are not valuable *per se* but are valuable in the context of a particular positioning. He makes the same point about the resource-based view of competition, arguing there is no dichotomy between his positioning view and the skills-based view. For Porter, successful companies do not have to skate to where the puck is—they define it. They do this, he argues, with continuity of strategy rather than by changing strategy. (For a wider discussion of Porter's ideas on what constitutes strategy, see Porter 1996.)

The role of complements and a dynamic theory of strategy

Porter accepts that a relationship may exist between complements and the overall size of an industry. However, he argues that a relationship between complements and industry profitability is less clear. Instead, he argues against a monotonic relationship, stating that complements may be consistent with high industry profitability at one point in time, and with low profitability at other times. Therefore, for Porter, the issue is how complements affect the five forces.

A question remains as to whether there are alternative routes, such as the use of game theory, which may increase our understanding of competition and provide a revision or extension of Porter's work. In answering this question we can turn our attention to the work of Brandenburger and Nalebuff on co-opetition, which was briefly alluded to above.

3.4 **The Value Net**

In an extension of Porter's five forces framework Brandenburger and Nalebuff (1996) use game theory to help factor the dynamic nature of markets into their analysis. They developed the **value net** which represents a map of the whole game, the players in the game, and their relationship to each other. In seeing business as a game they do not mean traditional games, such as chess, where there are winners and losers. Since in business success for one player can also mean success for another player, there can be win–win solutions. They also recognize that in business the rules of the game are not fixed, as in most games, but that the game itself can be changed. The players in the game are usually seen as the customers, suppliers, and competitors (where competitors include rivals, threat of new entrants, and substitute products or services). However, Brandenburger and Nalebuff (1995) introduce a new player called a **complementor**.

Complementors are organizations that supply complements to the industry; in so doing they create value for the industry and can affect its dynamics through their bargaining power. Brandenburger and Nalebuff (1995) use the example of

VALUE NET

this represents a map of the competitive game, the players in the game, and their relationship to each other

COMPLEMENTOR

a player is a complementor if customers value your product more when they have that player's product than when they have your product alone

Nintendo's domination of the video games industry in the 1990s to show how an organization can successfully add and appropriate value. Nintendo effectively reduced the bargaining power of its buyers by keeping its games cartridge in short supply. Although buyers were highly concentrated, Nintendo's strategy of deliberately restricting its games cartridge ensured retailers lost added value. Nintendo's complementors were games developers. To reduce the value to complementors Nintendo developed software in-house. They put security in the hardware and licensed the right to develop games for their system to outside programmers. Therefore, Nintendo controlled its complementors, reducing their added value but increasing its own added value through royalties on each game cartridge sold. By utilizing chip technology that was not cutting edge Nintendo ensured that its suppliers produced a commoditized product from which they would derive little added value. This allowed Nintendo to keep the cost of their games console down which enhanced their market share.

For further information on complementors and their impact on competitive behaviour go to the Online Resource Centre and see the Key Work feature. www.oxfordtextbooks.co.uk/orc/henry2e/

The value net is illustrated in Figure 3.4. This shows a map of the game, the players in the game, and their relationships to one another. If we look at the relationship between Microsoft and Intel it becomes apparent that this is not one of customer and suppliers but one of complementor, that is, the dual-core microprocessors provided by Intel allow the software provided by Microsoft to run more quickly and efficiently. Without Intel's innovative processors Microsoft's upgraded software would be less valuable to the consumer. Similarly, without Microsoft's upgraded products which require faster processor speeds there would be less reason to buy Intel's improved processors.

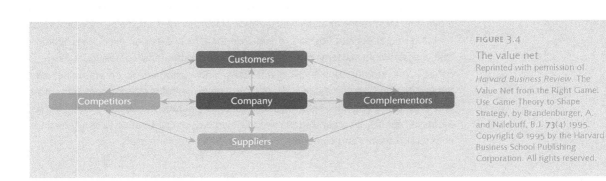

FIGURE 3.4

The value net
Reprinted with permission of *Harvard Business Review*. The Value Net from the Right Game: Use Game Theory to Shape Strategy, by Brandenburger, A. and Nalebuff, B.J. **73**(4) 1995. Copyright © 1995 by the Harvard Business School Publishing Corporation. All rights reserved.

*A player is a complementor if customers value your product more when they
have that player's product than when they have your product alone. A player is
a competitor if customers value your product less when they have that player's
product than when they have your product alone. (Brandenburger and
Nalebuff 1997)*

Brandenburger and Nalebuff use the concept of added value to help determine
how the profits will be divided. They argue that it is important to think about the
entire value chain in order to understand where an organization's value comes
from. In addition to trying to increase your organization's own complement's added
value, you must also be thinking of ways in which you can limit the added value of
another player's complement. A strategy to achieve this is to create a shortage
of your organization's differentiated product, which builds up its market dominance.
At the same time you encourage more suppliers of a complementary product into
the game, which has the effect of commoditizing that product. The reduction in value
of the complementary product will ensure that greater profit is appropriated by
your product.

In essence, an organization needs to try to create value and a larger market, which
is best undertaken by cooperating with customers and suppliers. At the same time an
organization is concerned with how this larger market is to be divided, that is, its
competitive position. As Brandenburger and Nalebuff (1997) suggest, 'a company
has to keep its eye on both balls, creating and capturing, at the same time'. They call
this **co-opetition** because 'it combines competition and cooperation'.

CO-OPETITION

competitive behaviour that
combines competition and
cooperation

3.4.1 A Complementary Sixth Force

Some critics of Porter's five forces have suggested that his framework would benefit
from the inclusion of government as a sixth force. This may or may not be the case.
However, we can say that Porter recognizes that complements have a role to play in
competitive analysis. If we extend Porter's five forces framework to take account of
complements, it evolves as shown in Figure 3.5. The inclusion of complementors into
Porter's five forces makes the framework more defensible, precisely because it adds
a dynamic facet to the analysis which allows players in the game to be more aware of
their interdependencies. Instead of win–lose there now exists an explicit recognition
that a sustainable strategy can involve both cooperation and competition. There is
cooperation among suppliers, organizations, and customers to create value, and
competition in how this value is divided up. The same holds true for complementors
and substitutes. Instead of viewing substitutes as inherently adversarial and complements as friendly, an organization can have elements of cooperation in its interactions
with its substitutes and competitive elements with complementors.

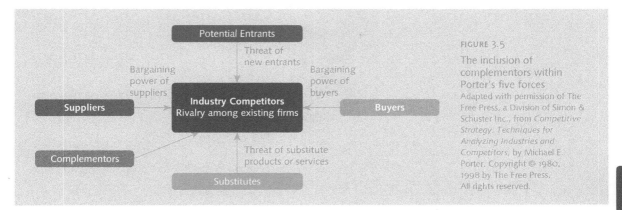

3.5 Strategic Groups

The analysis so far has been at the level of the entire industry. An industry is a group of organizations producing a similar product or service. Economists define an industry as a group of firms that supply a market. Therefore, in order to ascertain the boundary of an industry we need to identify the relevant market for the organization (see Grant (2005) for a discussion of industry boundaries). This will also allow us to see who the competitors in that industry are. For instance, we can ask: Are the inputs and product technologies of organizations similar? And is there a significant degree of overlap between the different products' customers? We can then define a market's boundary by its degree of substitutability on the demand and supply side. For example, to determine the range of products to be included in the market for Lexus cars, we can ask whether consumers would substitute buying a van instead of a car on the basis of their differences in price. Given the answer is likely to be 'No, customers are not willing to substitute purchasing a van instead of buying a car,' we can deduce that cars and vans are in different markets. Therefore, Lexus cars do not supply the same market as vans. Similarly, if customers are willing to substitute among the different makes of automobiles which make up the automobile industry (see Figure 3.6), such as sports cars and luxury models, based on their relative price differences, we are able to say that this constitutes a market, and Lexus occupies this automobile market rather than just the luxury car market.

If manufacturers find it relatively easy to switch their production from luxury cars to sports cars and high-volume cars, this supply-side substitutability suggests that Lexus is competing within the broader automobile market. In fact Toyota, which traditionally competes in the high-volume end of the market, showed that it is also capable of competing in the luxury market when it introduced its Lexus brand of cars. Toyota's success in competing in the luxury car market tells us that any car manufacturer in the luxury segment, such as BMW or Mercedes, would make a mistake in

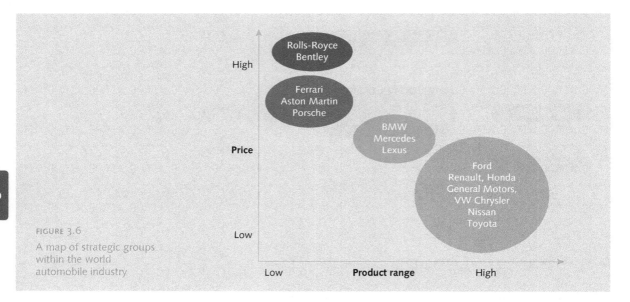

FIGURE 3.6

A map of strategic groups
within the world
automobile industry

assuming that their market was merely other cars in that luxury car segment. Rather, they need to be aware of the high degree of supply-side substitutability between mass market and luxury cars.

In addition to analysis at the whole-industry level it is also possible to undertake structural analysis *within* an industry. Just because organizations are in the same industry does not make them competitors. At first glance this may seem like a contradiction. For example, how can car manufacturers in the automobile industry not be in competition with each other? However, a closer analysis of the industry shows that strategic group or clusters of organizations tend to exist. Porter (1980, p. 29) states that, 'a strategic group is the group of firms in an industry following the same or a similar strategy'. Strategic group analysis is about identifying firms within an industry who possess similar resource capabilities and are pursuing similar strategies. If we recognize the capabilities and strategies of firms that are most like our own organization, we have a greater understanding of our competitors. Why? Because in any industry an organization's greatest competitors are going to be the firms most like it.

STRATEGIC GROUP

is a group of firms in an industry
following the same or a similar
strategy

Strategic groups of firms within an industry constitute a cluster and inform us that just because competitors occupy the same industry does not make them direct competitors. As we have seen, this does not mean that a firm within the same industry does not have the capability to be a potential competitor even if it is not a direct competitor. In the US, Ford, General Motors, and Chrysler occupy the same strategic group within the automobile industry. They are clearly in competition for the same consumers. In the UK, Morgan, a family-owned car company, and Ford are in the same industry but do not compete with each other. Morgan produce a limited number of hand-made cars and have a waiting list for their products that is counted in years. Therefore, Ford and Morgan would occupy different strategic groups. Firms in the same strategic groups tend to have similar market shares and respond in similar ways to external trends or competitor moves in the industry. Strategic group analysis falls between analysing each organization individually and looking at the industry as a whole.

3.5.1 Mobility Barriers

In the same way that an organization may be prevented from entering an industry by barriers to entry, mobility barriers inhibit movement between strategic groups. Porter (1980, p. 135) defines mobility barriers as 'factors that deter movement of firms from one strategic position to another'. For example, if barriers which derive from economies of scale exist, they will be more likely to protect a strategic group that includes organizations who have large plants. If the factors that prevent mobility result from an organization's strategy it simply increases the cost to other organizations of adopting that strategy. Porter suggests that organizations in strategic groups with high mobility barriers will achieve greater profits than those in groups with lower mobility barriers. However, there is conflicting evidence on this point (Grant 2005, Chapter 4).

MOBILITY BARRIERS

factors that prevent the movement of organizations from one strategic group to another

Mobility barriers may be changed by an organization's strategy. For example, where an industry exists that has a commoditized product, an organization may try to create a new strategic group. It might do this by spending on promotion and advertising to try to establish differentiation and brand loyalty. In the same way, external trends such as changes in buyers' behaviour or a change in technology can impact on strategic groups by creating new groups and making others obsolete. Organizations will face different hurdles in overcoming mobility barriers which will depend on their existing strategic positions and their resources and capabilities. For example, Toyota has successfully managed to overcome mobility barriers to entering the luxury car market. Its Lexus brand now competes with BMW and Mercedes.

We should note that a certain amount of judgement is required for determining the dimensions or axis on which strategic groups are based. Figure 3.6 represents a simplified illustration of the world automobile industry. Clearly there may be other strategic groups which could be represented here. Price and product range are the dimensions used to show strategic groups which may be following similar strategies. Other categories could be used and some may indeed disagree with Ferrari's strategic group being placed below Rolls-Royce, citing examples of Ferraris that are comparable to Rolls-Royces and Bentleys on price. This simply reinforces the fact that judgement needs to be exercised in developing a strategic group.

Figure 3.6 shows some of the competitors in the world automobile industry and their strategic groups. At the luxury end of the market are cars such as Rolls-Royce and Bentley with limited product ranges. These cars are often bought as status symbols that denote wealth and success. Also at the luxury end of the market, with comparable prices in some cases, are the sports models of Ferrari and Lamborghini. These cars are in a different strategic group as individuals who desire a Ferrari would probably be comparing it against other high-performance sports cars.

The strategic group that includes Mercedes, BMW, and Lexus produces a lower product range but at a higher quality and price than the high-volume market vehicles which comprise the strategic group occupied by Ford and VW. That said, there has been movement within the automobile industry as manufacturers such as BMW have introduced more compact saloons and a BMW Series 1 at a lower price to compete with the volume manufacturers. This strategy carries a risk of alienating customers loyal to the brand who may perceive it as being denigrated. Notice also that BMW and Porsche have introduced sports utility vehicles in an attempt to capture a share of the lucrative SUV market. At the lower end of the market are the volume manufacturers characterized by Ford and Honda. These competitors have the broadest product range and increasingly compete on design as well as price and reliability.

By mapping rivals following similar strategies into strategic groups an organization can ascertain their most direct competitors, the viability of a strategic group's mobility barriers in keeping competitors away from their market share, and, importantly, forecast the impact of industry trends on the sustainability of strategic groups. It is important to realize that the relevance of strategic group analysis depends upon the characteristics or dimensions used to map these firms. The aim should be to establish which characteristics can clearly differentiate one group of firms from another. Such characteristics might include price, product portfolio and geographical coverage, R&D capability, extent of vertical integration, and marketing expenditure, among others. In reality, some strategic groups might overlap as issues such as globalization force many firms to compete on converging characteristics. It is worth noting that industry dynamics will alter strategic groups over time. (See Case Study: The Semiconductor Industry. This explains the structural changes taking place in the semiconductor industry and the challenges facing European competitors as they try to compete against their Asian counterparts set against a backdrop of a global recession.)

CASE STUDY 3.2

The Semiconductor Industry

MOST tourists come to Dresden to view the city's architectural wonders. But the capital of the German state of Saxony also has more contemporary attractions— It is the hub of one of Europe's biggest technology clusters. Silicon Saxony, as the region has come to be called, boasts 1,500 high-tech firms employing 43,000 people, most of them in the semiconductor industry.

On 1 April [2009] Qimonda, a maker of memory chips and the cluster's largest employer, mothballed its factory, having been forced into insolvency earlier this

© AFP/Getty Images/Norbert Millauer

Globalfoundries in Dresden

year. At Dresden's other big 'fab', as chip-fabrication plants are called, is an indicator of another change that may prove just as damaging. There is a new logo at the entrance: visitors are no longer welcomed to AMD but to Globalfoundries. AMD, a maker of microprocessors for personal computers (PCs), decided last year to spin off its fabs into a separate company and to sell a majority stake to investment funds controlled by the government of Abu Dhabi.

The likely death of Qimonda and the birth of Globalfoundries . . . is a visible token of how hard recession around the world has hit the semiconductor industry . . . Just as important, it demonstrates the longer-term upheavals in the industry. The semiconductor business is becoming less vertically integrated and more concentrated. And its centre of gravity is shifting eastwards.

Despite a few signs that the worst may be over—If market researchers are right, it will shrink again in 2009 before resuming growth in 2010—iSuppli, one such forecaster, thinks that revenues will fall by more than 20% this year, to $205 billion (see chart 1).

To understand why the semiconductor industry has been so pummelled, think of integrated circuits (i.e. chips) not as tiny pieces of silicon engraved with millions of transistors, but as an essential resource. Before long every man-made object will come with at least one embedded microchip (see chart 2). Jerry Sanders, AMD's founder, once called chips 'the crude oil of industry'. The flip side is that chip makers have come to depend increasingly on the health of the rest of the economy.

The chip cycle

However, the industry's own economics are also to blame. Even without the world's wider troubles, these would have caused problems. In explaining how,

3

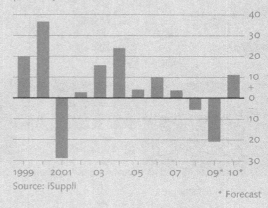

Wafer thin

Worldwide semiconductor industry revenue % change on previous year

CHART 1

Source: iSuppli

* Forecast

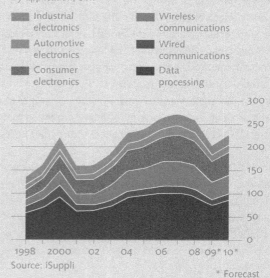

Chips with everything

Worldwide semiconductor industry revenue by application, $bn

- Industrial electronics
- Automotive electronics
- Consumer electronics
- Wireless communications
- Wired communications
- Data processing

CHART 2

Source: iSuppli

* Forecast

Dan Hutcheson, chief executive of VLSI Research, a consultancy, likens semiconductor manufacturing to a different industry: farming. Investment decisions have to be made long before products can be sold. Chip farmers have to spend billions and wait years before they can start etching circuits onto 'wafers', those thin disks of semiconductor material, the size of pizzas, which are sliced into hundreds of chips at the end of the production process.

This goes a long way towards explaining why chip makers, like farmers, have a tendency to oversupply the market, particularly if they sell memory chips, an undifferentiated product (like winter wheat). Even if prices fall below costs, they have an interest in keeping their fabs humming, in order not to lose their heavy upfront investment and to recover the variable costs. What is more, they are caught on a 'technology treadmill', in the words of Mr Hutcheson. Competition forces them always to employ the latest technology, which both increases output and puts pressure on prices.

Finally, just as in agriculture, governments further fuel this innate tendency to oversupply. In prestige, national security, industrial policy or just a desire to create jobs, politicians have always found a reason to support their semiconductor industries, mostly with cash. Silicon Saxony . . . received more than €1.5 billion (nearly $2 billion at today's exchange rate) from the state of Saxony alone, much of it to coax AMD into investing.

Asian governments have been the most active. Thanks to Taiwan's industrial policy, more than half of the world's chips are now made there. Support from the South Korean government made Samsung and Hynix the world's biggest makers of memory chips; they supply about 50% of this segment. China seems intent on turning its semiconductor companies into market leaders at almost any price . . . All this explains why of the 40 fabs under construction in 2007, 35 were in Asia, three in America and only two in Europe.

From 2002 until last year Asian makers of memory chips, especially, invested as if capital were free—which explains why everybody is now bleeding money. In July 2007 the price of a DRAM (dynamic random access memory) chip with a capacity of 512 megabits was more than $2. In early April it was about 50 cents. Smaller makers cannot cope. Qimonda, for instance, piled up losses of about €1.5 billion between October 2007 and June 2008. Its revenues were only €1.3 billion.

Even Taiwan is having second thoughts about an ambitious plan to merge and bail out the country's six makers of memory chips, which have lost $12.5 billion in the past two years and accumulated $11 billion in debts. Whatever happens to Qimonda and its Taiwanese rivals, the current crisis is sure to speed up two seemingly contradictory long-term trends in the industry. It is consolidating, in that the manufacture of chips is becoming concentrated among fewer companies. At the same time, it is splitting up, in that more companies are specialising in design, and contracting out or quitting the making of chips. Both developments are mainly the consequence of what has come to be called 'Moore's Second Law', an economic counterpart to a better known observation by Gordon Moore, one of the founders of Intel, the world's biggest chip maker by revenue.

The original Moore's Law is usually summarised thus: the number of transistors on a chip doubles every 18 months. In fact Mr Moore first predicted this would happen every year and later changed his forecast to every two years; the average has become his law. Mr Hutcheson points out that Mr Moore made more than a purely technical prediction. He also stated that the cost of an integrated circuit would stay the same, a halving of the cost per transistor with every doubling of the number.

The ever more sophisticated equipment required to make semiconductors has been getting dearer with every iteration of Moore's Law. The most advanced chips are built using 32-nanometre technology, meaning that transistors are now so tiny that more than 4 million can fit on this full stop. To reach the economies of scale needed to make such investments pay, chip makers must build bigger fabs.

Rising fixed costs give rise to Moore's Second Law: as the cost of transistors comes down, the cost of fabs goes up, albeit not at quite the same rate. In 1966 a new fab cost $14m. By 1995 the price had risen to $1.5 billion. Today, says Intel, the cost of a leading-edge fab exceeds $6 billion, including all the preparatory work. And the Taiwanese Semiconductor Manufacturing Company (TSMC) has built two 'GigaFabs' for between $8 billion and $10 billion each. The output . . . depends on the mix of products, but they each could easily churn out 3 billion chips a year.

These ever-increasing costs and the need for specialisation have caused the industry to splinter, says Derek Lidow, iSuppli's chief executive. Originally, all chip makers were vertically integrated, meaning they designed the chip, built the tools to make them, ran the fabs and added the necessary connectors. As costs went up and certain activities became more and more complex, they were spun out to spread expenses and know-how. Semiconductor equipment, design software and packaging have long been done by separate companies. But the past ten years have seen the rise of 'fabless' firms, which merely design integrated circuits.

Now established chip makers can no longer afford to develop their own manufacturing processes or even to run their own fabs. To share the pain, IBM, Samsung and others have teamed up to use chip-making technology jointly. Some firms, such as Texas Instruments, have chosen to go 'fab-lite', meaning that they have their own fabs only for certain chips. Others, such as AMD, have spun off manufacturing completely.

Hence the rise of 'foundries', the smelters of the information age. These are essentially contract manufacturers. Although far from household names, they are huge companies, churning out about one quarter of the world's semiconductors. The biggest, TSMC, has a manufacturing capacity greater even than Intel's. Its revenues grew at an annual average rate of 13% for several years, topping $10.6 billion, before falling by almost a third in the last quarter of 2008.

TSMC also illustrates a corollary of Moore's Second Law: even the biggest chip makers must keep expanding. Intel today accounts for 82% of global microprocessor revenue and has annual revenues of $37.6 billion because it understood this long ago. In the early 1980s, when Intel was a $700m company— pretty big for the time—Andy Grove, once Intel's boss, was not satisfied.

'He would run around and tell everybody that we have to get to $1 billion,' recalls Andy Bryant, the firm's chief administrative officer. 'He knew that you had to have a certain size to stay in business.'

Grow, grow, grow

Intel still appears to stick to this mantra, and is using the crisis to outgrow its competitors. In February Paul Otellini, its chief executive, said it would speed up plans to move many of its fabs to a new, 32-nanometre process at a cost of $7 billion over the next two years. This, he said, would preserve about 7,000 high-wage jobs in America. The investment will also make life even harder for AMD, Intel's biggest remaining rival in the market for PC-type processors.

Two other long-term developments also point towards further concentration of chip making. The first is technological change beyond that ordained by Moore's Law. Fully automated 'lights-out' fabs are in operation. Within a few years fabs will be producing wafers with a diameter of 450mm, up from 300mm now, making them even more productive. 'When the industry goes to 450mm and this happens at 22 or even 11 nanometres, it is conceivable to have one factory handle all our needs as a company,' says Mr Otellini.

The other development is the maturing of the industry. Its annual growth has slid from double digits in the mid-1990s to an average of around 5% since then. And since 2004 the profitability of chip firms has dropped steadily as many chip makers have lowered prices to expand their markets. In the future, only three types of semiconductor firm will make a decent return, predicts Mr Lidow: those with unique intellectual property; those happy to make commodity chips; and those with enough cash to achieve unprecedented scale.

High-ranking executives at leading firms give similar answers. In the long run, they say, there will be only three viable entities, at least at the leading edge of chip making: Samsung in memory chips, Intel in microprocessors and TSMC in foundries. The rest will be 'nationalistic' ventures in need of regular government bail-outs.

Yet such predictions may be a little off the mark. Largely because of that nationalism, the semiconductor industry is unlikely to end up as a bunch of near-monopolies. The Taiwanese are unlikely to let the South Koreans rule the memory roost. The newly founded Taiwan Memory Company (TMC), which is to take over the six local firms, could become the core of a global memory giant. It will hook up with Elpida Memory, Japan's sole maker of memory chips. TMC is also said to be interested in Qimonda.

As for microprocessors, in the fast-growing market for netbooks and other mobile devices, Intel has to do battle with many 'fabless' firms, most of which build chips based on designs by ARM, a British company. What is more, after spinning off manufacturing, 'our customers no longer have to ask: is AMD able to invest in the next generation of manufacturing?' says Dirk Meyer, the firm's chief executive. And Abu Dhabi's investment in Globalfoundries is part not just of its preparations for the post-oil age, but also of a long-term plan to create a 'global' alternative to foundries in Taiwan and mainland China.

Whatever the precise number of firms, the semiconductor industry will be highly concentrated and much of it will be dominated by Asian companies. The industry's extreme capital intensity is certainly a barrier to entry, and in theory a market with only a few suppliers is ripe for rigging. But chip makers are unlikely to be able to extract a disproportionate rent or restrict supply—or even to try. For one thing, the industry has a history of intense competition. This is especially fierce among Asian national champions, for which prestige plays a big role. More important, the global production network of the information-technology industry is much too interdependent. If foundries, for instance, took a much larger piece of the pie, others in the value chain, such as chip designers, would find it hard to survive.

Worse, over the past ten years Europe's market share in semiconductors has dropped from more than 23% to about 15%, according to Future Horizons, a consultancy. If governments do not act soon chip makers will continue to migrate elsewhere and put Europe's competitiveness at risk.

What Europe's semiconductor industry—and its technology sector as a whole, for that matter—badly needs is a better environment for entrepreneurs, says Dan Breznitz of the Georgia Institute of Technology, a specialist in the global IT industry. Because Europe's semiconductor industry has been dominated by big, hierarchical companies, fabless firms are still rare. In Israel, by contrast, with its newly entrepreneurial culture, they have multiplied. Europe, argues Mr Breznitz, is still too focused on manufacturing.

Europe could stage a comeback, some say, should an old idea finally take off: 'mini-fabs'—small, flexible and agile production units. Such a revolution has happened before, in steel: giantism once seemed insuperable, yet today plenty of steel is made in 'mini-mills', which use scrap as raw material. Might the foundries of the information age one day be under a similar threat? Maybe. But experts are right to be sceptical: transistors may get ever smaller, but in chip making scale rules.

Source: 'Under new management' *The Economist*, 2nd April 2009

⬛ Questions

1. Outline the structural changes taking place in the semiconductor industry.

2. Map the strategic groups that currently exist in this industry using appropriate dimensions.

3. Evaluate any mobility barriers that may exist. Track the direction organizations' strategies seem to be moving towards and explain what this will mean for industry competition.

To summarize, strategic groups are helpful to show competitive relationships within an industry and how industry trends might impact on competition. A strategic group map can help an organization to do the following:

- Identify who their direct competitors are and the extent of competitive rivalry within their strategic group.

- Identify mobility barriers which prevent organizations moving from one strategic group to another. These barriers to entry between groups include access to capital, which would prevent Morgan competing with Ford, or expert knowledge, which might prevent Ford producing a vehicle that can compete with Morgan's hand-made cars.

- Track the direction in which organizations' strategies are moving to determine industry competition. By drawing arrows from each strategic group to show in which direction the groups may be moving it becomes possible to determine the extent of competition. For instance, if strategic groups are moving farther apart, this may mean that strategic 'spaces' exist which can be exploited without increasing competition. If groups are converging, this implies greater volatility.

- Analyse trends in the general and competitive environment. For example, the trend towards consolidation in the UK financial services sector as a result of a decrease in customer loyalty has increased competitive rivalry within strategic groups. We have also seen that some supermarkets in the UK have entered this market offering savings and insurance products. Taken together, these trends might help predict a change in industry evolution. Organizations in a strategic group are likely to respond in the same way to trends given their similar strategies.

For more information on strategic groups go to the Online Resource Centre and see the Key Work feature.
www.oxfordtextbooks.co.uk/orc/henry2e/

3.6 Hypercompetition

The term hypercompetition was introduced by D'Aveni (1994) to explain a relentless mode of competitive behaviour which aims to force competitors out of the industry. This fierce competition is often seen in the video games and software industries, for example, the dominant market share of Microsoft within the software applications industry. Microsoft's closed systems prevent competitors gaining access to their software code, and their huge financial reserves which run to tens of billions of dollars have allowed them to compete aggressively by buying up potential threats while they are still minnows. More important, Microsoft's constant upgrading of new product

HYPERCOMPETITION

where organizations aggressively position themselves against each other and create new competitive advantages which make opponents' advantages obsolete offerings has the effect of destabilizing the software industry and forcing competitors to react. D'Aveni argues that organizations can no longer build a sustainable competitive advantage as this advantage is eventually eroded. In fact, he argues that organizations must consciously disrupt their own competitive advantages as well as the advantages of competitors. (See Strategy Focus: Gillette, which examines Gillette's introduction of a five-blade razor in order to stay ahead of competitors.)

STRATEGY FOCUS
Gillette

Gillette's announcement of a razor with five blades was greeted with scepticism last year. But four weeks after it went on sale, the Fusion has grabbed 55 per cent of new razor purchases. Its early success will encourage food and consumer goods companies as they scramble to revamp basic products to appeal to higher-paying customers. Gillette insisted that American males were ready for five blades, and were willing to pay a premium for them as consumers 'traded up' to better-performing products. The Fusion retails for $9.99, with a replacement pack of four blades costing $13–$14.

The company has spent millions of dollars on the launch. It claims that 70 per cent of retailers who stock Gillette have committed to in-store displays for three to six months. Fusion and a battery-powered, vibrating version called Fusion Power are priced at a 30 per cent premium to Mach3, a three-blade product that itself cost 50 per cent more than its predecessor. Data from Information Resources Inc, a consumer researcher, show that the two Fusion products together accounted for over half of all purchases of complete new razor sets in the four weeks to 19 February.

Gillette expects Fusion to be a $1bn brand within three years. Mach3 has generated retail sales since launch in 1998 of $16bn. Rival razor maker Schick, owned by Energizer, will next month launch a new three-bladed razor for women, with the blades embedded in a 'skin softening' strip containing aloe, cocoa butter, and vitamin E. Replacement blades will cost $2.29 — double the current product.

Source: 'Gillette's Fusion at cutting edge of trading up' *Financial Times*, 8 March 2006

Under conditions of hypercompetition, 'the frequency, boldness, and aggressiveness of dynamic movement by players accelerate to create a condition of constant disequilibrium and change . . . environments escalate towards higher and higher levels of uncertainty, dynamisms, heterogeneity of players, and hostility' (D'Aveni 1995).

The driving force of competition is the pursuit of profit, which is obtained by establishing a competitive advantage. However, a competitive advantage will only be transitory as rival organizations look for ways to undermine it or make it obsolete. Under conditions of hypercompetition organizations must continually recreate their competitive advantage if they are to gain market dominance. Christensen (2001) argues that the existence of competitive advantage will set in motion creative innovations that cause the advantage to be eroded as competitors try to catch up. For Christensen, the pursuit of competitive advantage is not futile, but the real issue for strategists is to understand the processes of competition and how competitive advantage comes about.

For further information on hypercompetition and its impact on competitive behaviour go to the Online Resource Centre and see the Key Work feature. www.oxfordtextbooks.co.uk/orc/henry2e/

We saw in Porter's five forces framework that where an organization incurs huge fixed costs in setting up a plant, competition for market share will be intense. Networks of consumers and the rapid rate of technological change exacerbate the effects of extreme-scale economies. By networks of consumers we simply mean that unless others are using the same technology our use of that technology becomes redundant. This forces converge around a single technical standard such as Microsoft Windows. At the same time, the rate of technological change continues to accelerate as organizations such as Intel continually shorten the lifespan of technologies and products, which further intensifies competition. Taken together these factors produce intense competition, particularly in emerging markets for new technologies. They create high-stakes industries where the successful competitor has the opportunity for complete domination. (See Strategy Focus: Microsoft, which illustrates the continual cannibalization of their source of competitive advantage in order to stay ahead of competitors.)

STRATEGY FOCUS
Microsoft

Microsoft is a classic example of an organization operating in a hypercompetitive environment. Its founder and Chief Software Architect, Bill Gates, has exercised visionary zeal in dominating the operating system and software applications market. In the early 1990s Microsoft held 90 per cent of the market for operating systems using its Windows programmes. Instead of protecting this dominance in the operating system market, Bill Gates chose to develop new Windows products such

Microsoft product screen shot reprinted with permission from Microsoft Corporation

Windows 7 desktop: by developing new Windows products, Bill Gates effectively destroyed the market share of the previous version of Windows.

as Windows 95, Windows 98, Windows NT and XP, and Vista, each time effectively destroying the market share of the previous version of Windows. This is not the way that companies are supposed to compete—producing new products and services that eat into the market share of a successful product. In 2009 Microsoft introduced a new operating system—Windows 7—in a bid to get consumers to upgrade from Windows XP and Windows Vista.

What Bill Gates and President and CEO Steve Ballmer understand is that in this turbulent marketplace Microsoft must constantly innovate and respond rapidly to achieve success. In a hypercompetitive environment any competitive advantage can quickly be eroded. Therefore, the challenge is to move with speed through a series of competitive advantages which effectively keep trumping a competitor's attempt to gain competitive advantage. In this way Microsoft has maintained its massive market dominance in both operating systems and software applications such as Word and Excel.

In hypercompetitive industries such as software, competitive advantage requires an understanding of environmental trends and competitor activities, and a willingness to risk a current advantage for the promise of a new advantage. Organizations aggressively position themselves against each other and create new competitive advantages which make opponents' advantages obsolete. At best only a temporary competitive advantage can be achieved until your competitors catch up or outmanoeuvre your last competitive move. In effect, hypercompetition requires an organization to replace successful products before its competitors do and thereby sustain market dominance by constantly recreating its competitive advantage.

Summary

It is clear that the competitive environment has a more direct impact on an organization's performance. Porter's five forces framework is a useful tool of analysis for evaluating some of the determinants of industry profitability and assessing firm performance. The five forces are: bargaining power of buyers, bargaining power of suppliers, threat of new entrants, threat of substitutes, and competitive rivalry. The framework enables an incumbent firm to assess the attractiveness of its industry based on the relative strength of these five forces. Given its resources, a firm can take a decision as to which industries it can most effectively compete in and position itself to reduce the adverse effects of these forces. According to critics, a major limitation of the five forces framework is its static nature; a charge contested by Porter.

Brandenburger and Nalebuff use game theory and introduce the concept of the value net in assessing the competitive environment. The value net represents a map of the whole game, the players in the game, and their relationship to each other. In taking account of the dynamic nature of the competitive environment they also introduce a new player called a complementor. A player is a complementor if customers value your product more when they have that player's product than when they have your product alone. As we have seen, the five forces can be extended by adding complementors as an additional competitive force. Furthermore, Brandenburger and Nalebuff's inclusion of co-opetition moves us beyond Porter's adversarial win–lose analysis and instead shows that it may be beneficial to cooperate with complementors to enlarge the market but compete with them to divide the market up.

A strategic group is a group of firms in an industry following the same or a similar strategy. A strategic group map is useful for identifying mobility barriers which prevent organizations moving from one strategic group to another. They help track the direction in which organizations' strategies are moving to determine industry competition. By analysing the effects of industry trends on strategic groups this can help organizations predict a change in the industry.

We concluded the chapter with a discussion of hypercompetition. In hypercompetitive environments organizations must consciously disrupt their own competitive advantages as well as the advantages of opponents. Competitive advantage is seen as temporary and lasts only as long as it takes for competitors to catch up or outmanoeuvre your last competitive move. Hypercompetition is characterized by intense and rapid competitive moves, and is more likely to be seen in industries characterized by rapid technological innovation.

A useful tool for assessing the competitive environment and future industry structure is the *industry life cycle*. We will consider this when we look at strategy formulation in **Chapter 7**.

▪ Review Questions

1. To what extent does the inclusion of complementors to Porter's five forces framework help in our understanding of competitive strategy?

2. What does hypercompetition teach us about the pursuit of a sustainable competitive advantage?

✦ Discussion Question

The effect of government policy on industry structure is too pervasive not to consider government as a *sixth* competitive force. Discuss.

▪ Research Topic

Use strategic groups to analyse the newspaper industry, paying particular attention to what mobility barriers, if any, exist and the trends that are bringing change to this industry.

▤ Recommended Reading

For a discussion of the five forces framework and strategic groups see:

- **Porter, M.E.** (1980). *Competitive Strategy: Techniques for Analysing Industries and Competitors*. Free Press, New York.

For an insight into the need for organizations to cooperate as well as compete with players in their competitive environment see:

- **Brandenburger, A.** and **Nalebuff, B.J.** (1996). *Co-opetition*. Currency Doubleday, New York.

An informative read on the use of game theory for strategy formulation is:

- **Brandenburger, A.** and **Nalebuff, B.J.** (1995). The right game: use game theory to shape strategy. *Harvard Business Review*, **73**(4), 57–71.

For a discussion of hypercompetition see:

- **D'Aveni, R.A.** (1994). *Hypercompetition: Managing the Dynamics of Strategic Manoeuvring*. Free Press, New York.

www.oxfordtextbooks.co.uk/orc/henry2e/
Visit the Online Resource Centre that accompanies this book for activities
and more information on the competitive environment

online resource centre

Notes

1   The discussion of Porter's five forces is drawn from Porter (1980), especially
    Chapter 1.
2   For a more detailed discussion of Porter's response to his critics, see Argyres and
    McGahan (2002).

References

Argyres, N. and **McGahan, A.M.** (2002). An interview with Michael Porter.
Academy of Management Executive, **16**(2), 43–52.

Brandenburger, A. and **Nalebuff, B.J.** (1995). The right game: use game theory to
shape strategy. *Harvard Business Review*, **73**(4), 57–71.

Brandenburger, A. and **Nalebuff, B.J.** (1996). *Co-opetition*. Currency Doubleday,
New York.

Brandenburger, A. and **Nalebuff, B.J.** (1997). Co-opetition: competitive and
cooperative business strategies for the digital economy. *Strategy and Leadership*,
25(6), 30.

Christensen, C.M. (2001). The past and future of competitive advantage.
Sloan Management Review, **42**(2), 105–9.

D'Aveni, R.A. (1994). *Hypercompetition: Managing the Dynamics of Strategic
Manoeuvring*. Free Press, New York.

D'Aveni, R.A. (1995). Coping with hypercompetition: utilizing the new 7S's
framework. *Academy of Management Executive*, **9**(3), 46.

Grant, R.M. (2005). *Contemporary Strategy Analysis*. Blackwell, Boston, MA.

Hamel, G. and **Prahalad, C.K.** (1993). Strategy as stretch and leverage. *Harvard
Business Review*, **71**(2), 75–84.

Hamel, G. and **Prahalad, C.K.** (1994). *Competing for the Future*. Harvard Business
School Press, Boston, MA.

Mintzberg, H. and **Waters, J.A.** (1985). Of strategies, deliberate and emergent.
Strategic Management Journal, **6**(3), 257–72.

Porter, M.E. (1980). *Competitive Strategy: Techniques for Analysing Industries
and Competitors*. Free Press, New York.

Porter, M.E. (1996). What is strategy? *Harvard Business Review*, **74**(6), 61–78.

Prahalad, C.K. (2000). Changes in the competitive battlefield. In *Mastering
Strategy* (ed. T. Dickson), pp. 75–80. Prentice Hall, Harlow.

4 The Internal Environment: Value-Creating Activities

4.1 Background to Differential Firm Performance

Key Work
Differential firm performance

4.2 Value Chain Analysis

Main Reference
Porter, M.E. (1985).
Competitive Advantage.
Free Press, New York.

4.3 Evaluating the Value Chain

Key Work
Value chain activities with reference to organizations

4.4 SWOT Analysis

Tools and Techniques
Undertaking a SWOT analysis

Learning Objectives

After completing this chapter you should be able to:

- Explain differential firm performance
- Discuss value chain analysis and the value system
- Evaluate the role of linkages for creating competitive advantage
- Undertake a SWOT analysis and discuss its limitations

Introduction

In **Chapters 2** and **3** we looked at some of the tools of analysis that can be used by the organization to understand its general and competitive environment. This included a discussion of PEST analysis and how PEST can be applied by the organization to help discern trends in its external environment. It is these trends which ultimately impact upon its competitive environment. We discussed the work of Kees van der Heijden (1996) and the role of scenario planning in helping organizations such as Shell make sense of highly uncertain markets by producing a set of stories about alternative futures. Scenario planning allows organizations to detect the all-important *weak signals* and formulate strategies to exploit them. SWOT analysis was also introduced in **Chapter 2**.

In **Chapter 3** we analysed the organization's competitive environment and the nature of competition within it. Porter's five forces framework, which concentrates on the industry structure facing organizations, was used to assess industry attractiveness. We noted that Porter's five forces analysis is best undertaken at the level of the strategic business unit (SBU). This framework was further evaluated by assessing the role of complements in creating industry value. We discussed how organizations might use strategic groups to help them identify competitor relationships. Lastly, we assessed the impact of hypercompetition on competitive behaviour.

We can now turn our attention to the internal environment facing the organization. It is important to realize here that, as with strategy formulation, a debate exists about what constitutes differential firm performance. The answer to the question of why firms with similar resources and which face the same industry structure perform differently is by no means concluded. What we can say is that a common criticism made about industry analysis is that it fails to answer this question. Indeed, many contributors within the field of strategic management would argue that a focus upon industry analysis has diverted attention away from this question in pursuit of matching the organization's resources to the needs of its external environment (the views of some of these protagonists will be discussed in detail in **Chapter 5**). This will become more apparent in **Chapter 7** when we discuss how an organization might position itself against the five forces.

DIFFERENTIAL FIRM PERFORMANCE refers to the observation that firms which possess similar resources and operate within the same industry experience different levels of profitability

This chapter is devoted to an analysis of the internal environment and how the organization might usefully analyse its value-creating activities.

- Section 4.1 introduces the background to differential firm performance and opens the debate on whether the industry in which the organization competes is the key determinant of its performance, or whether the answer to how well different firms perform lies within the organization itself.

- Section 4.2 deals with value chain analysis and how an organization can configure its value-creating activities in order to achieve competitive advantage.

- Section 4.3 evaluates the role of linkages within the value chain and how an organization can add value by analysing not only its own value chain but also that of its suppliers, distributors, and consumers.

- Section 4.4 evaluates SWOT within the context of the general and competitive environment and highlights some of its limitations.

- The chapter concludes by briefly revisiting the differential firm performance debate and introducing a different perspective. This suggests that relative firm performance is determined by an organization's resources and competencies, and is referred to as the resource-based view.

4.1 Background to Differential Firm Performance

Since Porter's seminal work on industry and competitor analysis (Porter 1980), a debate continues about what it is that drives an organization's performance. Is the industry context in which the firm finds itself the main determinant of its perform-ance? Or, are there factors contained within each individual organization which may more readily account for how well that organization performs? (See Segal-Horn (2004) for a collection of seminal articles which deal with differential firm perform-ance.) Put another way, in devising strategy, should the firm's main focus be the characteristics of its industry or the characteristics of its own organization?

For Porter (1980), as we saw in our discussion of the competitive environment, industry characteristics are paramount. For this reason his approach is referred to as part of the 'positioning' school, that is, the organization is viewed as capable of adopting a strategy which allows it to position itself within the industry to take advantage of the prevailing industry structure. Thus, for Porter, the attractiveness or profitability of an industry is determined by his five forces framework. As we will see when we come to look at strategy formulation in **Chapter 7**, if we adopt this view the corollary is that an organization is faced with a limited number of strategies on which to compete.

Rumelt (1991) argues that, contrary to the assertions of the positioning school, the defining factor in differential firm performance is not the industry structure within which the firm finds itself. Rather, it is more to do with factors at the individual firm level such as its resources and the strategy being adopted. This, in turn, is contested by Hawawini *et al.* (2003) who suggest that the external environment or industry effects are more important than firm-specific factors. If Rumelt is correct, it has implications for exactly what the firm should be focusing its strategic attention on and provides a broader arena for the importance of strategic formulation. Therefore, it is not surprising to find that strategic management as a discipline has become increas-ingly concerned with the internal environment of the organization. This approach is characterized by the resource-based view of strategy associated with the work of Prahalad and Hamel (Prahalad and Hamel 1990; Hamel and Prahalad 1993) and Grant (1991) which we will consider in **Chapter 5**.

For more information on differential firm performance go to the Online Resource Centre and see the Key Work feature.
www.oxfordtextbooks.co.uk/orc/henry2e/

4.2 Value Chain Analysis

Value chain analysis, which was devised by Porter (1985), is a technique which helps us assess an organization's resources and in so doing determine its strengths and possible weaknesses. Value chain analysis looks at the activities that go to make up a product or service with a view to ascertaining how much value each activity adds. (See Porter (1996) for a discussion of the role of activity systems within strategy.) The value or margin of a product is calculated by the amount of revenue it earns, in this case total revenue, which is calculated by the price of the product (or service) multiplied by the quantity consumed. If we know the total cost of each product, then the difference between the total revenue and total cost is the profit margin for the organization. Thus, the greater the difference between the organization's revenue and its costs, the greater the value it is adding.

If we desire to increase the value an organization adds for the consumers of its products, be they the end consumer or an intermediate such as a distributor, we need to know where and how much value each activity adds, and, importantly, how we might enhance this value added further by reconfiguring parts (or all) of the value-added process. However, it is increasingly recognized that organizations can also add value through cooperation with their suppliers, customers, and distributors. This process is referred to as the value chain system and recognizes that an organization's own value chain will interact with the value chain prevalent in other organizations. For example, a supplier's value chain, referred to as *upstream value*, will influence an organization's performance. Similarly, an organization's product will ultimately become part of a buyer's value chain, providing *downstream value*. How an organization manages the linkages between itself and other firms will have an impact on how value is created within the supply chain system. If this is done correctly it will result in a non-zero-sum game in which all parties within the supply chain system will benefit and provide the organization with a sustainable competitive advantage.

Competitive advantage derives from specific activities within the organization and how these activities relate to each other, and to supplier and customer activities. Where competitive advantage is a result of the configuration of many different activities, clearly it will be more difficult to imitate and therefore more sustainable. Strategy then can be seen to be about how an organization configures its range of activities *vis-à-vis* its competitors. Therefore, if an organization wishes to pursue a low-cost strategy this implies that it engages in a particular configuration of its activities (see Strategy Focus: Re-engineering the Value Chain at Ahold, where the CEO, Anders Moberg, is re-engineering its value chain to help reduce costs). If an organization wished to pursue a differentiation strategy, it would need a different configuration of its value chain activities. A discussion of strategy formulation at the individual firm level is covered in detail in **Chapter 7**.

VALUE CHAIN

describes the activities within an organization that go to make up a product or service

VALUE CHAIN ANALYSIS

allows an organization to ascertain the costs and value that emanate from each of its value activities

VALUE OR MARGIN

is the difference between the total value received by the firm from the consumer for its product or service and the total cost of creating the product or service

VALUE CHAIN SYSTEM

refers to the relationship between the value chain activities of the organization and its suppliers, distributors, and consumers

4

 STRATEGY FOCUS

Re-engineering the Value Chain at Ahold

As chief executive of IKEA, Anders Moberg would occasionally wander into the forest to see for himself that the trees being felled were the right ones to keep the Swedish home furnishing group's supply chain humming. These days he is applying a similar hands-on approach as chief executive at Ahold, the world's fourth largest food retailer. It is Mr Moberg's belief that the strength of Ahold's impressive turnround from a €1bn (£700m) accounting scandal disclosed three years ago today will ultimately be determined . . . by little-recognized opportunities in cost management that lie at the heart of the Dutch retail group. Now comes the task of 're-engineering the value chain'— squeezing every cent out of each element of the supply chain. 'It is all about how we look at the value chain,' says Mr Moberg. 'At IKEA we went out into the forest to see which were the right trees to pick to optimize production and cost efficiency in the sawmills.'

© iStockphoto.com/Justin Horrocks

The key to cost management is a detailed analysis of the cost of goods sold.
For one bottle of tomato ketchup, what are the components of the value chain, production, marketing, packaging, and distribution?

The key is a detailed analysis of the cost of goods sold. Take a bottle of tomato ketchup. 'What are the costs of the growers of the tomatoes? What are the components of the value chain, production, marketing, packaging, and distribution? Can you add a component in a different way, for example with standardized bottles? You are looking at how to re-engineer the value chain (in order) to lower the price.' Armed with intricate knowledge of supply chain costs, Ahold can press big brand manufacturers to cut the prices they ask of the retailer.

Adapted from: 'It is all about the value chain' *Financial Times*, 24 February 2006.

4.2.1 **Primary Activities**[1]

We can see that an organization is a collection of activities which aid it in the design, production, marketing, and support of its product. All these activities can be captured using value chain analysis. In assessing an organization's activities it is important to analyse these at the level of the strategic business unit (SBU). The activities contained within the value chain are classified by Porter as primary activities and support activities (see Figure 4.1). These primary and support activities provide the link between an organization's strategy and its implementation. This is because once the organization is seen as a collection of activities, and every employee is involved in an activity, it becomes apparent that everyone has a role to play in strategy implementation. Therefore, it becomes crucial that an organization's strategy is clearly communicated throughout the organization so that individuals understand why they are involved in particular activities, and how this relates to other activities.

PRIMARY ACTIVITIES

are activities which are directly involved in the creation of a product or service

SUPPORT ACTIVITIES

are activities which ensure that the primary activities are carried out efficiently and effectively

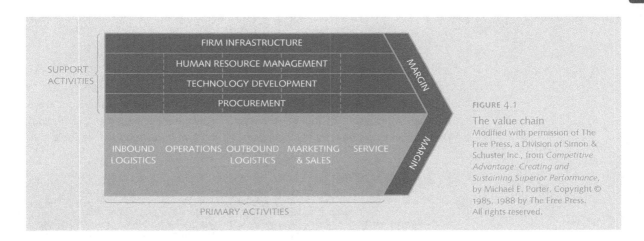

FIGURE 4.1

The value chain
Modified with permission of The Free Press, a Division of Simon & Schuster Inc., from *Competitive Advantage: Creating and Sustaining Superior Performance*, by Michael E. Porter. Copyright © 1985, 1988 by The Free Press. All rights reserved.

Primary activities are those activities which are directly involved in the creation and sale of a product or service. They include the following five generic categories: *inbound logistics*, *operations*, *outbound logistics*, *marketing and sales*, and *service*. These are explained in Table 4.1. Each primary activity can be subdivided into a number of distinct activities to reflect a particular industry and the organization's strategy.

Depending on the industry within which the organization competes, each of these primary activities can have an impact on its competitive advantage. For example, a distribution company such as UPS will clearly be more concerned about its inbound and outbound logistics—how it receives and stores products and gets them to the end user. The fact that UPS can accurately track the whereabouts of any of its parcels using sophisticated satellite technology and convey this to its customers is a means of adding value.

	Inbound logistics	These are the value chain activities that cover receiving, storing, and distributing inputs to the product. They include material handling, warehousing, inventory control, vehicle scheduling, and returns to suppliers.
	Operations	These activities deal with transforming an organization's inputs into final products such as machining, packaging, assembly, testing, printing, and facility operations.
	Outbound logistics	These activities are associated with collecting, storing, and distributing the product or service to buyers. Outbound logistics include warehousing, material handling, delivery, order processing, and scheduling.
	Marketing and Sales	This includes activities that make a product available for buyers to purchase and induces them to buy. It includes advertising, promotion, sales force, quoting, channel selection, channel relations, and pricing.
	Service	These activities enhance or maintain the value of products, such as installation, repair, training, parts supply, and product adjustment.

TABLE 4.1

Primary activities within the value chain

4.2.2 Support Activities

Support activities are there to ensure that the primary activities are carried out efficiently and effectively. The four generic support activities are *procurement*, *technology development*, *human resource management*, and *firm infrastructure* (see Table 4.2).

	Procurement	This value chain activity deals with the process of purchasing resource inputs to support any of the primary activities. Inputs to the organization's productive process include such things as raw materials, office supplies, and buildings. (See Strategy Focus: Procurement, which provides an insight into the growing importance of this activity.)
	Technology development	This activity covers an organization's 'know-how', its procedures, and any use of its technology that has an impact upon product, process, and resource developments.
	Human resource management	These activities include selection, recruitment, training, development, and remuneration of employees. They may support individual primary and support activities, as occurs when an organization hires particular individuals such as economists. They may also support the entire value chain, as occurs when an organization engages in company-wide pay negotiations.
	Firm infrastructure	This consists of activities which usually support the entire value chain, such as general management, planning, finance, accounting, and quality management. An organization's infrastructure is usually used to support the entire value chain.

TABLE 4.2

Support activities

The first three support activities may be associated with specific primary activities in addition to supporting the entire value chain, while firm infrastructure supports the entire value chain. As we saw with primary activities, each support activity can be divided into a number of distinct activities to reflect a particular industry.

Each category of primary and support activities includes a further three activities which impact on competitive advantage. These are *direct* and *indirect activities*, and *quality assurance*. Direct activities involve creating value for the buyer, for example through product design. Indirect activities allow direct activities to take place, such as regular maintenance. Quality assurance ensures that the appropriate quality of the other activities is maintained, for example through monitoring and testing.

STRATEGY FOCUS

Procurement

Is there a less exciting topic in management than procurement? Yet the reality of business today is that this is precisely where a lot of the vital action is—and not just in the private sector . . . A quiet under-reported revolution has been taking place within organizations in the past few years. Where once procurement was simply a matter of getting the best (which is to say lowest) price on a long list of unglamorous basic commodities—stationery, furniture, and laptops—the disciplines and attitudes of the procurement department are now being unleashed on an ever wider array of goods and, crucially, services.

The tone and nature of the conversations between companies and their service providers have changed. In the past, for example, in-house counsel would have been left to negotiate terms with the company lawyers. But there was always a danger that these 'negotiations' could end up being a bit too cosy. Managing these sorts of contracts, with their 'service level agreements', professional indemnity insurance, and liability clauses, is a task better suited to the experienced procurement professional. But, as well as basic contract management, procurement teams are increasingly being asked to find new and better (and preferably but not necessarily cheaper) service providers. A classic dodge is to seek out inefficient costly service providers to tender for a contract. When procurement then rides to the rescue with a much cheaper alternative, vast (but illusory) savings can be claimed. The other risk is that the intervention of procurement teams may disrupt successful existing relationships . . . Partnership, not antagonism, should be the goal. The danger is that formerly peaceful if inefficient relationships turn into unpleasantly adversarial—and no more efficient—ones.

Adapted from: 'The new-found power wielded by procurement departments' *Financial Times*, 20 June 2006.

4.3 Evaluating the Value Chain

A generic value chain provides a blueprint on which an organization can build in order to define its own value chain which is pertinent to the industry in which it competes. In deciding which activities to include in the categories that make up its value chain, an organization needs to be aware of their contribution to its competitive advantage. The value activities included will involve an element of judgement and subjectivity. Value chain analysis is much more than an evaluation of the discrete activities within the value chain. To be effective, value chain analysis needs to recognize and understand the relationship or linkages between these activities. The linkages between activities will not always be apparent. However, if the organization is to add value it must appreciate how the manner in which one activity is performed impacts upon the cost and performance of other activities.[2] The aim is to see if a given activity can be undertaken differently and thereby improved, which might also provide some form of competitive advantage. In addition, an organization must understand the relationship between its own value activities and those activities outside the firm such as suppliers, distributors, and customers, that is, it needs to appreciate its value chain system.

LINKAGES

the relationships between the way one value activity is performed and the cost or performance of another activity

The Japanese car producers Honda and Toyota[3] are well-known examples of organizations which add value by working with suppliers and distributors to identify ways in which their value chains can be reconfigured to reduce lead times and cut costs. The use of just-in-time (JIT) production methods allows parts to be delivered only when they are ready for assembly, thereby reducing lead times and cutting inventory costs.

4.3.1 The Importance of Linkages within the Value Chain

An organization's value chain activities represent the cornerstone of competitive advantage. However, its value chain should be seen not as a series of independent activities but rather as a system of interdependent activities, that is, each value chain activity is related to the others by way of linkages in the value chain. Porter (1985, p. 48) describes linkages as 'the relationship between the way one value activity is performed and the cost or performance of another activity'. For example, Toyota's just-in-time production methods reduce inventory and material handling. Therefore, competitive advantage can derive from the linkages between its different activities as well as from the activities themselves.

Porter suggests that linkages can lead to competitive advantage in two ways: *optimization* and *coordination*. This is a recognition that linkages will often involve trade-offs. For example, an organization may spend more on product design and the quality of its materials in order to avoid greater maintenance costs during the product's use. By optimizing these linkages between its activities an organization can achieve competitive advantage. Similarly, an organization can reduce its costs or improve its ability to differentiate by better coordinating activities in its value chain. An understanding of linkages helps an organization to achieve competitive advantage by focusing on the relationship between interdependent activities as well as individual activities. While the linkages between primary and support activities are apparent, the linkages between primary activities may be more difficult to discern; for instance, better servicing and maintenance of machinery will lead to a reduction in its downtime. A key to benefiting from linkages is actively to search out and understand how each value chain activity can impact on or is impacted by other activities. The Case Study: Risks of Outsourcing shows how important it is for an organization to identify all the linkages within its value chain if it is to mitigate the associated risks of outsourcing.

CASE STUDY 4.1
Risks of Outsourcing

In the end it wasn't just the bitter winter cold that did for Napoleon's march on Moscow in 1812, or even Tsar Alexander's rallying of the Russian peasantry to harry his army with hit-and-run guerrilla tactics. It was the fact that the general's supply chain was stretched so far that his soldiers could not feed their horses.

Some experts and consultants have been stressing for years that the trend of outsourcing parts of a business to other companies, and extending supply chains across the world to locate the cheapest inputs, is not without risk. Graham Stevens, a member of the management group at PA Consulting, says far too many companies have thoughtlessly pursued the cheapest option at too high a risk. 'A lot of companies outsource for the wrong reasons,' he says. 'You can't outsource your risk, your brand or your problems.' The mentality that Mr Stevens labels 'out of mind, out of sight outsourcing' is, he says, a serious mistake.

Well before the problems experienced by the European retailers, there was a litany of cases where companies and industries received a rude shock about the vulnerability of their businesses to their suppliers. The petrol crisis in the UK in 2000, which brought the economy close to a halt, resulted from road tankers—operated by outsourced hauliers rather than the oil companies themselves—being prevented from leaving refineries by a few hundred protestors.

There is a distinction between outsourcing proper—buying in functions previously undertaken 'in-house', as BA did after selling off its airline meals service—and simply extending or shifting supply chains, as European clothes retailers have done. But both expose companies to the same kinds of risk: political, reputational and logistical.

The political risk of operating in developing countries with unstable and often corrupt governments is well known. A thriving industry of consultants such as

Control Risks Group and organisations such as the World Bank's Multilateral Investment Guarantee Agency has grown up to deal with them. Perhaps more of a shock to the German and Danish clothes retailers whose supplies from China have been interrupted was their exposure to political risk in Brussels. The Commission's deal with China to restrict textile imports was negotiated and signed at short notice under pressure from some EU member states months after the global regime of textile quotas ended.

'The problem was not with outsourcing per se but the policy response of governments,' says Stefano Bertasi, director of policy and business practices at the International Chamber of Commerce in Paris. 'These are very difficult to anticipate.'

Others say that companies that fail to anticipate such responses will lose out. Pietra Rivoli, an economist at Georgetown University in Washington, is the author of a book on the globalisation of the garment industry, *Travels of a T-Shirt in the Global Economy*. One of the themes she found was the remarkable persistence of political interference in global economic integration. The fact that cotton is grown in Texas, for example, before being shipped to China and then back again as fabric or T-shirts, is testament less to the power of the free market than to the lobbying power of a small number of subsidised American cotton farmers.

Prof Rivoli says that before companies source exclusively from China, with a lead time measured in months, they must understand the political risks. 'You have to have a sophisticated understanding of the political relationship between China and the West,' she says. 'You have to be on top of the trade issue, the currency issue and a lot else besides. Retailers such as M&S and Gap are big enough to have their fingers on the pulse. Smaller ones may not be.'

Indeed, the political risk within modern democracies, where politicians move quickly to placate public opinion, can be considerable. Few could have predicted the firestorm of protectionist protest in the US last year when Greg Mankiw, then chairman of the White House council of economic advisers, made some apparently innocuous remarks about information technology offshoring being simply another form of trade. Subsequently Nicolas Sarkozy, then French finance minister, set off a wave of concern across the global IT industry when he proposed that, as part of his campaign against the 'de-localisation' of jobs from France, call centre workers in francophone Africa should be compelled to state from where they were speaking.

The reputational risk, as Nike discovered, is especially strong when brand and image are central to the business model. And on the logistical risk side, BA's sale of its catering business in 1997 and decision to buy in food from Gate Gourmet did not outsource its industrial relations problems.

The extension of supply chains magnifies any logistical disruption to the business, whether it stems from unreliability of supply, simple mistakes or failure of communication. Management theorists have invented a term for it—the 'bullwhip effect'—where a small movement towards one end of the supply chain can cause destabilising volatility at the other. 'Companies deciding to source in China rather than producing in-house may think they are adding a single link to their supply chain,' Mr Stevens says. 'In fact they are probably adding at least five: the production agent in China, a logistics company in China, Chinese customs, the freight shipper, customs and transport in the domestic market.' A hitch at any stage—an order missing a shipment date, for example—can multiply problems and delay at the next.

Though supply-chain risks can never be eliminated, companies can use a variety of strategies to mitigate them.

To reduce reputational risks, some businesses buy in credibility from elsewhere. Oil and mining companies, much as they might like to do all their work in Sweden, frequently have to operate in countries with unpleasant governments. The World Bank and its private-sector arm, the International Finance Corporation, are often asked to participate in projects in countries with poor governance—less for the finance they provide than for their human rights and environmental standards, which act as a seal of international approval. For logistical and political risks the obvious solution is to use multiple suppliers. Some clothing retail companies have continued to source from other producers in Turkey, Sri Lanka and Bangladesh to spread risks, for example. Prof Rivoli says the US has a useful 'safety valve' close at hand in the Central American and Caribbean clothing industry, which can ramp up production rapidly to take care of sudden shortfalls.

If using a single source is necessary because of the complexity of the product, as in the car industry, the buyer can insist that suppliers maintain buffer stocks and spare capacity.

Some go further. Zara, the successful Spain-based clothes company, keeps a remarkable proportion of its supply chain in-house. It buys cloth in a small number of basic colours from east Asia, and dyes, cuts and sews most of its own garments with a network of factories in Spain and Portugal. Because this supply chain delivers quickly and with little waste because of rapid feedback from shops about what is selling well, it compensates for what it costs in higher wages. Ironically, in its last set of earnings, Inditex, which owns Zara, said a supply disruption to the small proportion of clothes it sources from Asia and eastern Europe had affected otherwise healthy sales.

Some risks will always be hard to mitigate. Whether any of the above strategies would have prevented BA's problems, for example, is questionable. BA has had plenty of industrial relations problems with its own staff. Keeping its catering in-house, which would make it unusual in the airline industry, may not have reduced this risk.

But as Napoleon discovered, threats to supply chains should never be ignored. Outsourcing and globalisation have benefited companies and consumers immensely. They are not without hazards.

Source: 'Unchained malady: business is becoming ever more exposed to supplier problems' *Financial Times*, 25 August 2005.

▣ Questions

1. Why should an organization seek to understand and apply value chain analysis to all its activities rather than simply pursuing outsourcing as an end in itself?
2. How might an emphasis on the linkages between activities in the value chain be the route to a more sustainable competitive advantage?
3. What can organizations do to prevent an over-reliance on outsourced partners?

4.3.2 Managing Linkages within the Value Chain System

In most industries organizations do not undertake all the activities constituting the value chain system but will usually focus on a specific number of activities. This can be traced back to the eighteenth century and the work of the British economist Adam Smith on specialization and the division of labour.[4] In addition, the extent to which an organization can manage the linkages between the value chains of others within the value chain system may become an important competence and area of competitive advantage. Therefore, Porter argues that in addition to analysing and improving its own activities, an organization should also seek to analyse the benefits to be accrued from better links with the value chain of its suppliers, distributors, and consumers.

These linkages are similar to the linkages within an organization's own value chain in that the manner in which they are undertaken impacts upon the cost or performance of an organization's activities. For example, if a supplier is able to undertake frequent deliveries, this reduces an organization's inventory requirements. Japanese automobile manufacturers are a good example of managing external value chains in order to facilitate just-in-time deliveries of parts which can be put to immediate use rather than being tied up in expensive and unproductive inventory. The American retailer Wal-Mart is well known for the way it manages the linkages between itself and its suppliers. This enables Wal-Mart to leverage its massive buying power while at the same time providing suppliers with scale economies for their products through Wal-Mart stores. The way in which their UK counterparts manage the linkages between themselves and their suppliers has often ended in acrimonious exchanges. Suppliers claim that the sheer buying power of supermarket retailers allows them to dictate prices and terms to their detriment.

How an organization manages the linkages between its own and other value chains will have an impact on how value is created within the value chain system.

For example, if an organization can change the configuration of a supplier's value chain to optimize the performance of their respective activities, it will benefit itself and the supplier, leading to a win–win situation. In the same way, by improving the coordination between its own value chain and a supplier's value chain, both benefit. This provides an opportunity for the organization to improve its competitive advantage. The extent to which an organization can appropriate some of these benefits will reflect the bargaining power of its suppliers. Therefore, an organization must be prepared to influence the coordination of its suppliers' value chains and be prepared to negotiate to appropriate some of the rewards. The organization needs to undertake the same analysis with its distributors if it is to lower its costs or improve its differentiation.

The consumer also has a value chain, and an organization's product is an input into the buyer's value chain. With buyers, the key for organizations is to construct a value chain for them based on the activities that are relevant to how the product is used. This is important because the consumers of an organization's product will assess that organization on the benefits they derive from it. For example, in 2005 the UK Competition Commission, which regulates competition, found that retail outlets which issued store cards were not acting in the consumer's interest. This ruling provides retail stores with an opportunity to reconfigure the linkages between their buyers' value chains to improve customer loyalty and therefore performance, thus avoiding a zero-sum game in which 'losing' consumers simply vote with their wallets. An organization's ability to differentiate its offering will be a product of how its value chain relates to the buyer's value chain. Value for the consumer is created when an organization is able to lower the buyer's costs or improve differentiation for the buyer. The buyer's perception of the value to be derived from a product will determine the organization's ability to charge a premium price. This in turn provides the organization with competitive advantage.

In seeking to influence the value chain of its suppliers, distributors, and consumers, an organization needs also to address the *make or buy* decision. That is, does the organization want to undertake all activities of the product or service itself, or might it prefer to outsource some of the activities in its value chain? This evaluation should be integral to the analysis it undertakes as part of its assessment of its own value chain. Many organizations in both the public and private sectors make a conscious choice as to the value activities they perform internally and those value activities that they are prepared to purchase. The Case Study: Managing Linkages in the Value Chain System illustrates how BMW is making use of partners who can add greater value through their expertise in logistical activities. There is a recognition here of transaction cost and that some organizations may be able to provide certain value chain activities at a lower cost. Clearly, where these activities constitute a core competence, organizations may prefer to keep them in-house.

4

CASE STUDY 4.2

Managing Linkages in the Value Chain System—TNT Logistics*

A visitor to BMW's North American factory near Spartanburg, South Carolina, might assume the fork-lift truck drivers shuttling components around the assembly line were employees of the German car maker. In fact, they work for TNT Logistics, part of TPG, the Dutch post and package group. TNT manages BMW's North American supply chain from the moment a part is dispatched by a supplier until its installation in one of the Z4 sports cars or X5 sports utility vehicles made in Spartanburg. The arrangement is not unique to BMW; nearly 80 per cent of big European and North American companies outsource parts of their logistics operation to outside contractors, up from 71 per cent three years ago, according to research by the Georgia Institute of Technology.

Companies have long outsourced functions such as freight transport and warehouse management. With the increasing complexity of supply chains, however, many are now handing over bigger portions of their logistics operations to companies such as TNT. US companies surveyed by Georgia Tech predicted the proportion of their supply chain expenditure paid to outside contractors, known as third-party logistics providers (3PLs), would increase from 44 per cent this year to 49 per cent by 2009.

'Our customers do not want to spend time and money worrying about logistics; they want to get on with building products or providing services. We allow them to do that,' says Jeffrey Hurley, managing director of TNT Logistics in North America.

TNT is the world's second-largest logistics contractor, after UK-listed Exel but ahead of Nippon Express of Japan, UK-based Wincanton, and Germany's DHL Solutions. These companies promise to use their expertise and access to global freight networks to reduce their customers' costs and bring greater efficiency to their supply chains, which often stretch thousands of miles from suppliers in China and other low-cost countries to the big consumer markets of Europe and North America.

Logistics costs, which already amount to an average 7 per cent of sales at large US companies, are being pushed up by rising fuel prices, transport capacity shortages, and increased security checks on international cargo because of the threat of terrorism.

'The majority of companies still do most of their logistics in-house, so there is huge potential to grow,' Mr Hurley says. 'We can usually take 10–15 per cent off a customer's logistics costs and increase efficiency by a large percentage.'

In an office inside BMW's facility in Spartanburg, TNT managers monitor computer screens showing the flow of parts from suppliers all over the world.

* TNT was rebranded as CEVA Logistics in December 2006.

'We micro-manage the supply chain in a way our customers have not had time to do before,' says Mr Hurley. 'We know where every part is, right down to a gear. If something hasn't left a supplier in Mexico, we're on the phone to them.' Greater reliability in the supply chain has allowed BMW to reduce the inventory in its Spartanburg warehouse from a fortnight's supplies to just three days' worth. The usage rate of inbound delivery trucks has increased from 61 per cent to 79 per cent and the on-time delivery rate has exceeded TNT's target of 99.2 per cent.

'Before, BMW would not know what was arriving until they opened the back of the truck. Sometimes there would be the wrong part or wrong quantity but by then it was too late to correct, so you got hold-ups on the assembly line,' says Allen Melton, TNT's project manager at the BMW plant.

Once parts have arrived at the warehouse, TNT feeds them to the nearby assembly line along a conveyor belt connecting the buildings. Parts are delivered in the precise order needed by assembly-line workers. Such a lean operation brings risks: when the wrong-sized sunroof arrived at the assembly line recently production was halted for 33 minutes while the correct model was rushed from a supplier 16 miles away. TNT paid BMW a $19,000 penalty for the mistake. 'The aim is to make sure those sorts of discrepancies do not reach the assembly line by checking for defects at every stage of the supply chain,' Mr Melton says.

John Langley, professor of supply chain management at Georgia Tech, says TNT's relationship with BMW shows how companies are starting to view third-party logistics providers as strategic partners rather than contractors. 'Companies have tended to see 3PLs primarily as a way to reduce costs but a more efficient supply chain can create value throughout the business,' he says.

As the relationships become deeper, companies are entrusting logistics partners with more responsibility. At a warehouse in Indianapolis, Indiana, TNT conducts basic sub-assembly work for Eaton, a truck components maker. 'When we started this contract two years ago, Eaton did not trust us to talk to their suppliers and customers,' recalls Ted Wade, TNT's quality manager at the Indianapolis facility. 'But as you develop more trust they are prepared to outsource more functions and allow you further up the value chain.'

As well as reducing costs and improving efficiency, companies can offload some risks on to 3PLs. When TNT took control of Michelin's North American distribution network two years ago, it also bought the French tyre maker's 18 warehouses in the US and Canada and hired most of the company's 600 logistics staff 'The warehouses were getting old and needed upgrading,' says Bob Brescia, Michelin's head of logistics in North America. 'By handing them to TNT we got them off our balance sheet and avoided the investment.'

However, not all companies have embraced 3PLs as fully as BMW, Eaton, and Michelin. Many, such as Wal-Mart, the world's biggest retailer, believe logistics is too important to outsource. 'It is one of our core competencies,' says Gus Whitcomb, spokesman for Wal-Mart. 'It is certainly something we prefer to control internally.'

In Europe, logistics outsourcing is well developed but powerful labour unions limit its scope. For example, it would be difficult for TNT to work as closely with BMW in Europe as it does in Spartanburg because the car maker has an agreement with German unions that 3PLs cannot be involved in assembly-line work.

The greatest potential for 3PL growth lies in China, where logistics services are urgently needed to support manufacturing growth. Chinese TNT managers from Shanghai recently visited Spartanburg to learn about BMW's supply chain, and at TNT's North American headquarters in Jacksonville, Florida, Mandarin-speaking staff are testing Chinese-language software to communicate with Chinese customers and suppliers.

Analysts and executives forecast annual growth of about 8–10 per cent in the 3PL sector but competition is intensifying. David Kulik, managing director of TNT Logistics, says: 'When you compete on price there is always someone willing to do a job cheaper. So, we have to differentiate ourselves by adding more value.'

Source: 'Outsiders tighten the supply chain' *Financial Times*, 7 December 2004.

▪ Questions

1. Evaluate the German automaker BMW's decision to outsource part of its North American value chain system.
2. Why is BMW willing to relinquish these value chain activities while the US retail giant, Wal-Mart, considers these activities too important to trust to a third party?
3. To what extent might Wal-Mart be losing out on value creation by not employing third-party logistics?

An organization's own value chain analysis will help it to understand where it can add value in its activities and where its costs in some activities may exceed its value. Financial considerations are important, but so too is an organization's strategic capability. If an activity underpins an organization's strategic capability, that is, its ability to compete successfully in the marketplace, it will want to retain that activity. The decision an organization faces as to whether to continue with an activity or outsource it to a lower-cost producer will depend on the extent to which that activity is of strategic importance to the firm. Most organizations would be unwise to outsource what may constitute the source of their competitive advantage, but instead would seek to outsource lower-value activities to organizations that specialize in these activities.

Campbell and Goold (1998) state that identifying the extent of value chain overlaps between different businesses can be a source of synergy opportunity. For example, if two businesses within the same corporation purchase similar components, economies of scale may result by combining these purchases. Or, if two businesses have overseas offices in the same country, they could reap synergies by sharing premises, sales forces, or management.

Value chain analysis looks at the activities that go to make up a product or service with a view to ascertaining how much value each activity adds. It helps to identify the linkages between value activities within the organization to see if these can be improved. This involves assessing how these activities are best optimized and coordinated with a view to reducing the cost impact of one activity upon another or enhancing its performance. At the same time, the organization should identify if there is further value to be added by more effective management of the links with its suppliers, distributors, and customers within its value chain system (see Figure 4.1). The end result allows an organization to ascertain if it possesses a strategic capability or core competence within its activities, or more likely within its configuration of activities, which can be used as the basis for sustainable competitive advantage.

For a discussion of value chain activities with reference to organizations go to the Online Resource Centre and see the Key Work feature.
www.oxfordtextbooks.co.uk/orc/henry2e/

4.4 SWOT Analysis

We briefly introduced SWOT analysis in **Chapter 2** when we discussed the general environment. Those within the positioning school would argue that external analysis precedes the internal analysis of a firm's resources and capabilities. SWOT analysis can usefully be conducted once an audit of the external environment and the firm's own internal environment has been completed. Knowledge of an organization's own value chain helps indicate where its strengths and any weaknesses may reside. Equally, we might conduct a SWOT analysis following the discussion of the resourced-based view (RBV) of the firm in **Chapter 5**.

4.4.1 Integrating the General and Competitive Environments

SWOT analysis (Andrews 1971) refers to strength, weaknesses, opportunities, and threats. Strengths and weaknesses refer to the organization's internal environment, over which the organization has control. Strengths are areas where the organization excels in comparison with its competitors, while weaknesses are areas where the organization may be at a comparative disadvantage. Opportunities and threats refer to the organization's external environment, over which the organization has much less control. We noted that a SWOT analysis may prove useful in both the general environment and the competitive environment. However, the unpredictable nature of events in the general environment tends to make the use of SWOT analysis more problematic.

A SWOT analysis allows an organization to determine the extent of the strategic fit between its capabilities and the needs of its external environment. This implies that the organization has some understanding of the value chain activities that underpin its strengths and weaknesses. In addition, its analysis of the markets and industries in which it competes needs to be sufficiently robust if it is to be aware of real opportunities and threats that exist. SWOT analysis becomes more complicated when existing strengths can quickly become a weakness. For example, such things as changes in consumer tastes, innovative technologies, and new competitors will cause markets to change, thereby eroding an organization's current strengths and the source of its competitive advantage. A problem occurs when competitors are so busy investing in the capabilities that provide them with their current strengths that they fail to recognize threats in their external environment which will turn these strengths into a weakness. This is particularly the case where these threats emanate from outside their industry.

Therefore, in formulating strategy an organization should seek to match its strengths and weaknesses to the opportunities and threats it faces in its external environment. This analytical audit provides the organization with a better understanding of how it might best serve its markets. It illuminates the strategic choices which best match the organization's capabilities with the needs of its external environment. Yet, as we have noted, there can be a contradiction inherent in pursuing a strategic fit between an organization's strengths and the needs of its markets. As a result SWOT analysis should not simply be about matching an organization's existing strengths to the needs of the external environment, but also about being aware of how the external environment may evolve. Over time these can move in different directions, making strategy formulation problematic.

A number of issues faced by oil company Chevron emanate from the general environment, such as a social trend that sees people much more concerned about the impact of organizations' activities on the environment, and the political and economic impact as China and India continue to industrialize and simultaneously push up raw material prices and increase the threat of global warming. Other issues, such as a probable increase of 50 per cent in the number of cars in the world by 2030 and the need for alternative energy sources can also be seen to emanate from trends in the general environment, such as increasing affluence and growing environmental concerns. At the same time, the need for alternative energy sources is a prime concern within the oil industry (competitive environment) as competitors find it increasingly difficult to seek new substantive oil reserves. Given that these general environment concerns will ultimately play out in Chevron's competitive environment, we need to be aware of the relationship between the two.

We can amalgamate the tools of analysis drawn from the general environment, the competitive environment, and an internal analysis of the organization to produce a SWOT analysis. We can use scenario planning and PEST analysis to identify the external opportunities and threats (OT) facing an organization. The firm's internal strengths and weaknesses (SW) can best be determined following an appraisal of its resources and capabilities, which reside within the activities of its value chain. Why use this analysis? SWOT analysis allows an organization to assess the fit of its current strategy to its changing environment, and to help turn potential threats into opportunities, and weaknesses into strengths. It can help an organization to identify its resources and capabilities more clearly, and to assess whether these are a benefit or a constraint to exploiting opportunities in the marketplace. Ultimately it can be used to help formulate the organization's strategy.

For guidance on how to undertake a SWOT analysis go to the Online Resource Centre and see the Tools and Techniques feature.
www.oxfordtextbooks.co.uk/orc/henry2e/

4.4.2 Limitations of SWOT Analysis

Although SWOT analysis can be a powerful tool if used correctly, it also suffers from some drawbacks. One of these is that it is not an end in itself but more part of a process. It can provide useful signposts for the organization but, as with all tools of analysis, it will not supply the strategic decisions. Some common criticisms of SWOT are given below.

- It often produces lengthy lists which are each accorded the same weighting, when in fact not all strengths or weaknesses facing the organization will be weighted the same. For example, the effects of some weaknesses may seriously undermine the competitive advantage of the organization while others may have a less detrimental effect.

- Strengths and weaknesses may not be readily translated into opportunities and threats. For instance, an organization's strength embodied in its resources and capabilities may be moving in the opposite direction to how its market is developing.

- Ambiguity: the same factor can simultaneously be characterized as both a strength and a weakness. For example, the UK stationer and bookseller WH Smith has a store on most high streets. This makes it readily accessible for consumers. At the same time the fixed costs of its premises make it increasingly difficult to compete with online retailers not encumbered with the same cost structure.

- The same factor can also be an opportunity and a threat. For example, the trend in home entertainment means that consumers buy or rent films on DVD format, which benefits the film industry, but are less likely to attend the cinema, which is a threat to the industry.

- The analysis may be too focused within the industry boundary and miss the *weak signals*, *strategic inflexion points*, or *tipping points* which can restructure the firm's industry. (See Gladwell (2000) for tipping points; Grove (1996) for a discussion of strategic inflexion points; and Morgan (1988) for a discussion of fractures and discontinuities.)

 # Summary

In this chapter we have introduced an important debate within strategic management, that is, whether the industry context in which the firm finds itself is the main determinant of its performance, or whether there are internal factors within organizations which may more readily account for how well that organization performs. The former approach is characteristic of the positioning school and the work of Michael Porter. The latter is associated with the resource-based view of competition and will be addressed in **Chapter 5**. The answer to this question has implications for strategy formulation.

We evaluated value chain analysis as a technique which helps us to assess an organization's activities by showing where and how an organization adds value. It is a recognition by the positioning school of the internal factors that contribute towards profitability. The value chain comprises primary activities and support activities. Primary activities include inbound logistics, operations, outbound logistics, marketing and sales, and services, while support activities ensure that primary activities operate efficiently and effectively. Organizations add value through the configuration of their value chain activities and the linkages between these activities. We also noted that organizations add value through the linkages with their suppliers, distributors, and consumers. This process is referred to as the value chain system and recognizes that an organization's own value chain will interact with the value chain of others. How an organization manages the linkages between itself, suppliers, distributors, and consumers will have an impact on how value is created within its value chain system. The aim is to reduce costs or improve differentiation which provides a competitive advantage resulting in a win–win situation for all parties. Indeed, Brandenburger and Nalebuff (1996) note that organizations can add value through forming alliances and joint ventures as well as by competing.

Lastly, we revisited SWOT analysis in greater detail, pointing out that to be of greatest benefit it should include a prior analysis of the general and competitive environments. SWOT is a useful and much-used tool of analysis primarily because it is easy to use. That said, it has limitations: for example, the analysis may be too focused within the firm's industry boundary. Another limitation is that some factors can be seen as both a strength and a weakness.

We conclude the chapter with a reminder that the debate on differential firm performance continues. Value chain activities are clearly part of the internal resources that an organization possesses. However, a different perspective exists which emphasizes the organization's internal resources and capabilities. This suggests that relative firm performance, and therefore profitability, is determined by an organization's resources and competencies. This is referred to as the *resource-based view* and is discussed in **Chapter 5**.

Review Questions

1. Other things being equal, why do some organizations perform better than other organizations when competing in the same industry?
2. What factors should an organization take into account when it considers whether to undertake or outsource activities within its value chain?

Discussion Question

It is not value chain analysis *per se* which is important for competitive advantage but an understanding of the linkages in the value chain system. Discuss.

Research Topic

Identify the value chain activities for the Italian retailer Benetton. How is Benetton able to manage successfully the linkages in its value chain system?

Recommended Reading

A key reading to understand value chain analysis is the work of Michael Porter. It was Porter who developed value chain analysis and remains the best expositor.

- **Porter, M.E.** (1985). *Competitive Advantage*, Chapter 2. Free Press, New York.

www.oxfordtextbooks.co.uk/orc/henry2e/
Visit the Online Resource Centre that accompanies this book for activities and more information on value-creating activities.

online resource centre

4

Notes

[1] This section draws heavily upon Porter (1985), especially Chapter 2 which contains a discussion of value chain analysis and competitive advantage.

[2] Where an organization's activities are embedded within its routines and form part of its culture it is often difficult to identify clearly where value may be derived.

[3] That Toyota is able to add value within its activities is perhaps best seen in its rivalry with General Motors Corporation as the number one automobile manufacturer.

[4] These ideas were first discussed by Adam Smith in his book *The Wealth of Nations*, first published in 1776, in which he pointed out that greater productivity gains result from workers who specialize in an activity.

References

Andrews, K.R. (1971). *The Concept of Corporate Strategy*. Irwin, New York.

Brandenburger, A. and **Nalebuff, B.J.** (1996). *Co-opetition*. Doubleday, New York.

Campbell, A. and **Goold, M.** (1998). *Synergy: Why Links Between Business Units Often Fail and How to Make Them Work*. Capstone, Oxford.

Gladwell, M. (2000). *The Tipping Point—How Little Things Can Make a Big Difference*. Little Brown, Boston, MA.

Grant, R. (1991). The resource-based theory of competitive advantage: implications for strategy formulation. *California Management Review*, **33**(3), 114–35.

Grove, A.S. (1996). *Only the Paranoid Survive*. Random House, New York.

Hamel, G. and **Prahalad, C.K.** (1993). Strategy as stretch and leverage. *Harvard Business Review*, **71**(2), 75–84.

Hawawini, G., Subramanian, V., and **Verdin, P.** (2003). Is performance driven by industry or by firm-specific factors? A new look at the evidence. *Strategic Management Journal*, **24**(1), 1–16.

Morgan, G. (1988). *Riding the Cutting Edge of Change*. Jossey Bass, San Francisco, CA.

Porter, M.E. (1980). *Competitive Strategy*. Free Press, New York.

Porter, M.E. (1985). *Competitive Advantage*. Free Press, New York.

Porter, M.E. (1996). What is strategy? *Harvard Business Review*, **74**(6), 61–78.

Prahalad, C.K. and **Hamel, G.** (1990). The core competence of the corporation. *Harvard Business Review*, **68**(3), 79–91.

Rumelt, R.P. (1991). How much does industry matter? *Strategic Management Journal*, **12**(3), 167–85.

Segal-Horn, S. (ed.) (2004). *The Strategy Reader*, 2nd edn. Blackwell, Oxford.

Van Der Heijden, K. (1996). *Scenarios: The Art of Strategic Conversation*. Wiley, New York.

The Internal Environment: A Resource-Based View of Strategy

5

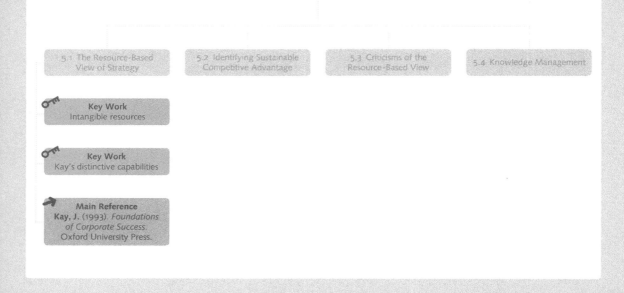

| 5.1 The Resource-Based View of Strategy | 5.2 Identifying Sustainable Competitive Advantage | 5.3 Criticisms of the Resource-Based View | 5.4 Knowledge Management |

 Key Work
Intangible resources

Key Work
Kay's distinctive capabilities

Main Reference
Kay, J. (1993). *Foundations of Corporate Success*. Oxford University Press.

Learning Objectives

After completing this chapter you should be able to:

- Discuss the resource-based view of strategy
- Explain the role of resources, competencies, and capabilities in helping an organization achieve a sustainable competitive advantage
- Explain how the resource-based view can guide strategy
- Evaluate the importance of knowledge management within organizations

Introduction

The previous chapter was devoted to an analysis of the internal environment and how the organization might usefully analyse its value-creating activities. In order to help assess the importance of the firm's internal environment we placed our discussion in the context of the factors which account for an organization's performance. In **Chapter 3** we saw that the answer to the question 'What drives an organization's performance?' was rooted in an understanding of an organization's markets and industry. This 'positioning approach' accepts the importance of an organization's resources but argues that in formulating strategy an analysis of the competitive environment is a more appropriate starting point.

What determines an organization's performance will continue to be our backdrop as we evaluate an alternative approach to this question. We have already noted that a criticism made about the positioning approach is that it fails to answer this question adequately. In this chapter we will explore a radically different perspective which suggests that relative firm performance, and therefore profitability, is determined by an organization's resources and competencies. This has been termed the resource-based view of the firm.

- In Section 5.1 we continue the debate on differential firm performance by introducing the resource-based view of strategic management. We evaluate the role of resources, core competencies, and distinctive capabilities in helping the organization to achieve a competitive advantage.

- Section 5.2 considers some of the attributes an organization's resources must possess in order for them to provide it with a source of sustainable competitive advantage. We also briefly discuss the *make or buy* decisions facing organizations.

- In Section 5.3 we discuss some of the criticisms of the resource-based view.

- The chapter ends in Section 5.4 with a discussion of the importance of knowledge management and how tacit knowledge might provide a competitive edge in the knowledge economy.

5.1 The Resource-Based View of Strategy

The resource-based view of strategy has a long antecedent, with links stretching back to Edith Penrose (1959). However, it is more commonly associated with the work of Prahalad and Hamel (1990), Rumelt (1991), Barney (1991), Grant (1991), and Peteraf (1993). The resource-based view also deals with the competitive environment facing the organization but takes an 'inside-out' approach, that is, its starting point is the organization's *internal* environment. As such, it is often seen as an alternative perspective to Porter's (1980) five forces framework, examined in **Chapter 3**, which takes the industry structure (outside-in) as its starting point.

The resource-based view emphasizes the internal capabilities of the organization in formulating strategy to achieve a sustainable competitive advantage in its markets and industries. If we see the organization as made of resources and capabilities which can be configured (and reconfigured) to provide it with competitive advantage, then its perspective does indeed become inside-out. In other words, its internal capabilities determine the strategic choices it makes in competing in its external environment. In some cases an organization's capabilities may actually allow it to create new markets and add value for the consumer, such as Apple's iPod and Toyota's hybrid cars. Clearly, where an organization's capabilities are seen to be paramount in the creation of competitive advantage it will pay attention to the configuration of its value chain activities. This is because it will need to identify the capabilities within its value chain activities which provide it with competitive advantage.

If we look at Toyota's much admired manufacturing system we see it manages *inbound logistics* in the form of excellent material and inventory control systems. This ensures that inventory levels are sufficient to meet customer demand by having parts delivered prior to their assembly. If we look at other primary activities in the value chain, such as *operations*, we find automated and efficient plants with embedded quality control systems. This is backed by *marketing and sales* through advertising and dealership networks, and *service* through the use of guarantees and warranties. Toyota's value chain activities, its linkages across them, and its linkages with the value chain of its suppliers are configured in such a way that they provide the Japanese competitor with a core competence or distinctive capability. It is this capability which provides it with competitive advantage and which its competitors have found difficult to match. Toyota is also able to appropriate the added value that is derived from these activities. For instance, Toyota makes more profit than the three largest automobile companies in the USA combined.

If firms in an industry face similar industry conditions we might expect, other things being equal, these firms to exhibit some degree of similarity with respect to profitability. Yet, if we compare the profitability of the UK supermarket retailer Tesco with its arch-rival Sainsbury's, we see a great divergence in profitability between firms that compete in the same industry. Porter (1980) argues that it is the industry structure within which organizations compete and how they position themselves against that structure which determines how profitable individual firms will be. In contrast, the resource-based view of strategy points not to industry structure but to the unique cluster of resources and capabilities that each organization possesses (Collis and Montgomery 1995; Stalk *et al.* 1992). Therefore, for proponents of the resource-based school, the answer to why firms within the same industry experience different levels of performance is to be found by looking inside the organization.

As is so often the case, the differences between competing perspectives can be overdone. For example, Amit and Schoemaker (1993) argue that the resource-based view can be seen as a complement to the positioning school. Hamel and Prahalad

(1993) concede that Porter's approach which embodies the notion of *strategic fit*, matching an organization's resources to the needs of the external environment, is not so much wrong but more what they refer to as *unbalanced*. For many managers the concept of strategy implies pursuing opportunities that *fit* the company's resources. Hamel and Prahalad suggest that this approach is not wrong but tends to obscure an approach in which *strategic stretch* supplements strategic fit. They argue that being strategic means creating a chasm between ambition and resources. In other words, an organization with a relatively small amount of resources but with big ambitions can leverage its resources to achieve a greater output for its smaller inputs.

We should keep in mind that both the positioning school (see also Porter 1996) and the resource-based view have relative merits and criticisms.

5.1.1 Resources

The resource-based view of competition draws upon the resources and capabilities that reside within an organization, or that an organization might want to develop, in order to achieve a sustainable competitive advantage. Resources may be thought of as inputs that enable an organization to carry out its activities. Where organizations in the same industry have similar resources but differing performance we might deduce that they vary in the extent to which they utilize their resources. Resources in and of themselves confer no value to organizations. It is only when they are put to some productive use that value follows. Resources can be categorized as tangible or intangible.

Tangible Resources

Tangible resources refer to the physical assets that an organization possesses and can be categorized as physical resources, financial resources, and human resources. Physical resources include such things as the current state of buildings, machinery, materials, and productive capacity. To add value these physical resources must be capable of responding flexibly to changes in the marketplace. Clearly, organizations with the most up-to-date technology and processes which possess the knowledge to exploit their potential will be at an advantage. The extent to which an organization can achieve an acceptable return on its capital employed will determine the extent to which it can attract outside capital or financial resources. This will be linked to expectations about its future growth. Its financial resources will include its cash balances, debtors and creditors, and gearing (debt-to-equity ratio).

The total workforce employed and their productivity, as measured by criteria such as profit or sales per employee, form a tangible human resource. In the knowledge-based economy the tacit knowledge and specialist skills of many employees form an intangible resource that it is difficult for competitors to imitate. It is interesting to note that it is tacit knowledge that can provide developed nations with a comparative advantage over low-cost manufacturing economies such as China and India.

RESOURCES

can be thought of as inputs that enable an organization to carry out its activities. They can be classified as tangible or intangible

TANGIBLE RESOURCES

refer to the physical assets that an organization possesses and include plant and machinery, finance and human capital

KNOWLEDGE-BASED ECONOMY

the tacit knowledge and specialist skills of employees which constitute an intangible resource that is difficult for competitors to imitate

Intangible Resources

Intangible resources comprise intellectual/technological resources and reputation. Technological resources include an organization's ability to innovate and the speed with which innovation occurs. Intellectual resources include patents and copyrights which themselves may derive from the organization's technological resources. For example, an intangible resource for the manufacturing company, Dyson, is the creative innovation of its founder, James Dyson, which competitors have been unable to successfully imitate. Organizations with valuable tacit knowledge built up through their culture, processes, and employees possess an intangible resource which cannot readily be transferred.

The reputation or 'goodwill' of an organization is increasingly recognized as a valuable intangible asset which can easily be damaged by ill-thought-out strategies and marketing campaigns. Some organizations, such as Benetton, have made a point of courting debate with their controversial advertising campaigns. In their case it seems to draw supporters and detractors in equal measure while generating useful free publicity. Johnson & Johnson's response to malicious tampering with their Tylenol product (see **Chapter 1**) ensures that it consistently remains top of organizations ranked according to their reputation.[1]

For a more detailed discussion of intangible resources go to the Online Resource Centre and see the Key Work feature.
www.oxfordtextbooks.co.uk/orc/henry2e/

5.1.2 Competencies

Whilst the existence of resources is important, resources *per se* do not confer any benefit on an organization. It is the efficient configuration of resources that provides an organization with **competencies**. A competence is a group of attributes that firms require in order to be able to compete in the marketplace. In this respect, all firms possess competencies. It is a prerequisite for competing within an industry. However, competencies in and of themselves do not confer any competitive advantage for the organization. It may be useful to think of competencies as deriving from the bundle of resources that a firm possesses. For example, in order to be able to compete in the automobile industry organizations must possess knowledge about design and engine and body manufacture. Without this base knowledge, firms would simply be unable to compete effectively in that industry irrespective of their resources.

There is a degree of confusion with the plethora of terms that circulate around the resource-based view of strategy. We will try to use common terms with the proviso that even here these may mean different things to different authors. For example, some advocates of the resource-based view use the term core competencies to refer to activities in which the firm can achieve a sustainable competitive advantage. Others use the term distinctive capabilities to make the same point.

5.1.3 Core Competencies

Prahalad and Hamel (1990) argue that the critical task of management is to create an organization capable of creating products which customers need but have not yet even imagined. To achieve this management must successfully operate across organizational boundaries rather than focus on discrete individual strategic business units (SBUs). Core competencies derive from the collective learning of individual members within an organization and their ability to work across organizational boundaries. Prahalad and Hamel (1990, p. 82) argue:

> The skills that together constitute core competence must coalesce around individuals whose efforts are not so narrowly focused that they cannot recognize the opportunities for blending their functional expertise with those of others in new and interesting ways.

Thus, a core competence or strategic capability can be thought of as a cluster of attributes that an organization possesses which in turn allow it to achieve competitive advantage. It may simply be that the organization has configured its collection of resources in such a way that allows it to compete more successfully. Dell and Benetton clothing are classic examples of firms that have achieved core competence in the way they configure their respective value chains. Many organizations have tried to copy Michael Dell's example but found his direct-sales model less easy to imitate than might be first thought. (See Case Study: Dell—Embedded Routines.)

Similarly, the Japanese motor manufacturer Toyota has achieved a core competence in the production of petrol-and-electric hybrid cars (see Strategy Focus: Toyota's Core Competencies). This in no small measure results from their first-mover advantages. This refers to organizations which benefit from the learning and experience they acquire as a result of being first in the marketplace. Other motor manufacturers are placed in the unenviable position of playing 'catch-up'. Prahalad and Hamel (1990) point out that many major corporations have had the potential to build up core competencies, but senior management lacked the vision to see the company other than as a portfolio of discrete businesses. This is what Prahalad and Hamel refer to as the *tyranny of the SBU*. They provide three tests that can be applied to core competencies in an organization.

1. A core competence should provide access to a wide variety of markets. For example, Honda's capabilities in engine design and production have enabled it to leverage its core competencies to compete in markets such as cars, lawnmowers, and powerboats.

DISTINCTIVE CAPABILITIES

are important in providing an organization with competitive advantage. They derive from three areas: an organization's *architecture, innovation,* and *reputation*

CORE COMPETENCE OR STRATEGIC CAPABILITY

a cluster of attributes that an organization possesses which in turn allow it to achieve competitive advantage

FIRST-MOVER ADVANTAGES

refers to organizations which benefit from the learning and experience they acquire as a result of being first in the marketplace

5

2. A core competence should make a significant contribution to the perceived customer benefits of the end products. For example, BMW has distinctive capabilities in engineering which allow it to produce high-quality cars that sell at a premium.

3. A core competence should be difficult for competitors to imitate. For a core competence to have any lasting value to the organization the competitive advantage that derives from its use must be sustainable. In order for that condition to hold, the core competence must be difficult for competitors to imitate. This is the case in the USA with Southwest Airlines; competitors have found that having similar resources to the airline has not enabled them to deconstruct what makes the airline so successful. In the UK, the competitors of the supermarket retailer Tesco have been unable to replicate its success despite having similar resources.

A core competence is enhanced as it is applied and shared across the organization. For Prahalad and Hamel, competencies are the glue that binds businesses together and spurs new business development. For example, Toyota's core competencies derive from its ability to blend core competencies across the whole organization. Nonetheless, competencies still need to be protected if the organization is to appropriate the rewards that derive from their use.

STRATEGY FOCUS
Toyota's Core Competencies

It is going awfully fast, and they are not sure where it is leading them, but Toyota's rivals reckon they have no choice but to give chase. The Japanese carmaker is so pleased with the success of its Prius, an electric-and-petrol hybrid car that has sold well in America, that it is pressing ahead with plans to put hybrid engines in a range of other cars and sport-utility vehicles (SUVs). Competitors, ranging from America's General Motors to Germany's BMW and DaimlerChrysler, are scrambling to roll out hybrids of their own. Ford has already announced that it could increase production of hybrid cars tenfold by 2010. Adding a hybrid engine costs thousands of dollars; this puts off many consumers. But Toyota is pressing ahead anyway, confident that, with practice, it can master fuel-saving technologies more quickly than rivals. Since it launched the new Prius in America in 2003, Toyota has sold over 150,000.

The Prius is an odd-looking machine. Some buyers who would never go near a Prius may choose an existing SUV or luxury car over a rival model if it comes with a fuel-saving and eco-friendly hybrid option that is partly subsidised by the maker. Toyota began offering hybrid versions of its Highlander and Lexus SUVs earlier this year. Although Americans love their oversized SUVs, they are heavy machines that guzzle petrol. So buying a hybrid version might ease some of the guilt, even if the savings at the pump do not end up offsetting the higher price. Toyota will also put a hybrid engine into one of its Lexus luxury sedans, and Honda will do the same for its Acura. That will give wealthy greens a chance to tout their eco-friendly credentials without sacrificing style. Honda has just launched a new hybrid version of its popular Civic in America, and Toyota will begin selling hybrid versions of its Camry sedan in 2007. Overall, Toyota is racing towards its target of selling 1m hybrid vehicles worldwide by 2010.

That is the last thing that its American, European, and Korean rivals want to hear. Many of their executives complain that hybrids are unprofitable and over-hyped. Rivals are upset with Toyota, for setting the agenda so deftly; with themselves, for failing to keep pace; and with consumers, for having the temerity to buy what they do not want to sell. The European carmakers have trumpeted diesel technology as a fuel-efficient and eco-friendly alternative. Toyota also sees merit in diesels—it opened a new diesel-engine plant in Poland last week—but it has no intention of making life easy for its rivals by taking its foot off the hybrid accelerator. So everyone else is now playing catch-up. Toyota may leave them in the dust anyway. While its rivals struggle to integrate hybrid engines into their vehicles, the Japanese giant hopes soon to cut the extra costs of those engines in half.

Source: 'Battery assault' *Economist*, 22 September 2005

5.1.4 Distinctive Capabilities

Kay (1993) argues it is the distinctive capabilities of an organization's resources that are important in providing it with competitive advantage. However, an organization's capabilities are only distinctive when they emanate from a characteristic which other firms do not have. Furthermore, possessing a distinctive characteristic is a necessary but not sufficient criterion for success; it must also be *sustainable* and *appropriable*. For a distinctive capability to be sustainable it needs to persist over time. For a distinctive capability to be appropriable it needs to benefit the organization which holds it rather than its employees, its customers, or its competitors. These distinctive capabilities derive from three areas: *architecture*, *reputation*, and *innovation*. These in turn are linked to relationships between an organization and its stakeholders: its employees, customers, shareholders, and suppliers, as well as a group of collaborating firms to which it may network. It is these relationships which allow an organization's resources to provide it with distinctive capabilities through the conduit of its architecture, reputation, and innovation.

Architecture

An organization's architecture comprises the system of relational contracts which exist inside and outside the organization. We can differentiate between internal architecture, which refers to an organization's relationships with its employees, and between employees, and external architecture, which refers to its relationships with its customers and suppliers. In addition, an organization may engage in relationships with other firms working in related activities; this form of architecture is referred to as networks. There is a myth about great leaders of organizations which detracts from the reality of organizational behaviour. Organizations depend far less on individual leaders and groups than they do on their established structures, dominant styles, and organizational routines—what might be termed their existing ways of working. It is these organizational routines that have developed over time and are continually used in changing competitive conditions that allow the organization to get the best out of their ordinary employees. As Kay (1993, p. 69) states, 'Architecture does not create extraordinary organizations by collecting extraordinary people. It does so by enabling very ordinary people to perform in extraordinary ways.'

However, because a distinctive architecture is based upon the output of all employees rather than a few individuals, it allows the added value created to be more readily appropriated by the organization. In the same way, for a distinctive architecture to be sustainable the relational contracts that an organization enters into must be difficult for its competitors to identify and imitate. The relationships will inevitably be implicit, complex, and subtle, based in and around the organization. This lack of formalization inhibits imitation and ensures that architecture remains a source of competitive advantage. Architecture, then, refers to the ability of the organization to create organizational knowledge which is more than just the sum of individual employees. It includes an organization's ability to respond effectively to changes taking place in its external environment, as well as its exchange of information both within and outside the company.

Reputation

Reputation as a source of distinctive capability is particularly important in those markets where consumers can only ascertain the quality of a product from their long-term experience. An example would include the use of a firm of architects. An organization's reputation is built up through its reliable relationships, which may have taken considerable time to nurture and develop. However, once this element of trust is achieved, it can provide the organization with a distinctive capability. A reputation for providing good-quality products and services endows an organization with competitive advantage which can be used to secure repeat business and charge premium prices. In addition, such a reputation can be leveraged when entering related markets, as witnessed by Sony across the consumer electronics industry. Indeed, reputation can be used to help facilitate a more successful entry into unrelated markets, as seen with Virgin and the easyGroup. In independent tests,[2] Johnson & Johnson scores higher than any other organization on reputation, which in no small measure results from their insistence that managers conduct themselves responsibly and their credo of putting the customer first.

Innovation

An organization's ability to innovate successfully is also a source of distinctive capability which is sustainable and appropriable. For example, it may produce innovative products such as Apple with its iTunes, iPod, and more recently its iPad. In a survey of senior executives around the world to find the 50 most innovative companies (*BusinessWeek* 2007a), Apple came top for the third year running. Apple's unrivalled innovation in product design and functionality is proving a hard act for competitors to follow. It remains at the forefront of the digital media with its iPod portable music and video players and iTunes online stores. Rather than sit back complacently, Apple entered the mobile phone market in 2007 with the introduction of its iPhone and in 2010 introduced the iPad—its touch-screen computer. This constant innovation and product development keep competitors guessing about which products Apple will bring out next and provide a source of sustainable competitive advantage as competitors struggle to imitate their success (see Case Study: Apple's Innovation Machine).

Courtesy of Apple

Apple's ability to innovate with products such as the iPod has provided a route for competitive advantage

In many respects the competitive advantage that appears to emanate from innovation may be seen to derive from an organization's architecture. An organization may develop innovative processes which are embedded within the routines of the organization and therefore difficult for competitors to copy. By seeking patents and copyrights, organizations can protect innovative products and ensure that they appropriate the value deriving from their use. The use of patents and copyrights may not suit hyper-competitive markets, as we saw in **Chapter 3**. In such a marketplace, D'Aveni (1999) argues for continuous new product development which allows you to stay one step ahead of competitors. The deliberate cannibalization of a successful product by its successor ensures that the firm is able to appropriate the rewards from its innovations.

In fact, Apple's iconoclastic co-founder and CEO, Steve Jobs, is doing both: constantly developing new products while also seeking to appropriate more of the value from these products. Apple developed its first in-house microprocessor, the A4, to power their iPad. This, along with its battery technology, allows Apple to control what components go into its products and reduces its dependence on third-party manufacturers. At the same time Apple also has its own software—its iWork suite of programmes that are similar to Microsoft Office. This combination of in-house hardware and software has the advantage of making Apple's technology more proprietary, difficult to imitate, and importantly, allows Apple to appropriate more of the value from its activities. It also allows Apple to blend all these technologies in a way that no other competitor can.

 CASE STUDY 5.1
Apple's Innovation Machine

'HEROES and heroics' is one of the central themes of the current season at the Yerba Buena Center for the Arts in San Francisco, which prides itself on showcasing contemporary artists who challenge conventional ways of doing things. On 27 January the centre played host to one of the heroes of the computing industry: Steve Jobs, the boss of Apple, who launched the company's latest creation, the iPad. Mr Jobs also has a reputation for showcasing the unconventional. He did not disappoint.

The iPad, which looks like an oversized Apple iPhone and boasts a colour screen measuring almost ten inches (25cm), promises to change the landscape of the computing world. It is just half an inch thick and weighs 1.5lb (680 grams). 'It's so much more intimate than a laptop, and so much more capable than a smartphone,' Mr Jobs said of the device, which will be available in late March.

The Apple iPad

Courtesy of Apple

The new iPad has important limitations, which critics were quick to point out. It does not have a camera or a phone and users cannot run multiple applications on it at the same time. But Apple should be able to correct such flaws in due course.

Together with a host of other touch-screen 'tablet' computers that are expected to reach shops over the next year or so, the iPad looks set to revolutionise the way in which digital media are consumed in homes, schools and offices.

The flood of devices is likely to have a profound impact on parts of the media business that are already being turned upside-down by the internet. The move from print to digital has not been easy for newspaper or magazine publishers. Readers have proved reluctant to pay for content on the web. Companies are unwilling to pay as much for online advertisements as for paper ones—hardly surprising, given the amount of space on offer. The iPad will probably accelerate the shift away from printed matter towards digital content, which could worsen the industry's pain in the short term. Yet publishers hope that tablets will turn out to be the 21st-century equivalent of the printed page, offering them compelling new ways to present their content and to charge for it. 'This is really a chance for publishers to seize on a second life,' says Phil Asmundson of Deloitte, a consultancy.

It does not come as a surprise, then, that Apple has already attracted some blue-chip media brands to the iPad's platform. During his presentation Mr Jobs revealed that the company had struck deals with leading publishers such as Penguin and Simon & Schuster. They will provide books for the iPad, to be found and paid for in Apple's new iBooks online store. More agreements ought to be signed before the first iPads are shipped in March. Users will also be able to download applications that give them access to electronic versions of newspapers such as the *New York Times*, which presented an iPad app at the launch.

Apple's media partners no doubt have mixed feelings about dealing with Mr Jobs. Apple is now widely demonised in the music industry for dominating the digital downloading business with its iTunes store. The firm has been able to control the price of music, boosting sales of iPods but not bringing the record companies a great deal of money. That said, Apple did provide a way for the music business to make a profit online, which had hitherto eluded it. Apple's sleek iPhone has also given plenty of content producers a platform on which they can charge for their wares.

The firm's record suggests that it will be able to make one of the computing industry's most fervent wishes come true. Technology companies have repeatedly tried to make a success of tablets or similar devices. But the zone between laptops and mobile phones has been something of a Bermuda Triangle for device-makers, points out Roger Kay of Endpoint Technologies, a consultancy. 'Products launched in there have usually disappeared from the radar screen,' he says.

Among them are previous generations of tablet-style computers. In the 1990s various companies experimented with the machines, including Apple. When its Newton personal digital assistant failed to take off, Mr Jobs killed the project. Tablets were once again briefly in the limelight when Microsoft's Bill Gates predicted they would soon become people's primary computing device—powered, of course, by his company's software. That did not come to pass because consumers were put off by tablets' high prices, clunky user interfaces and limited capabilities. Instead the devices, which cost almost as much as proper PCs, have remained a niche product used primarily in industries such as health care and construction.

Why are tablets causing so much excitement these days? One reason is that innovations in display, battery and microprocessing technologies have greatly reduced their cost. Apple's iPad is priced at between $499 for the basic version and $829 for one with lots of memory and a 3G wireless connection, bringing it within the reach of ordinary consumers. Another reason for optimism is that interfaces have improved greatly. The iPad boasts a big virtual keyboard, which pops up when needed. It also features multi-touch, meaning that two fingers can be used to change the size of a photo. Furthermore, tablets will benefit from the fact that people have become accustomed to buying and consuming content in digital form.

All this explains why other firms are eyeing the tablet market too. Dozens of prototypes were on show at a consumer-electronics trade fair in Las Vegas earlier this month, including ones from Motorola, Lenovo and Dell. Jen-Hsun Huang, the chief executive of NVIDIA, a maker of graphics chips, reckons this is the first time he has seen telecoms firms, computer-makers and consumer-electronics companies all equally keen to produce the same product. 'The tablet is the first truly convergent electronic device,' he says.

Netbooks and e-books

The iPad and other tablets could shake up the computing scene. There has been some speculation that they could dent sales of low-end PCs, including Apple's MacBook. But a more likely scenario is that they eat into sales of netbooks, the cheap mini-laptops that are used mainly for web surfing and watching videos. Netbooks have been on a roll recently, with global sales rising by 72% to $11.4 billion last year, according to DisplaySearch, a market research company. That makes them a tempting target.

Apple's new device also poses a threat to dedicated e-readers such as Amazon's Kindle, though these will probably remain popular with the most voracious bookworms. Apple's long-expected entry into the tablet market has already forced e-reader firms to consider making their devices more versatile and exciting. 'You will see more readers using colour and video over the next five years,' predicts Richard Archuleta of Plastic Logic, which produces the Que proReader. And more makers of e-readers may mimic Amazon's recent decision to let third-party developers create software for its line of Kindles.

Book publishers are quietly hoping that Apple's entry into e-books will help to reduce the clout of Amazon: the Kindle has 60% of the e-reader market, according to Forrester, a research firm. They are also excited by the opportunities that tablets offer to combine various media. Bradley Inman, the boss of Vook, a firm that mixes texts with video and links to people's social networks, believes the iPad will trigger an outpouring of creativity. 'Its impact will be the equivalent of adding sound to movies or colour to TV,' he says.

Newspaper and magazine publishers are also thrilled by tablets' potential. Their big hope is that the devices will allow them to generate revenues both from readers and advertisers. People have proven willing to pay for long-form journalism on e-readers. But these devices do not allow publishers to present their content in creative ways and most cannot carry advertisements. Skiff, a start-up spun out of Hearst, is a rare exception to this rule. Its 11.5-inch reader is large enough to show off all elements of a magazine's design and accommodates advertising too.

Apple's arrival in the tablet market means that publishers will have to develop digital content for these devices, as well as for e-readers and smartphones. Many will prove unable or unwilling to do so themselves. That may boost firms such as Zinio, which has developed a digital-publishing model called Unity. This takes publications' content, repurposes it for different gadgets and stores it in 'the cloud', the term used to describe giant pools of shared data-processing capacity. Users pay once for the content and can access it on various Zinio-enabled devices, increasing the chances that it will be consumed.

Apple has other ambitions for the iPad. It hopes it will become a popular gaming machine and has designed the device so that many of the games among the 140 000 apps available for other Apple products will run on it straight away. The company has also revamped its iWork suite of word-processing, spreadsheet and presentation software for the iPad in an effort to ensure that the new device will catch on with business folk.

Apple's shareholders are no doubt hoping that the iPad will live up to its billing as a seminal device in the history of computing. They have already seen the company's share price soar. Defying the recession, on 25 January Apple announced the best quarterly results in its 34-year history, with revenues rising to $15.7 billion and profits to $3.4 billion—an increase of 32% and 50% respectively over the previous year. They will be keeping their fingers crossed that the iPad turns into another billion-dollar hit. Whether or not that turns out to be the case, Mr Jobs has already proven heroic enough to merit a portrait on the Yerba Buena Center's walls.

Source: 'Apple's innovation machine churns out another game-changing device' The *Economist*, 27 January 2010.

Questions

1. Identify the resources and distinctive capabilities that reside inside the Apple corporation. What value, if any, do you believe Apple derives from the reputation of Steve Jobs as a creative innovator?

2. To what extent do you believe Apple is able to revive the ailing fortunes of newspaper and magazine publishers who are willing to embrace digital technology and work in partnership with the technology company?

3. Which organizations inside (and outside) the computer industry have the most to fear from Apple's latest innovation?

The concern for innovation is not limited to organizations. The US Department of Commerce formed an advisory committee in 2007 to look at how best to measure innovation initiatives. It is made up of individuals who include Steve Ballmer of Microsoft, IBM's Sam Palmisano, an entrepreneur, and members of the academic community including a professor of economics at Harvard. The fifteen-strong panel is intended to represent the diversity of the US economy. Innovation is defined by the panel as the design, invention, development, and/or implementation of new or altered products, services, processes, systems, organizational structures, or business models for the purpose of creating new value for customers and financial returns for the firm (*BusinessWeek* 2007b). The ultimate aim of the advisory committee is not simply to develop new metrics for innovation but to try to ensure that US businesses remain competitive in a global environment.

In an article entitled 'Strategy and the delusion of grand design', Kay (2000) summarizes *distinctive capability* as the characteristics of a company that either cannot be copied by competitors or can only be copied with great difficulty. As we have seen, these will include such things as patents and copyrights, a strong brand image, patterns of supplier or customer relationships, and skills, knowledge, and routines that are often embedded within the organization and, therefore, are difficult for a competitor to unravel. It is these distinctive capabilities that are the basis of sustainable competitive advantage. The task then is to identify and match these distinctive capabilities with the needs of the marketplace.

Kay points out a contradiction inherent in the question 'How do organizations create distinctive capabilities?', since if distinctive capabilities can be replicated they fail to be distinctive capabilities. What is truly irreproducible has three sources: (1) market structure that limits entry; (2) a company's history which by definition will require time to replicate; (3) tacitness in relationships—the routines and behaviours—which cannot be copied since the participants themselves are unsure how they work. Therefore, organizations would do well to identify what distinctive capabilities they already possess rather than what distinctive capabilities they would like to have. We will have more to say on this topic when we examine sustainable competitive advantage below.

For a discussion of Kay's distinctive capabilities go to the Online Resource Centre and see the Key Work feature.
www.oxfordtextbooks.co.uk/orc/henry2e/

Grant (1991) distinguishes between resources and capabilities. He sees resources as inputs into the production process. These include capital equipment, the skills of individual employees, patents, brands, finance, and so on. On their own these resources are rarely productive. To be productive requires the cooperation and coordination of teams (or bundles) of resources. A capability is the capacity for a team of resources to perform some task or activity. Therefore, resources are the source of an organization's capability. And it is capabilities that are the main source of its competitive advantage.

Grant (1991) proposes a framework for strategy formulation comprising five stages:

1. Identify and classify the organization's resources. Appraise strengths and weaknesses relative to those of your competitors. Identify opportunities for better resource utilization.

2. Identify the organization's capabilities, that is, what it can do better than its rivals. Identify the resource input to each capability, and the complexity of inputs.

3. Appraise the rent-generating potential of resources and capabilities by (a) their potential for sustainable competitive advantage, and (b) the appropriability of their returns.

4. Select a strategy which best exploits the organization's resources and capabilities relative to the opportunities that exist in the external environment.

5. Identify whether any resource gaps exist which need to be filled. Invest in improving the organization's resource base.

There are two fundamental reasons for making the resources and capabilities of the firm the foundation for its strategy. First, internal resources and capabilities provide the basic direction for a firm's strategy and, second, resources and capabilities are the primary source of profit for the firm.

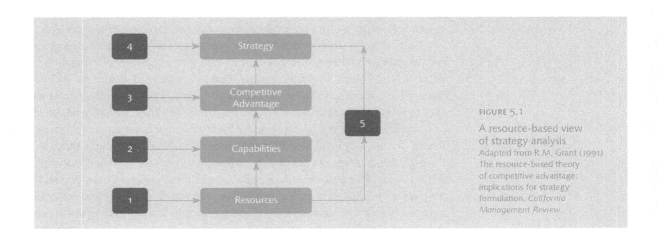

FIGURE 5.1

A resource-based view of strategy analysis
Adapted from R.M. Grant (1991) The resource-based theory of competitive advantage: implications for strategy formulation, *California Management Review*.

5.2 Identifying Sustainable Competitive Advantage

Barney (1991) argues that all the resources that the firm has access to may not be strategically relevant, since some may actually prevent an organization from conceiving and implementing a valuable strategy. Also, some resources may lead it to implement strategies that reduce its effectiveness and efficiency. A competitive advantage arises when an organization is implementing a value-creating strategy that is not also being implemented by current or potential competitors. A sustained competitive advantage occurs when an organization is implementing a value-creating strategy that is not being implemented by current or potential competitors *and* when these competitors are unable to duplicate the benefits of this strategy.

The use of the term *sustainability* here does not refer to permanence. Rather, it implies that a competitive advantage will not be competed away because competitors are unable to duplicate it. The competitive advantage may indeed be eroded by structural changes within the industry such that what was once a competitive advantage in one industry setting may not transcend industry changes. It then becomes a weakness or an irrelevance. This has resonance with the concept of *creative destruction*, highlighted by Joseph Schumpeter, which causes economies to advance through transformational changes. An organization's resource must have four attributes to provide the potential for a sustainable competitive advantage: (1) it must be valuable; (2) it must be rare; (3) it must be difficult to imitate; and (4) there should be no strategic substitute for this resource. We can explore each of these in detail.

1. Valuable resources. Organizational resources can only be a source of competitive advantage or sustainable competitive advantage when they are valuable. Resources are valuable when they enable a firm to formulate and implement strategies that improve its *efficiency and effectiveness*. Environmental models such as *Porter's five forces* (discussed in **Chapter 3**) and *SWOT analysis* (discussed in **Chapter 4**) seek to identify the organization's resources which can exploit opportunities and/ or neutralize threats. It is in this sense, of exploiting opportunities and mitigating threats and thereby improving efficiency and effectiveness, that some attributes the organization possesses can be called a resource. The resource-based view goes further in suggesting the additional characteristics these resources must possess if they are to provide sustainable competitive advantage. Clearly, there are links between the work of Porter and the resource-based view, and differences between the two approaches can be overstated.

2. Rare resources. If valuable organizational resources reside within a large number of competitors or potential competitors then they cannot be a source of sustainable competitive advantage. The reason is that each competitor would have the capability to exploit that resource in the same way. The same analysis also applies

SUSTAINED COMPETITIVE ADVANTAGE occurs when an organization is implementing a value-creating strategy that is not being implemented by competitors *and* when these competitors are unable to duplicate the benefits of this strategy

VALUABLE AND RARE RESOURCES provide a means of competitive advantage. However, if the organization is to achieve sustainable competitive advantage, it is necessary that competing organization cannot copy these resources

to bundles of valuable organizational resources since some strategies require a mix of resources to be implemented. A valuable resource for implementing a strategy is undoubtedly leadership, but if this resource is not rare then many organizations will also be able to formulate and implement the same strategies. That a resource is valuable is a necessary but not sufficient condition for sustainable competitive advantage.

3. **Can the resource be imitated?** Valuable and rare resources provide a means of competitive advantage. However, if the organization is to achieve sustainable competitive advantage it is necessary that competing organizations cannot copy these resources. Where resources can easily be imitated, competitors will simply compete away an organization's ability to generate above-average returns. An example is the dot.com companies of the 1990s, some of whom had innovative ideas and gained a competitive advantage largely by first-mover advantages. Unfortunately, others quickly followed, acquiring the resources to imitate their strategies and eroding any lasting value. An organization's resources will be difficult to imitate if it embodies a *unique location*, *path dependency*, *causal ambiguity*, and *social complexity*.

French wines are an example of competitive advantage through unique location: their climate, soil, and expertise handed down through generations.

© iStockphoto.com/Christopher Messer

French wines

Unique location. An organization based in a unique location will be able to add value to its products, which allows it to generate superior returns. The unique location it possesses is a resource that is difficult to imitate. French wines have long experienced a competitive advantage through the uniqueness of their climate, soil, and expertise handed down through generations.

Path dependency. Competitors will find it extremely difficult to replicate resources that an organization possesses as a result of the path it has followed to arrive at its current position. In effect, path dependency can be seen as the unique experiences an organization has acquired to date as a result of its tenure in business. Competitors

PATH DEPENDENCY

is a way of describing the unique experiences a firm has acquired to date as a result of its tenure in business simply cannot acquire these resources on the open market and therefore cannot copy the firm's value-creating strategy.

Causal ambiguity. Causal ambiguity exists when the link between the resources controlled by an organization and its sustainable competitive advantage is not understood or is only partially understood. Therefore, competitors are unsure as to which resources to acquire and, if required, how to configure them. This issue becomes a sustainable competitive advantage when the organization itself is unsure of the exact source of its competitive advantage. The strategies of 3M, Apple, and W L Gore and Associates (makers of Gore-Tex fabric) are cases in point; competitors simply cannot imitate their success because they are unable to replicate their resource combinations or their unique history.

Social complexity. A final reason why an organization's resources may be difficult to imitate is because they may be based on complex social interactions. These may exist between managers in an organization, in an organization's culture, and in its reputation with its suppliers and customers. When it is known how these socially complex resources add value to the firm, there is no causal ambiguity between the resources and competitive advantage of the organization. However, the fact that competitors may know, for example, that the culture within an organization improves efficiency does not mean that they can readily imitate that culture.

4. Substitutability. Substitutability implies that there must be no strategically equivalent valuable resources that are themselves not rare or that can be imitated. Two valuable firm resources (or bundles of resources) are strategically equivalent when they can be exploited separately to implement the same strategies. Substitutability can take at least two routes. First, although it may not be possible for a firm to imitate another firm's resources exactly, it may be able to substitute a similar resource that allows it to formulate and implement identical strategies. For example, an organization may seek to copy a competitor's top management team. Although this will not be done exactly as the teams will be different, they may be seen as strategic equivalents and therefore as substitutes. Second, very different firm resources can be strategic substitutes. In one organization an inspirational leader may have a clear vision of future consumer trends. In a competing organization a similar vision about the future may require focus groups, and teams of managers thinking, sharing, and debating what the future might hold. The two firm resources may be strategically equivalent, and thus substitutes for one another.

The Case Study on Dell illustrates the difficulty that competitors face in trying to imitate Michael Dell's direct-sales business model. Although the model appears transparent, in reality there exist substantial causal ambiguity and social complexity that make it very difficult to imitate.

CASE STUDY 5.2
Dell—Embedded Routines

AS TECHNOLOGY executives go, Michael Dell is not, you might say, as colourful as some of his peers. Larry Ellison of Oracle has his huge new yacht and his fighter jet; Jeff Bezos of Amazon is funding a space-rocket start-up; Bill Gates of Microsoft has his enormous, high-tech house and a penchant for Leonardo manuscripts; Steve Jobs of Apple somehow combines counter-cultural cool with business smarts and a second job as a movie mogul. What about Mr Dell? He has four kids, a wife and three dogs, he shrugs. And no, he does not invest in rockets. His company, the world's largest maker of personal computers, is fashioned in Mr Dell's own forthright, no-nonsense image. It does not make sexy products—but, thanks to its straightforward direct-sales model, its brutally efficient lean-manufacturing approach and its unrivalled expertise in logistics and supply-chain management, it does make an enormous amount of money.

The way Dell makes and sells PCs is, in fact, the antithesis of the way Apple makes and sells its iPod music-players, which are arguably the sexiest technological devices around at the moment. Dell's PCs are based on industry-standard technologies. They are sold direct, through Dell's website. And the company's efficiency allows it to offer low prices, squeezing out less competitive rivals while still making a profit. The iPod, by contrast, is based on proprietary standards, is sold through Apple's glitzy chain of retail stores, and is priced at a premium to rival players. This week Dell launched a new music-player, the DJ Ditty, as a challenge to Apple. As you would expect, it is cheap, powerful, but not terribly exciting. 'Tape-backup drives are a far bigger business for us, or LCD projectors,' says Mr Dell. Such products, along with storage-area networks, servers, and other bits of corporate-computing gear—only 15 per cent of Dell's sales are to consumers—may not be as glamorous, but are far more lucrative.

Dell's ability to churn out profits in a predictable and reliable manner has made it a favourite among investors. Look at the last 10 years of sales data in the firm's 15 biggest markets—a total of 150 data points—and you will find that it increased its market share in 144 cases, says Mr Dell. That is strong evidence, he says, that his firm's business model 'works everywhere, in a multitude of market conditions'. But might the Dell machine be in danger of running out of steam? Last month, Dell announced that, despite record earnings, its second-quarter sales had grown by a mere 14.7 per cent, rather than the 16–18 per cent it had forecast, and that sales in the current quarter would also be slightly lower than expected. Its share price immediately fell by nearly 10 per cent, and has since declined further.

The case against Dell was made most strongly by Laura Conigliaro, an analyst at Goldman Sachs, who downgraded Dell from 'outperform' to 'neutral'. Dell is unlikely to return to reliable double-digit revenue growth in future, she argues.

It faces increasing competition from Asian vendors such as Acer and Lenovo, and a widening gap between unit growth and revenue growth. And it is a far less nimble company than it used to be. 'The company has now come up short of revenue expectations four quarters in a row, with each quarter's miss caused by a different combination of market conditions and execution miscues,' she wrote. In short, Dell is a victim of its own success: its scale means it is running out of room for growth, cannot respond quickly to changing market conditions, and no longer deserves to be valued at a premium to its rivals. Really?

Room for Growth, Outside America

Mr Dell says he has heard all this before, 'maybe ten thousand or twenty thousand times'. Back in the 1990s, he recalls, critics claimed there were limits to the firm's direct-sales model, and suggested that Dell would never be able to make laptops or servers. 'People say the sky has fallen, that it's the beginning of the end,' he says. 'I don't agree. There are lots of markets with room to grow.' This week Kevin Rollins, who took over from Mr Dell as chief executive officer in 2004, said the company hopes to double or even triple its market share in Europe, which is around 13 per cent, compared with 32 per cent in America. Sales in The Netherlands, for example, are growing by 40 per cent a year.

Dell's worldwide market share of around 19 per cent means there is also room for growth in other regions, notably Asia. But won't low-cost Asian vendors be difficult for Dell to elbow aside? No, says Mr Dell. The firm is, in effect, an Asian vendor itself, with factories in China and Malaysia. Dell is more efficient than Lenovo, he says, and more profitable, thanks to its direct-sales model. Other growth areas are printers, storage systems, and services. In printing, profit margins are unusually high, notes Mr Dell. 'We'll fix that,' he says, just as the company did when it undercut the high-margin incumbents in the server business. Dell's services arm, meanwhile, which installs and manages computers for large companies, now represents 10 per cent of its business, and is growing twice as fast as its PC division.

What of the charge that Dell's size means it is less responsive to shifts in demand? Mr Dell makes a point of making regular visits to the company's call centres—and even takes a few calls himself—to make sure that he still understands consumer demand. On one of these visits, the deluge of calls received convinced him that the company had gone too far in slashing the prices of its consumer PCs—a move that had compensated for slowing demand from the American government, but hurt the firm's margins. Mr Dell enjoys his spells in the call centre—they are, he says with relish, 'lots of fun'.

Evidently Mr Dell's idea of fun is different from that of his peers, with their yachts, planes, and spaceships. Like his firm, he is predictable rather than glamorous. But that is the way investors like it, and he intends to keep things that way.

Source: 'Technology's Mr Predictable' *Economist*, 22 September 2005.

● Questions

1. Identify the extent to which Dell embodies each of the following: a unique location; path dependency; causal ambiguity; and social complexity.

2. Why do competitors find it so difficult to imitate Dell's direct-sales model given that its products are based on standard industry technology?

3. Examine Dell's current financial performance and state whether Michael Dell's optimism about the future of Dell is warranted.

5.2.1 Make or Buy Decision

The recognition of an organization's core competence or activities that it performs exceptionally well can be the basis for its decision to provide a product or service itself, or to outsource it. If the organization is to focus on its core competencies as the basis of its sustainable competitive advantage, then the corollary of this is that activities which do not constitute a core competence for the firm can be given to outside firms who can provide these at a lower cost. This decision is intrinsically linked with an understanding of the activities contained within the firm's value chain. For example, British Airways recognize that the provision of in-flight meals and snacks adds little value to their overall activities and that they have no core competencies in these activities. As a result they took a decision that this activity would best be attended to by an outsourced catering organization. However, it must be stated that such decisions are not without risk. British Airways lost around £45 million in 2005 when Gate Gourmet, its outsourced catering supplier, caused 670 staff to lose their jobs as the caterer struggled to meet its contractual obligations to BA. The labour dispute spread to BA's own workforce. In the UK a petrol crisis in 2000 nearly caused the economy to falter. This resulted from road tankers which were operated by outsourced hauliers rather than the oil companies themselves being prevented from leaving oil refineries by hundreds of protestors. In the past Nike has been the object of consumer revolts over conditions in factories run by their East African subcontractors, over which they experienced little direct control. Oil and mining companies operating in West Africa and Latin America have been blamed for the brutal actions of local security firms hired to protect their property.

The make or buy decision, or what is more appropriately termed *transaction costs*, will be discussed in greater detail in **Chapter 8**.

5.3 Criticisms of the Resource-Based View

Most would agree that the resource-based view of the firm represents a leap forward in strategic management. There are clear links and complementarity with the work of Michael Porter and the positioning school, and equally sharp departures. Whether one would go so far as classifying the resource-based view as a new paradigm within strategic management is a matter of debate. Furthermore, although there are benefits to the resource-based view of strategy, it is not without criticisms. A common criticism made of the resource-based view is that it says very little on the important issues of how resources can develop and change over time. Similarly, the dynamic role played by individuals within organizations is often assumed to be self-evident and therefore seldom addressed. Others have argued that the resource-based view of strategy lacks detail and is therefore difficult for organizations to implement (Priem and Butler 2001). A more detailed road map is required if it is to prove useful to organizations. Lastly, we are back in the realm of deliberate strategies (see **Chapter 1**) with no formal recognition of emergent strategies and the role that these might play.

5.4 Knowledge Management

The Internet has given rise to talk of a new economy which plays by different rules from the old economy. Whereas in the old economy an organization's capital assets are crucially important, in the new economy intellectual assets predominate. The real question regarding the Internet is: Does it represent a new paradigm or new way of doing business? Porter (2001) disagrees with those who argue that the Internet represents a new way of doing business. He points out that it is the established organizations that are benefiting from their use of the Internet to improve their product offerings and strategy. Whilst the Internet may simply be conducive to aiding existing business practices it has undoubtedly helped with the wide dissemination of knowledge.

KNOWLEDGE MANAGEMENT

refers to processes and practices through which organizations generate value from knowledge

Grant (2005) argues that much current thinking about resources and capabilities has been shaped by an interest in knowledge management. Much of the literature has been dominated by organizational learning. It has exhorted firms to become learning organizations and offered remedies for teaching smart people how to learn. We will say more on these issues in **Chapters 10** and **11**. Grant suggests that the single most important contribution of knowledge management is the recognition that different types of knowledge have different characteristics. We might also add that, unlike other resources, knowledge tends not to be depleted with use. Furthermore, the leveraging of knowledge across organizational boundaries is an active pursuit of most corporations in their search for sustainable competitive advantage.

This search can also be achieved by the organization entering into strategic alliances (see **Chapter 9**).

Nonaka and Takeuchi (1995) differentiate between knowledge that can be seen as *tacit* and knowledge that can be seen as *explicit*. Explicit knowledge or 'knowing about' is revealed through communication and can be readily transferred. Examples might include company accounts, or how to put up a tent. It is precisely because explicit knowledge is so readily transferred that it requires some form of protection, such as copyright, if it is to remain within the organization. Tacit knowledge or 'know-how', in contrast, cannot be codified. It is highly personal, and difficult to formalize and disseminate to others. It is revealed through its application and acquired through practice. It consists of mental models, beliefs, and perspectives. No matter how many times one explains how to ride a bicycle to a four-year-old he will only acquire the knowledge through practice. Transfer of tacit knowledge can be slow, costly, and uncertain. Tacit knowledge will require individuals to coalesce around the provider of that knowledge if it is to be *eventually* acquired.

For the organization, managing knowledge will require an understanding of its characteristics. If organizations are to learn and grow they need to be able to share tacit knowledge effectively. However, managing this tacit knowledge throughout all areas of the organization is a daunting task. If an organization is to learn in ways that benefit its performance, individuals and groups within the organization must be willing to modify their behaviour accordingly. What is apparent is that the knowledge-based economy is here to stay. Therefore, the question for organizations is not *should we?* but *how do we?*

Summary

The resource-based view has shaken up strategic management by questioning industry selection and positioning which results in organizations pursuing similar strategies. Instead, this approach emphasizes the organization's own set of resources and capabilities as a determinant of competitive advantage.

In this chapter we have explored and delineated resources, core competencies, and distinctive capabilities in order to identify how competitive advantage might be achieved. We also looked at the issue of sustainable competitive advantage. There is slight confusion among the terms used by different adherents to the resource-based view but, as we have seen, this is readily overcome. Where Prahalad and Hamel discuss core competence, Kay uses the term distinctive capabilities; both are a means of achieving sustainable competitive advantage. Grant distinguishes between resources and capabilities and proposes a five-stage framework for strategy formulation. We examined four attributes an organization's resources must possess in order to provide it with the potential for sustainable competitive advantage. We also addressed some of the criticisms of the resource-based view which relate to difficulties that organizations may experience in trying to implement this approach. We concluded the chapter with a discussion of knowledge management and the challenges facing organizations as they try to manage tacit knowledge.

We end by arguing that Porter's industry analysis remains important and the choice should not be seen as one of *either/or* but rather one of complementarity. Organizations cannot neglect the industries within which they operate, but neither can they afford to focus slavishly upon them at the expense of their internal resources and miss opportunities to establish sustainable competitive advantage.

Review Questions

1. Evaluate the key differences between Porter's five forces framework and the resource-based view of competition.

2. What do you believe is the contribution of the resource-based view to strategic management?

Discussion Questions

1. The pursuit of core competencies and distinctive capabilities requires a unique organizational culture. Discuss.

2. Once an organization's reputation becomes tarnished it loses a distinctive capability which can never be recovered. Discuss.

Research Topic

Identify the internal resources and capabilities that reside within India's Tata Group. Evaluate whether these provide the group with a sustainable competitive advantage.

Recommended Reading

A good introduction to the resource-based view is provided by:

• **Barney, J.** (1991). Firm resources and sustained competitive advantage. *Journal of Management*, **17**(1), 99–120.

An article that is widely credited with popularizing the views of the resource-based approach is:

• **Prahalad, C.K.** and **Hamel, G.** (1990). The core competence of the organization. *Harvard Business Review*, **68**(3), 79–91.

For an explanation of how organizations with fewer resources but bigger aspirations than their competitors can compete successfully, see:

- **Hamel, G.** and **Prahalad, C.K.** (1993). Strategy as stretch and leverage. *Harvard Business Review*, **71**(2), 75–84.

For a most informative and detailed discussion of distinctive capabilities, see:

- **Kay, J.** (1993). *Foundations of Corporate Success*, Oxford University Press, Oxford.

www.oxfordtextbooks.co.uk/orc/henry2e/
Visit the Online Resource Centre that accompanies this book for activities and more information on a resource-based view of strategy.

 online resource centre

Notes

1   See www.harrisinteractive.com for a list of companies and their reputation quotient (the Reputation Index).
2   See www.harrisinteractive.com.

References

Amit, R. and **Schoemaker, P.J.H.** (1993). Strategic assets and organizational rents. *Strategic Management Journal*, **14**(1), 33–46.

Barney, J. (1991). Firm resources and sustained competitive advantage. *Journal of Management*, **17**(1), 99–120.

BusinessWeek (2007a). The 50 most innovative companies. *BusinessWeek Online*, 3 May 2007 (available online at: www.businessweek.com).

BusinessWeek (2007b). An official measure of innovation. *BusinessWeek Online*, 20 April 2007 (available online at: www.businessweek.com).

Collis, D.J. and **Montgomery, C.A.** (1995). Competing on resources: strategy in the 1990s. *Harvard Business Review*, **73**(4), 118–28.

D'Aveni, R.A. (1999). Strategic supremacy through disruption and dominance. *Sloan Management Review*, **40**(3), 117–35.

Grant, R.M. (1991). The resource-based theory of competitive advantage: implications for strategy formulation. *California Management Review*, **33**(Spring), 114–35.

Grant, R.M. (2005). *Contemporary Strategy Analysis*, 5th edn. Blackwell, Boston, MA.

Hamel, G. and **Prahalad, C.K.** (1993). Strategy as stretch and leverage. *Harvard Business Review*, **71**(2), 75–84.

Kay, J. (1993). *Foundations of Corporate Success*. Oxford University Press, Oxford.

Kay, J. (2000). Strategy and the delusion of grand design. In *Mastering Strategy*, pp. 5–10, Pearson Education, Harlow.

Lieberman, M.B. and **Montgomery, D.G.** (1988). First mover advantages. *Strategic Management Journal*, **9**(5), 41–58.

Nonaka, I. (1991). The knowledge creating company. *Harvard Business Review*, **69**(6), 96–104.

Nonaka, I. and **Takeuchi, H.** (1995). *The Knowledge Creating Company*. Oxford University Press, Oxford.

Penrose, E.T. (1959). *The Theory of the Growth of the Firm*. John Wiley & Sons, New York.

Peteraf, M. (1993). The cornerstones of competitive advantage: a resource-based view. *Strategic Management Journal*, **14**, 179–91.

Porter, M. (1980). *Competitive Strategy: Techniques for Analysing Industries and Competitors*. Free Press, New York.

Porter, M. (1996). What is strategy? *Harvard Business Review*, **74**(6), 61–78.

Porter, M.E. (2001). Strategy and the Internet. *Harvard Business Review*, **79**(3), 62–78.

Prahalad, C.K. and **Hamel, G.** (1990). The core competence of the organization. *Harvard Business Review*, **68**(3), 79–91.

Priem, R.L. and **Butler, J.E.** (2001). Is the resource-based 'view' a useful perspective for strategic management research? *Academy of Management Review*, **26**(1), 22–40.

Rumelt, R.P. (1991). How much does industry matter? *Strategic Management Journal*, **12**(3), 167–85.

Stalk, G., Evans, P., and **Schulman, L.E.** (1992). Competing on capabilities: the new rules of corporate strategy. *Harvard Business Review*, **70**(2), 57–69.

6 Assessing Organizational Performance

6.1 What is Performance?	6.2 Maximizing Shareholder Value	6.3 Meeting the Needs of Stakeholders	6.4 Financial Analysis	6.5 The Balanced Scorecard	6.6 Benchmarking
		Key Work Stakeholders in the John Lewis Partnership	**Tools and Techniques** Example of discounted cash flow	**Tools and Techniques** Application of a balanced scorecard approach	**Key Work** Benchmarking

Main Reference
Kaplan, R.S. and **Norton, D.P.** (1996). Using the balanced scorecard as a strategic management system. *Harvard Business Review*, 74(1), 75–85.

Learning Objectives

After completing this chapter you should be able to:

- Discuss the importance of assessing organizational performance
- Evaluate shareholder and stakeholder perspectives for an organization
- Explain the role of financial ratios in assessing organizational performance
- Discuss economic value added (EVA) as a performance measurement
- Explain the role of discounted cash flow (DCF) in making decisions
- Evaluate the balanced scorecard approach to an organization's performance
- Explain benchmarking as a means of improving performance

Introduction

In **Chapter 4** we addressed the internal environment facing the organization and how an organization might usefully analyse its value-creating activities. In **Chapter 5** we explored a radically different perspective to industry analysis. This suggests that relative firm performance, and therefore profitability, is determined by an organization's resources and competencies. This is the resource-based view of the organization. We move now from what *determines* an organization's performance to an *assessment* of its performance. In this chapter we will address some of the different ways in which an organization can assess its performance and keep its attention on its strategic aims. The choice of performance measures is a challenge because these play a key role in strategy formulation, evaluating whether an organization's objectives have been achieved, and in compensating managers. Therefore, the purpose of assessing organizational performance is to help the organization ascertain whether the strategies being implemented are actually adding value.

- In Section 6.1 we start the chapter with a discussion of why organizations exist. This will help us to answer the question: What are we measuring and for whom? This touches on the debate between organizations pursuing value for shareholders or meeting the needs of wider stakeholders. This debate will be revisited in greater detail in **Chapter 12**.

- Section 6.2 discusses whether the purpose of companies is to maximize shareholder value. It compares accounting profit with economic profit and asks whether a different performance measure—*economic value added*—may be more beneficial for shareholders.

- Section 6.3 evaluates the proposition that the purpose of organizations is *not* to maximize shareholder value but rather to meet the needs of the stakeholders.

- Section 6.4 explains traditional financial ratios and how they can be used and interpreted by organizations. Also included here is the role of discounted cash flow in decision making.

- In Section 6.5 the balanced scorecard is introduced and evaluated as an alternative means of assessing organizational performance. The case study used in the chapter will draw attention to the difficulty of using a balanced scorecard approach.

- The chapter concludes in Section 6.6 with a discussion of how benchmarking can be used to improve performance. We shall see that to achieve the fullest benefit a firm should be willing to compare itself against competitors outside its industry. In this way best-practice frameworks can be adopted and, if necessary, adapted to suit the firm's own unique needs.

6.1 **What is Performance?**

At first glance this question may seem a little glib, perhaps even absurd. However, as we shall see, the use of different performance criteria can produce conflicting results and lead to inappropriate or suboptimal resource allocation decisions. To address performance issues we must first address the fundamental question: *Why do businesses exist?*[1]

SHAREHOLDERS

are individuals or groups who have invested their capital within an organization, and are therefore deemed to be the owners

PRINCIPAL–AGENT PROBLEM

refers to the separation of ownership from control within corporations, where the owners are the principal but the control of the organization is by salaried managers who act as the agent

There is an assumption that the primary objective of organizations is to maximize profits to benefit shareholders. In their seminal work, Berle and Means (1932) cast doubt on profit-maximizing theories. They were not questioning whether the objective of organizations should be to maximize profits for the shareholders but whether this actually occurs. This is because of the existence of the principal–agent problem. This refers to the separation of ownership from control within corporations. The owners are the principal who provide the capital but control is in the hands of managers who act as agent on the principal's behalf. A key issue is that both parties have different access to information which may allow the agent to act on his or her own behalf and against the principal's interests. Therefore, the question arises as to how the agent should be monitored and the costs that result from this. Much more will be said on this in **Chapter 12**.

This profit-maximizing assumption was contested by behavioural psychologists claiming that organizations consist of shifting coalitions (Cyert and March 1963). This approach argues that organizational behaviour is determined by the interests and beliefs of the dominant coalition(s). Some economists eschewed profit maximization and argued instead for market share or sales maximization. Others suggested that managers actually run companies based upon utility functions which included profit but also other elements. This idea of coalitions within and around organizations has found its expression in stakeholder theory. However, whether the overriding objective of shareholders' interest can be subordinated to a multiplicity of other interests is an ongoing debate.

6.2 **Maximizing Shareholder Value**

If we consider privately owned and public limited companies (companies quoted on the stock market), there is an assumption that these organizations are in business to create value and that the profit they produce is to be distributed among the owners of the business—the shareholders. This perspective is associated with Friedman (1962) who advocated that an organization has only one social responsibility, which is to make as much profit for its shareholders as it can. If we look at the reasons why some people hold shares, then it would appear that Friedman's assertion has validity. Many shareholders purchase shares in the anticipation that they will increase in value over time, that is, they expect capital growth. Of course, this capital growth must exceed what it costs them to buy shares in the first place and what they could have earned if they had placed their money elsewhere—in other words, their opportunity cost. Some corporations, such as utilities, which operate in mature markets tend to pay relatively high dividends which may be attractive to those on fixed incomes, such as the elderly, who may require an additional income stream.

If the role of corporations is to create value and distribute profit to their shareholders this brings us neatly to how corporate performance will be measured. There are accounting conventions that organizations follow but these vary from country to country. Even within the same country managers can use their discretion to interpret and state profitability figures. The main purpose of financial statements is to show the underlying economic performance of an organization. The balance sheet and profit-and-loss account are the primary financial statements. The balance sheet shows a snapshot of a company's assets, liabilities, and capital at one moment in time. The profit-and-loss account shows the difference between a company's total revenue and its total expenses. The standard measures of accounting profit may not only misrepresent to owners what the true profit might be, they may also lead to a misallocation of the organization's resources as managers pursue opportunities they believe to be profitable but which may not fully cover their cost of capital.[2] Herein lies a distinction between what an accountant may count as profit and what constitutes profit for an economist.

The classical economist David Ricardo pointed out that profit, or what he termed economic rent, is the surplus left over when the inputs to a productive process, which includes the cost of capital being employed, have been covered. This is the basis of economic profit. In an attempt for organizations to include a more realistic Ricardian profit figure, economic value added (EVA) was developed (this measure of economic profit is widely associated with the consultancy organization SternStewart & Company). This is worked out by taking a company's operating profit after tax minus its annual cost of capital. As a company's investments occur over time we need to discount this revenue stream to find out its present value. If the net present value of the resulting figure is positive, the organization can be seen to be adding value for its shareholders. If it is negative, the organization's resources could be usefully employed elsewhere. Organizations such as Coca-Cola, AT&T, and the US bank JPMorgan Chase, formerly known as Chase Manhattan, have adopted this measure of profitability to improve their returns to shareholders instead of the more usual return on investment (ROI), which is discussed later.

In an attempt to measure the extent of wealth created for shareholders by companies, consulting firm Stern Stewart has proposed a wealth added index (WAI). The idea is that organizations create value for shareholders when their returns to these investors, which include capital growth and dividends, are greater than investors expect for keeping their money in shares. The WAI is not without its disadvantages, but when assessing some of the world's largest corporations it shows some surprising results. (See Case Study: Measuring Shareholder Value (WAI) which illustrates the winners and losers of over 5000 organizations when ranked according to the WAI.)

ACCOUNTING PROFIT

measures the difference between the total revenue generated by the organization and its total cost

ECONOMIC RENT OR ECONOMIC PROFIT

is the surplus left over when the inputs to a productive process, which include the cost of capital being employed, have been covered

ECONOMIC VALUE ADDED

is an attempt for organizations to include a more realistic profit figure. It is worked out by taking the difference between a company's operating profit after tax and its annual cost of capital, and discounting this to find out its present value

CASE STUDY 6.1

Measuring Shareholder Value (WAI)

The world's stock markets have taken investors on a bumpy ride over the past five years. Look beyond the broad indices, though, and the picture is more nuanced. Some companies have created great wealth for their shareholders, while others have destroyed vast amounts. First, a note of caution: any league table based on share values should be treated with some scepticism. Even so, a long-term global perspective can give a much-needed view above the daily market clamour.

One attempt to gain such a view is the Wealth Added Index (WAI), compiled by Stern Stewart, a consulting firm . . . This ranks the world's 5069 largest quoted companies by shareholder wealth created (or destroyed) between June 1996 and June 2001. Central to the WAI rankings is the idea that companies create value for shareholders only if their returns to investors—from share-price rises and dividends—exceed their 'cost of equity' (defined as the minimum return that investors require for putting their money in risky shares).

For all companies, the cost of equity on this basis ought to be greater than the return that is available from a riskless alternative such as government bonds. And the greater the risk investors bear, the greater the returns they should require. If a firm's returns do not exceed the cost of its equity, shareholders' capital could be better used elsewhere. In Stern Stewart's analysis, companies whose share values not only grow, but grow by more than the return required by investors, are creating value; those that return less, over time, are destroying it.

Risky Business

The trickiest part of this calculation is to work out this 'required return', taking into account a company's riskiness. A company's capital typically consists of a mixture of debt and equity. Debt has an obvious cost: the interest rate on a bond or loan. The cost of equity is less simple. For this, Stern Stewart relies on the Capital Asset Pricing Model (CAPM). The CAPM, a cornerstone of corporate-finance theory, is more commonly used to analyse large portfolios of shares than individual companies. Still, everyone agrees that equity capital has an economic cost—though the dotcom boom made it seem free for a while—and the CAPM is a widely used way to measure it. Another caveat is that Stern Stewart's WAI assumes that stockmarkets are efficient . . . meaning that all investors are rational and agree on the best way to measure risk. Many market observers would question that assumption, especially after experiencing the technology bubble. Moreover, the WAI is skewed by size: big firms tend to add or destroy more wealth, because the index is expressed in absolute terms rather than in percentage outperformance.

Against these caveats, the WAI has several virtues. One is that it avoids the pitfalls of the majority of benchmarks which are relative measures within an industry. These can be misleading since they always produce some winners, even if every company in the industry does badly for its shareholders (consider airlines and film studios). Because it does not depend on reported profits, the index also avoids tricky cross-border accounting differences that bedevil Stern Stewart's other popular measure of returns, economic value-added (EVA). Comparative EVA figures can be produced only for individual countries, not for the world as a whole. The WAI also gives an alternative view to 'total shareholder returns' (TSR), a common metric of share performance that reflects the returns to 'buy and hold' investors.

An investor who has held shares in Britain's Vodafone ever since June 1996, for example, has chalked up a 248 per cent TSR. But Stern Stewart's methodology, which takes into account those who bought during the period as well as those who held throughout, produces a startlingly different result. It reckons that overall Vodafone destroyed some $145 billion between 1996 and 2001, more than any other company in the study. Most of that value was lost as Vodafone bid dearly for third-generation (3G) mobile-phone licences and paid a hefty price for Mannesmann, a German group. Vodafone's loss was Mannesmann's gain; the German company ranks as the world's third-biggest wealth creator over the same period, with $121 billion of gains to its credit. This seems to confirm Warren Buffett's observation that shareholders of target companies are the only winners in mergers.

In general, telecoms companies feature prominently among the biggest wealth destroyers. AT&T is responsible for vaporizing $137 billion, thanks to its failed forays into broadband and data, along with a devastating price war in its core long-distance markets. Lucent Technologies, spun off from AT&T in 1996, is also among the worst performers, having laid to waste $101 billion as its networking-equipment market collapsed.

The big American car makers also did badly. DaimlerChrysler, conceived in 1998, ranks 14th from bottom, with an average annual return of 11 per cent, the mirror image of its cost of equity. Ford and GM have also been plagued by overcapacity as well as by costly acquisitions in Europe. GM's average annual return of 13 per cent is respectable, but does not meet its 15 per cent cost of equity. European and Japanese car makers, though smaller, did far better; Toyota, BMW, PSA Peugeot Citroën, and Renault together added around $50 billion in wealth.

General Electric is the clearest winner. Its strategy of striving to be number one or two in each of its business lines apparently paid off with $227 billion in wealth creation over the period. But even the legendary Jack Welch is not perfect. Between June 2000 and June 2001, GE's shares fell short of investors' required return by ten percentage points. Citigroup has the only unblemished record in the table, having added value consistently throughout the period. The giant American bank delivered an average annual return of 37.3 per cent, nearly four times its cost of equity.

One lesson from the rankings is that costly acquisitions are a good way to destroy value. Another is that volatile markets can quickly turn a wealth creator into a wealth destroyer. As the recent woes of the telecoms industry suggest, the quest for shareholder value creates as many spectacular failures as successes.

Source: 'Marked by the market' *Economist*, 29 November 2001.

▪ Questions

1. What is the benefit to shareholders of companies measuring their performance using a wealth added index (WAI)?

2. To what extent does the creation of shareholders' wealth stem from the efficient use of capital rather than a company's strategy and innovation?

3. If Warren Buffett is right, that only shareholders of target companies benefit from mergers and acquisitions—why do companies continue to bid for other firms?

6.3 Meeting the Needs of Stakeholders

STAKEHOLDERS

are those individuals or groups which affect or are affected by the achievement of an organization's objectives

We have seen that when the focus is on shareholders there is a presumption that shareholder value is the dominant objective of the organization. An alternative approach is a view of the organization that serves the interest of stakeholders. According to Freeman (1984), stakeholders are those individuals or groups who affect or are affected by the achievement of an organization's objectives. These include customers, suppliers, employees, government, competitors, the local community, and, of course, shareholders. Those who advocate a stakeholder model dispute that the primary role of organizations is to create shareholder value.

Stakeholder theorists would argue that many different stakeholders are affected by an organization's decisions. They argue that the role of management is to balance these stakeholder needs rather than simply focus on shareholders. Indeed, the growth of modern corporations requires executives to recognize that their actions have effects far beyond their nation's borders as a result of their linkage in a globalized economy. The collapse of the Enron Corporation in the US is a case in point, as its impact was felt far beyond the capital loss to shareholders.

However, stakeholders have conflicting needs, making the task of management in balancing these different interests more fraught. This is because stakeholders may have different objectives which leave managers trying to balance multiple objectives. One way of trying to prioritize the different interests of stakeholders is to assess the influence they exert on an organization's objectives. Mendelow (1991) proposed a model which ranks stakeholders according to their *power* and *interest*. This is shown

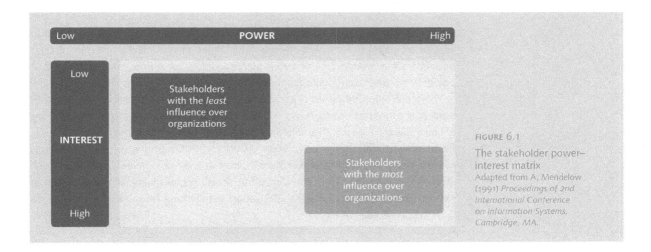

FIGURE 6.1

The stakeholder power–
interest matrix
Adapted from A. Mendelow
(1991) *Proceedings of 2nd
International Conference
on Information Systems*,
Cambridge, MA.

in Figure 6.1 which categorizes stakeholders according to how much power they possess and the level of interest they show in what the organization does.

Power refers to stakeholders' ability to influence the organization's objectives, while interest refers to their willingness to influence the organization's objectives. Clearly, if the stakeholders exhibit both high power and high interest the organization would be wise to consult them before committing itself to any major decisions. Such a stakeholder might be a regulatory body concerned with competition and consumer affairs: for example, the Office of Fair Trading in the UK. Other stakeholders may exhibit high power but relatively low interest. Institutional shareholders are commonly placed within this sector. However, a trend is for institutional investors to be increasingly interested in the objectives of organizations in which they choose to invest. This is as a result of the concerns of the individuals whose funds institutional shareholders manage. Therefore, they need to be seen to be taking a more active role in discussions with organizations.

Similarly, the government or government agencies may have a benign interest in the activities of organizations but be forced to exercise their legislative powers when organizations behave in an unacceptable manner. An example would be when governments introduce new health and safety legislation following the negligent behaviour of corporations. Sternberg (1997) argues that trying to balance different stakeholder needs does not work. Freeman's definition of stakeholders can lead to a vast number of different stakeholder needs, and stakeholder analysis is unable to differentiate which stakeholders should be selected.

Even where stakeholders have low interest, they can be moved into a high-interest space by their response to activities the company engages in that are attracting unwanted media attention. Similarly, stakeholders who have low power but a high level of interest in the organization's activities can form coalitions, often temporarily coalescing around a single social issue, and be a powerful force for change. This is often seen during environmental disasters, for instance when the oil tanker Exxon Valdez spilt oil in Prince William Sound, Alaska, resulting in substantial damage to wildlife and the environment. During such times environmental pressure groups benefit from a groundswell of public opinion which, for a time, may increase their power when negotiating with corporations.

Therefore, even when an organization's priority is to create value for its shareholders it cannot afford to do so without some understanding of the expectations of stakeholders. As such, their criteria for successful performance may differ markedly from purely shareholder maximization. As we saw in **Chapter 1**, some organizations make a point of including stakeholder interest in their core values and vision. (See Strategy Focus: John Lewis and Corporate Social Responsibility, which provides an extract from the British retailer's CSR report highlighting how John Lewis engages with its stakeholders.)[3]

STRATEGY FOCUS

John Lewis and Corporate Social Responsibility (CSR)

Retailer John Lewis Partnership

Engaging with our stakeholders

We believe that being a responsible retailer means respecting the interests of all our stakeholders. This involves listening and actively responding to their concerns and acting on their behalf, as well as being honest in our expectations and intentions and reporting our performance fairly. Understanding the interests of our stakeholders helps inform our thinking and feeds into our CSR risk and opportunity assessment, which in turn shapes our CSR vision, programmes and commitments. Below, we outline some of the ways we actively involve our key stakeholders.

Partners

Why We Engage

Because our Partners are all owners of the business and share in its success, they get to have a say in how the business is run, as well as an equal percentage share in its profits. Giving our Partners a 'voice' is central to the principles of co-ownership and we engage the views and opinions of our Partners through a number of key channels. Our Partners also have an 'external voice' through their vital role as advocates for our business and all that we do.

How We Engage

- Conduct an annual Partner Survey
- Hold AGMs and other meetings to foster loyalty and understanding
- Provide printed publications, including letters pages in the *Gazette* and the *Chronicle*, hold regular roadshows and presentations, including video presentations by the Chairman and Managing Directors and provide online communication tools – such as the 'Ask Mark' (Mark Price) section on our intranet
- Through Councils, forums and committees at local, divisional and Partnership level
- CSR governance groups

Outcomes

90% of Partners responded to the 2009 Partner survey. Following this, individual branches are looking at what the scores are saying and are working to understand what actions can be taken at a local level as well as what can be fed into our divisional and Partnership Councils. 2010 will see the launch of a revised Partner survey to reflect the new Partner Strategy Commitments. A number of Partner focus groups have been held, as well as invaluable feedback gained from the Partnership Council to ensure the revised survey is easy to understand and resonates with Partners. Questions raised by our Partnership Council have focused on our work to reduce carrier bags and how we collaborate on CSR across our business. Our Partners are also keen to understand what tangible action they need to take to support our CSR commitments and how we can arm them better to respond to customer enquiries on sustainability issues. We will be addressing these points in 2010.

Our letters pages in the *Gazette* and other internal magazines continue to provide a means for Partners to express any view on the Partnership. These are a keystone of the Partnership's open culture, playing a vital role in keeping Partners informed as co-owners of the business and in holding management to account. Letters are handled in a way unique to the Partnership, allowing Partners greater freedom of expression than would generally be permitted elsewhere.

Customers

Why We Engage

We aim to deal honestly with our customers and secure their loyalty and trust by providing outstanding choice, value and service. We want to hear what our customers think and how we can do things better. Only by gathering feedback on our performance can we maintain and raise our standards of customer service and keep our customers satisfied.

How We Engage

- Focus groups
- Customer satisfaction and opinion research and surveys
- Feedback through customer service teams and online feedback forms
- Customer forums on waitrose.com

Outcomes

Focus groups have told us that the issues that matter most to our customers are reducing packaging, improving the nutritional value of food and responsible sourcing, both in terms of the standards in the supply chain and the sustainability of our products. We are already making good progress in these areas. We communicate our policies and positions via customer-facing websites, magazines and other instore point-of-sale material, as well as through our Partners. We are working with our marketing teams to further develop our customer communications.

Source: http://www.johnlewispartnership.co.uk

For a better understanding of the different stakeholders involved in
the John Lewis Partnership go to the Online Resource Centre and
see the Key Work feature.
www.oxfordtextbooks.co.uk/orc/henry2e/

We will return to these issues in **Chapter 12** when we evaluate the shareholder and
stakeholder perspectives in much greater detail.

6.4 Financial Analysis

A view of the role of organizations as simply to create value for shareholders is
increasingly disputed, and the needs of wider society continue to be placed on the
corporate agenda. Clearly, the organization must assess the performance criteria its
managers believe to be important. The choice of financial and other performance
measurements will reflect the corporate governance frameworks in each country. For
example, some European countries, such as Germany, which adopt a two-tier board
of directors including employee representation will look to include more than simply
financial measurements, while what Sternberg (2004) calls the Anglo-American
model will adopt performance measurements which reflect shareholder value. Even
here, as we shall see below, a number of major organizations use performance
measurements, such as the balanced scorecard, which take account of stakeholder
needs. However, we would be unwise at this juncture to stretch the stakeholder
model's reach too far. The overriding concern in quoted companies, particularly in the
US and the UK, continues to reflect shareholder value.

We can see that measuring an organization's performance is necessary to
understand whether the strategies being implemented actually add value to the
organization (Buzzell and Gale 1987). If not, the question is whether an alternative
strategy would be more appropriate. Therefore, the use of performance measurements acts as a control on management to ensure that they fulfil their fiduciary duty
to shareholders. An organization undertakes activities whose outcomes will only
be known with certainty at some point in the future. This necessitates some form
of discounted cash flow in order to try to approximate what the net present value of
future income streams or capital sums is worth. The problem is that these future
cash flows are uncertain, which makes any calculation based upon them fraught
with difficulties.[4] Therefore, management tends to rely upon more traditional accounting measures.

The result of using traditional financial measures is that the emphasis is upon past
financial performance. In addition, the financial measures often used by corporations

tend to draw attention to short-term performance only. We mentioned earlier that managers need to be aware of the economic profit the organization makes and that this is related to the actual cost of capital being employed by the firm. We will briefly review some of the traditional financial measures used by corporations to assess their past performance.

1. **Return on capital employed (ROCE)** is a performance ratio commonly used by organizations. It is calculated by dividing profit before interest and tax by capital employed. Capital employed in accounting terms usually means fixed assets plus current assets less current liabilities (creditors: amounts due within one year). As there is some variation of the terms in the denominator and the numerator, it is useful to find out what definitions have been used in any ratios quoted. The formula is:

$$\frac{\text{Profit before interest and tax}}{\text{Capital}} \times 100$$

The ROCE figure should ideally reflect the level of risk in the investment and can be compared with interest rates for other investments where risk is minimal, such as bank accounts. It is useful to compare the figure over time. If managers want to know how this figure can be improved, they need to work out two subsidiary ratios.

2. **The profit margin or return on sales (ROS)** measures the percentage return on sales (*net profit per £1 of sales*). The formula is:

$$\frac{\text{Profit before interest and tax}}{\text{Sales}} \times 100$$

Organizations can operate on thin profit margins as long as they have substantive volume sales. Profit margin can be improved therefore by increasing the selling price and/or reducing costs.

3. **Capital turnover** measures the level of activity in the organization as reflected by sales in relation to the capital employed, that is, it measures the number of times the assets (the capital employed) are utilized or turned over to achieve those sales. The formula is:

$$\frac{\text{Sales}}{\text{Capital employed}}$$

For capital turnover we require a high level of activity for a low level of investment. Capital turnover can be improved by increasing sales activity or decreasing capital employed, or by selling off fixed assets that are no longer used.

These three performance ratios are interrelated as the profit margin multiplied by the capital turnover gives the return on capital employed. A business can improve its return on capital employed by reducing costs and/or raising prices, which will improve its profit margin. Alternatively, it can increase its sales volume and/or reduce its capital employed, which will improve its capital turnover. It is important to remember that financial ratios require comparison if they are to be useful. The fact that an organization makes a return on investment of 15 per cent may sound great, until you discover that the industry average is 23 per cent. Similarly, comparison with key competitors can draw attention to where an organization might need to benchmark its performance. This is discussed later in the chapter.

Discounted Cash Flow Analysis

We mentioned earlier that the outcome of current organizational activity will only be known with certainty at some point in the future. This is true of current investments that yield an estimated return in the future. To help managers choose between different investment decisions it is useful if they can estimate the present value of these future income streams. That way they can compare the relative benefits of each investment decision. To do this we can use discounted cash flow (DCF) analysis. Discounted cash flow is a method for determining the future value of cash flows in the present. At its simplest an organization can determine the present value of a payment received 'n' years in the future discounted at x% per annum. The rate of interest chosen to discount the future cash flow is based on the cost of capital. This discount rate will in turn determine the discount factor used to discount the future cash flow. With short-term investment projects with fairly reliable cash flows which may vary over a number of years, discounted cash flow analysis can be used to make choices between them.

However, an inherent problem with discounted cash flow is that the further one forecasts these cash flows into the future the more unreliable they become. Do most strategic decisions contain discrete cash flows that can be readily discounted? In reality, the answer is likely to be no. This is because of the nature of strategic management. Once formulated, a strategy is consistent with a range of possible outcomes that will depend on the business environment facing the organization. If we accept D'Aveni's assertion that markets are hypercompetitive this makes the use of discounted cash flow analysis highly problematic.

For a worked example of discounted cash flow go to the Online Resource Centre and see the Tools and Techniques feature.
www.oxfordtextbooks.co.uk/orc/henry2e/

6.5 The Balanced Scorecard

BALANCED SCORECARD

provides managers with a more comprehensive assessment of the state of their organization. It enables managers to provide consistency between the aims of the organization and the strategies undertaken to achieve those aims

The balanced scorecard was developed by Kaplan and Norton (1992) as a means for organizations to measure their performance from a wider perspective than the traditional financial measures. Kaplan and Norton's research identified two major problems with corporate strategies. The first was that most companies measure their performance using financial ratios. These measures only provide a snapshot of how a company performed in the past. What they do not do is show how well an organization might perform in the future. When Kaplan and Norton tried to find out which factors determine an organization's success, they uncovered factors such as customer satisfaction and loyalty, employee commitment, and the speed at which organizations learn and adapt. The second issue was a gap between an organization's strategy and its implementation by employees. This was because many organizations simply issued strategic statements that their employees failed to understand. Kaplan and Norton found that strategy was rarely translated into action because it was simply not translated into measures that employees could make sense of in their everyday work.

The balanced scorecard is an attempt to overcome these two weaknesses. It is not about formulating strategy but rather it helps in understanding and checking what you have to do throughout the organization to make your strategy work. Financial measures are important, but they reflect the results of actions that have already been taken. Kaplan and Norton propose supplementary operational measures which include customer satisfaction, internal processes, and innovation and improvement activities which more clearly highlight an organization's future performance. As they state, 'the scorecard wasn't a replacement for financial measures; it was their complement'. The balanced scorecard then provides managers with a more comprehensive assessment of the state of their organization. It enables managers to provide consistency between the aims of the organization and the strategies undertaken to achieve those aims.

The balanced scorecard allows an organization to evaluate its respective strengths and weaknesses from four different perspectives: a customer perspective, an internal perspective, a financial perspective, and a future perspective. The idea is that an organization's perspective of how it sees itself and how the outside world views it can be shown by integrating these four perspectives into a single balanced view. Assume, for example, that an organization wants to improve its market share. Using a balanced scorecard approach the organization would need to translate what this actually means. For instance, what are the measures that it needs to undertake to increase its customers? This then leads management to assess what changes it needs to make within the organization to accomplish this. Once the need for internal change is understood, it is then possible to assess what new skills and competencies the organization needs to acquire to improve its performance. Norton and Kaplan outline a set of measures and yardsticks that organizations can use for each of these steps. (See Strategy Focus: GPs in the Firing Line, which highlights how a balanced scorecard is being used to measure and control the performance of doctors in the UK by their funding bodies—primary care trusts—on behalf of the Department of Health.)

STRATEGY FOCUS
GPs in the Firing Line

GP practices across the country are facing a series of punitive measures including suspension of contracts and threat of closure as primary care trusts (PCTs) escalate their use of controversial traffic-light ratings. The Department of Health's balanced scorecard scheme, which rates practices against a range of clinical and organisational indicators, has now been rolled out across 40% of trusts.

A further 40% plan to introduce the hugely contentious rating system during the current financial year, after a set of national indicators were developed for the DH by management consultancy McKinsey. And where PCTs are using scorecards, some are imposing severe contractual sanctions on low-rated practices. In one case, a practice is facing closure because of its refusal to offer extended hours.

Last October as many as 70% of GP practices in trailblazer PCTs were failing at least one element of the ratings system, with small practices and those in deprived areas most likely to struggle. Responses from 116 PCTs find the number with scorecards in place has soared from just a handful last year to around 50. And managers are increasingly using the scorecards to ramp up pressure on practices.

These include NHS Walsall, which has suspended a GP for failing to meet scorecard stipulations. A spokesperson said: 'We have used remedial notices for minor surgery, opening times and GP cover. Using information from balanced scorecards has assisted in recent GP suspension and investigation.' NHS Camden is investigating 16 breaches identified through balanced scorecards. One practice has been warned of a possible default on a remedial notice for failing to 'ensure that the practice is open for a minimum of 10 hours outside 9am–6.30pm', and is being warned that it 'would lead to a loss of contract and possible closure'.

Elsewhere, NHS Greenwich stated: 'Two practices have been subject to remedial notices due to poor performance' flagged up by their scorecards. But GPs raised concerns that the bullying approach taken by some trusts could be in breach of the DH's new guidance offering NHS providers two chances to improve before their contracts are put under threat. Dr Peter Graves, chief executive of Bedfordshire & Hertfordshire LMC, is planning to submit a motion to the LMC's conference condemning use of balanced scorecards, which he said had infuriated GPs locally.

He said: 'They only include easily measurable criteria, ignoring large chunks of general practice. We're putting a motion to the LMC's conference to outlaw them.' The motion accuses PCTs of spreading 'lies, damn lies and statistics'. Dr George Moncrieff, a GP in Bicester, Oxfordshire, said it was essential GPs had confidence that any scoring system was properly validated before using it for disciplinary action.

Source: 'GPs face sanctions as scorecards go national' *Pulse*, 14 April 2010.

The balanced scorecard approach looks at an organization from four perspectives (Kaplan and Norton 1996).

1. **How do we look to shareholders?** This financial perspective would include measures such as cash flow, increase in sales, and return on capital employed (ROCE) which we covered when we looked at traditional financial measures earlier.

2. **How do customers view us?** The customer perspective measures might include an organization's market share since this will be driven by customers' perceptions of its products *vis-à-vis* its competitors' products. It can also include the extent to which customers are prepared to endorse new product offerings.

3. **What must we excel at?** The internal business perspective measures will reflect such things as cycle times, productivity, and quality.

4. **Can we continue to improve and create value?** The innovation and learning perspective might include measures that take account of the speed and efficiency of new product development, reflecting a technological leadership goal.

In the 75th anniversary edition of the *Harvard Business Review* the balanced scorecard was listed as one of the fifteen most important management concepts to be introduced within its pages. Forrester Research (www.forrester.com) states that 25 per cent of world businesses use it. According to a survey of 960 global executives by Bain & Company in 2005 (www.bain.com), 57 per cent said their organization use the balanced scorecard. In 1996 the use was 39 per cent of organizations. However, when assessed in terms of satisfaction by these organizations, the balanced scorecard rated below average. The list of companies that have used this approach include the Royal Bank of Scotland, Exxon Mobil, Ericsson, the Swedish insurance company Skandia, BP Chemicals, and Xerox. In addition, the balanced scorecard is also popular with public sector and non-profit-making organizations (see Strategy Focus: GPs in the Firing Line).

Criticisms of the balanced scorecard coalesce around the measurements it leaves out, such as employee satisfaction and supplier performance. However, this might be because what an organization chooses to measure is often what it finds easy to measure. The balanced scorecard requires that organizations start to measure things that they may have previously neglected. Another problem is that many organizations suffer from information overload as they go from measuring a few factors to measuring too many factors. One of the greatest failings is that organizations do not use the measurements to motivate people because management do not sufficiently link measures to a programme of actions. In this respect, identifying the right things to measure is merely the starting point. If organizations are to achieve a sustainable competitive advantage, they need to understand better the role of intangibles, such as brands, as well as their own people.

The balanced scorecard may provide a bridge between the needs of shareholders and the needs of stakeholders. Concern about the impact of their activities on the environment is forcing some companies to think hard about ways in which they can

© Marks & Spencer plc

Stuart Rose, chairman and former CEO, launches Marks & Spencer's £200 million, five-year, 100-point 'eco-plan' which includes commitments for M&S to become carbon neutral and send no waste to landfill by 2012.

reduce their carbon footprint. For example, in an effort to make the company carbon neutral, the British retailer Marks & Spencer plans to make its polyester clothing from recycled plastic bottles instead of oil. Clearly, taking the needs of wider stakeholders into account can be good for business. The Case Study: Applying a Balanced Scorecard illustrates how a balanced scorecard approach to assessing organizational performance can be used. It also highlights some of the issues to be considered when trying to measure important competitive factors.

In summary, Kaplan and Norton's balanced scorecard takes the traditional financial performance measures and complements these with criteria which measure performance from three additional perspectives: customers, internal business processes, and learning and growth. The balanced scorecard helps prevent the underachievement of strategic goals by an overemphasis on short-term financial measures. By adopting a more balanced approach, the organization can actively pursue strategies that achieve its aims by setting performance measures that have some correlation with these strategies. In addition, this approach also takes account of the different expectations of stakeholders, recognizing perhaps that maximizing shareholder value is not a prime motivator for employees or customers.

CASE STUDY 6.2

Applying a Balanced Scorecard

Of all the management tools designed to improve corporate performance, the balanced scorecard is by far the most popular. More than 80 per cent of large US companies use it, as do many government departments. In Europe, the proportion of users is lower, but the numbers are growing and there is no sign of a peak as yet. Everyone is desperate to raise performance, in the public sector and the private, and if the balanced scorecard offers a solution, then surely it must be worth trying? The concept of the scorecard is deceptively simple. At the end of the 1980s, it was apparent that the usual array of hard financial measures was no longer an adequate means of navigating a company (if, indeed, it ever was) because it was retrospective and essentially short term.

Managers needed to look to the future, and in the electronic era, the future was increasingly intangible. More and more, factors such as innovation, customer satisfaction, and skills would ultimately determine the company's fortunes, not earnings per share or return on invested capital. In the boardroom, however, soft measures always lost out to hard ones. One solution, which became known as the balanced scorecard, was to combine three new sets of measures with the customary financial ones, embracing the customer, learning and growth, and internal issues, such as quality improvement and cost control. Developed by representatives from a dozen companies and led by Harvard professor Robert Kaplan and consultant David Norton, the scorecard idea grew wings following the pair's famous *Harvard Business Review* article in 1992.

One of the contributors was Shell Canada, and some three years later, the Royal Dutch Shell group was among the global companies that decided to take up the idea. This became part of its major 1995–6 restructuring programme to improve flagging performance. 'At first,' says group HR director John Hofmeister, 'there was a group scorecard confined to a small number of people. But as the new business groups took the place of the old regions, scorecards using the same architecture and assumptions were applied in each business, and in the local operating units.' 'The balanced scorecard has helped our performance,' believes Mr Hofmeister. 'It gives us better and better alignment (between all operating units) and focuses attention on what's important and on results. In addition,' he adds, 'the group's reward structure is linked directly to the scorecard.'

Selecting the measures, however, requires great care. Following Shell's recent crisis concerning the overstatement of its oil reserves, there was a suspicion that the inclusion of reserves on the scorecard was partly to blame. Reserves are, after all, the future of Shell's business, and intangible in the sense that they are managers' estimates. The snag was that they were linked to individual reward structures. Mr Hofmeister emphatically denies that this had anything to do with the overstatement. He says that he has examined the detailed records over the past seven years, and in only two years did the reserve replacement measure trigger some reward. Even then, it only formed a small part of the total package. Nonetheless, the reward system has now been changed to put more emphasis on the group and less on the individual. The incident demonstrates the truth that, despite being simply management tools, scorecards can have a big impact on business—for good or ill. Some observers believe that linking personal rewards to scorecard measures is bad in principle, whereas others claim that, unless there is some personal consequence of good or bad performance, there is no incentive for change. Whatever the truth, it is evident that few companies have yet reached Shell's level of sophistication in scorecard use.

The latest research from the Hackett Group, a US-based benchmarking company that advises clients on 'how to drive world-class performance', indicates that although 82 per cent of their 2700-strong database of companies claim to use scorecards, only 27 per cent have 'mature systems that use a mix of financial and operational metrics'. It concludes that 'most companies are having significant difficulty taking balanced scorecards from concept to reality.'

John McMahan, senior business adviser at the company, explains: 'Given the way the scorecard has evolved in practice, it's no wonder that many financial executives look on the concept as an expensive, bloated, and useless substitute for the traditional paper reports. Most companies get very little value out of scorecards because they haven't followed the basic rules that make them effective.'

One reason for this difficulty is the number of measures normally included in a scorecard. In the US, the average is an astonishing 132 per month and of these, 80 per cent are internal, historical financial, and operating data. The company's future is restricted to the other 20 per cent. In contrast, Kaplan and Norton suggested that management should focus on just 20 or 30 measures.

The question is: which ones? The choice depends on the company's strategic objectives, which seems an obvious point to make, and yet it is surprising how many organizations fail to take this into account. Jonathan Chocqueel-Mangan, now an independent consultant but, until a few years ago, European vice-president for Mr Norton's company, the Balanced Scorecard Collaborative, recalls: 'One company I reviewed had 30 unconnected business units. They used 23 different scorecard formats: some had objectives but no measures; some had measures but no objectives. None had both.'

As the scorecard concept has evolved, the emphasis has shifted from measurement to strategy and communication. But unless the strategic objectives fit with each other and with the measurements, the scorecard is likely to create more confusion than clarity. It is no use listing customer satisfaction as an objective if, for example, the unreliability of component suppliers is overlooked. And unless everyone knows what the strategy is, and their part in it, performance will not change. To produce a consistent 'story' takes time and goodwill from all the parties concerned. One of Mr Kaplan and Mr Norton's star companies is the Swedish office furniture maker, Kinnarps, which, after four years, now uses the scorecard throughout the organization and is very satisfied with the result. However, Charlotte Bhiladvala, head of business development at the company, admits that the process almost failed. 'Initially,' she explains, 'there was a lot of resistance to the academic concept, and it took a long time to adapt it and translate it to suit our culture. You always start with the strategic maps and work on the linkages, and then ask: "How do we get there and what are the measures?" You can't hurry it—you must let people understand it.'

Source: 'Understanding performance' *Financial Times*, 6 October 2004. © Andrew Bibby

▪ Questions

1. What is the rationale for using a balanced scorecard?

2. In deciding which balanced scorecard measures to use why is it important to understand your organization's objectives?

3. The balanced scorecard, in reality, is dominated by historical financial information. Discuss.

For examples of how organizations apply a balanced scorecard approach go to the Online Resource Centre and see the Tools and Techniques feature.
www.oxfordtextbooks.co.uk/orc/henry2e/

6.6 Benchmarking

Why do some organizations excel at some practices and activities while others do not? Can something be learned from the way in which successful companies carry out their practices that will improve your own company's performance? This is the essence of benchmarking. Benchmarking involves comparisons between different organizations with a view to improving performance by imitating or, indeed, improving upon the most efficient practices. This should not be limited to competitors within the same industry but instead be measured against *any* organization that has a reputation for being the best in its class.

In Japan benchmarking is practised through what is called *Shukko* (Zairi 1996). This is where employees work with other organizations and acquire new practices which will benefit their organization. *Shukko* may lead to the transfer of technology between

BENCHMARKING

is a continuous process of measuring products, services, and business practices against those companies recognized as industry leaders

Courtesy of Xerox Corporation

In the USA, the Xerox Corporation is widely credited with having developed benchmarking.

employees and/or organizations, and also provide for management development. However, its key advantage is the acquisition of specific knowledge which is lacking in the organization. In the US, the Xerox Corporation is widely credited with developing benchmarking, defining it as 'a continuous process of measuring our products, services, and business practices against the toughest competitors and those companies recognized as industry leaders'. A key to successful benchmarking will be the open learning that is allowed to take place between organizations. Clearly, organizations that are not competitors will be less concerned about sharing best practice.

For example, in order to improve the service on its frequent-flyer programme, British Airways visited the Oriental Hotel in Bangkok. The Oriental Hotel has a reputation for looking after and pampering its guests. Thus, British Airways was able to improve upon its practices on how to record details of its customer preferences. The Xerox approach to benchmarking is included in Table 6.1 and involves ten sequential steps. The starting point is for an organization to identify what it wants to benchmark in order for it to identify suitable companies to benchmark against. Benchmarking should not be confined to your own industry but the net should be spread wide to truly capture best practice. The end goal is for the organization to reach a level of maturity in which it attains a leadership position by having benchmarked practices fully integrated into its processes.

Benchmarking exposes organizations to state-of-the-art practices and, by inculcating a continuous learning process, can help to engender an organizational culture

Planning	1	Identify what is to be benchmarked
	2	Identify comparable companies
	3	Determine data collection method and collect data
Analysis	4	Determine current performance 'gap'
	5	Project future performance levels
Integration	6	Communicate benchmark findings and gain acceptance
	7	Establish functional goals
Action	8	Develop action plans
	9	Implement specific actions and monitor progress
	10	Recalculate benchmarks

TABLE 6.1

The Xerox approach to benchmarking
Source: M. Zairi 1996

that actively pursues change and innovation. In this respect it can be a vehicle for empowering employees and optimizing their creative potentials. The downside is that some organizations may harbour unrealistic expectations about what benchmarking can achieve. The choice of companies to benchmark against will require managerial skill and time to ensure that an appropriate match is obtained. Even where benchmarking practices can be formulated into organizational objectives, unless managers can facilitate a cultural environment that embraces change and innovation, these 'best practices' will simply fail at the implementation stage.

For a further discussion of benchmarking go to the Online Resource Centre and see the Key Work feature.
www.oxfordtextbooks.co.uk/orc/henry2e/

 Summary

We have seen that the choice of performance measure must first address a more fundamental issue, which is: Who is the organization there to serve? We have discussed the dominant approach within publicly quoted UK and US corporations of shareholder maximization. This assumes that the purpose of organizations is to add value for their shareholders. This is contrasted with a stakeholder approach which argues that corporations need to take account of wider societal needs if they are to grow in a responsible and sustainable manner.

We have explored different financial measurements of organizational performance and noted their tendency to be backward looking and focus on short-term time horizons. In order to complement financial measurements, Kaplan and Norton developed the balanced scorecard. This is an attempt to actively link strategy to an organization's objectives. Instead of merely looking at financial data, managers are expected to look at indicators which measure, for example, customer satisfaction and market share. Therefore, the balanced scorecard includes stakeholders in the assessment of an organization's performance. A common criticism of the balanced scorecard approach levelled by organizations is the difficulty of translating its concepts into implementation (see Case Study: Applying a Balanced Scorecard).

We concluded the chapter with a discussion of benchmarking by looking at Xerox, the company widely credited with its introduction to the West. We noted that benchmarking should not be limited solely to direct competitors or those within your industry, but a firm should be willing to compare itself against competitors outside its industry. In this way best-practice frameworks can be adopted and, if necessary, adapted to suit the firm's own unique needs.

Review Questions

1. Why does an organization's choice of performance measures depend on whom it seeks to serve?
2. Compare and contrast the balanced scorecard measure of performance with economic value added (EVA). Why might an organization choose to adopt the balanced scorecard approach?

Discussion Questions

1. What is the role of the modern corporation and who *should* it serve?
2. Why is the assumption of profit maximization still a powerful driving force for many organizations?

Research Topic

Identify a well-known company in Japan and one in Germany that are seeking to reduce the impact on society of their carbon footprints. What do you believe is the reason for their engagement with environmental issues?

Recommended Reading

There are many books dealing with the responsibilities of organizations. One that benefits from being written by a practitioner who has influenced the corporate governance debate is:

- **Cadbury, A.** (2002). *Corporate Governance and Chairmanship—A Personal View*. Oxford University Press, Oxford.

For a discussion of qualitative as well as quantitative measures of performance, see:

- **Kaplan, R.S.** and **Norton, D.P.** (1992). The balanced scorecard—measures that drive performance. *Harvard Business Review*, **69**(1), 71–9.

See also the Caux Round Table website (www.cauxroundtable.org) for a rationale for the inclusion of moral responsibility within business decisions.

online resource centre

www.oxfordtextbooks.co.uk/orc/henry2e/
Visit the Online Resource Centre that accompanies this book for activities and more information on assessing organizational performance.

Notes

1. These fundamental questions are discussed by the Caux Round Table, an organization of business leaders which seeks to include moral responsibility within business decisions (see www.cauxroundtable.org).
2. See Grant 2005 for a discussion of the relative benefits of economic profit over accounting profit.
3. More in-depth information about the relationship between John Lewis and its stakeholders, including its policy towards suppliers, government, local authorities and regulators, NGOs, campaign groups, and consumer associations is available on their website (http://www.johnlewispartnership.co.uk).
4. For a helpful discussion on assessing organizational performance see Grant 2005.

References

Berle, A.A. and **Means, G.C.** (1932). *The Modern Corporation and Private Property*. Macmillan, New York.

Buzzell, R.D. and **Gale, B.T.** (1987). *The PIMS Principles: Linking Strategy to Performance*. Free Press, New York.

Cyert, R.M. and **March, J.G.** (1963). *A Behavioural Theory of the Firm*. Prentice-Hall, Englewood Cliffs, NJ.

D'Aveni, R.A. (1994). *Hypercompetition: Managing the Dynamics of Strategic Manoeuvring*. Free Press, New York.

Freeman, R.E. (1984). *Strategic Management: A Stakeholder Approach*. Pitman, Boston, MA.

Friedman, M. (1962). *Capitalism and Freedom*, p. 133. University of Chicago Press, Chicago, IL.

Grant, R.M. (2005). *Contemporary Strategy Analysis*, 5th edn. Blackwell, Boston, MA.

Kaplan, R.S. and **Norton, D.P.** (1992). The balanced scorecard—measures that drive performance. *Harvard Business Review*, **69**(1), 71–9.

Kaplan, R.S. and **Norton, D.P.** (1996). Using the balanced scorecard as a strategic management system. *Harvard Business Review*, **74 (1)**, 75–85.

Mendelow, A. (1991). *Proceedings of Second International Conference on Information Systems, Cambridge, MA*. Cited in Johnson, G., Scholes, K., and Whittington, R. (2005). *Exploring Corporate Strategy: Text and Cases*, 7th edn, pp. 181–2. Prentice Hall, Harlow.

Sternberg, E. (1997). The defects of stakeholder theory. *Corporate Governance: International Review*, **5**(1), 3–10.

Sternberg, E. (2004). *Corporate Governance: Accountability in the Marketplace*, 2nd edn. IEA, London.

Zairi, M. (1996). *Benchmarking for Best Practice—Continuous Learning Through Sustainable Innovation*. Butterworth Heinemann, Oxford.

PART 2 CASE STUDY
The Battle for Brainpower

© istock.com/Felix Möckel

In a speech at Harvard University in 1943 Winston Churchill observed that 'the empires of the future will be empires of the mind'. He might have added that the battles of the future will be battles for talent. To be sure, the old battles for natural resources are still with us. But they are being supplemented by new ones for talent—not just among companies (which are competing for 'human resources') but also among countries (which fret about the 'balance of brains' as well as the 'balance of power').

The war for talent is at its fiercest in high-tech industries. The arrival of an aggressive new superpower—Google—has made it bloodier still. The company has assembled a formidable hiring machine to help it find the people it needs. It has also experimented with clever new recruiting tools, such as billboards featuring complicated mathematical problems. Other tech giants have responded by supercharging their own talent machines (Yahoo! has hired a constellation of academic stars) and suing people who suddenly leave.

But a large and growing number of businesses outside the tech industry—from consulting to hedge funds—also run on brainpower. When the Corporate Executive Board (CEB), a provider of business research and executive education based in Washington, DC, recently conducted an international poll of senior human-resources managers, three-quarters of them said that 'attracting and retaining' talent was their number one priority. Some 62 per cent worried about company-wide talent shortages. The CEB also surveyed some 4000 hiring managers in more than 30 companies, and was told that the average quality of candidates had declined by 10 per cent since 2004 and the average time to fill a vacancy had increased from 37 days to 51 days. More than one-third of the managers said that they had hired below-average candidates 'just to fill a position quickly'. The CEB found, too, that about one in three employees had recently been approached by another firm hoping to lure them away.

Can't Get Enough of It

All this brings back memories of the dotcom boom in the late 1990s, when management consultants were writing books such as *The War for Talent* (by Ed Michaels, Helen Handfield-Jones, and Beth Axelrod of McKinsey), telling companies that they must move heaven and earth to recruit and promote the best talent. No sooner had the bubble burst than many former masters of the universe were begging for work.

Indeed, companies do not even know how to define 'talent', let alone how to manage it. Some use it to mean people like Aldous Huxley's alphas in *Brave New World*—those at the top of the bell curve. Others employ it as a synonym for the entire workforce, a definition so broad as to be meaningless.

Nor does stocking up on talent seem to protect companies from getting it spectacularly wrong. Enron did everything that Mr Michaels and his colleagues recommended (indeed, McKinsey was both a consultant and a cheerleader for the Houston conglomerate). It recruited the best and the brightest, hiring up to 250 MBAs a year at the height of its fame. It applied a 'rank-and-yank' system of evaluation, showering the alphas with gold and sacking the gammas. And it promoted talent much faster than experience. Another corporate disaster, Long-Term Capital Management, was even more talent-heavy than Enron, boasting not only MBAs but Nobel prizewinners among its staff. But despite all this talent, the companies still succumbed to greed and mismanagement.

The Coming Shortage

Clearly there is more to good management than hiring the best and the brightest. Among other things, it requires rewarding experience as well as talent, and applying strong ethical codes and internal controls. Indeed, talent-intensive businesses have a particular interest in maintaining high ethical standards. Whereas in manufacturing industries a decline in such standards is often slow, in talent-intensive ones it can be terrifyingly sudden, as Arthur Andersen and Enron found to their cost.

All the same, structural changes are making talent ever more important. The deepest such change is the rise of intangible but talent-intensive assets. Baruch Lev, a professor of accounting at New York University, argues that 'intangible assets'—ranging from a skilled workforce to patents to know-how—account for more than

6

half of the market capitalization of America's public companies. Accenture, a management consultancy, calculates that intangible assets have shot up from 20 per cent of the value of companies in the S&P 500 in 1980 to around 70 per cent today.

McKinsey makes a similar point in a different way. The consultancy has divided American jobs into three categories: 'transformational' (extracting raw materials or converting them into finished goods), 'transactional' (interactions that can easily be scripted or automated), and 'tacit' (complex interactions requiring a high level of judgement). The company argues that over the past six years the number of American jobs that emphasize 'tacit interactions' has grown two and a half times as fast as the number of transactional jobs and three times as fast as employment in general. These jobs now make up some 40 per cent of the American labour market and account for 70 per cent of the jobs created since 1998. And the same sort of thing is bound to happen in developing countries as they get richer.

A second change is the ageing of the population. This will be most dramatic in Europe and Japan: by 2025 the number of people aged 15–64 is projected to fall by 7 per cent in Germany, 9 per cent in Italy, and 14 per cent in Japan. But it will also make a difference to China, thanks to its one-child policy. And even in America, where the effect will be less marked, the retirement of the Baby Boomers (which has just started) means that companies will lose large numbers of experienced workers over a short period. RHR International, a consultancy, claims that America's 500 biggest companies will lose half their senior managers in the next five years or so, when the next generation of potential leaders has already been decimated by the re-engineering and downsizing of the past few decades. At the top of the civil service the attrition rate will be even higher. This means that everyone will have to fight harder for young talent, as well as learning to tap (and manage) new sources of talent.

At the same time loyalty to employers is fading. Thanks to all that downsizing, the old social contract—job security in return for commitment—has been breaking down, first in America and then in other countries. A 2003 survey by the Society for Human-Resource Management suggested that 83 per cent of workers were 'extremely' or 'somewhat' likely to search for a new job when the economy recovered.

As well as becoming more footloose, the workforce is becoming less standardized. Today employees come in all shapes and sizes. Some 16 per cent of American workers telecommute some of the time. A quarter of the staff at B&Q, a British DIY chain, are over 50; the oldest is 91. And these diverse workers are often part of a global supply chain that keeps going 24 hours a day. Managers not only need to deal with lots of different sorts of people, but also to manage workers in different countries and often across different functions. That means even more competition for people with up-to-date management skills.

Obsession with talent is no longer confined to blue-chip companies such as Goldman Sachs and General Electric. It can be found everywhere in the corporate world, from credit-card companies to hotel chains to the retail trade. Many firms reckon that they have pushed re-engineering and automation as hard as they can. Now they must raise productivity by managing talent better.

With opportunities at home running dry, the hunt for talent has gone global. Over the past decade multinational companies have shipped back-office and IT operations to the developing world, particularly India and China. More recently they have started moving better jobs offshore as well, capitalizing on high-grade workers with local knowledge; but now they are bumping up against talent shortages in the developing world too.

Even governments have got the talent bug. Rich countries have progressed from simply relaxing their immigration laws to actively luring highly qualified people. Most of them are using their universities as magnets for talent. India and China are trying to entice back some of their brightest people from abroad. Singapore's Ministry of Manpower even has an international talent division.

The Dark Side

Competition for talent offers many benefits—from boosting productivity to increasing opportunities, from promoting job satisfaction to supercharging scientific advances. The more countries and companies compete for talent, the better the chances that geniuses will be raked up from obscurity.

But the subject is strewn with landmines. Think of the furore that greeted Charles Murray's and Richard Herrnstein's book *The Bell Curve*, which argued that there are differences in the average intelligence of different racial groups; or the ejection of Lawrence Summers as president of Harvard University because he had speculated publicly about why there are so few women in the upper ranks of science.

It would be wonderful if talent were distributed equally across races, classes, and genders. But what if a free market shows it not to be, raising all sorts of political problems? And what happens to talented Western workers when they have to compete with millions of clever Indians who are willing to do the job for a small fraction of the price?

Source: 'The battle for brain power' *Economist*, 5 October 2006.

Questions

1. Outline some of the structural changes that are taking place in different industries and the impact this has on how workers perform their roles.

2. In an era of low-cost manufacturing how might Western economies benefit from an understanding of talent or knowledge management?

3. If China and India continue to upskill their workers, what are the ramifications for Europe, Japan, and the US?

PART 3

Strategy Formulation

7 Business-Level Strategy

| 7.1 What is Business-Level Strategy? | 7.2 Generic Competitive Strategies | 7.3 A Resource-Based Approach to Strategy Formulation | 7.4 The Industry Life Cycle | 7.5 Strategy Formulation and Market Turbulence |

Key Work
Blue ocean strategies

Key Work
Environmental turbulence and the choice of strategy

Main Reference
Porter, M.E. (1980).
Competitive Strategy: Techniques for Analysing Industries and Competitors.
Free Press, New York.

Main Reference
Grant, R.M. (1991).
The resource-based theory of competitive advantage: implications for strategy formulation. *California Management Review*, **33**(Spring), 114–35.

Learning Objectives

After completing this chapter you should be able to:

- Define business and corporate strategy
- Discuss the role of business strategy in achieving competitive advantage
- Evaluate Porter's generic competitive strategies
- Discuss a resource-based approach to strategy formulation
- Evaluate the industry life cycle
- Assess the impact of turbulent markets on strategy formulation

Introduction

In Part 2 on strategy analysis we discussed and evaluated different analytical tools to help organizations make sense of their general and competitive environment.

Analytical tools and frameworks which can be used to better understand the general (or macro) environment include PEST analysis and scenario planning. A key task for the strategist is to identify the *weak signals* in the general environment that have the potential to change an industry's structure (see **Chapter 2** for a discussion of the general environment). This might be through technological change; for example, the advent of microprocessors ushered in the era of personal computers which made industries based on older technologies, such as typewriters, obsolete. It can also include a change in the rules of the industry game. Michael Dell's business model has allowed Dell to successfully dominate the personal computer manufacture market by utilizing a customer-focused direct-sales approach. It is these weak signals which form trends that have the potential to change the competitive environment. Therefore, they are a useful link between the general and competitive environment. Identifying and monitoring these takes managerial judgement, resources, and time. There is no guarantee that the weak signals being monitored will amount to a *trend* that impacts the competitive environment. Nonetheless the risk from ignoring weak signals can be devastating to an organization's markets and industry.

To help organizations make sense of their competitive environment we evaluated Porter's five forces framework in **Chapter 3**. Porter identified five forces that impact upon an industry's structure and therefore its potential profitability. The strength of each of these five forces—the bargaining power of buyers and suppliers, the threat of entry to the industry, the threat of substitutes, and competitive rivalry—will determine how attractive the industry is for its incumbent players. In order to assess internal resources and capabilities **Chapter 4** was devoted to an analysis of the internal environment and how an organization might usefully analyse its value-creating activities. In **Chapter 5** we explored a radically different perspective of industry analysis. This suggests that relative firm performance, and therefore profitability, is determined by an organization's resources and competencies. This is the resource-based view of the organization. In **Chapter 6**, the last chapter in Part 2, we looked at the different ways in which an organization can assess its performance and keep its attention on its strategic aims. The choice of performance measures is a challenge because these play a key role in strategy formulation, evaluating whether an organization's objectives have been achieved, and in compensating managers. Having analysed the external and internal environment facing organizations, we now turn our attention to strategy formulation, which we deal with in this part of the book. In this and subsequent chapters we will address strategy formulation at the *business*, *corporate*, and *global* levels.

Strategy formulation should be undertaken with a view to allowing an organization to achieve sustainable competitive advantage. The strategy being formulated will derive from the objectives and mission that the organization has set itself. It is perhaps prudent at this stage to mention that, although we have separated out the chapters on strategy formulation from those on strategy implementation for ease of exposition, in reality an organization must be mindful of its ability to implement strategy during the strategy formulation stage. Similarly, strategy may best be viewed as a non-linear incremental process in which persuasion is as important as rationally formulated plans (Quinn 1978). The best formulated strategy will avail the organization naught if it is poorly implemented. In the same way, simply adopting a strategy without any understanding of an organization's internal strengths and capabilities and how these meet the needs of the external environment will surely be a recipe for disaster. Although strategy formulation implies a deliberate form of decision making, we would do well to remember that at any given moment in time the strategy actually being pursued may be as a result of deliberate and emergent factors (Mintzberg and Waters 1985; Mintzberg 1996). This was discussed in detail in **Chapter 1**.

- In Section 7.1 we start the chapter with a discussion of business-level strategy. We discuss the differences between business strategy and corporate strategy. We also discuss the role of business strategy in achieving competitive advantage.

- Section 7.2 evaluates Porter's generic competitive strategies. The generic strategies are: *overall cost leadership*, *differentiation*, and *focus*. These strategies provide a way in which organizations can position themselves against the five forces (discussed in **Chapter 3**) and generate a superior return on investment. We explore the risks inherent in the pursuit of each generic strategy.

- In Section 7.3 we address an alternative approach to strategy formulation. This is the resource-based view of strategy (first discussed in **Chapter 5**). We assess the implications of this approach for strategy formulation.

- In Section 7.4 we look at the industry life cycle. We explore how an understanding of the different stages of the life cycle helps an organization to formulate an appropriate business strategy.

- The chapter concludes in Section 7.5 with an evaluation of market turbulence and hypercompetition. We look at four different competitive environments and assess how market leaders and challengers might achieve strategic supremacy in each.

7.1 What is Business-Level Strategy?

MARKET

is defined by demand conditions and based on an organization's customers and potential customers

INDUSTRY

is determined by supply conditions and based on production technology

Any given organization may comprise a number of different businesses, each operating in distinct markets and serving different customers. A market is defined by demand conditions and based on an organization's customers and potential customers. The industry in which it competes is determined by supply conditions such as a common technology or distribution channels. In choosing which markets to serve, an organization will *de facto* determine the industry in which it competes. For example, white goods such as refrigerators and washing machines are distributed through the same channels yet only refrigerators chill food and washing machines clean clothes. The markets, based on consumer demand, are for chilled food storage and laundry services. Therefore, we can see that although a domestic appliance industry exists based on a common technology (white boxes with motors in them), a domestic appliance market does not (Kay 1993).[1]

Business-level strategy is a means of separating out and formulating a competitive strategy at the level of the individual business unit. This is sometimes referred to as a strategic business unit (SBU). A strategic business unit is a distinct part of an organization which focuses upon a particular market or markets for its products and services. It should be remembered that a parent company sets the overall or corporate strategy. The role of the business unit is to devise a strategy which allows it to compete successfully in the marketplace and to contribute to the corporate strategy. In this respect the managers of a business unit may have considerable autonomy to devise their business-level strategy. This reflects their knowledge of local markets, customers, and competitors. However, this cannot be decided in isolation from the corporate strategy being pursued. The business unit managers must ultimately show that their business strategy contributes to the corporate strategy.

In contrast, corporate strategy focuses upon the fundamental question: What business (or businesses) do we want to be in? Kay (1993) argues that the problem with this formulation is that the term *business* can denote a market, industry, or strategy group. We have seen that a market is determined by consumer demand whereas supply factors define an industry. We know from **Chapter 3** that a strategic group is a group of companies following a similar or identical strategy. Therefore, organizations need to identify clearly when they use the phrase *business*—are they discussing their market, industry, or strategic group? As they are distinct concepts, to use the term *business* can tend to confuse rather than help. Many organizations now talk about their *core business*, in which core business is defined as the market(s) in which their distinctive capability gives them a competitive advantage. Although an organization might choose to look at its strategy group, industry, and market, its primary focus should be on those markets where it can best utilize its distinctive capabilities to secure a sustainable competitive advantage. The market is all about consumers and it is only by meeting consumer demand in ways that your competitors cannot match that you are able to secure competitive advantage. The way to achieve this is by using your core competencies or distinctive capability.

Therefore, when organizations discuss their core business they need to ask what markets they can compete in that allow them to translate their distinctive capability into a competitive advantage. An organization's boundaries are determined by the market it chooses to compete in, while the industry boundaries are determined by the markets which similar firms decide to compete in. In deciding which markets to compete in the rule should be to compete where the organization can gain competitive advantage. The task is to match the firm's distinctive capabilities to the markets that exist and, indeed, to use its distinctive capabilities to create new markets (Hamel and Prahalad 1993).

It is the task of the most senior executives to formulate a coherent corporate strategy. However, this is seldom undertaken in a vacuum, particularly given the distance between the board of directors and the markets they serve. In reality one would expect these executives to canvass input from senior managers running the individual business units. Equally important are the opinions of major shareholders and other

COMPETITIVE STRATEGY

is concerned with the basis on which an organization will compete in its chosen markets

STRATEGIC BUSINESS UNIT

is a distinct part of an organization which focuses upon a particular market or markets for its products and services stakeholders who possess sufficient power and influence to undermine the corporate strategy. For example, billionaire US investor Carl Icahn has accused media giant Time Warner of not doing enough for its shareholders. Icahn suggested major changes to the strategy of the world's biggest media company, recommending that it separates its cable business and buy back at least $20 billion (£11 billion) of its stock. If corporate strategy answers the question 'What business should we be in?', or more accurately 'Which markets do we want to serve?', it remains for competitive strategy to answer the question: How are we going to compete in our chosen markets? The key to bear in mind with business strategy is that it is always in pursuit of a sustainable competitive advantage. The question is *how* it achieves this. To answer this we will start by evaluating Porter's generic competitive strategies.

7.2 Generic Competitive Strategies

A sustainable competitive advantage is about performing different activities or performing similar activities in different ways. In other words, the firm must be capable of producing value for the consumer that is recognized as being superior to that of its competitors. It is precisely because competitive advantage is determined *vis-à-vis* your competitors that Porter's analysis is concerned with the competitive environment of industry structure and the five competitive forces. Porter (1980) argues that competitive strategy is about developing a defendable position in an industry which enables you to deal effectively with the five competitive forces and, thus, generate a superior return on investment for the firm. To achieve superior value that is recognized by the consumer the firm can do one of two things. First, it can offer its products or services at a lower price than rivals but without sacrificing the quality of the product. Second, it can produce a differentiated product which consumers perceive to be of better value than the product offerings of rival firms, and hence charge a premium price for its goods. In addition, the firm must choose which market segments it wants its products to compete within. That is, does it want to try to cover all or most market segments and adopt a broad-based approach? Or, would it be content to compete within a particular market niche which may require a different set of resources and capabilities, and which may be overlooked by rivals seeking to gain dominant market shares?

Whilst recognizing that the best strategy for an organization will actually be unique and reflect its individual circumstances, Porter (1980) developed three generic strategies to help an organization outperform rivals within an industry, and so successfully position itself against the five forces we discussed in **Chapter 3**. These strategies are referred to as *generic* because they apply to different types of organizations in different industries. The first of the three strategies is called *overall cost leadership*. A cost-leadership strategy involves a firm being the lowest-cost producer within the industry. This allows the firm to outperform rivals within the industry because it can charge lower prices and its lowest-cost base still allows it to earn a profit. In effect, this firm can charge the *lowest* price within the industry which rivals simply cannot match. Therefore, a cost-leadership strategy allows the firm to make superior profits.

A *differentiation* strategy is based on an organization producing products or services which are perceived by customers as unique or different. A differentiated product has the opportunity to meet different customer needs more closely. It is this difference that is the basis on which customers are prepared to pay a premium price. Clearly, the cost of producing the differentiation must not outweigh the price being charged. Or, put another way, customers should be prepared to pay a price which exceeds the cost of the differentiation, thereby allowing the organization to earn superior profits.

The third generic strategy is referred to as a *focus* strategy. A focus strategy allows an organization to target a segment or niche within the market. The segment may be based on a particular customer group, geographical markets, or specific product lines. Unlike overall cost-leadership and differentiation strategies which are industry-wide, a focus strategy is aimed at serving a particular target market efficiently. These generic strategies are shown in Figure 7.1.

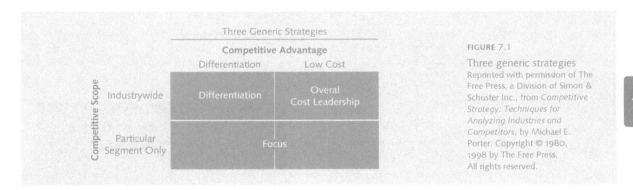

FIGURE 7.1

Three generic strategies
Reprinted with permission of The Free Press, a Division of Simon & Schuster Inc., from *Competitive Strategy: Techniques for Analyzing Industries and Competitors*, by Michael E. Porter. Copyright © 1980, 1998 by The Free Press. All rights reserved.

Figure 7.1 illustrates Porter's generic strategies and shows how an organization can choose to adopt a broad-based approach which seeks to cover most (or all) markets within the industry, that is, engage in a broad target. Alternatively, the firm may choose to focus upon a narrow strategic target (segment) of the industry. Whichever strategic target, broad based or narrow segment, the organization chooses to concentrate its resources and capabilities on, it must then adopt either a cost-leadership strategy or a differentiation strategy. As we shall see later, Porter warns organizations about the dangers of attempting to pursue these three strategies simultaneously.

7.2.1 Overall Cost-Leadership Strategies

We should note that implementing each of the three generic strategies will involve organizations in utilizing different internal resources and capabilities. For example, the resources and capabilities required to be a low-cost producer will often differ markedly from the capabilities required to produce a differentiated product. A **cost-leadership strategy** is adopted when an organization seeks to achieve the lowest costs within an industry and targets its products or services at a broad market. A cost-leadership strategy requires an organization to pursue (Porter 1980, p. 35):

COST-LEADERSHIP STRATEGY

where an organization seeks to achieve the lowest-cost position in the industry without sacrificing its product quality

- aggressive construction of efficient-scale facilities,
- vigorous pursuit of cost reductions from experience,
- tight cost and overhead control,
- avoidance of marginal customer accounts,
- cost minimization in areas like R&D, service, sales force, and advertising.

In reality, the organization must concentrate on all the activities that occur within its value chain and ensure that the costs associated with each activity are sufficiently pared down (see Strategy Focus: Low-Cost Airlines). At the same time it must also ensure that all these activities are properly coordinated across the value chain. Value chain analysis is discussed in **Chapter 4** (see also Porter 1985).

STRATEGY FOCUS
Low-Cost Airlines

After only three months as chief executive of easyJet, Andrew Harrison is pushing out the boundaries of Europe's second-biggest low-cost airline with the launch of its first routes to Morocco, Turkey, and Croatia. The extension of the low-fare airline model from the UK to more far-flung destinations will support easyJet's steady growth in capacity and

An easyJet plane

© easyJet Airline Company Ltd.

passenger numbers by about 15 per cent a year. But investors will draw more comfort from Mr Harrison's commitment to improving profitability. easyJet's profit margins lag behind those of Ryanair, its Irish rival, and Mr Harrison, the former chief executive of RAC until its takeover last year by Aviva, the leading UK insurance group, said yesterday he was determined to narrow the gap.

Mr Harrison said: 'We now make £2 profit per passenger. That is a relatively low profit margin, but the goal is £4 per passenger in the next three years.

Ryanair makes £5 per passenger. It sells more heavily on their flights. It manages costs very tightly. There's no one thing that makes them that much more profitable. We will improve our revenues and our costs.' Mr Harrison, who last December replaced Ray Webster, the New Zealander who led the airline's operations for most of its first decade, believes that easyJet can raise its yields (average fare levels) by attracting a growing share of business passengers, who tend to book later and pay correspondingly higher fares.

'The opportunity is there to market ourselves better, in particular to small and medium-sized businesses.' He said the easyJet business model, with its greater emphasis than Ryanair on flying to primary airports, offering greater convenience and high-frequency schedules, would be key to attracting more business traffic.

Source: 'easyJet chief plots a more profitable route' *Financial Times*, 2 March 2006.

An overall cost-leadership strategy implies a high market share and standardized products which utilize common components. This allows the organization to achieve economies of scale and reduce costs. Therefore, the organization may have to invest in the latest technology to reduce manufacturing costs and production processes. Such a decision will only be undertaken if it allows the organization to achieve its lower-cost strategy. A low-cost position within the industry can create a virtuous circle in which the higher margins achieved by the low-cost company allow it to continually reinvest and update plant and equipment, which in turn further reduces costs, which increases margins, and so on. For some time now car manufacturers have ensured that new models, which are expensive to develop, share common platforms with existing cars, thereby reducing their manufacturing cost. Toyota has achieved a low-cost position within the automobile industry and now earns more revenue than the three largest American auto producers, General Motors, Ford, and Chrysler, combined. Toyota continues to perpetuate this position by constant innovation within and across its value chain. In Toyota's case this low-cost production has achieved above-average quality standards. Notice also that any differentiation that does occur within the industry is matched by, or more accurately driven by, Toyota.

The Experience Curve

The concept of the experience curve was developed by the Boston Consulting Group in 1968 and helps an organization identify a relationship between its costs of production and its accumulated experience. The experience curve suggests that as output doubles the unit cost of production falls by 20–30 per cent. The actual percentage reduction in costs will vary between different industries. However, as a general rule, we can say that if a product costs, for example, £10 per unit to produce, and a firm produces 100 units, if the organization doubles its output to 200 units, the cost will fall to between £7 and £8 per unit.

If we apply this concept to the overall cost leader, we can see that a result of its dominant market share is that it will have accumulated the greatest experience, and it is this experience (or learning) which allows it to reduce its costs. As its market share continues to grow so its costs differential with rivals within the industry widens as it moves further down the experience curve. The corollary of this is that an organization should pursue a strategy of growth which enhances its accumulative experience and further lowers its costs. The experience curve allows an organization to anticipate cost reductions based upon future growth in sales. The idea then is to price its current products on this anticipated cost reduction. The effect is to undercut competitors, increase market share, and thereby benefit from cost reductions which increase profit margins. Where cumulative experience is less important within an industry, one would expect other factors to outweigh the experience curve.

Cost-Leadership Strategies and Porter's Five Forces

A major benefit of being the lowest-cost competitor within an industry is that it allows an organization to generate above-average profitability even where intense competition exists. Its lower cost base allows it to still earn a return after the other (higher-cost) competitors have competed away their profit through *rivalry*. Similarly a low-cost position allows the firm to defend itself against *buyers* who can only drive prices down to the level of the next most efficient competitor. Even in this unlikely situation the overall cost leader can still generate positive returns. When faced with the bargaining power of *suppliers*, being a low-cost producer provides a hedge against any increases in their input prices. Should there be a *threat of entry* from firms outside the industry, the low-cost producer will be in an advantageous position to compete on price which effectively acts as a barrier to entry. Lastly, the low-price competitor will be in a better position than its competitors to counter *substitutes* given its superior price–performance ratio. Porter (1980, p. 45) argues: 'fundamentally, the risks in pursuing the generic strategies are two: first, failing to attain or sustain the strategy; second, for the value of the strategic advantage provided by the strategy to erode within industry evolution'.

The Risks of Following an Overall Cost-Leadership Strategy

A low-cost position protects the organization against all of the five forces. However, there are risks associated with this strategy.

- A cost-leadership strategy can prove expensive as the organization continually updates its capital equipment.
- There is also the ease with which competitors may be able to imitate the activities of the cost leader.

- A change in technology may nullify past investments in capital equipment and allow competitors to take market share.

- Customer tastes may change, which results in them being less price sensitive and more willing to pay a higher price for a differentiated product. An organization following an overall cost-leadership strategy may not be able to readily adjust to these market changes.

7.2.2 Differentiation Strategies

A **differentiation strategy** is aimed at a broad market and involves the organization competing on the basis of a product or service that is recognized by consumers as unique. This difference must be sufficiently valued by consumers to the extent that they are willing to pay a premium price for it. A major benefit of producing a differentiated product is that rivals will find it difficult to imitate. We might reinforce that the choice of a differentiation strategy by an organization will involve different resources, capabilities, and organizational arrangements from a strategy based on cost leadership. It is for this reason that Porter believes an organization which seeks to follow more than one of the generic strategies is confused or is what he refers to as 'stuck in the middle' (Porter 1980, p. 41).

Organizations may differentiate their product offerings in a variety of ways. These include:

- design or brand image (e.g. BMW cars),

- customizing products to suit consumers' specific requirements (e.g. Dell personal computers),

- state-of-the-art technology (e.g. Intel microprocessors),

- marketing abilities (e.g. Procter & Gamble),

- reliability (e.g. Toyota cars),

- product engineering skills (e.g. Bosch),

- creativity (e.g. Apple's iPod), and

- customer service (e.g. the British retailer John Lewis).

In reality, we would expect the organization to use a number of dimensions on which it can differentiate its product. That is, when evaluating its value chain the organization would be able to point to different activities where it is clearly differentiated from its competitors. Although the aim of a differentiation strategy is not to focus primarily on costs, it is clearly important that the organization has some knowledge of its cost structure such that any differentiation achieved can be set at a price customers will be prepared to pay, and that easily covers the cost of the differentiation.

DIFFERENTIATION STRATEGY

involves the organization competing on the basis of a unique or different product which is sufficiently valued by consumers for them to pay a premium price

Differentiation Strategy and Porter's Five Forces

A differentiation strategy allows an organization to achieve above-average profits in an industry by creating a defensible position for coping with the five forces. For instance, differentiation provides a defence against competitive *rivalry* because it creates brand loyalty which helps protect the organization from price competition. This brand loyalty and unique product offering have to be overcome by entrants thinking of entering the market, which acts as a *barrier to entry*. The power of *buyers* is constrained as they lack a comparable alternative. A differentiation strategy provides the organization with higher margins which enables it to deal more easily with *suppliers*. In addition, suppliers may value the benefits that derive from being associated with a successful product or service. Lastly, a successfully differentiated product has customer loyalty which protects the organization from the use of *substitutes*. The more difficult it is for competitors to imitate the differentiation, the more likely it will be for the organization to achieve a sustainable competitive advantage. This implies that the basis of the differentiation is not readily identifiable, and even when known, is far from easy to replicate.

The Risks of Following a Differentiation Strategy

As with an overall cost-leadership strategy, a differentiation strategy has inherent risks.

* The organization must ensure that the high price charged for differentiation is not so far above competitors that consumers perceive the difference as not worth paying, and it results in reduced brand loyalty.
* Buyers may decide that their need for a differentiated product has declined. For example, the use of the Internet has greatly reduced the search costs involved in comparing products.
* Competitors may narrow the attributes of differentiation which results in consumers being faced with a viable substitute.

7.2.3 Focus Strategies

FOCUS STRATEGY

occurs when an organization undertakes either a cost or differentiation strategy but within only a narrow segment of the market

Whereas the low-cost and differentiation strategies we have discussed are aimed at the entire industry, a focus strategy is aimed at serving a segment (or segments) of the market. This might be a particular group of consumers or a specific geographical market—in effect, any viable segment of the market. Examples of focus strategies include Cartier for jewellery, Burberry for fashion, and Toyota for hybrid cars. Porter argues that by focusing on a narrow segment or niche of the market, the organization may be better placed to meet the needs of buyers than competitors who are trying to compete across the whole industry. By focusing on the needs of particular segments that exist within the industry, an organization can achieve competitive advantage either through lower costs or differentiation. The organization following a focus strategy does not accomplish this for the whole industry but only achieves competitive advantage within a specific niche. For example, hybrid cars currently serve a niche within the automobile industry (see Strategy Focus: Hybrid Cars).

STRATEGY FOCUS
Hybrid Cars

Not so long ago, most of the world's carmakers were trumpeting plans to do away with traditional petrol engines altogether. Revolutionary fuel cell powered cars running on hydrogen and emitting no carbon dioxide were supposed to go into mass production by about 2005. That year has come and gone. But the sector has still made some progress. High oil prices have renewed interest in more economical diesel engines and flex-cars that can run on ethanol. Especially in the US, the biggest buzz has been over hybrid electric vehicles, which capture and store braking energy.

Toyota, the leader in the area, has already sold over 600,000 hybrids and looks well on track to sell 1m a year, or about 10 per cent of its total global volume, by 2010. Honda is starting from a lower base, but growing fast. Others are scrambling to catch up. An alliance of General Motors, BMW, and DaimlerChrysler* recently unveiled plans to spend $1bn on developing a new hybrid transmission system and integrating it with other vehicle components.

Such ambitions are not without risk. But the dangers of being left behind in hybrids may be even larger. Political pressures are increasing, while Toyota is rapidly reaching the point where its famed capacity for reaping scale efficiencies kicks in. Toyota's rivals can still fight back. After all, the petrol engine was only one of many competing approaches to powering cars a century ago. But they will have to move fast, particularly as hybrids look like a stepping-stone on the path towards fuel cell powered cars—still a likely ultimate destination.

Source: 'Hybrid cars' *Financial Times*, 21 August 2006.

* Note that in May 2007 Daimler Benz sold Chrysler to Cerberus, a private equity group.

With a cost-focus strategy the firm seeks to become the cost leader but only within a particular segment of the market. Similarly, with a differentiation-focus strategy, the firm seeks to differentiate its products or services to effectively meet the needs of a particular segment of the market. Therefore, the purpose of a focus strategy is to achieve cost leadership or differentiation but within a narrow segment of the market. A focus strategy is predicated upon the firm being able to exploit only some of the differences within the industry. The firm may target segments that it believes it can more readily defend from competition. A cost-focus strategy may be possible because larger competitors within the industry have cost advantages that derive from economies of scale, but may be unable to produce cost-effective small production runs. The same logic applies to custom-built orders which do not allow larger competitors to exploit their economies of scale based upon standardization.

A cost-focus strategy differs from an overall cost-leadership strategy in that the organization is seeking to serve a narrow segment of the market. For example, the German retailer Aldi continues to thrive in the discount segment of retailing. A typical Aldi store is relatively small (around 15,000 square feet) and has about 700 products, 95 per cent of which are store brands. This compares with the 25,000 plus products that a more traditional supermarket carries. As with a cost-leadership strategy, quality cannot be sacrificed for cost savings. For instance, in taste tests many of Aldi's own-label products have beaten branded products. Aldi stores its products on pallets rather than shelves to cut the time it takes to restock and therefore to cut costs. It is difficult to see traditional supermarket retailers wanting to imitate this practice or, indeed, having the capability to manage costs in this niche market. In 2006, Germans voted Aldi the third most trusted brand after Siemens and BMW (Kumar 2006).

A differentiation-focus strategy offers a unique product that is highly valued within a segment of the market. The special needs within that segment are perceived to be more effectively met by the niche player than by rivals who compete across the market (see Strategy Focus: Hybrid Cars). This in turn helps to develop brand loyalty which makes entry by other competitors more difficult. As with broad-based cost leadership and differentiation, the extent to which a focus strategy achieves a sustainable competitive advantage will depend upon the organization's resources and distinctive capabilities and the ease with which these can be imitated. In addition, the durability of the segment may be an issue, as it may be less durable than the industry as a whole.

Focus Strategies and the Five Forces

The same factors that apply to overall cost-leader and differentiation strategies discussed above also apply to a focus strategy. As with low-cost and differentiation strategies, a focus strategy can provide a defence against competitive forces.

The Risks of Following a Focus Strategy

The risks of a focus strategy are:

• The segment may not be durable, for instance customer preferences may change and the niche player may be unable to respond.

- Broad-based competitors believe the segment represents an attractive submarket and out-focus the focuser.
- The difference between the segment and the main market narrows, leaving focus-based competitors at a disadvantage.

Stuck in the Middle

Porter's generic strategies represent alternative approaches to dealing with competitive forces. In contrast an organization that fails to pursue at least one of these generic strategies is referred as *stuck in the middle*. A firm stuck in the middle:

> *lacks the market share, capital investment, and resolve to play the low cost game, the industrywide differentiation necessary to obviate the need for a low-cost position, or the focus to create differentiation or a low-cost position in a more limited sphere. (Porter 1980, p. 41)*

Similarly, an organization should not try to pursue both a low-cost strategy and a differentiation strategy since it too will become stuck in the middle. Whilst the actual choice of generic strategy will be dictated by the organization's resources and capabilities, Porter believes it should seek to make a definitive choice as each generic strategy is mutually inconsistent. (see Case Study: Gatwick Airport's Search for a Business Strategy, which highlights the issues its owner—Global Infrastructure Partners—faces in devising a relevant business strategy.

CASE STUDY 7.1

Gatwick Airport's Search for a Business Strategy

The new owner of Gatwick has pledged to upgrade the airport's ageing facilities and to improve passengers' experience. Global Infrastructure Partners (GIP), which already owns London City airport, is required to spend about £900 million over the next four years to bring the tired buildings of Gatwick, in West Sussex, up to standard.

The airport, Britain's second-busiest, with 32 million passengers a year, has long been considered the poor relation to Heathrow, west of London. GIP, which is to buy Gatwick from BAA for £1.5 billion, is understood to want to reinvigorate the airport, attracting new airlines and passengers. The investment fund, which is part-owned by Credit Suisse and General Electric, the world's largest company, has briefed some of Gatwick's large airline customers on what it wants to achieve at the airport.

Courtesy of Gatwick Airport

London Gatwick Airport

The carriers, including easyJet, British Airways and Virgin Atlantic, have also given GIP a wish list of things that they want improved. It is understood to include upgrading Gatwick's railway station so that passengers do not have to lug suitcases up multiple flights of stairs. The airlines also want Gatwick's 120,000 sq m South Terminal to be overhauled, with security areas expanded to reduce queuing. They want to make Gatwick's shops less intrusive to create more space and to speed up the flow of passengers from check-in to boarding gate.

Paul Charles, a spokesman for Virgin Atlantic, said: 'Gatwick has the longer-term opportunity to leapfrog Heathrow in terms of offering much better facilities. We are looking forward to working with the new owner, but expect it to be committed to improving Gatwick and offering us and our passengers better standards of service.'

GIP declined to comment on its plans for Gatwick yesterday, but it has committed itself to upgrading the airport. Michael McGhee, the GIP partner leading the acquisition, said: 'We will upgrade and modernise Gatwick to transform the experience for both business and leisure passengers. We plan to work closely with the airlines to improve performance, as we have done successfully at London City airport.'

BAA, which is owned by Ferrovial, the Spanish infrastructure company, put Gatwick up for sale at the end of last year. Its decision to sell was driven by a need to reduce debt and to pre-empt a ruling from the Competition Commission that forced it to dispose of the airport. The commission ruled in March that BAA's ownership of the London airports Heathrow, Gatwick and Stansted had resulted in poor services and facilities for passengers.

BAA has long been accused by airlines of putting more investment into Heathrow, the world's busiest international airport, at Gatwick's expense.

Andy Harrison, chief executive of easyJet, Gatwick's largest carrier, said: 'We welcome this change in ownership and look forward to working with GIP. Regardless of who owns Gatwick, it is still a monopoly. Therefore, it is vital that Gatwick is properly regulated to protect airline passengers from the new owners exploiting their market power.'

Gatwick's sale price of £1.5 billion was below the £1.6 billion regulated asset value placed on the airport by the Civil Aviation Authority. BAA had hoped to receive upwards of £2 billion for Gatwick, but was forced to drop its aspirations when the credit crunch hit. Lack of financing meant that potential bidders kept dropping out, leaving BAA to pick between offers from GIP; Manchester Airports Group; Borealis, a Canadian pension fund; and the Lysander consortium, which includes Citigroup and Vancouver Airports. The price was also affected by a decline in passenger numbers at Gatwick, which is more exposed to the leisure market than Heathrow and more susceptible to families reducing their holiday spending. Passenger numbers in the past year are down 8.4 per cent and a number of airlines based at Gatwick, including XL and Oasis, have collapsed since the start of the downturn.

BAA insiders said that the company was comfortable with the sale price, although it was lower than had been hoped for, because it would allow BAA to focus on improving Heathrow. The funds from the sale of Gatwick will also enable BAA to reduce its £10 billion debt burden. Ferrovial bought BAA three years ago for £10.2 billion. Colin Matthews, BAA's chief executive, said: 'This marks a new beginning for both Gatwick and BAA. We wish Gatwick well for the future and are confident that the airport will flourish under new ownership. BAA will focus on improving Heathrow and our other airports.' GIP said yesterday that it was qualified to own Gatwick because it had proved its competence in running London City, which it bought in 2006.

However, some of Gatwick's airline customers noted that City, with only two million passengers a year, was much smaller than GIP's latest acquisition. 'We need results, and there is a concern that GIP has bitten off more than it can chew,' one observer said. A spokesman for British Airways said: 'We want to see Gatwick run as efficiently as possible while maintaining the highest levels of customer service for passengers and airlines.'

GIP is not thought to be planning significant job cuts at Gatwick and is likely to keep most of the existing management team in place. However, the investment fund does need to explain its business strategy for the airport. Gatwick was originally run by the British Airports Authority as a second hub to Heathrow, offering flights to similar destinations. In recent years, though, Gatwick has seemed to lack a coherent strategy. It sought to attract low-cost carriers, such as easyJet, as well as charter flights and traditional carriers, including Delta and US Airways. The British airlines, meanwhile, started to use Gatwick as a leisure hub. Virgin Atlantic flies all its 'holiday' flights from Gatwick, while BA's long-haul flights from the airport are also to destinations such as Barbados. Analysts said yesterday that the new owner would have to develop a clearer strategy, with speculation that it will increasingly concentrate on the leisure market.

Airports tend to specialise in certain types of travel. Stansted and Liverpool, for example, are bases for low-cost carriers. Heathrow is a hub that connects leading world cities. Regional airports, such as Manchester, have focused on the leisure market and Gatwick is expected to follow that model.

Half the sale price will be funded by debt. BAA said that, of the price, £10 million was conditional on Gatwick's traffic performance and £45 million on GIP's future capital structure. BAA expects capital markets to improve, allowing GIP to borrow more. Insiders said that if GIP had been able to borrow more, the sale price could have been higher. It is demanding, therefore, an extra payment if GIP is able to use its balance sheet more aggressively.

Up in the air

— BAA owns seven airports in Britain: Heathrow, Gatwick, Stansted, Southampton, Glasgow, Edinburgh and Aberdeen.
— The Competition Commission ruled in March that BAA should dispose of Gatwick, Stansted and one of either Glasgow or Edinburgh.
— It argued that BAA's monopoly control of airports in London and Scotland was bad for airlines and passengers.
— BAA has taken the case to the Competition Appeal Tribunal in an attempt to overrule the Commission's decision. The hearing is this week, with a judgment likely by the end of the year. If BAA's appeal is unsuccessful, it will have to put Stansted and, probably, Glasgow up for sale.
— Stansted is Britain's third-largest airport with 20 million passengers a year. It has a regulated asset value of £1.1 billion, but possible bidders have said that they may demand an 'O'Leary Discount'. Michael O'Leary, chief executive of Ryanair, Stansted's largest customer, is notorious for moving flights to other airports if owners do not cut costs.
— Glasgow is the eighth-largest airport in the UK with 7.5 million passengers a year. It is unregulated and is likely to fetch up to £500 million. Manchester Airports Group is an early favourite to acquire Glasgow.

Source: 'Gatwick's new owner, Global Infrastructure Partners, promises £900m facelift' *TheTimes*, 22 October 2009.

Questions

1. What is the distinctive capability of Gatwick airport?
2. Identify the different markets in which Gatwick airport might successfully compete.
3. Which generic strategy might Global Infrastructure Partners pursue to achieve a competitive advantage for Gatwick airport?

Criticisms of the Generic Strategies

While many firms may choose to adopt a low-cost strategy or differentiation strategy, it may not be true to suggest that these are inconsistent. Organizations are increasingly finding that a route to competitive advantage is being able to combine being a low-cost producer with some form of differentiation; this is referred to as a hybrid strategy. Such a strategy is adopted by the Swedish furniture manufacturer IKEA, which provides low-cost manufacture with a differentiated product. Often the two are complementary, so that being a cost leader allows an organization to invest in differentiation required by the market. Consider, for example, the Japanese auto manufacturer Toyota. It has an enviable record on cost reductions while at the same time its cars are differentiated from other major players such as Ford and General Motors. Therefore, it occupies a position in which it is the *overall cost leader* in the auto industry, but its products are also renowned for reliability providing them *differentiation* and brand loyalty. Far from being inconsistent this strategy is proving to be the business model—differentiation and low-cost manufacturing—that the rest of the industry is desperately trying to emulate.

In the UK supermarket retailers selling similar foodstuffs have sought to differentiate themselves through selling clothing, consumer electronics, savings products, and garden furniture, in the process turning themselves into department stores selling food! For example, Tesco, the market leader, continues to expand its range of non-food items as it moves into higher-margin goods and services. The problem for all supermarkets is that such products are easily imitated by rivals. In contrast, the previous market leader Sainsbury's was stuck in the middle trying to sell higher-priced foods but with the slogan that 'Good food costs less at Sainsbury's'. In the 1990s it found itself losing market share to Tesco. Its foodstuffs were not perceived by consumers to be sufficiently differentiated to warrant a premium price when compared with other supermarkets, nor were its operations sufficiently low cost to be able to compete on price.

In the same way the British retailer Marks & Spencer found that its clothes were no longer perceived by consumers to be differentiated on the basis of outstanding value for money. Instead, the retailer saw its fortunes decline as it grappled with tired clothing lines, loss of identity, incoherent objectives, and no clear vision. It was unable to compete effectively with competitor retailers more closely matching customer needs who outsourced their manufacture to low-cost countries in the Far East. In time, M&S who historically prided themselves on their quality British-made goods were forced to source their supplies from similar low-cost economies. Its famous customer service and no-quibble money-back guarantee was no match for poor product lines. It is interesting to note that after years of lacklustre performance M&S has begun to see a substantial increase in its profitability, driven by increases in the sale of women's clothing. Clearly this important segment of its business is now sufficiently differentiated from other clothing retailers to warrant consumer expenditure.

HYBRID STRATEGY

this is where an organization is able to combine being a low-cost producer with some form of differentiation

7.3 A Resource-Based Approach to Strategy Formulation

The resource-based view of strategy (discussed in **Chapter 5**) argues there are two fundamental reasons for making the resources and capabilities of the firm the foundation for its strategy. First, internal resources and capabilities provide the basic direction for a firm's strategy and, second, resources and capabilities are the primary source of profit for the firm. Grant (1991) distinguishes between resources and capabilities. He sees resources as inputs into the production process. A capability is the capacity for a team of resources to perform some task or activity. Therefore, resources are the source of an organization's capability. And it is capabilities that are the main source of its competitive advantage. We might reiterate that although we separate out strategy formulation from strategy analysis for ease of exposition, in reality these are part of the same process.

In a constantly changing world Grant argues that a focus solely upon the external environment may not provide a sufficient foundation for a long-term strategy.

> When the external environment is in a state of flux, the firm's own resources and capabilities may be a much more stable basis on which to define its identity. Hence, a definition of a business in terms of what it is capable of doing may offer a more durable basis for strategy. (Grant 1991, p. 116)

In other words, a focus upon which markets the organization competes in and, therefore, which customer needs it seeks to satisfy may be inappropriate when faced with a rapidly changing environment. Given this type of environment, the focus instead should be on internal factors. The resource-based view argues that even the choices articulated by Porter, competing on cost or differentiation within a broad or narrow market, are themselves predicated upon the resources within the organization, since no organization can hope to follow an overall cost-leadership strategy if it does not possess economies of scale and technically proficient plant and machinery.

The aim of the resource-based approach to strategy formulation is to maximize Ricardian rents. We defined Ricardian rents in **Chapter 6** as the surplus that is left over when the inputs to a productive process, which includes the cost of capital being employed, have been covered. As resources depreciate or are imitated by competitors, so the rents they generate also begin to diminish. To appreciate rents fully we need to understand the relationship between resources and capabilities. A difficulty we previously alluded to is that resources that reside within an organization are not always transparent and, therefore, are not easy to identify. In the same way an organization may not be capable of assessing its capabilities objectively but instead may assess them according to some past chimera. What is essential is that an organization can assess its capabilities in terms of those that its competitors possess, thereby allowing it to exploit any differential advantage.

Organizational capabilities require that the knowledge of individuals is integrated with an organization's resources such as its capital equipment and technology. This is accomplished by organizational routines (Nelson and Winter 1982). Organizational routines are regular, predictable, and sequential patterns of work activity undertaken by members of an organization. Therefore, an organization's capabilities comprise a number of interacting routines. For resources and capabilities to operate effectively the organization must achieve cooperation and coordination between routines. Therefore, the type of management style within the organization, its vision, and its values are all crucial ingredients to achieve the efficient operation of routines.

ORGANIZATIONAL ROUTINES
are regular, predictable, and sequential patterns of work activity undertaken by members of an organization

According to Grant the profits that accrue to a firm's resources and capabilities depend upon two factors: first, the sustainability of the competitive advantage which resources and capabilities confer and, second, the ability of the firm to appropriate the profits (or rents) earned from its resources and capabilities. The characteristics of resources and capabilities that provide for the sustainability of a competitive advantage are: *durability*, *transparency*, *transferability*, and *replicability*.

Durability refers to the rate at which an organization's resources and capabilities depreciate or become obsolete. While resources such as plant and machinery may be quickly depreciated by technological changes, other resources such as an organization's brand tend to depreciate far slower. In fact the tendency for the external environment to change rapidly may actually benefit established brands as consumers opt for tried and tested choices. In contrast with resources, an organization's capabilities may experience greater longevity. This is because the organization may be able to replace the resources on which the capabilities are based more readily as they wear out. Interestingly, corporate culture plays a part in sustaining competitive advantage (Barney 1986, 1995) by ensuring the continuity of capabilities through its socialization of employees.

DURABILITY
refers to the rate at which an organization's resources and capabilities depreciate or become obsolete

Another factor which helps determine sustainable competitive advantage is how quickly a firm's competitors can imitate its strategy. Transparency refers to the ease with which a competitor can identify the capabilities which underpin a rival's competitive advantage and, therefore, which resources it requires in order to duplicate these capabilities. Clearly the more complex and embedded the resources and capabilities are, the more difficult it will be for a competitor to duplicate them. The more difficult the strategy is to imitate, the more sustainable the competitive advantage. Transferability refers to how easily a competitor can access the resources and capabilities necessary to duplicate an incumbent's strategy. If organizations can acquire resources and capabilities on similar terms to their rival, then its competitive advantage will be unsustainable. However, we might expect that a firm that is first to acquire such resources and capabilities may acquire some advantage through its experience and knowledge of these resources which competitors will lack (first-mover advantages). Similarly, capabilities may be less transferable as they represent a collection of interactive resources. It may be that the only way to imitate the competitive

TRANSPARENCY
is the ease with which a competitor can identify the capabilities which underpin a rival's competitive advantage

TRANSFERABILITY
refers to how easily a competitor can access the resources and capabilities necessary to duplicate an incumbent's strategy

advantage of a rival is to transfer capabilities in their entirety. However, the dynamics present in one organization that allow a capability to flourish may not be present to the same extent in another organization.

It might be possible for an organization to gain resources and capabilities through replication. Replicability is the use of internal investments to copy the resources and capabilities of competitors. Where the capabilities are based upon complex organizational routines this will be far more difficult. Even where an organization's routines seem relatively straightforward they may be difficult for competitors to imitate successfully (e.g. Dell). The extent of the profits deriving from a firm's resources and capabilities will depend not only on its ability to sustain its competitive advantage but also on its ability to appropriate or capture these profits for itself. This will depend upon the balance of power between the firm and its employees. Where an employee's contribution to the firm is readily identifiable, and their skills are scarce and easy to take from firm to firm, we would expect the employee to be in a strong bargaining position for a share of the profits. However, where the employee's contribution is not so clearly defined and is enhanced by the organizational routines within the firm, we might expect the firm to appropriate greater returns.

REPLICABILITY

is the use of internal investments to copy the resources and capabilities of competitors

7.3.1 Implications for Strategy Formulation

We have seen that an organization's most valuable resources and capabilities are those that are difficult to identify, imperfectly transferable, and difficult to imitate, and in which it has clear ownership. Given this, its strategy should be based upon exploiting these resources and capabilities, which limit its activities to where it possesses a competitive advantage. For example, the British car manufacturer Morgan builds hand-made sports cars for a specific segment of the market (Porter's narrow market or niche), thereby playing to its strengths rather than trying to compete on price against mass-market players such as Ford. Where an organization's resources and capabilities are easy to imitate, a sustainable competitive advantage may derive from competing within a niche which may be unable to support myriad competitors. The dynamic of the marketplace necessitates that competitors constantly focus upon updating their competitive advantages rather than trying vainly to shore up their existing advantages, which will simply be imitated.

Figure 7.2 shows a five-stage model to help guide organizations in their strategy formulation. The focus is upon the internal capabilities of the organization. The starting point is to analyse a firm's resources and then to assess the firm's capabilities, that is, what activities it can perform better than its rivals. Stage 3 involves an appraisal of the rent-generating potential of its resources and capabilities. That is, are the firm's resources and capabilities able to provide a sustainable competitive advantage, and can the profits that accrue be appropriated by the firm? In stage 4, the firm is in a position to formulate a strategy which allows it to exploit its internal resources and capabilities in relation to the opportunities that exist in the external environment. In

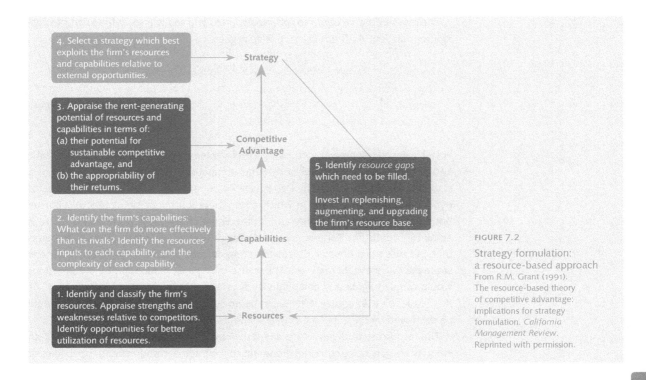

FIGURE 7.2

Strategy formulation:
a resource-based approach
From R.M. Grant (1991).
The resource-based theory
of competitive advantage:
implications for strategy
formulation. *California
Management Review*.
Reprinted with permission.

stage 5, the firm identifies any resource gaps that may exist and upgrades its current resources and capabilities to ensure that it can achieve a sustainable competitive advantage. (For a more recent example of this model which subsumes stages 4 and 5 into a single stage, see Grant 2005, p. 171.)

To ensure sustainable competitive advantage an organization needs to upgrade its resources and capabilities based on what it believes will be the basis of its *future* competition. In other words, the organization needs to be able to assess its external environment correctly and to evaluate the trends, some of which start within the general environment but which have their greatest impact in the competitive environment. These trends will determine the resources and capabilities required to compete successfully in the future. Prahalad and Hamel (1990) refer to these capabilities as core competencies. Kay (1993) tends to dismiss the concept of generic strategies, arguing instead that each organization is different. As we saw in **Chapter 5**, Kay uses the term distinctive capabilities to describe how organizations achieve competitive advantage. One approach to assessing the external environment is to try to identify the weak signals we discussed in **Chapter 2**. Another is to produce a series of scenarios (also discussed in **Chapter 2**) based on what the organization believes may occur in the future. The goal is for an organization's strategy to go a little beyond its current resources and capabilities (Hamel and Prahalad 1993) to ensure that the resources and capabilities necessary to address future competitive challenges are being built up.

The resource-based approach places resources and capabilities at the heart of strategy formulation. As Grant (1991, p. 133) argues:

> *The key to a resource-based approach to strategy formulation is understanding the relationships between resources, capabilities, competitive advantage, and profitability . . . this requires the design of strategies which exploit to maximum effect each firm's unique characteristics.*

Porter's generic approach to business-level strategy is often characterized as static and incapable of dealing with a dynamic competitive landscape. (This notion of a static framework is rejected by Porter (see Porter 1999).) Others point to the use of hybrid strategies (Hill 1988) in which an organization might simultaneously pursue both a cost-leadership strategy and a differentiation strategy. Nonetheless, there is empirical support for Porter's generic strategies (Campbell-Hunt 2000). Kay argues that, because the distinctive capabilities of organizations differ, any search for generic strategies will inevitably fail. This is because their general adoption by organizations would simply negate any competitive advantage that might have been derived. As Kay (1993, p. 368) argues: 'There can be no such recipes because their value would be destroyed by the very fact of their identification.'

The resource-based view shifts the discussion for competitive advantage from an emphasis on the competitive environment to the internal resources and capabilities of the organization. A criticism made of the resource-based view is that it is unclear how resources and capabilities evolve over time (Porter 1991). However, the purpose of strategy remains the same in each perspective: for the organization to exploit the opportunities within its external environment. It is how the organization gets to this position that generates contention. There is empirical support for both views, suggesting perhaps that they should not be seen so much as incompatible but more as occupying different positions on the same continuum. (Empirical support for the resource-based view can be found in Henderson and Cockburn 1994.)

BLUE OCEANS

comprise untapped market space, demand creation, and the possibility of highly profitable growth

Kim and Mauborgne (2005) argue that organizations need to create and capture what they call **blue oceans** of uncontested market space. A blue ocean represents a strategic position unoccupied by competitors that has the potential for demand creation and highly profitable growth. They contend that in formulating strategy the analysis of neither the company nor the industry will lead to the creation of blue oceans and sustained high performance. What is important is the strategic move. A strategic move is defined as 'the set of managerial actions and decisions involved in making a major market-creating business offering' (Kim and Mauborgne 2005, p. 10). Their research suggests that companies which create blue oceans focus on value innovation.

Value innovation occurs when organizations shift their focus from beating the competition to making the competition irrelevant by placing equal emphasis on *both* value and innovation. Value innovation goes against Porter's assertion that an organization can pursue either differentiation *or* a low-cost strategy. It implies that companies which seek to create and capture blue oceans can pursue differentiation and low cost at the same time. A key feature of value innovation is a belief that 'market boundaries and industry structure are not given but that they can be reconstructed by the actions and beliefs of industry players' (Kim and Mauborgne 2005, p. 17). An example is Cirque du Soleil, which created a new product offering by expanding existing industry boundaries to go beyond the traditional circus. Instead it substantially upgraded the tired format of tent venues and blended circus with theatre, dance, and music. In the process it created an entirely new group of consumers prepared to pay a premium for unique entertainment. At the same time, it eliminated the high-cost elements of the circus such as star performers and the use of animals, thereby reducing its cost structure. By not trying to compete with the existing circus format, Cirque du Soleil made traditional circus offerings irrelevant to it and created uncontested market space. We might note that in creating and capturing blue oceans an organization still needs the requisite capabilities to do so.

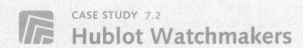

CASE STUDY 7.2
Hublot Watchmakers

Once a year, at his farm overlooking Lake Geneva, Jean-Claude Biver makes cheese. He uses milk collected only during the brief few weeks when the Alpine meadows on which his cows graze are in flower. The milk is heated over an open fire made with hand-cut wood, the cost of which alone exceeds the price most cheese

Watch mechanism

would fetch. He leaves it to age all summer. This painstaking process yields five tonnes a year, but he cannot bear to sell a gram of it.

If Mr Biver changed his mind, he could probably name his price. His cheese can send the authors of Michelin guidebooks into rapture; Switzerland's best chefs regularly call him begging for some. But he parcels it out only to family and friends, and to restaurants that he particularly likes. And he always refuses payment for the stuff. 'If I don't sell it,' explains Mr Biver, 'then I will decide who gets it and who doesn't. I will be the master of my cheese until the last piece.'

Oddly, Mr Biver is also a talented salesman. At Hublot, a watchmaker that he has run since 2004, sales are down by only 15% this year—a considerably better performance than Switzerland's luxury-watch business as a whole, which has seen sales slump by about 30%. Hublot's sales increased more than fivefold between 2004 and 2007, a record that enticed LVMH, a luxury-goods conglomerate, to buy the firm last year.

Hublot's success stems in part from Mr Biver's penchant for rationing his products. He was careful to restrict supply when business was booming, delivering only seven watches, say, when ten were ordered. Jewellers pay cash for stock, so it seems foolish not to sell as many watches as possible. Yet for Mr Biver it is an essential strategy. 'You only desire what you cannot get,' he says. 'People want exclusivity, so you must always keep the customer hungry and frustrated.'

This approach has helped shield Hublot from the downturn in two ways. Cash-strapped retailers who have cut costs by running down stocks of other firms' watches keep buying his, since they did not have many on hand to begin with. And they have not slashed prices for Hublot's watches, as they have with those of its rivals (watchmakers get only about a third of the final selling price of a watch). That has helped preserve the brand's image of luxury and exclusivity.

Keeping inventories tight is a strategy Mr Biver refined in 1981 after he and a friend bought the rights to the name Blancpain—all that was left of a firm that had once supplied watches to divers in the American navy but had gone out of business in the 1970s. Two things attracted him to the brand: it claimed to be Switzerland's oldest watchmaker and it had missed out on the technological revolution of quartz timers powered by batteries.

Mr Biver decided to turn this anachronism into a strength. At the time the Swiss watch industry had been in decline for 15 years as Asian digital watches selling for $20 displaced Swiss ones costing ten times as much. Even Rolex, the undisputed champion of Swiss watchmakers, eventually relented and started adding electronics to its timepieces.

Mr Biver developed a new, backward-looking slogan for the firm: 'Since 1735 there has never been a quartz Blancpain watch. And there never will be.' It turned out to be an industry-changing move. Last year mechanical watches accounted for 70% of the value of Swiss watch exports. A decade after restarting Blancpain, Mr Biver sold it for SFr60m ($43m) to the Swatch Group, having initially paid SFr22,000.

The shock of the old

Swatch promptly charged Mr Biver with turning around its own ailing brand, Omega. Although Omega had made the first watch taken to the moon, it had become something of a national joke by the 1980s. Mr Biver's approach was pure marketing. He pioneered techniques that would seem commonplace now, such as product placements in James Bond films and celebrity sponsorships. Under his leadership Omega's sales almost tripled. Following a brief spell in retirement, Mr Biver then took the reins at Hublot.

His success coincides with a broader revival. The Swiss watch industry has staged a remarkable recovery since its nadir in the early 1980s. Last year exports of Swiss watches were valued at SFr17 billion, a 70% increase from 2003. Yet the outlook appears less certain in recessionary times. The most expensive watches have been hit especially hard: in September sales of platinum watches, for instance, were down by nearly half compared with last year. For all his marketing prowess, Mr Biver nonetheless relies on the existence of free-spending consumers with a penchant for showing off. At the best of times, he freely admits, it is hard to justify spending $100,000 on a watch. But the fact that they keep time well, he hopes, will continue to serve as 'the little bit of rationality that lets you sell the irrational'.

Source: 'Salesman of the irrational' *The Economist*, 12 November 2009.

▣ Questions

1. What are the resources and capabilities of Hublot, the Swiss watchmaker?
2. Identify which elements of Jean-Claude Biver's approach to business are *explicit* and which are *implicit*.
3. What part does *social complexity* play in Jean-Claude Biver's success?

For a discussion of blue ocean strategies and how an organization might create uncontested market space go to the Online Resource Centre and see the Key Work feature.
www.oxfordtextbooks.co.uk/orc/henry2e/

7.4 **The Industry Life Cycle**

The industry life cycle suggests that industries go through four stages of development: *introduction, growth, maturity,* and *decline* (see Figure 7.2). There will clearly be variations between different industries as to the length of each life cycle. McGahan (2000) points out that even within an industry, different strategic groups may be experiencing different stages of the life cycle. The life cycle is frequently applied to

INDUSTRY LIFE CYCLE

suggests that industries go through four stages of development which include: introduction, growth, maturity, and decline product markets where a product life cycle can be discerned which follows the same stages as the industry life cycle. The product life cycle allows an organization to vary its marketing mix to produce an appropriate response according to each stage in a product's development. The industry life cycle is the supply-side equivalent of the product life cycle.

The industry life cycle helps an organization to see how it is positioned in terms of the development of its markets. The different stages of the industry life cycle will have an impact upon competitive conditions facing the organization. For example, one would expect the level of competitive rivalry during the introduction stage, when a market is being opened up, to be different from that in the maturity stage, when the market is saturated and market share comes at the expense of your competitors. Therefore, an organization can benefit from an understanding of the industry life cycle and formulate its strategy to match the needs of each stage more closely.

7.4.1 Introduction Stage

The introduction stage of the industry life cycle (Figure 7.3) is characterized by slow growth in sales and high costs as a result of limited production. Organizations invest in research and development to produce new products. These command a premium price and confer upon the organization a first-mover advantage (Lieberman and Montgomery 1988). During this stage profits will be negative as sales are insufficient to cover the capital outlay on research and development. An advantage of being the first mover is that an organization may set the industry standard (Shapiro and Varian 1999) even in the face of a superior technology. Consider the VHS standard set by Matsushita for video recording in the face of a superior product, Betamax, developed by Sony. However, the tendency is for product life cycles to be compressed, as each stage is cut short by rapid change, which means that any first-mover advantage is quickly eroded. This also means that the timescale for a firm to recoup its capital expenditure is shortened, which brings a greater risk for the first mover.

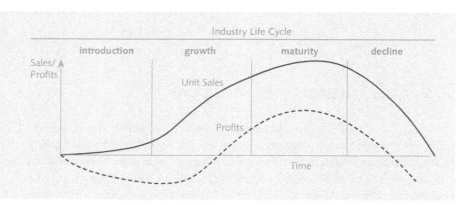

FIGURE 7.3
Industry life cycle

7.4.2 Growth Stage

In the growth stage sales increase rapidly as the market grows, allowing firms to reap the benefits of economies of scale. The increase in product sales brings greater profits which in turn attracts new entrants to the market. As consumer awareness of the product grows, so firms vie to have their brands adopted and increase spending on marketing activities. A goal for the firm is not merely to attract new customers but to ensure that customers repeat their purchases.

7.4.3 Maturity Stage

The maturity stage of the life cycle sees a slowing in sales growth and profits as the market becomes saturated. Firms will begin to exit the industry, and low-cost competition based on efficient production and technically proficient processes becomes more important. As market share can only be achieved at the expense of competitors, rivalry becomes more intense within the industry. With exit barriers the rivalry will be more intense still as marginal firms find it difficult to exit the industry. During the maturity stage of the life cycle it is conceivable that a product may benefit from innovation or finding new consumer markets. It may become *rejuvenated*. For example, Johnson & Johnson have successfully targeted their baby-oil products at female consumers and thereby created a new market. Somewhat controversially, the pharmaceutical industry has found that drugs which are deemed unacceptable on health grounds in Western economies can be marketed to developing nations where regulatory requirements are less stringent.

7.4.4 Decline Stage

In the decline stage firms experience a fall in sales and profitability. Consumer loyalty shifts to new products based on newer technologies. For example, fewer consumers bother to write cheques, preferring instead to use debit and credit cards. DVDs (digital versatile disks) have superseded the market for video cassettes. Competition within the industry will be based on price as consumers shun the old products. Firms will continue to exit the industry and consolidation may occur as a strategy for firms to achieve acceptable profits. Therefore knowledge of the industry life cycle is useful to help an organization understand how each stage can affect its competitive environment. In line with its rivals, it must ensure that its strategy formulation is sufficiently robust to meet the needs of each stage of the cycle.

7.5 Strategy Formulation and Market Turbulence

If markets are becoming increasing turbulent and hypercompetitive, how can organizations formulate successful strategies to achieve sustainable competitive advantage? The answer lies in a clearer understanding of the competitive conditions which operate in the marketplace, and the relationship between an environment's turbulence and the choice of strategy.

For more information on environmental turbulence and the choice of strategy go to the Online Resource Centre and see the Key Work feature. www.oxfordtextbooks.co.uk/orc/henry2e/

Christensen (2001) states that the practices and business models that constitute advantages for today's most successful companies only do so because of particular factors at work under particular conditions at this particular point in time. He argues that strategists need to get to grips with *why* and under what conditions certain practices lead to competitive advantage. Christensen points out that even tacit knowledge which is difficult to imitate confers only a temporary advantage. This is because scientific progress which results in better understanding has a tendency to transform knowledge that once resided within an organization's proprietary routines into explicit and replicable knowledge. The task for organizations then is to be sufficiently aware of the factors which underpin their competitive advantage such that they will know when old competitive advantages are due to disappear and how new ones can be built.

Others suggest that more attention needs to be paid to the differences between the strategies of dominant incumbent players and those of challengers who are seeking to disrupt the current environment. By better understanding the interaction between strategy and the environment, managers can better tailor their strategies to the environment, or attempt to change the environment to their benefit. D'Aveni (1999) argues that the firm with strategic supremacy shapes the basis of competition for its rivals, that is, it determines the rules on which rivals will compete within the industry. For example, in the 1970s and 1980s, Gillette's heavy investment in R&D put it at a disadvantage in a market increasingly dominated by its competitor Bic's disposable razors. Instead of trying to compete according to industry rules that suited Bic, Gillette redefined the rules of the game for razors.

In 1989 Gillette introduced its Sensor razor, which defined winning in terms of brand image and shaving quality. This disruption of the competitive environment by Gillette continued with the introduction of Sensor Excel and Mach3 razors. Gillette has successfully changed the rules of the game, which in turn has changed the competitive environment. The new competitive environment is characterized by periods of stability punctuated by disruptions. Gillette deliberately disrupts the market with a new product offering (e.g. its Fusion razor) and consolidates its gains around the new standard. In the same way Sony's PlayStation 3 (PS3) is trying to redefine the games console market by making its console the main home entertainment system (see Strategy Focus: Disrupting the Competition—Sony's PlayStation 3). The lesson to be acquired in these hypercompetitive markets is that strategic paradigms which work well in one environment may not operate at all in another.

STRATEGY FOCUS

Disrupting the Competition— Sony's PlayStation 3

In truth, the PS3 is more than just a games console: it's Sony's attempt to make its unit the central home-entertainment system. The PS3 contains a 60GB hard disc capable of storing music, movies, games, and photos, and it can be hooked up to the internet for online play and community and chat features, allowing users to download games, movie trailers, and multimedia content from the PlayStation 3 Network. But the *pièce de résistance* has to be the high-definition Blu-ray DVD player that drives the console, and the PS3's ability to output games and films in true high-definition to HD-ready televisions and monitors.

The results are spectacular: even on a normal television set or computer screen, the graphics are crisp and richly rendered, but in high-definition they are stunning ... Incorporating a Blu-ray player within the PS3 could prove a masterstroke or a howler. With the next-generation DVD format war still unresolved (Blu-ray is competing with the Microsoft-backed HD DVD format), Sony clearly hopes that the popularity and pervasiveness of its new console will mean that Blu-ray becomes the *de facto* high-definition format.

The delay in launching the PlayStation 3 to the European market (largely because of problems with mass-producing some elements of the Blu-ray disc drives) means Sony faces some unexpectedly stiff competition from several already well-established consoles: Microsoft's Xbox 360, released at the end of 2005, is widely considered to be the most complete gaming platform available ... Nintendo's Wii console ... was a huge hit, and has already sold more than 4.5 million units worldwide thanks to its motion-sensitive controller and innovative gameplay.

While the price-tag of the PS3 will put off some casual gamers, it's unlikely to deter dedicated Sony fans. There has also been some confusion over the level to which European units will be backwards-compatible with PlayStation 1 and PlayStation 2 games, but Sony says that more than 1700 PS2 titles will work happily

Market turbulence can occur within an industry as a result of competence-enhancing or competence-destroying disruptions. Competence-destroying disruptions can occur through events such as changes in customers' tastes, technological substitution, or obsolescence of a competence. They may destroy the competencies of the industry leader by changing the industry's critical success factors; these are the factors in an industry necessary for an organization to gain competitive advantage. (See **Chapter 8** for a greater explanation of critical success factors.) In contrast, competence-enhancing disruptions have the effect of making the leader's competencies more valuable. Competence disruptions can occur infrequently or constantly, which results in different patterns of turbulence within an industry. They result in four different competitive environments: *equilibrium*, *fluctuating equilibrium*, *punctuated equilibrium*, and *disequilibrium* (D'Aveni 1999, p. 131). These are illustrated in Figure 7.4.

- **Equilibrium.** This environment is characterized by long periods of little or no competence-destroying turbulence. Incumbent leaders exercise control through barriers to entry. A challenger must make these barriers to entry irrelevant.

- **Fluctuating equilibrium.** The environment is characterized by rapid turbulence based on frequent competence-enhancing disruptions. Challengers try to destroy the underlying core competencies of the leader and move the environment to punctuated equilibrium or disequilibrium.

- **Punctuated equilibrium.** This is characterized by brief dynamic periods based on discontinuous change or competence-destroying revolutions. This is particularly so in industries which experience fast technological change followed by a dominant standard. The leader has to decide when and how to respond to the next revolution. The challenger seeks to disrupt the stability sought by the leader.

- **Disequilibrium.** This is the most challenging of the hypercompetitive environments, characterized by frequent and discontinuous disruptions. The leaders will constantly be creating new competencies, and deliberately disrupting themselves before their rivals do. Examples include Microsoft's continuous introduction of new software which intentionally cannibalizes their existing product. The challengers have to try to disrupt this environment in ways that cannot easily be matched or change the environment to become less disruptive.

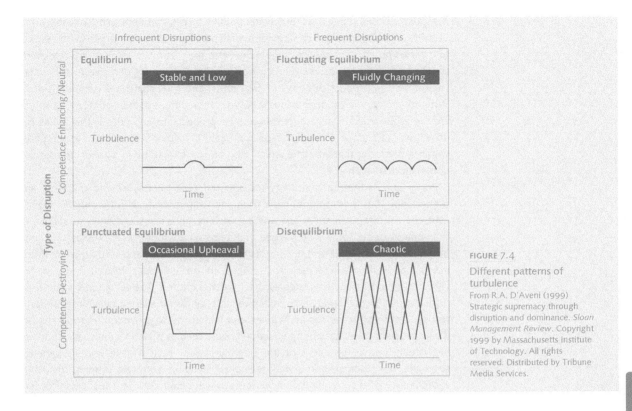

FIGURE 7.4

Different patterns of
turbulence
From R.A. D'Aveni (1999)
Strategic supremacy through
disruption and dominance. *Sloan
Management Review*. Copyright
1999 by Massachusetts Institute
of Technology. All rights
reserved. Distributed by Tribune
Media Services.

D'Aveni argues that the aim of industry leaders and challengers in each environment
is to achieve strategic supremacy by trying to control the degree and pattern of turbulence. As he states: 'By understanding the pattern of turbulence in the current
competitive environment, managers can develop better strategies that lead to and
maintain strategic supremacy' (D'Aveni 1999, p. 135).

Summary

Whereas corporate strategy asks *what* markets we should compete in, business strategy is concerned with *how* an organization is going to compete in its chosen industry
or market. Business-level strategy deals with individual business units which operate
within an industry or distinct market segments. The aim of business strategy is to
achieve a sustainable competitive advantage. In this chapter we evaluated Porter's
generic competitive strategies of overall cost leadership, differentiation, and focus.
We noted that each strategy provides the means for an organization to occupy a

defendable position against the five competitive forces that determine industry profitability. When pursuing a strategy of overall cost leadership, the organization seeks to offer its products or services at a lower price than its rivals. With a differentiated strategy the organization delivers a product which consumers perceive to be better value than the product offerings of rival firms, and thus charges a premium price. Whether the organization pursues a low-cost or differentiation strategy, it must choose which market segments it wants its products to compete within. That is, does it want to adopt a broadly based approach? Or would it be content to compete within a particular market niche which may be overlooked by rivals seeking to gain dominant market share?

Porter argues that each strategy requires different capabilities and therefore an organization that tries to adopt more than one strategy is *stuck in the middle*. However, there is disagreement about whether organizations can successfully adopt more than one strategy. Some would argue that a combination of low-cost leadership and differentiation, a hybrid strategy, is possible and point to the success of Japanese auto manufacturer Toyota. The generic strategies are not without risks and these, along with criticisms of generic strategies, have been explored. The resource-based view (RBV) suggests an alternative approach to strategy formulation in which the primary focus is upon the resources and capabilities within the organization. Proponents of this approach argue that an organization should seek to match its internal resources and capabilities to the needs of the external environment. Unlike Porter's generic strategies, the resource-based view sees profit deriving from two sources: first, the sustainability of the competitive advantage which resources and capabilities confer and, second, the ability of the firm to appropriate the profits (or rents) earned from its resources and capabilities.

The industry life cycle suggests that industries go through four stages of development: *introduction*, *growth*, *maturity*, and *decline*. We noted that the different stages of the industry life cycle will have an impact upon the competitive conditions facing the organization. Also, within an industry different strategic groups may be experiencing different stages of the life cycle. The life cycle is frequently applied to product markets where a *product life cycle* can be discerned which follows the same stages as the industry life cycle. The industry life cycle is the supply-side equivalent of the product life cycle.

Finally, we discussed the role of competitive strategies within turbulent and hyper-competitive markets. By better understanding the interaction between strategy and the environment managers can better tailor their strategies to the environment, or attempt to change the environment to their benefit. We noted that market turbulence can occur within an industry as a result of competence-enhancing or competence-destroying disruptions. Competence disruptions result in four different competitive environments: *equilibrium*, *fluctuating equilibrium*, *punctuated equilibrium*, and *disequilibrium*. We ended the chapter by reiterating that the aim of leaders and challengers in each competitive environment is to achieve strategic supremacy by trying to control the degree and pattern of turbulence.

Review Questions

1. Comment on Porter's assertion that an organization trying to pursue more than one generic strategy will end up *stuck in the middle.*

2. How can an understanding of the different stages of the industry life cycle help an organization formulate a coherent business strategy?

Discussion Question

Product life cycles are now so short as to be all but irrelevant for organizations when assessing their product offering and that of their competitors. Discuss.

Research Topic

Identify the many incarnations Microsoft Windows software has gone through and state the extent to which each incarnation is competence enhancing or competence destroying. How successful have competitors been in rewriting the rules of the game set by Microsoft?

Recommended Reading

For a discussion of generic strategies see:

- Porter, M.E. (1980). *Competitive Strategy: Techniques for Analysing Industries and Competitors*. Free Press, New York.

For a discussion of the importance of resources and capabilities for achieving sustainable competitive advantage see:

- Grant, R.M. (1991). The resource-based theory of competitive advantage: implications for strategy formulation. *California Management Review*, **33**(Spring), 114–35.

For an understanding of the transitory nature of competitive advantage see:

- Christensen, C.M. (2001). The past and future of competitive advantage. *Sloan Management Review*, **42**(2), 105–9.

For an insight into the need for organizations to formulate strategies that can change the rules of the game, based upon an understanding of turbulent markets, see:

- D'Aveni, R.A. (1991). Strategic supremacy through disruption and dominance. *Sloan Management Review*, **40**(3), 127–35.

online resource centre

www.oxfordtextbooks.co.uk/orc/henry2e/
Visit the Online Resource Centre that accompanies this book for activities and more information on business level strategy.

Note

1 The discussion of markets, industries, and strategic groups draws heavily upon Kay (1993).

References

Barney, J. (1986). Organizational culture: can it be a source of sustained competitive advantage? *Academy of Management Review*, **11**(3), 656–65.

Barney, J. (1995). Looking inside for competitive advantage. *Academy of Management Executive*, **9**(4), 49–61.

Campbell-Hunt, C. (2000). What have we learned about generic strategy? A meta-analysis. *Strategic Management Journal*, **21**(2), 127–54.

Christensen, C.M. (2001). The past and future of competitive advantage. *Sloan Management Review*, **42**(2), 105–9.

D'Aveni, R.A. (1999). Strategic supremacy through disruption and dominance. *Sloan Management Review*, **40**(3), 127–35.

Grant, R.M. (1991). The resource-based theory of competitive advantage: implications for strategy formulation. *California Management Review*, **33**(Spring), 114–35

Grant, R.M. (2005). *Contemporary Strategy Analysis*, 5th edn. Blackwell, Boston, MA.

Hamel, G. and **Prahalad, C.K.** (1993). Strategy as stretch and leverage. *Harvard Business Review*, **71**(2), 75–84.

Henderson, R. and **Cockburn, I.** (1994). Measuring competence? Exploring firm effects in pharmaceutical research. *Strategic Management Journal*, **15**(Special Issue), 63–84.

Hill, C.W.L. (1988). Differentiation versus low cost or differentiation and low cost. *Academy of Management Review*, **13**(3), 401–12.

Kay, J. (1993). *Foundations of Corporate Strategy*. Oxford University Press, Oxford.

Kim, W.C. and **Mauborgne, R.** (2005). *Blue Ocean Strategy*. Harvard Business Press, Boston, MA.

Kumar, N. (2006). Strategies to fight low-cost rivals. *Harvard Business Review*, **84**(12), 104–12.

Lieberman, M.B. and **Montgomery, D.G.** (1988). First mover advantages. *Strategic Management Journal*, **9**(5), 41–58.

McGahan, A. (2000). How industries evolve. *Business Strategy Review*, **11**(3), 1–16.

Mintzberg, H. (1996). Learning 1, Planning 0. *California Management Review*, **38**(4), 92–3.

Mintzberg, H. and **Waters, J.A.** (1985). Of strategies, deliberate and emergent. *Strategic Management Journal*, **6**(3), 257–72.

Nelson, R.R. and **Winter, S.G.** (1982). *An Evolutionary Theory of Economic Change*. Harvard University Press, Boston, MA.

Porter, M.E. (1980). *Competitive Strategy: Techniques for Analysing Industries and Competitors*. Free Press, New York.

Porter, M.E. (1985). *Competitive Advantage*. Free Press, New York.

Porter, M.E. (1991). Towards a dynamic theory of strategy. *Strategic Management Journal*, **12**(Special Issue), 95–117.

Porter, M.E. (1999). What is strategy? *Harvard Business Review*, **74**(6), 61–78.

Prahalad, C. and **Hamel, G.** (1990). The core competence of the organization. *Harvard Business Review*, **36**(3), 79–91.

Quinn, J.B. (1978). *Strategies for Change: Logical Incrementalism*. Irwin, New York.

Shapiro, C. and **Varian, H.R.** (1999). Standard wars. *California Management Review*, **41**(2), 8–32.

8 Corporate-Level Strategy

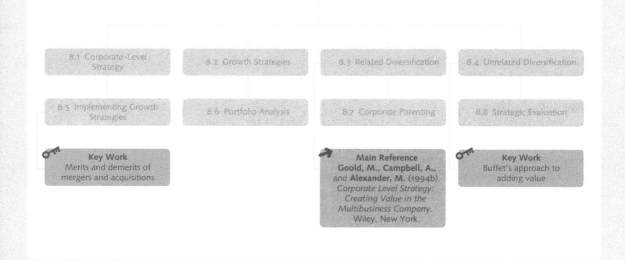

| 8.1 Corporate-Level Strategy | 8.2 Growth Strategies | 8.3 Related Diversification | 8.4 Unrelated Diversification |
| 8.5 Implementing Growth Strategies | 8.6 Portfolio Analysis | 8.7 Corporate Parenting | 8.8 Strategic Evaluation |

Key Work
Merits and demerits of mergers and acquisitions

Main Reference
Goold, M., Campbell, A., and Alexander, M. (1994b). *Corporate Level Strategy: Creating Value in the Multibusiness Company.* Wiley, New York.

Key Work
Buffet's approach to adding value

Learning Objectives

After completing this chapter you should be able to:

- Explain what is meant by corporate strategy
- Assess the effectiveness of different growth strategies
- Evaluate related and unrelated diversification strategies
- Assess the impact of portfolio analysis
- Explain the role of corporate parenting in creating value
- Discuss strategy evaluation

Introduction

In **Chapter 7** we looked at business-level strategy and how an organization competes in its chosen markets. In this chapter we turn our attention to corporate strategy. Corporate strategy is concerned with the question: what businesses do we want to compete in? Where an organization is made up of multiple business units, a question arises as to how resources are to be allocated across these businesses. How an organization determines which businesses to invest in and which to divest will be covered in this chapter. Clearly, the overall objectives of the organization will be paramount in guiding these decisions. These objectives and, therefore, the overall direction for the organization are determined by the corporate parent.

The role of a corporate parent is to add value across the business units. A measurement of the value being added by the corporate parent is whether it is greater than if the business units were managed independently of the organization. Where a corporate parent adds greater value, the organization is said to achieve synergy. In formulating a corporate strategy, executives must be mindful of the organization's internal resources and capabilities and how these meet the changing needs of the external environment. The impact of corporate strategy on stakeholders, such as major shareholders or trade unions, who possess sufficient power and influence to undermine the strategy, must also be considered. For example, in 2006 the Volkswagen Group's attempts to restructure were met by opposition from powerful trade unions resisting attempts to curb their members' wages. Senior executives argued that if the group were to compete successfully in the world automobile market it must tackle the disproportionately high wages of German auto workers.

- In Section 8.1 we start the chapter with a discussion of corporate-level strategy. We define corporate strategy and briefly discuss the role of the corporate parent in adding value to the organization.

- Section 8.2 includes a discussion of the role of growth strategies. These strategies include the choice of market penetration, product development, market development, and diversification.

- In Section 8.3 we address related diversification in greater detail and discuss vertical and horizontal integration. We consider the role of transaction-cost analysis to assess whether organizations should produce goods internally or purchase them on the open market.

- Section 8.4 evaluates unrelated diversification. We consider some of the research evidence surrounding the performance of the parent company as a result of unrelated diversification. We briefly discuss the performance of successful organizations involved in diverse business activities.

- In Section 8.5 we look at some of the different ways in which growth strategies can be achieved. This includes internal developments, mergers and acquisitions, joint ventures, and strategic alliances.

- Section 8.6 deals with portfolio analysis. We evaluate the Boston Consulting Group portfolio matrix and the General Electric screen matrix. We show how an understanding of portfolio analysis may help an organization to allocate resources more efficiently across business units.

- Section 8.7 deals with an assessment of the effectiveness of corporate parenting strategies. We look at instances in which a corporate parent may add value and where value can be destroyed.

- The chapter ends in Section 8.8 with a discussion of the different criteria that can be used to evaluate an organization's strategy.

8.1 Corporate-Level Strategy

We noted in previous chapters that all organizations exist for a purpose. Once the purpose of the organization is determined, for instance to maximize shareholder value, the role of corporate strategy is to enable the organization to fulfil that purpose. Therefore, corporate strategy defines the scope of the industries and markets within which the organization competes in order to achieve its organizational purpose. The role of the business unit is to devise a strategy that allows it to compete successfully in the marketplace and to contribute to the corporate strategy. The managers of a business unit may have considerable autonomy to devise their business-level strategy. This reflects their knowledge of local markets, customers, and competitors. However, business unit managers must ultimately show that their business strategy contributes to the corporate strategy.

The corporate strategy sets the direction in which the organization will go. Even where the organization simply comprises a single business with only one or a few products, corporate strategy is relevant. The organization must still consider the fundamental question of why it exists. And once the why (purpose) is answered, a corporate strategy can be formulated that enables an organization to achieve its purpose. Where an organization is made up of many businesses operating in different markets, corporate-level strategy is also concerned with how resources are to be allocated across the business units. Clearly the objectives of the organization will be paramount in guiding these decisions. These objectives and the overall direction of the organization are determined by the corporate parent. We noted in **Chapter 7** that to state corporate strategy as *what business(es) do we want to be in* can tend to oversimplify the issue since it combines three distinct concepts: the market, industry, and strategy group.

A question at the forefront of corporate strategy is how an organization adds value across the businesses that make up the organization. This is the role of corporate parenting. A corporate parent exists where an organization is made up of multiple business units. It refers to all those levels of management that are not part of customer-facing and profit-run businesses within the multi-business organization. Corporate parents are often described as corporate headquarters and derided as simply *cost centres*. This is because a corporate parent has no external customers and as such it cannot generate any direct revenues. Given that it incurs corporate overhead costs, the corporate parent must demonstrate that these costs are offset by the tangible benefits it provides to the business units in the portfolio. The question then becomes one of what the corporate parent is doing that allows these businesses to perform better collectively than they would as stand-alone units (Goold *et al.* 1994a).

CORPORATE PARENTING

is concerned with how a parent company adds value across the businesses that make up the organization

CORPORATE PARENT

refers to all those levels of management that are not part of customer-facing and profit-run business units in multi-business companies

Corporate parenting is of benefit if the corporate parent adds greater value by its management and coordination of these individual business units. The idea is that by effectively managing the related capabilities in each business unit, as well as leveraging its own management skills across these business units, a corporate parent may achieve synergy. Synergy occurs when the total output from combining businesses is greater than the output of the businesses operating individually. It is often described mathematically as $2 + 2 = 5$. For example, it can derive from economies of scale such as occur when two business units decide to combine their manufacturing facilities, which results in lower costs. Therefore, the value of the combined businesses is greater than the value that can be derived from two separate businesses.

SYNERGY

occurs when the total output from combining businesses is greater than the output of the businesses operating individually. It is often described mathematically as $2 + 2 = 5$

8.2 Growth Strategies

In order to grow organizations can pursue a number of different strategies depending on the level of risk they are prepared to countenance, their resources and capabilities, and their management expertise. The organization might choose to direct its energies to internal growth strategies or it may seek to diversify into other businesses. Ansoff (1965) devised a matrix to analyse the different strategic directions organizations can pursue.[1] There are four strategies that an organization might follow: *market penetration*, *product development*, *market development*, and *diversification*. These options are summarized below and shown in Figure 8.1:

- **Market penetration**: increase market share in your existing markets using your existing products.
- **Market development**: entering new markets with your existing products.
- **Product development**: developing new products to sell in your existing markets.
- **Diversification**: developing new products to serve new markets.

The first three strategies are particularly relevant to organizations that operate within the boundaries of an individual business. However, an organization that seeks to broaden its scope of activities will be concerned with how it can best diversify into

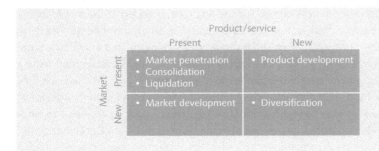

FIGURE 8.1

Ansoff's growth vector matrix
Adapted with permission from H.I. Ansoff (1965). *Corporate Strategy*, McGraw-Hill. The Ansoff Matrix was developed later.[1]

different businesses. This issue of the multi-business organization will be addressed in detail when we look at diversification.

8.2.1 Market Penetration

An organization pursuing a strategy of market penetration seeks to increase the market share in its existing markets by utilizing its existing products. Its aim is to attract new consumers, and to get existing consumers to increase their usage of the product or service. This strategy relies upon the organization's existing resources and capabilities and, therefore, is relatively low risk. To achieve market penetration the organization will usually improve its product quality and levels of service, backed by promotional spend. Its knowledge of both products and the marketplace should enable it to respond more readily to changing consumer needs. In an attempt to increase market share, the UK telecommunications provider, BT, offers a higher-speed broadband connection to telephone subscribers and free weekend calls to anywhere in the UK. Where the market is growing, market penetration is relatively simple to achieve. However, in a mature market, a strategy of market penetration implies taking market share from your competitor which will invite retaliation. If demand conditions are insufficient to permit market penetration, the organization must decide whether it can still retain its existing market share, or whether it would be wiser to exit the industry. This strategy is shown in the first quadrant of Figure 8.1.

8.2.2 Product Development

This strategy involves developing new products for your existing markets. The ability to innovate is crucial in developing products for rapidly changing consumer markets. As we saw in **Chapter 7**, rapid innovation is often a function of hypercompetitive markets. A strategy of product development is necessary where organizations are faced with shorter product life cycles. In industries such as consumer electronics and computer software, organizations are forced to continually develop new products to maintain and grow their market share, and keep competitors on the defensive. The phenomenal growth of Apple's iPod and iPhone is testimony to the rewards that successful product development brings. For the first quarter ended 31 December 2005, Apple reported what was at that time the highest quarterly revenue and earnings in the company's history. It produced revenues of $5.75 billion and a quarterly profit of $565 million. It sold a colossal 14 million iPods during this quarter, representing a 207 per cent growth over the same period in the previous year. At the same time the very success of this product carries with it the seeds of its potential downfall. Competitors will already be seeking to imitate its success, which forces Apple to innovate and develop product improvements. In the quarter ended 26 December 2009, Apple's financial results continued to reflect its distinctive capability of product innovation. The company posted revenue of $15.68 billion and a net quarterly profit of $3.38 billion, compared with revenue of $11.88 billion and net quarterly profit of $2.26 billion in the same quarter a year ago. In the same quarter Apple sold 3.36 million Macintosh computers, representing a 33 per cent increase over the same period a year ago; 8.7 million iPhones, representing 100 per cent growth over a year ago; and 21 million iPods, representing an 8 per cent decline from the year-ago quarter (www.apple.com). New product development can be expensive and carries a greater risk of failure. There is no guarantee that consumers will adopt the product. However, an organization that actively monitors consumers' requirements is better placed to match their products to consumers' needs, or as in Apple's case, develop products that create consumer need.

8.2.3 Market Development

Market development involves entering new markets with the firm's existing products. This may be done by targeting new market segments and new geographical areas, or by devising new uses for its products. The existing product may undergo some slight modification to ensure that it fits these new markets better. This is often the case where certain social and cultural adjustments are made to ensure that the product more closely meets the needs of particular geographical market segments. Many retailing organizations follow this route to growth. For example, the US giant Wal-Mart, French retailer Carrefour, and UK retailer Tesco have all sought to enter new geographical markets with only marginal changes to their product offerings. As with the previous strategies, market development builds upon an organization's existing resources and capabilities. Although the organization will have extensive knowledge of its product, its experience of the markets will be less complete, thus increasing the level of risk.

MARKET DEVELOPMENT

entering new markets with your existing products

∞

8.2.4 Diversification

The fourth quadrant in the growth vector matrix is diversification. Here we are dealing with an organization that seeks to broaden its scope of activities by moving away from its current products and markets and into new products and new markets. Although this will involve the greatest level of risk it may be necessary where an organization's existing products and markets offer little opportunity for growth. However, this risk can be mitigated by the organization diversifying into related businesses, that is, businesses which have some links with its existing value chain. In addition, broadening the scope of the organization can help to spread risk by reducing the reliance on any one market or product. When the scope of an organization takes it into unrelated markets, there may still be a sound business logic for the decision. This is particularly true where a business is cyclical in nature. By diversifying into

DIVERSIFICATION

occurs when an organization seeks to broaden its scope of activities by moving into new products and new markets another business it may be possible to smooth these cycles so that a peak period in one market coincides with a downturn in another market. This issue of the multi-business organization will be addressed in the next section when we discuss related and unrelated diversification.

8.3 Related Diversification

Related diversification refers to entry into a related industry in which there is still some link with the organization's value chain. Where an organization occupies a competitive advantage in an industry that is becoming increasingly unattractive, it may wish to diversify into a related industry. The aim is to choose an industry in which it retains a close match with the resources and capabilities which provide it with competitive advantage in its current industry, and thereby generate synergy. For example, Honda possesses distinctive capabilities in engine design and technologies. This capability allows Honda to leverage its core competence in engine design and production across cars, power boats, and lawn mowers. Related diversification can be separated into vertical integration and horizontal integration. Vertical integration occurs when an organization goes *upstream*, that is, it moves towards its inputs, or *downstream*, that is, it moves closer to its ultimate consumer. The more control the organization has over the different stages of its value chain, the more vertically integrated it is. Horizontal integration takes place when an organization takes over a competitor or offers complementary products at the same stage within the value chain. We can look at each of these in greater detail.

8.3.1 Vertical Integration

We can differentiate between two kinds of vertical integration. *Vertical integration backwards* occurs when an organization moves upstream towards its inputs. An organization may desire to have greater control over the inputs or raw materials that go to make up its products. For example, the British supermarket retailer Morrisons grows many of its own vegetables and is Britain's biggest abattoir owner. Vertical integration allows it to be more nimble in delivering promotions on fresh food which it believes may be a source of competitive advantage. Where the costs of inputs to its productive processes fluctuate, an organization may decide that it is in its best interest to own these inputs. Similarly, an organization may feel it necessary to have control over the quality of its inputs or may want to gain access to new technologies. Clearly, an organization must ask itself if the value it derives from owning an asset is greater than the value to be derived from outsourcing its use. In some instances, the input will simply be too important to the organization for it to allow it to be outsourced, whatever the benefits might be.

Vertical integration forwards occurs when an organization moves downstream towards its end consumers. In such a case an organization might acquire transport and warehousing to ensure its control over the channels of distribution to the consumer. It may acquire retail outlets to ensure that it chooses where, when, how, and at what price its products are sold. Whether the organization adopts vertical integration forwards or backwards, the end result is the same: it moves along its value chain and at secures greater control over its value-chain activities. A good example of vertically integrated companies occurs in the oil industry. Companies such as ExxonMobil, Shell, and BP often adopt a vertically integrated structure allowing them to operate along the supply chain from crude oil exploration all the way through to refined product sale. The downside of vertical integration is that the organization becomes increasingly dependent on a particular market and may be unable to respond quickly to market changes.

8.3.2 Horizontal Integration

Horizontal integration occurs when an organization takes over a competitor or offers complementary products at the same stage within its value chain. HSBC was able to acquire market share in the UK when it took over Midland Bank. easyJet took over the budget airline Go! from British Airways and was quick to re-badge all of Go!'s planes with easyJet's own distinctive brand. The rationale for horizontal integration is usually one of efficiency savings through economies of scale. By combining two separate organizations it is argued that economies of scale can be achieved far faster than through organic or internal growth.

8.3.3 Transaction-Cost Analysis

To understand transaction-cost analysis it is helpful to appreciate why organizations exist. Organizations exist because they are capable of undertaking transactions more efficiently than individuals can in the marketplace. All transactions undertaken between individuals, between firms, or between individuals and firms involve transaction costs. These transaction costs include the *search costs* involved in making a purchase, such as the time involved in collecting information about the quality or price of a product, the costs involved in *negotiating* and drawing up a contract which tries to cover as many eventualities as possible, and the costs of *monitoring* the other party to ensure their legal obligations are fulfilled. In the event of the agreement being reneged upon, there is the cost of *enforcement* through the courts.

According to Williamson (1975), transaction-cost analysis implies that organizations should produce goods and services internally where the transaction costs of doing so is less than purchasing these on the open market. Therefore, transaction-cost analysis provides a rationale for firms to assess whether to integrate vertically. For instance, when organizations integrate vertically and operate at different points along their value chain, there may be a tendency for them to be become too large and overly bureaucratic. Where the administrative costs of managing their internal transactions are greater than the transaction costs occurring within the market, outsourcing these activities to a third-party specialist is a more efficient option. Where this is the case, the imposition of contracts ensures that third-party producers supply products and services at an acceptable quality and price. Where transaction costs are much greater than administrative costs, the organization may choose vertical integration. As we saw briefly in **Chapter 5**, many organizations have actively sought to outsource those activities in which they add less value. The benefit is one of efficiency gains achieved through outsourcing to a specialist provider and flexibility in being able to respond more readily to market changes.

8.4 Unrelated Diversification

UNRELATED DIVERSIFICATION

refers to a situation where an organization moves into a totally unrelated industry

Unrelated diversification refers to a situation where an organization moves into a totally unrelated industry. It is sometimes called *conglomerate* diversification to reflect that it involves managing a portfolio of companies. The lack of any link between existing markets and products and the diversified industry carries the greatest element of uncertainty and, therefore, risk. It may be that the organization's management skills are sufficiently robust to provide it with a core competence that can be leveraged across different business units. This was certainly the case with the British conglomerate Hanson which experienced success in the 1980s. As with all strategic decisions, the rationale for diversification needs to be clearly thought out. Management complacency or poorly prepared analysis will simply multiply the likelihood of failure.

A common reason for diversification is where an organization's existing markets are saturated or declining. In such a case the organization will seek growth opportunities elsewhere. These opportunities may also more closely reflect the organization's development of its own resources and capabilities. Another reason for conglomerate diversification might be that regulatory authorities view vertical and horizontal integration by the organization as uncompetitive. A third reason for diversification is that management may believe that by not having all their eggs in one basket (focusing on one market or product range) they can diversify their risk. If an organization operates across many different businesses, the failure of one business as a result of adverse economic cycles will not cause the company to collapse.

Where the skills required to run a business are common to each business, an organization may leverage its management skills across different businesses. This might include production, marketing, R&D, and financial skills. This is often the case in turnaround (or failing company) situations where an organization's management might possess excellent financial skills. These management skills can then be transferred to poorly performing acquired companies. The idea is to put in place stringent financial controls that allow a business to be turned around, that is, returned to a profit-making position. In the short term the effect of these targets is often to improve cash flow and shore up losses. Diversified organizations such as Hanson were particularly adept at turning around poorly performing businesses and selling them on at a substantial profit.

In the 1990s organizations listened to the mantra of 'stick to the knitting' (Peters and Waterman 1982) as they began to de-layer, downsize, and divest themselves of all non-core business activities.

Porter's (1987) study of the activities of large prestigious US firms between 1950 and 1986 found that the majority of them had divested more acquisitions than they had retained. Porter suggests that the reason for some acquisitions is more the result of chief executives' ego than the existence of a market opportunity. Markides (1995) found that an organization's decision to focus upon its core business is the most useful form of restructuring. Other research (Daley *et al*. 1997) points to the increase in the share price of parent organizations that sell off unrelated activities. This adds weight to suggestions that unrelated diversification may be more in the interest of managers as agents rather than shareholders as principals. Hence the stock market rewards organizations that divest themselves of unrelated diversification with a rise in share price, signalling that this strategy is viewed as more appropriate for adding value.

Diversification may have become less popular but there still remain stellar examples of successfully diversified firms. The US giant GE (General Electric) operates in more than 100 countries and employs around 300,000 people worldwide. Under the leadership of chief executive Jack Welsh, GE transformed itself throughout the 1980s and 1990s from a maker of electrical appliances to a giant conglomerate. It continues to operate a series of diverse companies from power generation to financial services. (See Strategy Focus: A Question of Diversification for a discussion of organisations that continue to follow a diversification strategy.)

STRATEGY FOCUS
A Question of Diversification

In engaging in conglomerate diversification, business leaders adopted the rationale that there exists a number of companies which are poorly managed and underperforming. The aim then is to subsume these companies within the conglomerate with a view to restructuring them to release value. In the UK, Hanson Trust and BTR were industry giants that dominated the conglomerate game. In the 1980s Hanson regularly outperformed the FTSE 100 with its ever-growing revenues and profit. BTR was seen as one of the best managed companies into the 1990s. However by the mid 1990s market sentiment had moved against these conglomerates as the environment in which both firms competed had begun to change beyond their theory of the business. Undoubtedly leadership succession also played a role as the calibres of the original leaders were difficult to replicate.

Today diversified conglomerates still exist such as GE and Berkshire Hathaway in the USA. In India, the Tata Group has wide-ranging interests which include engineering, chemicals, consumer products, information technology and communications, and energy, among others. As part of its desire to become a global group it has acquired high-profile British companies such as Corus, the steel maker, and Jaguar and Land Rover, as well as Daewoo Commercial Vehicles in South Korea. The French company, PPR, tends to acquire related organizations specializing as it does in retail shops and luxury brands including the Gucci group. The Gucci Group itself owns such luxury brands as Gucci, Balenciaga, Yves Saint Laurent, and Sergio Rossi.

Where a company is poorly managed and underperforming, restructuring it using cost controls and customer-focused measures to release value may be relatively straightforward. However as we will see later in this chapter a question that needs to be addressed is: Can a parent company release more value from its acquisitions (related or unrelated) than can be released by a rival organization? Or, to adopt a resource-based view, can an acquirer deploy its distinctive capabilities effectively in an acquired business to release value? The value created by an acquisition must outweigh the cost of the acquisition. Where a substantial bid premium has been paid this becomes more difficult to achieve.

We might note that diversification is often rationalized by managers in terms of risk reduction. Yet if shareholders require a diversified portfolio of shares they can achieve this far more cheaply than an organization because the cost of buying shares in a company is cheaper than buying the company which inevitably attracts a bid premium. This is the reason many commentators argue that diversification is often in the interests of the managers of diversifying companies, and not their shareholders.

To diversify or not to diversify?

© iStockphoto.com/James Goldsworthy

Warren Buffet, the investor and second-richest man in the world (at the time of writing), is chairman of Berkshire Hathaway which he runs with his business partner, Charlie Munger. This is an investment firm which includes diverse interests in insurance, soft drinks, confectionery, furniture, restaurants, carpets, and plane rentals. His strategy appears to have little to do with exploiting synergies across these businesses.

Between 1965 and 2009 Berkshire experienced an average annual return of 20.3 per cent against 9.3 per cent for the S&P 500 index.[2] During the Internet boom of the 1990s, when fund managers talked of the new economy and a new investment paradigm, Buffet wisely sat out the fleeting dot.com era preferring instead to stick to his *old* economy portfolio. This became one more reason for his richly deserved accolade, the Sage of Omaha. In 2004, Berkshire increased its per-share book value (which it prefers to earnings per share as a measure of performance) by 10.5 per cent; the S&P 500 index rose by 10.9 per cent, with dividends included. In 2003, Berkshire also failed to match the S&P 500, increasing per-share book value by 21 per cent against the S&P's 28.7 per cent.[3] In 2009 Berkshire produced returns of 19.8 against the S&P's 26.5 per cent. Over time, however, the company has comfortably beaten the S&P 500 index.

Goold and Luchs (1993) point out that an assumption that the pursuit of synergy is the only rationale for a group of companies tends to contradict the available evidence. This suggests that not all corporations should focus their management effort on acquiring and managing portfolios of interrelated businesses. They argue that the ultimate test of diversification is that the businesses in the portfolio are worth more under the management of the corporate parent than they would be under any other rival organization. These ideas will be developed in detail when we discuss corporate parenting in Section 8.7. Where conglomerates exist with a sound rationale and clear vision, synergies can be achieved. An organization needs to be able to leverage its resources, capabilities, and core competence in order to achieve sustainable competitive advantage. A body of research exists that shows that unrelated diversification tends not to be as successful as related diversification (Singh and Montgomery 1987; Markides and Williamson 1994). Nonetheless, this issue is not clear cut as Goold and Luchs (1993, p. 15) point out, 'despite extensive research, empirical evidence on the performance of companies pursuing more and less related diversification strategies is ambiguous and contradictory'.

The examples of GE and Berkshire Hathaway show that a carefully managed conglomerate can produce a sound growth strategy.

For a discussion of Warren Buffet's approach to adding value go to the Online Resource Centre and see the Key Work feature.
www.oxfordtextbooks.co.uk/orc/henry2e/

8.5 Implementing Growth Strategies

We have seen that in pursuing a strategy of growth the organization is faced with either concentrating upon its existing industry or diversifying into new industries. We can now turn our attention to looking at how these different corporate strategies can be implemented. This includes *mergers and acquisitions*, *internal developments*, *joint ventures*, and *strategic alliances*.

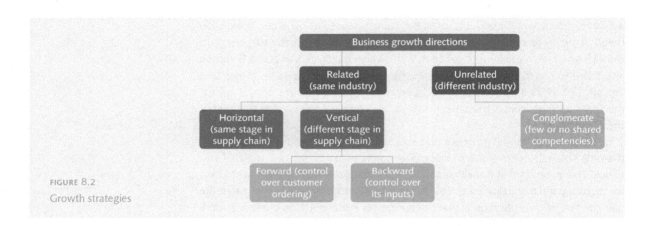

FIGURE 8.2
Growth strategies

8.5.1 Mergers and Acquisitions

MERGER

occurs when two organizations
join together to share their
combined resources

A merger occurs when two organizations join together to share their combined resources. A merger implies that both organizations accept the logic of combining into a single organization and willingly agree to do so. Shareholders from each organization become shareholders in the new combined organization. Mergers include the pharmaceutical giant GlaxoSmithKline which resulted from the merger of Glaxo Wellcome and SmithKline Beecham in 2000. In 2007 Reuters agreed to merge with its Canadian rival Thomson Corporation. As is the case with all mergers, a key topic of conversation was synergy, in this case an estimated £250 million ($500 million) in annual savings within three years. A driving force for the merger is a belief that consumers are prepared to pay for accurate and timely financial news and data provided by these organizations. In addition, there is believed to be a level of complementarity as each company has strengths in different geographical markets, and serve different clients.

ACQUISITION

occurs when one organization
seeks to acquire another, often
smaller, organization

An acquisition occurs when one organization seeks to acquire another, often smaller, organization. The acquisition may be in the interest of both organizations particularly where the acquiring company has substantial financial resources and the firm to be acquired possesses proprietary technology but needs funds to develop it further. The acquisition may be in the form of shares of the new organization and perhaps a cash payment. Where payment is only in the form of cash, the acquired shareholders will no longer be owners. Clearly, where the shareholders feel the price being paid for their shareholding represents fair value they will be more likely to concede ownership. However, where the acquisition is unwelcome and contested it is referred to as a *takeover*, specifically a *hostile takeover*. In a hostile takeover the board of directors of the takeover target is likely to say one of two things: first, that the offer being made undervalues the organization and, therefore, should be rejected; secondly, that the strategies being proposed by the takeover organization are incoherent and will not allow the true value embedded within the organization to be released.

An example of such a defence was put forward by National Westminster Bank in the midst of a hostile takeover by its smaller rival, the Royal Bank of Scotland (RBS); the defence failed. Despite the rhetoric of the chairman of Cadbury, Roger Carr, who argued that were Kraft to succeed in acquiring Cadbury, it 'would be absorbed into Kraft's low growth, conglomerate business model', this defence also failed. In its £11.6 billion ($18.9 billion) takeover battle for Cadbury the US food company Kraft was able to convince Cadbury's shareholders that it could release greater value for them than they were currently experiencing under their existing management. The disastrous takeover of Dutch bank ABN Amro by The Royal Bank of Scotland and two other European banks is a salutary lesson. The consortium—RBS, the Belgian-Dutch bank Fortis and Banco Santander of Spain—paid more than €71 billion for part of the Dutch lender—three times the book value. By the time that RBS, then led by its chief executive Sir Fred Goodwin, had secured the ABN Amro deal, the Dutch bank had sold on to Bank of America the asset which was most prized by RBS—its Chicago-based LaSalle unit. The price RBS paid for a lack of rigorous due diligence is the toxic assets it acquired with ABN and a second government bailout. The first rescue package saw HM Treasury take a 58 per cent stake in the bank. The Belgian-Dutch bank Fortis was nationalized by the Dutch government to avert a liquidity crisis.

An organization may seek to implement a mergers and acquisitions route to growth in order to enter new markets quickly and acquire resources and capabilities it does not currently possess. A key issue with acquiring another organization's assets is whether value is being created or destroyed. Many mergers and acquisitions which appear to exhibit sound business logic often fail miserably to live up to the pre-merger hype and expectations. A case in point was the merger of Germany's luxury carmaker Daimler Benz with US automobile maker Chrysler to form DaimlerChrysler in 1998. This was initially billed as a merger of equals. In fact, the merger with Chrysler cost Daimler Benz $36 billion (£18 billion) and an estimated $50 billion over the next ten years.[4] Chrysler was eventually sold to private equity group Cerberus in 2007 when Daimler's chief executive, Dieter Zetsche, conceded that the expected synergies between the organizations had been over-estimated, arguing that US consumers had not been prepared to pay more for German technology.[5]

When the objective of a merger and acquisition is to increase market share, one would expect the organization to engage in a strategy of horizontal integration. Where the organization is concerned about its inputs, for example, we might expect it to go upstream and engage in vertical integration. The benefits to be derived from mergers and acquisitions are speed, market entry, and rapid access to capabilities. The disadvantages of mergers and acquisitions include paying a premium price for the acquired company and thereby increasing your financial risk. Also, the problem of combining different cultures may not have been properly considered, such that any reorganization is slow to release value to shareholders. The legendary US investor Warren Buffett publicly derided Kraft's takeover of Cadbury as 'a bad deal' stating that Kraft's use of its shares in the Cadbury deal was 'very expensive currency'. Buffett, Kraft's largest shareholder with more than 9 per cent of shares, argued that the £1.3 billion (£798 million) of reorganization costs and $390 million of deal fees would mitigate any added value.

Porter (1987) suggests three criteria for increasing shareholder value in acquisitions:

1. **Attractiveness.** An organization should be capable of achieving above-average returns in the target firm's industry.

2. **Cost of entry.** This includes the capital sum paid for the acquisition, and costs such as the time it takes for management to integrate the organizations. The cost of entry should not be so expensive that it effectively prohibits the organization recouping its initial investment. This is all too often the case where management has paid a high premium for an acquisition.

3. **Competitive advantage or better-off.** The acquisition must present an opportunity for competitive advantage for the parent organization, or vice versa. An organization should only consider other businesses if substantial synergy can be achieved.

Kay (1993) argues that added value or synergy is *only* forthcoming when distinctive capabilities or strategic assets are exploited more effectively. In other words, a merger that results in the acquisition of distinctive capabilities that are already being exploited adds no value.

For more information on the merits and demerits of mergers and acquisitions go to the Online Resource Centre and see the Key Work feature. www.oxfordtextbooks.co.uk/orc/henry2e/

CASE STUDY 8.1
The Merger of British Airways and Iberia

Courtesy of British Airways

After the markets closed on Thursday night, the British Airways board marched into a meeting in its head office, close to Heathrow, for what would prove to be a defining moment for the airline.

Earlier in the day, the board of Iberia had met in Madrid to agree the terms of a deal with the British carrier, 16 months after the two sides had announced that they were in merger talks. BA chief executive Willie Walsh had previously suggested that corporate governance—the make-up of the board—had been a sticking point in the discussions. But the talks accelerated after a change in management at Iberia over the summer. Antonio Vázquez, who took over the Spanish carrier, sold tobacco firm Altadis to Britain's Imperial Tobacco in 2008 and has a reputation as a dealmaker.

It also seems likely that huge losses incurred by both airlines had sharpened the focus of the two companies on getting a deal done. After little more than an hour, the BA board emerged and the agreement was in place. An announcement was put out by 8.30pm that evening.

The two sides hope the deal will return the combined group to profitability, allowing them to slash costs and improve buying power on the likes of fuel and aircraft, generating savings of €400m (£357m) a year. It would also create potential for higher revenue by offering a far wider range of routes to passengers, combining

BA's strength across the Atlantic with Iberia's network across South America. 'Consolidation is happening in our industry and it is critical that BA starts participating in that,' Walsh said on Friday.

That is, if BA can sort out its pension deficit—thought to be about £2.6bn. Its schemes are subject to a valuation later this year, after which pension trustees and BA management will need to negotiate how much cash the airline needs to pump in to keep them afloat. Even then, the agreement will need rubber-stamping by the pensions regulator, which is not expected to make a ruling until next September, and the merger will not be completed until the issue is resolved. It has been a long courtship, and it will be a long engagement.

'It was a deal that was waiting to be done and that needed to be done,' said one source close to the agreement. 'Europe will ultimately be divided up into three or four full-service airlines and one or two low-cost carriers. Nine months ago, BA was talking about a merger with Qantas, a deal with Iberia and a transatlantic alliance with American. Qantas has fallen away . . . and Willie needed to pull off at least one of the others.'

By Walsh's own admission, BA has been in a 'fight for survival' for much of this year. Over the past decade, the airline industry has lurched from one crisis to another: the terrorist attacks of 2001, the threat of liquid bombs, Sars, swine flu and a soaring oil price. BA itself also suffered the troubled opening of its new base at Heathrow, Terminal Five, which most agree has now been turned into a success.

But it has been the global recession that has wrought the most damage: BA is losing £1.6m a day. Earlier this month, it reported half-year losses of £292m on top of record losses of £401m for the previous year. This will be the first time in the carrier's history that it has recorded two successive years in the red.

The deal with Iberia was broadly welcomed by the City. The new firm will generate annual revenues of £13.5bn—making it the third-largest airline in the world—carry 61.5m passengers and fly to 205 airports. It will be headquartered in London, although domiciled in Madrid for tax purposes, with Walsh chief executive and Vázquez as chairman. Both brands will continue to exist.

John Strickland, an airline consultant, says BA had been 'feeling more and more left behind' as rivals Air France and KLM merged and Lufthansa absorbed Swiss International Airlines in 2005 and subsequently Brussels Airlines, Austrian Airlines and the British carrier BMI.

'Air France-KLM is the shiny example of an airline merger,' he says. 'It was a deal that wasn't blood-laden for staff. Whether it was pragmatism or foresight, they kept two brands and two functioning head offices. They looked at cost savings but it wasn't brutal in human terms and customers have been kept happy. But there has been an enormous upturn in revenue. It really has been a case of one plus one equals three . . . It is a model that has worked and is something that BA and Iberia will have learned from.'

Walsh, 48, who joined BA in 2005, made his mark at Aer Lingus, where he joined as a pilot and worked his way up to chief executive. He turned the business into an aggressive low-cost operator and while he was there spent two years in Mallorca, where he ran Futura, a charter airline owned by the Irish group. His Spanish, apparently, is not so bad.

It seems unlikely that Walsh will have much pause for breath after sealing the deal. BA cabin crew have threatened a strike over job losses and changes to their terms; the airline is already cutting 4,900 posts. The unions are also a potential obstacle in the Iberia deal, seeking assurances that there will be no further compulsory redundancies in return for lending support. And BA is still awaiting a verdict from Washington and Brussels on its alliance with American Airlines.

'BA's problems are serious but they are arguably no worse than anyone else's,' says Strickland. 'And they are not paralysed, or twiddling their thumbs; they are working in a wide range of fields to improve the situation . . . And in the main, the staff have bitten the bullet and seen the need for change. Willie Walsh is very well regarded by investors and the deal with Iberia is a key plank in moving forward. It is a feather in his cap.'

Source: 'After a long wait, BA and Iberia make their connection' *The Guardian*, 14 November 2009.

Questions

1. What is the business rationale for a merger between British Airways and Iberia?

2. The experience of past mergers in other industries, for instance DaimlerChrysler, suggests that the benefits to be derived are often exaggerated by board members. Identify the potential downsides with the British Airways and Iberia merger.

3. Porter contends that many mergers and acquisitions tend to destroy shareholder value because they are based on the CEO's ego rather than sound business logic. Discuss with reference to BA and Iberia.

8.5.2 Internal Development

An alternative route to growth is **internal development**. This is sometimes referred to as organic growth. It involves the organization using its own resources and developing the capabilities it believes will be necessary to compete in the future. Many organizations start their growth trajectory using organic growth and consider mergers and acquisitions as their industry matures. In reality, organizations may simultaneously pursue a strategy of internal development and simply capitalize on acquisition opportunities as they arise. A benefit of internal development is that the organization

INTERNAL DEVELOPMENT

sometimes referred to as organic growth. This involves the organization using its own resources and developing the capabilities it believes will be necessary to compete in the future experiences less financial risk and grows at a rate that it is able to control. The learning that takes place within the firm is captured for its own benefit. Also, the organization does not need to use valuable resources trying to manage different cultures. The main disadvantage of internal development is the time it takes the organization to build up necessary strategic capabilities. Stalk (1988) argues that the ways in which leading companies manage time represent the most powerful source of competitive advantage. With product cycle times reducing, a firm developing internally may not be able to exploit market opportunities. In addition, where barriers to entry exist, a strategy of mergers and acquisitions may be necessary to enter the industry.

8.5.3 Joint Ventures and Strategic Alliances

An organization may decide that it is in its interest to collaborate with one or more firms in order to achieve a specific objective. The agreement between such organizations may only be temporary, and can range from the establishment of a formal entity to a looser organizational arrangement. Collaboration continues to grow over time as organizations recognize the benefits that cooperation may bring. A key reason for the expansion in cooperative ventures is the growth in international markets. An organization that lacks the crucial market intelligence necessary to operate in overseas markets stands a greater chance of success if it collaborates with an established overseas competitor.

JOINT VENTURE

when two organizations form a separate independent company in which they own shares equally

A **joint venture** exists when two organizations form a separate independent company in which they own shares equally. (The Case Study: Sony Ericsson illustrates how a joint venture between the Japanese consumer electronics company Sony and the mobile phone company Ericsson allows them to exploit their respective core competencies.) It is often formed when organizations feel it may be beneficial to combine their resources and capabilities to develop new technologies or gain access to new markets. For example, the cost of developing a European long-haul airliner proved prohibitive for any one country. By entering into a collaborative alliance Britain, France, Germany, and Italy have formed the European Airbus consortium and successfully developed the A380, the world's largest passenger plane, at a greatly reduced risk. Each nation has contributed its own distinctive capabilities to ensure that they develop a product which will successfully compete with their American competitor, Boeing. Organizations that are restricted from owning foreign assets outright may enter into a joint venture with a foreign partner as a means of gaining access to inputs or lucrative markets. For example, as China and India continue to industrialize they seek to benefit from access to Western technology by entering into joint ventures. At the same time Western organizations gain access to massive consumer markets.

CASE STUDY 8.2
Sony Ericsson

Miles Flint of Sony Ericsson likens the mobile phone maker's lot to that of the movie industry. 'You develop a product, you show it in focus groups, or you show it in screenings, but it is only when the box office opens, or the product is in the stores, that you really know how well it is going to do,' says the president of Sony Ericsson. Fortunately for Japan's Sony and Sweden's Ericsson, their joint venture's camera and music phones are proving popular, particularly with the target audience: young affluent people.

The Walkman music phones, launched last year, account for 25 per cent of Sony Ericsson's sales. The group is hoping to replicate that success with the Cyber-shot camera phones launched in February. These phones play to the joint venture's strengths by combining some of Sony's most famous consumer electronics devices with Ericsson's expertise in wireless technology. Today, Sony Ericsson is celebrating its fifth anniversary by usurping LG Electronics as the world's fourth biggest mobile phone maker. It has been able to do so while also maintaining one of the highest average selling prices to the mobile network operators: €145 ($184) in the second quarter of 2006.

Walkman music phones account for 25 per cent of Sony Ericsson's sales. These phones play to the joint venture's strengths by combining Sony's consumer electronics with Ericsson's expertise in wireless technology.

But it was not always like this.

Sony Ericsson's pre-tax profit of €514m for 2005 contrasts with a loss of €291m in 2002, the first full year of the joint venture. Things started off badly in 2001 because the mobile handset divisions of Sony and Ericsson were already struggling, and the joint venture was simply putting the Sony Ericsson logo on the partners' existing phones. The turning point came in 2003 when collaboration resulted in the T610, Sony Ericsson's first integrated camera phone. The black and silver phone developed a cult status, partly due to its 'stick' or rectangular shape. But challenges persisted because Sony Ericsson did not have a full range of phones to sell to the mobile network operators. It ramped up its research and development during 2004 and 2005, which led to the Walkman and Cyber-shot phones.

Sony Ericsson now has a range of 35 phones, and Mr Flint says the joint venture's confidence is rooted in how 'the broad portfolio is generating margins across the piste'. Pre-tax profit margins were 9 per cent in the second quarter of 2006, and Sony Ericsson is now seeking to raise its profile and boost sales through a new media campaign. The joint venture's research suggested that it and its peers' brands are regarded as lacking warmth and personality. So the Sony Ericsson logo, which combines an S and an E in a green and silver ball, has replaced a verb in a series of statements in advertisements.

'I SE my long commute' is supposed to convey the message that people love travelling long distances to work because they enjoy listening to their Walkman phone. Mr Flint says Sony Ericsson aspires 'to be a cool brand'. This month it will unveil a limited edition silver version of its Cyber-shot phone to mark its use by Daniel Craig in *Casino Royale*, the James Bond movie. In April it produced a Robbie Williams version of the Walkman phone in collaboration with the UK pop singer and T-Mobile.

Sony Ericsson is considering increasing sales of handsets to network operators through exclusive deals on music content. In March it announced a partnership with Orange to offer songs and videos by Christina Aguilera, a Sony BMG artist.

Having integrated cameras and MP3 players into mobiles, what does Mr Flint think will be the next big thing? He cautions about rapid take-up of mobile television, partly because of research suggesting people spend more time on the Internet than watching TV. Instead, he points to the mobile's increasing role in user generated content. Teenagers have flocked to social networking websites such as MySpace and Bebo that allow them to share messages, music, and pictures. Sony Ericsson is putting Google's Blogger facility on its Cyber-shot phone, which enables people to create their own blog and post photographs on it in just two or three keystrokes.

Mr Flint, 53, says the mobile is 'increasingly becoming the depository of our life: we keep our pictures, we keep our music, we keep our e-mail, and certainly when we look at younger people than I am there is a lot of sharing of ideas, sharing of pictures, sharing of music'.

Source: 'Collaboration in search of the ultimate 'cool brand' accolade' *Financial Times*, 2 October 2006.

Questions

1. Using Ansoff's growth matrix identify the growth strategy that Sony and Ericsson are pursuing with their joint venture.

2. Evaluate the distinctive capabilities of Sony and Ericsson. To what extent have these been shared across the Sony Ericsson joint venture?

3. What reasons might either partner provide to terminate the joint venture?

Strategic alliances take place when two or more separate organizations share some of their resources and capabilities but stop short of forming a separate organization. The idea is that each partner within the strategic alliance gains access to knowledge it would not otherwise possess and that would be expensive to develop. A useful alliance will involve complementary resources and capabilities which allow both organizations to grow and develop according to their strategic objectives. Hamel *et al.* (1989, p. 134) argue that a strategic alliance may be useful to strengthen both companies against outside rivals even if in the process it weakens one of them *vis-à-vis* the other. Therefore, alliances may be viewed as competition in a different form. The ultimate aim of strategic alliances is to learn from your partners. The more focused companies view each alliance as an opportunity to view their partners' broad capabilities. They use the alliance to build new skills and systematically diffuse all new knowledge they acquire throughout their organizations. Both joint venture and strategic alliances work well when each partner's objectives are clear and agreed, and when the working relationship is based on trust. Where managerial differences exist these must be resolved prior to entering into a strategic alliance.

STRATEGIC ALLIANCES

when two or more separate organizations share some of their resources and capabilities but stop short of forming a separate organization

8.6 Portfolio Analysis

Corporate strategy is concerned with the question: what businesses do we want to compete in? Or, more accurately, which markets have we identified in which we can effectively deploy our distinctive capabilities and translate them into a competitive advantage? Where an organization is made up of multiple business units, the question concerns how resources are to be allocated across these businesses. The subject of portfolio strategy is concerned with managing these strategic business units (SBUs) to decide which businesses to invest in and which to divest of in order to maintain overall corporate performance.

A portfolio is simply the different business units that an organization possesses. Portfolio analysis allows the organization to assess the competitive position and identify the rate of return it is receiving from its various business units. By disaggregating the organization into its individual SBUs, the organization can devise appropriate strategies for each. The aim is to maximize the return on investment by allocating re-sources between SBUs to achieve a balanced portfolio. In effect, the parent organization assumes the role of a proactive investor or banker which manages its investment to achieve the highest return based upon an acceptable level of risk. The two most widely used portfolio analyses are the Boston Consulting Group (BCG) growth-share matrix and the General Electric business screen. We can look at each of these in turn.

8.6.1 Boston Consulting Group Matrix

This matrix was developed by the Boston Consulting Group and was widely used in the 1970s and 1980s. Since then diversified organizations have largely fallen from favour as companies seek to focus upon their core competencies. The BCG matrix plots an organization's business units according to (1) its *industry growth rate* and (2) its *relative market share* (Figure 8.3). Industry growth rate can be determined by reference to the growth rate of the overall economy. Therefore, if the industry is growing faster than the economy we can say it is a high growth industry. If the industry is growing slower than the economy it is characterized as slow growth. A business unit's relative market share (or competitive position) is defined as the ratio of its market share in relation to its largest competitor within the industry. A business unit that is the market leader will have a market share greater than 1.0.

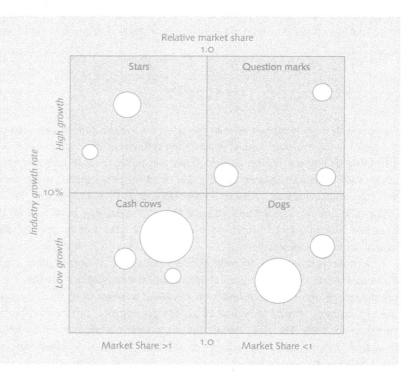

FIGURE 8.3

The BCG matrix
Reprinted from B. Hedley,
Strategy and the business
portfolio. *Long Range Planning*,
10(1), 12. © 1977, with
permission from Elsevier.

A key element of the BCG matrix is market share. The matrix draws heavily upon the experience curve which suggests that a high market share is a function of cost leadership achieved through economies of scale. This ability to reduce unit costs comes through the accumulated experience the business gains competing within the industry. In Figure 8.3 each business unit (or product) is represented by a circle and plotted on the matrix according to its relative market share and industry growth rate.

The size of the circle corresponds to the amount of revenue being generated by each business unit. The lines dividing the portfolio into four quadrants are somewhat arbitrary (Hedley 1977). A high industry growth rate is put at 10 per cent, whereas the lines separating relative market share are set equal to the largest competitor which is 1.

A business unit can fall within one of four strategic categories in which it will be characterized as a *star*, *question mark*, *cash cow*, or *dog*. These classifications can then be used to determine the strategic options for each business unit, that is, which business justifies further resource allocation, which generates cash for expansion, and which needs to be divested.

- **Stars** are characterized by high growth and high market share. They occupy the upper left quadrant of the matrix and are the business leaders, generating large amounts of cash. They represent the most favourable growth and investment opportunities to the organization. As such, resources should be allocated to ensure that they maintain their competitive position. At times stars may require funding in excess of their ability to generate funds, but this will act as a deterrent to competitors. Over the long term, investment in stars will pay dividends as their large market share will enable them to generate cash as the market slows and they become cash cows.

- **Cash cows** experience high market share but in low-growth or mature industries. Their high market share provides low costs which produces high profits and cash generation. Their position in low-growth industries means that they require little in terms of resource allocation. The cash surpluses they generate can be used to fund stars and question marks.

- **Question marks** compete in high-growth industries but have low market share. They occupy the upper right quadrant of the BCG matrix. Because they are in growth industries, question marks have high cash needs but they only generate small amounts of cash as a result of their low market share. The strategic options facing a question mark are to make the investment necessary to increase market share and manage the business to a star and finally a cash cow as the industry matures. The other option is immediate divestment or winding the business down with no further investment. In this way the question mark may provide the organization with some residual cash flow in the short term.

- **Dogs** have a low market share within a low-growth industry. The lack of industry growth guards against allocating further resources to a dog. Often the cash needed to maintain its competitive position is in excess of the cash it generates. Organizations need to ensure that only a minimal amount of its business units occupy this position. The strategic option would be one of divestment.

According to Hedley (1977) the primary goal of a portfolio strategy should be to maintain the position of cash cows. The cash from the cash cows can then be used to consolidate the position of stars which are not self-sustaining. Any surplus remaining can then be used to resource selected question marks to market dominance. An appropriate strategy for a multi-business organization is to retain a balanced portfolio. The cash generated by cash cows, and by question marks and dogs being liquidated, should be sufficient to support the organization's stars and help selected question marks achieve market dominance. What portfolio analysis shows us is that the strategy being formulated for each business unit should correspond to its position in the matrix. It should also align with the capabilities of the organization's overall portfolio of businesses. For instance, managers of stars should be accorded more recognition for maintaining market share. In contrast with stars, managers of cash cows might be given higher profit levels to achieve as a more appropriate objective. Therefore, the corporate parent must remain vigilant to ensure that its overall performance is not suboptimal as a result of inappropriate business unit objectives which lead to poor resource allocation decisions.

Criticisms of the BCG Matrix

The BCG matrix uses only industry growth rate and market share to assess a business unit's current performance. In particular, it overemphasizes the importance of market share and market dominance which stems from its belief in the experience curve. Its simplicity of use and persuasive results ensured a wide following throughout the corporate world in the 1980s. However, the BCG matrix is a tool of analysis and, therefore, requires managers to use their judgement. It is not an excuse to suspend one's judgement. Prahalad and Hamel (1990) note:

> *major companies that have had the potential to build core competencies*
> *but failed to do so because top management was unable to conceive of*
> *the company as anything other than a collection of discrete businesses.*

Hamel and Prahalad (1994) lament what they call 'the tyranny of the SBU', arguing instead for the modern business organization to be seen as a portfolio of competencies. Table 8.1 provides a comparison of the organization when viewed in terms of SBUs and core competencies.

8.6.2 The General Electric–McKinsey Matrix

General Electric and McKinsey & Company developed a more comprehensive measure of strategic success. In contrast with the BCG matrix's four quadrants, the General Electric (GE) matrix comprises a nine-cell matrix (Figure 8.4). The axes comprise (1) *industry attractiveness* and (2) *business strength/competitive position*. Unlike the BCG matrix there is an attempt to broaden the analysis of a business unit's internal and external factors. For example, industry attractiveness includes factors such as industry profitability, market growth, and the number of competitors, among others.

	SBU	Core competence
Basis for competition	Competitiveness of today's products	Inter-firm competition to build competencies
Corporate structure	Portfolio of businesses related in product-market terms	Portfolio of competencies, core products, and businesses
Status of the business unit	Autonomy is sacrosanct; the SBU 'owns' all resources other than cash	SBU is a potential reservoir of core competencies
Resource allocation	Discrete businesses are the unit of analysis; capital is allocated business by business	Businesses and competencies are the unit of analysis; top management allocates capital and talent
Value added of top management	Optimizing corporate returns through capital allocation trade-offs among businesses	Enunciating strategic architecture and building competencies to secure the future

TABLE 8.1

The organization: SBU and core competence.
Reprinted by permission of *Harvard Business Review*. Two concepts of the corporation, from C.K. Prahalad and G. Hamel (1990). The core competence of the corporation. *Harvard Business Review*, **68**(3). © 1990 by the Harvard Business School Publishing Corporation. All rights reserved.

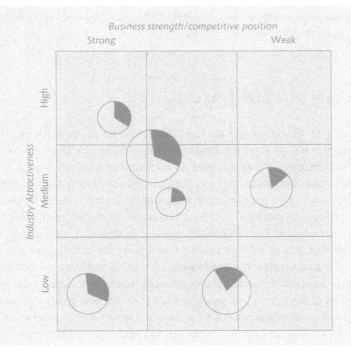

FIGURE 8.4

The General Electric–McKinsey matrix

Similarly, business strength and competitive position go beyond market share to include a wider analysis of the organization's internal strengths and weaknesses. This includes factors such as technological capability, product quality, and management ability as well as relative market share. These are the factors that managers believe will be important for achieving success.

As with the BCG matrix, each business unit is represented by a circle and plotted on the matrix. Each business unit (or product) is also identified by a letter. The size of the circles relates to the size of the industry and the shaded portion corresponds to the market share of each business unit. Each industry that a business unit operates within is graded on a scale of 1 (very unattractive) to 5 (very attractive). By mapping each business unit against the factors management believe to be important for success, each business unit can be assessed for its business strength and competitive position on a scale of 1 (very weak) to 5 (very strong).

The GE matrix overcomes some of the more simplistic analysis of the BCG matrix. The inclusion of a nine-cell matrix helps to broaden the criteria for assessing the performance of business units. Nonetheless, we should be aware that the analysis can become complex. It is also subjective. The different criteria which are used to measure industry attractiveness and competitive position are provided by the parent company. The parent company in turn uses these criteria to assess each business. In effect, the parent corporation is stating what it believes to be important and simply assessing its strategic business units according to this.

8.7 Corporate Parenting

In evaluating portfolio strategies the role of the corporate parent in the previous section is simply one of an investment manager; moving funds between businesses as it seeks to maximize its corporate returns. In contrast, Campbell *et al.* (1995a) seek to understand how, and under what conditions, corporate parents succeed in creating value. They argue that multi-business organizations create value by influencing or *parenting* the businesses they own. Sound corporate strategies create value through parenting advantage. Parenting advantage occurs when an organization creates more value than any of its rivals could if they owned the same businesses. For example, in the past Unilever has added value by sharing marketing and technological information across its business units in different countries. It added value through the provision of funds to its businesses for R&D to enable new product development. Left to its own devices the individual business unit would simply under-invest in this area (Buchanan and Sands 1994). However, this no longer appears to be the case. (See Strategy Focus: Unilever, in which the corporate parent is struggling to add value to its acquisitions and outperform its rivals.)

PARENTING ADVANTAGE

occurs when an organization creates more value than any of its competitors could if they owned the same businesses

STRATEGY FOCUS
Unilever

The years go by and the question remains. Can Unilever turn itself round? Improvements at the Anglo-Dutch consumer products group must be acknowledged. Pre-tax profits rose 16 per cent in the first half of 2006, on 6 per cent sales growth. Patrick Cescau, chief executive, congratulated himself yesterday on six consecutive quarters of growth. Unilever has a slimmed-down management team and a slimmed-down portfolio of businesses now it has sold some underperformers. It also communicates better with investors. But the question remains. Underlying first-half sales growth of 3.4 per cent is hardly stellar. Peers such as Procter & Gamble, which on Wednesday said underlying second-quarter sales rose 8 per cent, managed underlying sales growth of more than 6 per cent last year.

In Europe, Unilever's first-half underlying sales barely grew. There is little evidence of the group being able to raise sales volumes without price cuts. Spending on advertising and promotions is rising as a percentage of turnover—necessary to propel sales growth but one reason behind a deterioration in margins. Underlying operating margins, 14 per cent in the second quarter, were 1 percentage point lower than a year ago.

Although some might beg to differ, Mr Cescau believes Unilever has restored competitiveness. He has set a target of 3–5 per cent sustainable underlying sales growth, and an operating margin greater than 15 per cent by 2010. Such undemanding goals underline the main risk for investors—that the management does well enough to resist radical change, like a break-up, but not well enough to outperform. Add to that another danger—that Unilever's cash pile gets squandered on underperforming acquisitions. Both risks suggest there is little chance that Unilever's shares' discount to its peers, a legacy of its inferior operating performance over a long period, will disappear.

Source: 'Unilever' *Financial Times*, 4 August 2006.

The parent organization is seen as an intermediary between investors and businesses. In this respect, the parent competes against other parent companies and also against other intermediaries such as investment trusts. Therefore, the corporate-level strategies make sense as long as the parent organization is able to create sufficient value to compete with other intermediaries (Campbell *et al.* 1995a). If there is a good fit between the corporate parent's skills and the needs and opportunities that exist for its businesses, the corporation is likely to create value. However, if there is not a good fit, the corporation is likely to destroy value. The concept of corporate parenting is useful in helping an organization to decide which new businesses it should acquire. This is because unless the corporate parent is creating greater value than its costs, the businesses would be better off as independent companies. In addition, it helps the corporate parent focus when deciding how each business should be managed.

In their influential book, subtitled *Creating Value in the Multibusiness Company*, Goold *et al.* (1994b) argue that successful parents create parenting advantage through their *value-creation insights*. This is an essential feature of successful corporate parents. It states that corporate strategies should be based on insights into how they can create value in their portfolio of businesses. These insights tend to emanate from the corporate culture as well as the experience of the chief executive and his or her management team. Parenting advantage also involves creating a *fit* between how the parent operates, that is, the *parent's distinctive characteristics*, and the opportunities that exist within the business units. The key is not simply to identify some level of fit but rather to achieve a closer fit with its businesses than can be achieved by rival organizations (See Strategy Focus: Adding Value, in which Disney expects its parenting of Marvel Inc. to add value for the organization.) The idea of fit is a dynamic one, such that a fit in today's environment will not necessarily be a fit in tomorrow's environment. Therefore, corporate strategists need to be aware of the trends occurring in the general environment that will have an impact upon their business units. One way in which an organization might do this is scenario planning, which was discussed in **Chapter 2**.

STRATEGY FOCUS
Adding Value Marvel Style

NOT even the combined powers of Spider-Man, Iron Man, the Incredible Hulk, Captain America and the X-Men could keep The Mouse at bay. On August 31st Walt Disney announced it was buying Marvel Entertainment for $4 billion, just days after the comic-book publisher had celebrated 70 glorious years of independence, during which it had created many of the most famous cartoon characters not invented by Disney itself.

In fact, Marvel did not put up much of a fight, accepting what most analysts think was a generous price. Disney will get access both to Marvel's creative minds and—potentially far more valuable in an age when familiar stories rule the box office—an archive containing around 5000 established characters, only a fraction of which have yet made the move from paper to the silver screen.

Marrying Marvel's characters with Disney's talent for making money from successful franchises is a good idea. In recent years Disney has proved the undisputed master at Disney is bringing the exploiting the same basic content through multiple channels, including films, websites, commercial heft video games, merchandising, live shows and theme parks.

The edgier, darker Marvel characters should fill a hole in Disney's much cuddlier portfolio. This currently covers most people from newborn babies, through the addictive 'Baby Einstein' DVDs (popularly known as 'baby crack'), to adults, through its Touchstone label. Disney's own cartoons, and the newer ones created by Pixar, an animation studio it bought in 2006 for $7 billion, appeal to children. 'Hannah Montana', a hit television show, caters to pre-teen girls. The Marvel characters should be just the thing for boys of the same age, whom Disney has found especially hard to attract of late.

However, many of Marvel's best-known characters already have contractual obligations to various rival media conglomerates that will not be easily or quickly undone. Sony has an indefinite hold on Spider-Man; News Corporation exerts similar control over the X-Men. Universal owns distribution rights to the Hulk and long-term theme-park rights in Florida to several characters. This is a pity, because Disney's theme parks are a part of its business where teenage boys would particularly welcome the contrast that Marvel's superheroes would provide to the Magic Kingdom's oppressive wholesomeness.

Another risk is one that often presents itself in mergers, especially those involving creative types: a clash of cultures. Happily for Marvel, Disney is no longer the corporate control-freak it was under its former boss, Michael Eisner. His successor, Bob Iger, has turned out to be a relatively hands-off boss, with the Pixar acquisition a model of the sort of treatment Marvel can expect. Indeed, John Lasseter, the chief creative force behind Pixar, reportedly played an important role in reassuring Marvel's talent that their culture would be safe in Disney's hands.

Also fully behind the deal is Stan 'the Man' Lee, a living legend of the cartoon world who helped create many of Marvel's best-known characters during the 1960s. Mr Lee, who recently launched his first digital comic as part of a partnership between his new firm and Disney, has predicted that the Disney-Marvel merger will prove 'a terrific deal which will be extremely beneficial to both companies. The synergy between them is perfect.'

Ironically, in the 1960s, Mr Lee tried, without success, to convince his bosses to turn Marvel into a multimedia company like Disney. Now, albeit in a roundabout way, one of his outlandish fantasies is about to become a reality.

Source: 'Of mouse and X-Men' *The Economist*, 3 September 2009.

To understand fully the fit between a parent and its various businesses the organization needs to analyse its parenting opportunities and the critical success factors for each business.

8.7.1 Parenting Opportunities

Each business unit contains opportunities for the parent to create value. It may be that the business unit does not have a strong management team or lacks some specialized expertise such as marketing. A business will present the corporate parent with its own unique opportunities. Therefore, the issue is whether the business needs and opportunities identified can be exploited by the parent company. In other words, do the parent's skills and resources fit with the needs and opportunities of the business?

Critical Success Factors

Each type of business will have different critical success factors which determine its success in the marketplace. In one business it might be the ability to develop innovative solutions for consumers; in another it might be product development and the speed to market. In order to create value the parent's characteristics must be compatible with the critical success factors needed for the business. This is crucial, since a misunderstanding of critical success factors may lead the parent company to destroy value. Successful corporate strategy requires parents which possess value-creation insights and distinctive parenting characteristics, and which focus on businesses where they can create value. There are four ways in which the corporate parent can create value for their businesses: *stand-alone influence, linkage influence, functional and services influence*, and *corporate development activities*.

1. **Stand-alone influence.** This concerns the parent company's impact upon the strategies and performance of each business the parent owns. Stand-alone influence includes such things as the parent company setting performance targets and approving major capital expenditure for the business. There is an opportunity here for the parent to create substantial value. However, where the parent imposes inappropriate targets or fails to recognize the needs of the business for funds, it will destroy value.

2. **Linkage influence.** This occurs when parents seek to create value by enhancing the linkages that may be present between different businesses. For example, this might include transferring knowledge and capabilities across business units. The aim is to increase value through synergy.

3. **Functional and services influence.** The parent can provide functional leadership and cost-effective services for the businesses. The parent company creates value to the extent that they provide services which are more cost effective than the businesses can undertake themselves or purchase from external suppliers.

4. **Corporate development activities.** This involves the parent creating value by changing the composition of its portfolio of businesses. The parent actively seeks to add value through its activities in acquisitions, divestments, and alliances. In reality, the parent company often destroys value through its acquisitions by paying a premium which it fails to recover (Porter 1987).

In the same way that business-level strategy decisions are guided by their impact on competitive advantage, corporate parenting proposes that the main criterion for corporate strategy decisions is their impact on *parenting advantage*. In this way it aims to provide a measurement for corporate-level decisions which might improve corporate strategies. Parenting advantage—or creating better value than one's rivals—should be used to guide corporate strategy development. As Campbell *et al.* (1995b) state:

> parenting advantage is the only robust logic for a parent company to own a
> business . . . parenting advantage is the goal and criterion that should guide
> both the selection of businesses to include in the portfolio and the design
> of the parent organization.

8.7.2 Portfolio Decisions

We can now turn to the question of which businesses the corporate parent should include in its portfolio. Goold *et al.* (1994b) suggest that businesses can be classified into five types: *heartland*, *edge of heartland*, *ballast*, *alien territory*, and *value trap*. These business types are illustrated in the *parenting fit matrix* (Figure 8.5). To determine which of the above five types a business falls within two questions can be asked.

1. Do the parenting opportunities in the business *fit* with value-creating insights of the parent, such that the parent can create a substantial amount of value?

2. Do the critical success factors in the business have any obvious *misfit* with the prospective parenting characteristics, such that the parent might influence the business in a way that destroys value?

The answer to the first question will range from a high fit, where the value-creation insights of the parent fit well with the opportunities in the business, to a low fit, where the value-creation insights of the parent company do not address the important opportunities that exist within the business. Clearly, where the value-creation insights address all the important opportunities in a business, there is no room for a rival to create superior value-creation insights. Where the degree of fit between parent and business units is low, it is likely that another corporate parent could add greater value.

The second question requires the corporate parent to understand the critical success factors in the business and compare these with its own parenting characteristics.

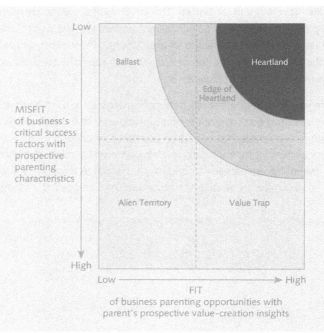

FIGURE 8.5

The parenting fix matrix
From M. Goold, A. Campbell, and
M. Alexander (1994). *Corporate
Level Strategy: Creating Value
in the Multibusiness Company*.
© John Wiley & Sons Ltd.
Reproduced with permission.

A misfit is likely to occur when the parent does not understand the critical success factors of the business. It lacks a 'feel' for the business and, therefore, inadvertently influences the business in ways that destroy value. Those businesses that the parent do not understand well enough to ascertain the extent of misfit should be categorized as having a high misfit.

Figure 8.5 is divided into four quadrants. A business will occupy one of these quadrants according to how well there is a fit between its needs and opportunities and the skills of the corporate parent.

The top right-hand quadrant comprises **heartland businesses**. These are businesses with needs and opportunities that the parent organization can address. The critical success factors of these businesses are clearly understood by the parent. Heartland businesses should be the main focus of the company's parenting. These are businesses the parent understands and can add the most value to. **Edge-of-heartland businesses** can come about where a parent company might acquire a new business that meets the value-creation insights of the parent but not all the heartland criteria. For example, the new business might be operating in markets with which the parent is unfamiliar. In such a case the parent should recognize that its feel for the business is less certain and this might require that it develop new parenting skills to deal with the business. The new business can be thought of as extending the boundaries around the heartland. For example, Canon's heartland includes businesses that involve precision mechanics, fine optics, and microelectronics (Goold *et al*. 1994b). However, Canon has extended its heartland to cover medical equipment, chemical products, and, importantly, office products. The new business should be seen as an experiment in which the boundaries of the heartland business are tested. This will involve greater risk than a heartland business but offer the upside of substantial value creation.

Ballast businesses are those in which there are few opportunities for the parent company to add value. Most portfolios will contain a number of ballast businesses. Although the parent understands ballast businesses and they do not present any misfits, the issue is likely to be one of opportunity cost. That is, as there are few parenting opportunities the parent's time and resources would be better spent on other businesses, particularly heartland businesses. Ballast businesses may offer the corporation a useful cash flow but ultimately the issue is: what effect does retaining a ballast business have upon the rest of the portfolio and is it worth more to the parent company than to its rivals?

Value trap businesses are businesses which appear attractive to the corporate parent on the surface but in reality there exist areas of misfit with the parent. Value trap businesses should be avoided and kept out of the corporate portfolio unless the parent is capable of learning to reduce or eliminate the misfits. Businesses which do not fit with the prospective corporate strategy are said to be part of **alien territory**. Businesses which lie within alien territory offer the parent little opportunity to create value. The parent company's value-creating insights are not relevant for such businesses and its parent characteristics do not fit the businesses. They may be in the portfolio as a result of being part of another business that was acquired. They are referred to as *alien* because their need is for a different corporate parent with a fundamentally different corporate strategy.

We should be aware that the parenting-fit matrix has its limitations. In line with similar portfolio tools of analysis, it depends on the subjectivity of those making decisions as to what constitutes a good fit between the parent and business units. Senior corporate managers spend less time with each business than their own managers do. In such a case their influence on these business units may be less soundly based than that of the managers who actually run them. Furthermore, corporate headquarters encourage managers of business units to compete with each other for resources. As a result these managers will filter information going to the corporate parent in order to show their business in the best possible light. Where this occurs some value will be destroyed as the information on which the corporate parent is making decisions is inevitably biased (Goold *et al*. 1994a).

There are similarities between parenting advantage and the resource-based view of core competencies (Prahalad and Hamel 1990). The key divergence is the role given to the parent organization. According to the parenting advantage framework, the onus is upon the resources and capabilities of the parent company, and how this is shared across the businesses (Campbell *et al*. 1995a). For the resource-based view, the core competencies that reside within the parent organization and individual businesses are not disaggregated but treated as uniform.

To summarize, the best parents have *value-creation insights* about the most appropriate parenting opportunities and focus their activities on trying to create added value from these insights. They possess distinctive parenting characteristics which enable them to create value. These will usually be superior to those of similar parents. Crucially, the best parents primarily focus their portfolios on those business units where their parenting skills can create substantial value—these are heartland businesses. They may make a conscious decision to invest time and resources in businesses which fall outside the heartland, such as ballast businesses. A point to bear in mind is that any such decision should be based on a clear understanding that ballast businesses are worth more to the corporate parent than to rival corporate parents. They should not be retained for emotional or historical reasons.

8.8 Strategic Evaluation

We have addressed in this and the previous chapter a variety of different strategies that organizations can implement. The question we now need to address is: how can the organization differentiate between the strategic options that it faces? We might include a caveat here that it is unrealistic to expect any form of evaluation to identify a 'best' or optimal strategy. However, strategy evaluation can help to surface the implications of pursuing different strategic options before they are implemented. One method is to assess the strategy according to its *suitability*, *feasibility*, and *acceptability*. We can assess each of these in turn.

Suitability

An organization will be concerned to evaluate how well the strategy matches the needs identified within its strategic analysis. There should be some consistency between the strategy, the opportunities within the external environment, the resources and capabilities of the organization, and the organizational objectives. For example, is the strategy capable of overcoming a threat identified in the external environment and mitigating any weaknesses in the organization? The strategy should leverage the organization's resources and capabilities to exploit external opportunities that may arise as a result of market changes. The strategy should also meet the organization's objectives which might be return on capital employed, profit per employee, or customer satisfaction. It may include some combination of qualitative and quantitative measures as suggested by the balanced scorecard (discussed in **Chapter 6**).

Feasibility

Feasibility concerns whether a strategy will work in practice. An organization must ensure that it possesses the necessary resources and capabilities, such as finance, technological expertise, marketing, and other factors necessary to implement the strategy. Where resources and capabilities are deficient, can the organization develop these and achieve a sustainable competitive advantage? As we have seen, each industry has its own critical success factors. A strategy will not be tenable if it fails to meet these critical success factors. These will include factors such as quality levels, price, product development, innovation, and customer support.

Acceptability

This criterion of acceptability addresses the response of stakeholders to the proposed strategy. Clearly, if a strategic change is to be implemented, it must have the support of those who will be most affected by it. For example, managers of an SBU often understand their business far better than staff at head office. However, a proposed strategy from a SBU which takes into account local market conditions must also fit within the overall strategy set by the corporate parent. Similarly, stakeholders, such as institutional investors, will be particularly concerned about the impact of the strategy on profitability. Their attentions will be drawn towards the return on capital employed, the cost–income ratio within the organization, and the perceived levels of risk that arise from the strategy. Other stakeholders, such as employees, customers, and key suppliers, will need to be assured that any changes will not negatively impact upon them. If the strategy is one of growth through mergers and acquisitions, the organization needs to consider if this will be acceptable to the competition authorities.

The criteria of suitability, feasibility, and acceptability help managers to be explicit about any assumptions that may underpin their strategies. In the real world it may be unlikely that an organization's strategy fulfils all three criteria. In this case the organization must decide on the strategy which fits its stated aims and objectives more closely. Inevitably this will involve compromise.

Rumelt (1995) proposes four tests of (1) *consistency*, (2) *consonance*, (3) *advantage*, and (4) *feasibility* to evaluate a strategy. He argues that any strategy can be tested for four types of critical flaw. We briefly discuss these below.

1. **Consistency.** Any proposed strategy must not present mutually inconsistent goals and policies. For example, a high-technology organization might face a strategic choice between offering a customized high-cost product or a more standardized low-cost product. Unless a choice is explicit throughout the organization, there may be conflict between the sales force, the design team, manufacturing, and marketing.

2. **Consonance.** The test of consonance allows the organization to evaluate the economic relationships that characterize the business. It also helps determine whether or not sufficient value is being created to sustain the need for the strategy over the long term. Consonance can include an assessment of why the organization exists, the economic foundation which supports the business, and the implications of changes.

3. **Advantage.** This addresses whether an organization can appropriate sufficient of the value that it creates. A strategy must create a competitive advantage in one or more of the following three areas: superior skills, superior resources, and superior position.

4. **Feasibility.** Lastly, the criterion of feasibility is to ensure that any proposed strategy does not overtax an organization's available resources or create insoluble problems for it.

Summary

Corporate strategy is concerned with the question: What businesses do we want to compete in? Corporate strategy helps define the scope of the different industries and markets within which the organization competes in order to achieve its organizational objectives. Where an organization is made up of multiple business units, a role arises as to how resources are to be allocated across these businesses. The purpose and objectives of the organization are paramount in guiding these decisions. Once the objective of the organization is determined, for instance to maximize shareholder value, the role of corporate strategy is to enable the organization to fulfil that objective. These objectives and, therefore, the overall direction of the organization, are determined by the corporate parent. The role of a corporate parent is to add value across its business units. Where a corporate parent adds greater value, the organization is said to achieve synergy. Synergy occurs when the total output from combining businesses is greater than the output of the businesses operating individually.

In order to grow, organizations can pursue four strategies: market penetration, product development, market development, and diversification. Each strategy carries a different level of risk and is predicated upon an organization's resources and capabilities. Where an organization seeks to broaden its scope of activities it will be concerned with how it can best diversify into different businesses. This may take the form of related or unrelated diversification. The methods by which an organization's corporate strategies can be implemented are internal developments, mergers and acquisitions, joint ventures, and strategic alliances. The organization's competitive position, cost implications, need for technology, speed, access to markets, and competitive threats will all help to guide the decision on which methods it chooses to implement its strategy. A popular method for assessing business performance in the past was portfolio analysis. Two approaches include the Boston Consulting Group matrix and the General Electric matrix. These approaches became less widely used as corporations focused upon their core activities and sought to 'stick to the knitting'.

The corporate parenting approach argues that the parent company should use its value-creation insights and distinction parenting characteristics to identify a heartland of businesses to which it can add substantial value. A measurement of the value being added by the corporate parent is whether it is greater than if the business units were managed independently of the organization. We have seen that there are similarities between the corporate parenting approach and the resource-based view. In evaluating strategies, executives must be aware of both the organization's internal resources and capabilities and how these meet the needs of the external environment. In addition, the opinions of stakeholders who have the power and influence to affect strategy must be taken into account.

Review Questions

1. If an organization's portfolio of businesses comprises some *dogs*, what are the options open to it according to the BCG matrix? State circumstances in which an organization might be prepared to tolerate dog businesses.

2. Evaluate the different criteria a parent company can use in assessing the value to be derived from its parenting of business units.

Discussion Question

If Warren Buffett is right, that only shareholders of target companies benefit from takeovers, why do some companies continue to bid for other organisations?

Research Topic

Discuss the reasons for the takeover of Cadbury by Kraft. Assess the impact on both organizations of the takeover paying particular attention to whether (and where) value has been created or destroyed.

Recommended Reading

- Markides, C.C. and Williamson, P.J. (1994). Related diversification, core competencies and corporate performance. *Strategic Management Journal*, **15**(Special Issue), 149–65.
- Seth, A. (1990). Value creation in acquisitions: a re-examination of performance issues. *Strategic Management Journal*, **11**(2), 99–115.

For a discussion of portfolio analysis and the growth share (BCG) matrix see:

- Hedley, B. (1977). Strategy and the business portfolio. *Long Range Planning*, **10**(1), 9–15.

For an understanding of the resource-based view and a critique of portfolio analysis with its focus upon strategic business units (SBUs), see the influential article:

- Prahalad, C.K. and Hamel, G. (1990). The core competence of the corporation. *Harvard Business Review*, **68**(3), 79–91.

For a corporate parenting approach to corporate strategy which argues that a parent company should ensure that the value it creates from its businesses is more than could be achieved by a rival organization, see:

- Goold, M., Campbell, A., and Alexander, M. (1994). *Corporate Level Strategy: Creating Value in the Multibusiness Company*. John Wiley & Sons Wiley, New York.

online resource centre

www.oxfordtextbooks.co.uk/orc/henry2e/
Visit the Online Resource Centre that accompanies this book for activities and more information on corporate-level strategy.

Notes

1. The 1965 version of the matrix was supplanted by a more articulate version in H.I. Ansoff (1988), *The New Corporate Strategy*, Wiley, New York, which is shown below:

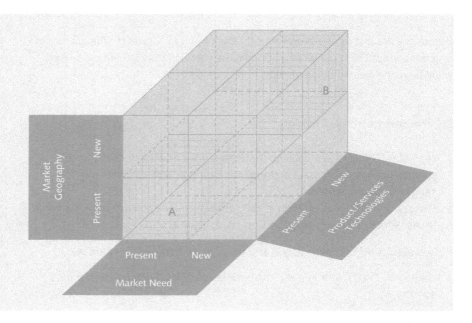

FIGURE 8.6
Ansoff's updated growth vector matrix
From H.I. Ansoff (1988).
The New Corporate Strategy,
pp. 82–9. New York:
John Wiley & Sons.

[2] Figures from www.berkshirehathaway.com.

[3] Figures from www.berkshirehathaway.com.

[4] *Daily Telegraph* (2007). Daimler offloads Chrysler for $7.4bn: private equity deal ends miserable decade for German engineer. *Daily Telegraph*, 15 May 2007.

[5] *Financial Times* (2007). Happily never after mergers, like marriages, fail without a meeting of minds. *Financial Times*, 15 May 2007.

References

Ansoff, I. (1965). *Corporate Strategy*. McGraw-Hill, New York.

Ansoff, I. (1988). *The New Corporate Strategy*. John Wiley & Sons, New York.

Buchanan, R. and **Sands, R.** (1994). Creating an effective corporate centre: the influence of strategy on head office role. *European Business Journal*, **6**(4), 17–27.

Campbell, A., Goold, M., and **Alexander, M.** (1995a). Corporate strategy: the quest for parenting advantage. *Harvard Business Review*, **73**(2), 120–32.

Campbell, A., Goold, M., and **Alexander, M.** (1995b). The value of the parent company. *California Management Review*, **38**(1), 91.

Daily Telegraph (2007). Daimler offloads Chrysler for $7.4bn: private equity deal ends miserable decade for German engineer. *Daily Telegraph*, 15 May 2007.

Daley, M., Mahotra, V., and **Sivakumar, R.** (1997). Corporate focus and value creation: evidence from spin-offs. *Journal of Financial Economics*, **45**(2), 257–81.

Financial Times (2007). Happily never after mergers, like marriages, fail without a meeting of minds. *Financial Times*, 15 May 2007.

Goold, M. and **Luchs, K.** (1993). Why diversify? Four decades of management thinking. *Academy of Management Executive*, **7**(3), 7–25.

Goold, M., Campbell, A., and **Alexander, M.** (1994a). Corporate strategy and parenting theory. *Long Range Planning*, **31**(2), 308–14.

Goold, M., Campbell, A., and **Alexander, M.** (1994b). *Corporate Level Strategy: Creating Value in the Multibusiness Company*. John Wiley & Sons, New York.

Hamel, G. and **Prahalad, C.K.** (1994). *Competing for the Future*. Harvard Business School Press, Boston, MA.

Hamel, G., Doz, Y., and **Prahalad, C.K.** (1989). Collaborate with your competitors and win. *Harvard Business Review*, **67**(1), 133–9.

Hedley, B. (1977). Strategy and the business portfolio. *Long Range Planning*, **10**(1), 9–15.

Kay, J. (1993). *Foundations of Corporate Success*. Oxford University Press, Oxford.

Markides, C.C. (1995). Diversification, restructuring and economic performance. *Strategic Management Journal*, **16**(2), 101–18.

Markides, C.C. and **Williamson, P.J.** (1994). Related diversification, core competencies and corporate performance. *Strategic Management Journal*, **15**(Special Edition), 149–65.

∞

Peters, T.J. and **Waterman, R.H.** (1982). *In Search of Excellence*. Harper & Row, New York.

Porter, M.E. (1987). From competitive advantage to corporate strategy. *Harvard Business Review*, **65**(3), 43–59.

Prahalad, K. and **Hamel, G.** (1990). The core competence of the corporation. *Harvard Business Review*, **68**(3), 79–91.

Rumelt, R. (1995). The evaluation of business strategy. In *The Strategy Process* (ed. H. Mintzberg, B. Quinn, and S. Ghoshal). Prentice-Hall, Hemel Hempstead.

Singh, H. and **Montgomery, C.A.** (1987). Corporate acquisition strategies and economic performance. *Strategic Management Journal*, **8**(4), 377–86.

Stalk, G. (1988). Time—the next source of competitive advantage. *Harvard Business Review*, **66**(4), 41–51.

Williamson, O.E. (1975). *Markets and Hierarchies: Analysis and Antitrust Implications*. Free Press, New York.

9 International Strategy and Globalization

9.1 Globalization or Localization

9.2 International Strategy

9.3 A Globalization Framework

9.4 Types of International Strategy

9.5 Entry Mode Strategies

9.6 Porter's Diamond of Competitive Advantage

9.7 The Myths of Global Strategy

9.8 The Challenge of Globalization

Key Work
Benefits and disadvantages of globalization

Key Work
Multidomestic strategies

Key Work
Entry mode strategies

Main Reference
Palmisano, S.J. (2006). The globally integrated enterprise. *Foreign Affairs*, 85(3), 127–36.

Learning Objectives

After completing this chapter you should be able to:

- Discuss different perspectives on globalization
- Explain what motivates organizations to expand abroad
- Describe a framework for globalization and explain how a multinational corporation can achieve competitive advantage
- Evaluate four basic types of international strategy
- Assess different entry mode strategies
- Use Porter's diamond to explain the competitive advantage of nations
- Discuss some of the myths associated with globalization
- Assess the opportunities and challenges associated with a globally integrated enterprise

Introduction

In **Chapters 7** and **8** we discussed strategy formulation at the business and corporate level. The key issue in business-level strategy is how an organization competes in its chosen markets. For corporate strategy, the concerns are what businesses we want to compete in and how resources should be allocated across these businesses. Whether formulating strategy at the business level or corporate level, the organization seeks to create value and achieve a sustainable competitive advantage. In this chapter we will discuss competitive advantage from an international perspective. There will be links with some of the topics discussed in **Chapter 8**, such as strategic alliances and joint ventures. We will also address comparative advantage and the role that different factors play in providing a nation with competitive advantage.

A crucial issue for organizations that operate across international borders is to what extent they can develop global brands and global products for all markets. Or, conversely, to what extent must their international strategy recognize and adapt to international diversities based on, for instance, consumer preferences? Central to this issue is the extent to which an organization believes globalization has led to a standardization of consumer tastes and preferences and, therefore, homogeneous markets. Or, as others have argued, that important national differences still exist which warrant that organizations provide different product offerings to different countries. Clearly, each manager's understanding of the changes taking place in the international environment will have an impact upon the type of strategy their organization pursues. In the same way, the level of risk an organization is prepared to countenance and the amount of control it requires over its international operations will determine the entry mode strategy it adopts.

Another important issue is how globalization affects the organizational structure and processes within a firm, that is, whether its existing structure is sufficiently flexible to enable the rapid dispersal of knowledge and distinctive capabilities across its borders. This is important if the organization is to achieve synergies and more readily cope with external changes. Lastly, we will evaluate some of the myths of globalization, and assess the opportunities and challenges that globalization brings.

- In Section 9.1 we start the chapter with a discussion of globalization. We look at the evidence for globalization as articulated by Theodore Levitt and consider alternative views.

- Section 9.2 deals with international strategy and looks at the motives for international expansion.

- In Section 9.3 we describe Ghoshal's globalization framework and discuss how an organization can achieve competitive advantage in the global economy.

- Section 9.4 evaluates four different types of international strategy that the organization can pursue: *multidomestic*, *international*, *global*, and *transnational*. The transnational strategy is then considered in detail.

- Section 9.5 considers different entry mode strategies based upon an organization's desire to control its overseas operations and its need to manage risk.

- Section 9.6 is an evaluation of Porter's diamond and how organizations achieve competitive advantage abroad based on factors that exist within their home nation.

- In Section 9.7 we consider some of the prevailing myths of globalization and whether truly globalized companies actually exist.

- The chapter ends in Section 9.8 with an assessment of the opportunities and challenges facing globally integrated enterprises and national governments in a globalized world.

9.1 Globalization or Localization

GLOBALIZATION

refers to the linkages between markets that exist across national borders. This implies that what happens in one country has an impact on occurrences in other countries

Globalization refers to the linkages between markets that exist across national borders. These linkages may be economic, financial, social, or political—in effect, anything that leads to increased interdependence among nations. This implies that what happens in one country has an impact on occurrences in other countries. In contrast, localization implies that national differences between countries are important and that organizations must take account of these differences in their product offerings, distributions, and product promotions if they are to be successful.

Levitt (1983), a proponent of globalization, argues that a major driving force for convergence between nations is technology. Technology has created a world in which consumers worldwide desire standardized products. The national differences that existed have gone, and only corporations which realize this will be in a position to take advantage of the huge economies of scale in production, distribution, marketing, and management that globalization brings. For Levitt, this spells the end for multinational corporations, that is, corporations that operate in a number of countries and adjust their product offering to suit each country. It marks the ascendancy of the global corporation—one that sells the same products to all nations in the same way, thereby achieving low costs through economies of scale. As Levitt states, somewhat emphatically, 'the world's needs and desires have been irrevocably homogenized'. Coca-Cola and Pepsi soft drinks are examples of globally standardized products that easily cross national borders.

Success in this globalized marketplace requires that organizations compete on price and quality, offering the same products sold at home to international markets. It requires organizations to search for similarities that exist in segments around the world in order to exploit economies of scale. Globalization and the resulting standardization of products both respond to homogenized markets and expand these markets by offering products at lower prices. In this respect Levitt's global corporation is a result of globalization but is also the cause of continuing convergence.

Contrary to Levitt's assertions, Douglas and Wind (1987) argue that success requires standardized products and global brands; organizations can make greater profits by adapting products and marketing strategies to suit individual markets. They point out that while there are global segments with similar needs, such as luxury goods, this is not a universal trend. For example, Nestlé's frozen food division Findus finds it necessary to market fish fingers to its UK consumers and *coq au vin* to the French, reflecting an understanding of the importance of national differences. For Douglas and Wind (1987, p. 22), 'The evidence suggests that the similarities in customer behaviour are restricted to a relatively limited number of target segments' and 'substantial differences between countries' still exist.

Douglas and Wind also reject Levitt's assertion that consumers worldwide are becoming more price-sensitive, trading product features for a lower price. Instead they point out that a strategy of offering low prices does not lead to a sustainable competitive advantage since it is readily imitated by your competitors. In the same way, technological innovations may lower a competitor's cost structure and therefore its prices. As for economies of scale from supplying a global market, Douglas and Wind state that technological improvements have actually allowed scale efficiencies at lower levels of output. This means that organizations can service differences in national markets more efficiently. Other impediments to globalization may also come from tariffs and import restrictions imposed by foreign governments. Even within the corporation, restrictions to globalization may arise from local managers of foreign subsidiaries who see standardization as demotivating. It deprives them of their autonomy to make decisions based on their local expertise. Therefore, Douglas and Wind argue that globalization is far from ubiquitous and that organizations would be unwise to ignore national differences. A similar point is made by Ghemawat (2005) who states that geographic and other differences have not been superseded by globalization but rather are increasing in importance. He argues that an understanding of regional strategies can help organizations boost their performance.

Hofstede (1991) argues that the national varieties that exist between countries are likely to survive for some time. In contrast to the advocates of globalization, he sees a worldwide homogenization of people's attitudes 'under the influence of a presumed cultural melting-pot process' as very far off indeed. Hofstede reminds us that:

> *Not all values and practices in a society, however, are affected by technology or its products. If young Turks drink Coca-Cola this does not necessarily affect their attitudes towards authority ... In the sphere of values, i.e. fundamental attitudes towards life and other people, young Turks differ from young Americans just as old Turks differ from old Americans. There is no evidence that the cultures of present-day generations from different countries are converging. (Hofstede 1997, p. 17)*

Levitt, and Douglas and Wind, occupy opposite sides of the globalization debate. The debate is not academic but pragmatic; the outcome affects corporations. For instance, if the world is becoming increasingly globalized, this impacts upon the strategic choices facing organizations. If the world is becoming increasingly localized, a different set of strategic responses are required. What is often lost sight of in the globalization debate is its effects on the lives of ordinary people. Clearly, one might take a Utilitarian approach and argue that, on balance, a greater good is accomplished. However, this often masks local tragedies. (see Case Study: The Impact of Globalization). We should point out that when referring to a multinational corporation or multinational enterprise, we mean all organizations competing internationally. This is different to Levitt who uses the term to characterize a particular strategic response. Bartlett and Ghoshal (1989) also use the term multinational corporation to define a particular strategic response. What these authors refer to as a multinational strategy we will refer to as a multidomestic strategy (see below).

CASE STUDY 9.1
The Impact of Globalization

Eight days ago, a 32-year-old France Télécom worker died after throwing herself from the fifth-floor window of company premises in Paris following news of further corporate reorganisation.

© iStockphoto.com/JurgaR

The suicide, the 23rd among staff at the former phone monopoly in 18 months, triggered anguish about stress at work. Didier Lombard, the company's chairman, was summoned to a meeting with Employment Minister Xavier Darcos and efforts to provide psychological support to employees during restructuring were stepped up at companies across the land.

The sense of workplace stress when you cross the threshold of a French office or factory doesn't seem notably greater than anywhere else in Europe in these difficult times. But in asides and emails, employees frequently complain about how over-loaded they are.

Hervé Juvin, president of strategic management advisory firm Eurogroup Institute and a respected social analyst, suggests that the problem lies not so much in workplaces, but in how the French regard work. Surveys consistently suggest that they are happy about their own lives, but alarmed about the wider world. 'When it comes to their family, their homes, their friends, all is fine,' he says. 'But beyond that, they see the world at large as hostile.'

French transport infrastructure and medical services are the envy of the world, the countryside is spacious and beautiful, Paris remains an architectural jewel, and there is an ample social safety net for those who lose their jobs or suffer illness.

Yet there is a collective fear that these anchors are all coming adrift, that the services available today will decline in the future. And that fear is not without foundation. The state deficit is forecast to reach almost 74% of GDP. The social security and healthcare overdraft limit has just been doubled to €20bn (£18bn), and endless media stories talk of service quality being eroded as the overblown state seeks to shed jobs and enhance public sector efficiency.

Stéphane Rozès, a political analyst and president of study firm Cap, says: 'The French say that now they are happy, but when you ask them about the future they are pessimistic. They feel they are not in control of their destiny. For the past 15 years, the French have been convinced that tomorrow will be worse than today. They want to conserve the present.'

This helps explain why work looms so large in perceptions of self-worth. Juvin says that staff 'cling to the company, which is their last point of outside certainty in an uncertain world'.

The vehemence of French reactions to site closures and restructuring this year is rooted in this desperate struggle to balk change. Factory occupations and boss-nappings have been commonplace. Ministers swarm to try to avert job losses and save doomed plants. When HIG Capital, an American private equity firm, agreed to invest €1m to save just 50 jobs at the troubled Molex car parts plant near Toulouse, the announcement was made personally by industry minister Christian Estrosi.

'There is a widespread perception that the state should guarantee jobs for life and rising incomes,' says Juvin. As the state pares the civil service, ministers play to the gallery, leaning on companies, sometimes strong-arming potential investors, standing shoulder-to-shoulder with employees to produce an adapted version of the status quo.

The French crave security, and the private sector no longer provides it. Three-quarters of parents want their children to get safe state jobs. Every year, 800,000 candidates compete for 60,000 public sector posts.

Graduates of elite colleges expected to join an executive élite this autumn, but now find themselves as low-paid, insecure interns. There are more than 20 types of employment contract, but more and more employees—particularly the young and unskilled—are signed on short-term rather than indefinite contracts that offer full employment protection.

Meantime, the 35-hour week, still nominally in force in some companies, increased time off in exchange for flexibility that benefits employers. Factory workers can find themselves working split shifts, or accountants protracted days during the company reporting season, increasing pressure on family life. In effect, staff are obliged to do as much work, in less time. Hence the stress.

Middle-class employees 'thought they had a deal with their employers', says Juvin. 'If I give a lot to the company, the company will give a lot to me.' Restructuring and job-shedding have shredded the contract.

Often reluctantly, workers have become highly mobile. A report to the Conseil d'Orientation pour l'Emploi last week showed that in 2005 a quarter of French people had previously worked outside the region where they now work, against an EU average of 15%. Because around half of households rent, the French can relocate far more readily than their UK counterparts in search of work or the good life.

Unemployment at the end of June reached 9.1% — 2.6 million — in mainland France, up from little more than 7% in the first quarter of 2008. But according to the accompanying quarterly survey from the national statistics institute, the number of people wanting work was actually 3.3 million.

The pervading sense of insecurity and job scarcity prompt saving. While British and American consumers hocked themselves up to the hilt with mortgages and credit card debt in the boom years, the French continued to save almost €15 for every €100 earned.

All this helps to explain why the dream of many French families remains enshrined in the 1995 film *Le Bonheur est dans le pré*, in which a harassed factory owner flees a northern industrial town to raise geese in the south-west. He finds happiness gazing over the meadow, companionship in the village café on market days, and professional fulfilment modernising the farm's production of foie gras.

But France cannot run away from globalisation, live on peasant-style craft production, or count the value of happiness derived from gazing at meadows. To become happy, Juvin believes, the French need to abandon the idea that the state should solve all problems. Rozès says they need to work together, locally, to shape their future. Both agree French workers need to regain the sense that they are in control of their destiny. How would you measure that?

Source: 'Workplace stress adds to the gloom for pessimistic French' *The Guardian*, 20 September 2009.

Questions

1. What, if anything, can French companies do to alleviate the growing sense of alienation being felt by their employees?
2. To what extent is this a symptom of a globalized marketplace and, therefore, outside French state control?
3. Evaluate the extent to which the French government can embrace globalization for economic prosperity whilst simultaneously 'dictating' terms of employment for foreign employers.

For further information on the benefits and disadvantages of globalization go to the Online Resource Centre and see the Key Work feature. www.oxfordtextbooks.co.uk/orc/henry2e/

9.2 International Strategy

What motivates organizations to pursue a strategy of international diversification? When a decision is made to expand abroad, what are the different types of market entry open to organizations? We will see later that some of these market entry strategies coincide with the growth strategies we evaluated in **Chapter 8**. The motives for firms to expand internationally can be evaluated by looking at *organizational factors* and *environmental factors*. The organizational factors occur within the firm while the environmental factors are exogenous, that is, outside the firm's control.

9.2.1 Organizational Factors

These can be divided into:

- the role of the senior management team, and
- firm-specific factors.

The Role of the Management Team

The perception of the senior management team about the importance of international activities will play a role in the decision of the organization to internationalize. This may arise from a saturation of the domestic market; for example, the mobile phone giant Nokia was forced to expand beyond the confines of its domestic economy in Finland. Where an organization faces large fixed costs, such as can be seen with R&D within the pharmaceutical industry, expansion overseas allows it to achieve economies of scale by spreading its costs over greater units of output. Similar economies of scale are achieved by firms which compete in the branded packaged goods industry such as Proctor & Gamble and Unilever. These firms have developed distinctive capabilities in managing and coordinating their marketing activities worldwide.

The extent to which managers possess knowledge and experience of overseas markets will have a bearing on their decision to expand abroad. Another factor will be the management perception of risks involved in overseas activities. In fact, the perceived level of risk can be correlated with the different types of market entry undertaken. We will discuss entry mode strategies in Section 9.5. An important consideration in

deciding whether to internationalize will be the locational advantages that an organization might gain from its value chain. The various activities that go to make up an
organization's value chain may be located in different countries to take account of
differential costs and other locational advantages that a country may possess. We
discussed the value chain in detail in **Chapter 4**. We will revisit locational advantages
when we consider national differences as a source of competitive advantage.

Firm-Specific Factors

These include the size of the firm and the international appeal of an organization's
product. Other things being equal, the likelihood is that larger firms will internationalize more than smaller ones. This is not surprising given that larger firms possess
greater resources, produce greater capacity, and are therefore likely to require wider
market coverage to attain economies of scale. That said, some firms may be relatively
small but the nature of their product offering may have an international appeal, such
as software, in which case a small firm may quickly internationalize. Products or
services which possess an international brand image and, therefore, international
appeal may explain why some firms expand internationally, for example Coca-Cola,
Starbucks, and high-end fashion goods such as Armani.

9.2.2 Environmental Factors

Environmental factors can be divided into:

- unsolicited proposals,
- the 'bandwagon' effect, and
- attractiveness of the host country.

Unsolicited Proposals

An unsolicited proposal may come about from an organization being approached by
a foreign government, distributor, or customer.

The 'Bandwagon' Effect

The bandwagon effect refers to organizations which follow competitors who have
gone international. Clearly, organizations will not want to be seen to be missing out
on new opportunities. In the same way organizations may come to the conclusion
that a presence in an overseas market is desirable.

Attractiveness of the Host Country

The market size of countries and a favourable regime towards foreign direct investment will be attractive to organizations. The rising per capita incomes of China and

Modern Beijing: The rising per capita incomes and high population of China are proving an irresistible lure for many businesses.

© istock.com/Xin Zhu

India, coupled with populations that together make up a third of the world's population, are proving an irresistible lure for many organizations.

9.3 A Globalization Framework

Ghoshal (1987) outlines a framework in which he argues that a multinational corporation can benefit from three different sources of competitive advantage when seeking to go global. In addition, he states three goals inherent to all multinationals:

- The organization must achieve efficiency in its current activities.
- It must manage the risks inherent in carrying out those activities.
- It must develop learning capabilities that allow it to innovate and adapt to the future.

In order to gain competitive advantage the organization will need to undertake actions that enable it to achieve these three goals. These may involve trade-offs as multinational corporations pursue goals that will at times be conflicting. This is not a cause for concern, as Ghoshal's framework allows a multinational to differentiate between the benefits and costs of alternative strategies. Ghoshal states that an organization has three fundamental tools by which it can build competitive advantage.

- It can exploit the differences in input and output markets that exist in different countries. For example, the cost of employing a software engineer in India is many times cheaper than in the US.

6

- It can benefit from economies of scale in its different activities.
- It can take advantage of synergies or the economies of scope that derive from its diversity of activities.

Table 9.1 gives a summary of the strategic objectives of the organization and the sources of competitive advantage open to the multinational corporation.

TABLE 9.1

Global strategy: objectives and the sources of competitive advantage. Sources of Competitive Advantage from *Strategic Management Journal* vol 8:5 by S. Ghoshal, 1987 © John Wiley & Sons Ltd. Reproduced with permission.

Strategic objectives	Sources of competitive advantage		
	National differences	Scale economies	Scope economies
Achieving efficiency in current operations	Benefiting from differences in factor costs—wages and cost of capital	Expanding and exploiting potential scale economies in each activity	Sharing of investments and costs across products, markets, and businesses
Managing risks	Managing different kinds of risks arising from market- or policy-induced changes in comparative advantages of different countries	Balancing scale with strategic and operational flexibility	Portfolio diversification of risks and creation of side-bets
Innovation, learning, and adaptation	Learning from societal differences in organizational and managerial processes and systems	Benefiting from experience—cost reduction and innovation	Shared learning across organizational components in different products, markets, or businesses

9.3.1 The Goals of a Multinational Corporation

Achieving Efficiency

The efficiency of an organization is the ratio of the value of its outputs to the costs of all its inputs (Ghoshal 1987, p. 428). In other words, the greater the ratio or the gap between an organization's costs and the value it generates, the more efficient it is. The differentiation of its products from competitor offerings allows an organization to premium price and, therefore, maximize the value of it outputs. Similarly, by pursuing low-cost factors, such as wages or more efficient manufacturing processes, the organization will minimize the costs of its inputs. (See Porter's generic strategies in **Chapter 7** for an explanation of the firm as a low-cost producer and differentiator.) In effect, this allows a multinational corporation to configure its value chain to optimize the use of its resources.

Managing Risks

The multinational corporation faces different types of risk. These include *macro-economic* risks which are outside its control, such as military conflicts, *political* risks which emanate from decisions taken by national governments, *competitive* risks which deal with the uncertainty about how competitors will react to its strategies, and, lastly, *resource* risks. Resource risks imply that the firm may not have or be able to acquire the resources it needs to undertake its strategy. This might be because it lacks a particular technology. A key point to bear in mind is that risks change over time, necessitating an awareness of the external environment.

Innovation, Learning, and Adaptation

Ghoshal argues that the multinational corporation, by virtue of the different and varied environments within which it finds itself operating, is able to develop diverse capabilities and better learning opportunities than a domestic based firm. Its diverse resource base may help the firm create innovations and exploit them in different locations. However, what is actually required for learning to take place is the existence of learning as an organizational objective which is actively supported and encouraged by senior management utilizing requisite systems and processes. In short, learning must pervade the organization's culture if it is to manifest itself in innovation.

9.3.2 The Sources of Competitive Advantage

We mentioned earlier that there are three tools for achieving global competitive advantage. These are *national differences*, *economies of scale*, and *economies of scope*.

National Differences

This deals with what are sometimes called *locational advantages*. Locational advantages derive from the observed fact that different countries have different factor endowments which provide these countries with different factor costs. For example, Russia has an abundant supply of natural gas, whereas Japan has very little. As a result of this factor endowment Russia is an exporter of natural gas whereas Japan is an importer. In the same way, the activities that go to make up a multinational corporation's value chain have different factor costs. The aim of the multinational corporation, then, is to configure its value chain in such a way that each of its activities is located in the country which has the lowest cost. National differences may also arise because of the clustering of key suppliers or technology firms around a particular location, for example, Silicon Valley in California. Increasingly, organizations in the UK from finance to telecoms have set up call centres in India for dealing with customer service matters. This allows organizations to exploit the cheap labour rates existing in India and keep their cost base down. This is fine as long as productivity and quality levels do not offset the benefits of lower wages.

Economies of Scale

The concept of economies of scale states that as a firm increases the volume of its output so it is able to achieve a reduction in its unit costs. One reason for this is that as firms produce ever larger outputs so their learning experience accumulates. This allows them to move down the experience curve, which in turn generates cost reductions. The firm should configure its value chain in order to ensure that it achieves economies of scale in each activity.

Economies of Scope

Economies of scope arise from an understanding that the cost of undertaking two activities together is sometimes less than the cost of undertaking them separately. For example, auto manufacturers use common platforms when making different types of cars. This allows them to achieve smaller production runs at a relatively low cost through economies of scope. This flexible manufacturing enables an organization to produce a customized offering for the consumer at relatively low unit costs. In managing its activities globally, the organization needs to use all three sources of competitive advantage in order to simultaneously maximize its efficiency, risk, and learning: 'The key to a successful global strategy is to manage the interactions between these different goals and means' (Ghoshal 1987, p. 427).

9.4 Types of International Strategy

When considering how to compete in international markets organizations are faced with a stark dilemma. On the one hand, to what extent should they produce standardized products for sale in different countries utilizing the locational advantages of low-cost countries? On the other hand, to what extent should they produce differentiated products which embody variations in local tastes and preferences but incur greater costs? This is the debate between *globalization and localization* which we discussed in greater detail in Section 9.1 when we assessed the work of Theodore Levitt. For now we can say that, other things being equal, globalization provides for greater efficiency through economies of scale brought about by standardization and locational advantages, while localization ensures that the organization's products are responsive to and meet the needs of local preferences.

The issue of globalization versus responsiveness to local needs highlights four basic strategies open to the organization seeking to diversify its activities overseas. These are: *multidomestic*, *international*, *global*, and *transnational*.

9.4.1 Multidomestic Strategy

A multidomestic strategy is aimed at adapting a product for use in national markets and thereby responding more effectively to the changes in local demand conditions. This assumes that each national market is unique and independent of the activities in other national markets. To this extent local managers are often given substantial autonomy to determine how the product will meet the needs of local consumers. A benefit of this decentralized multidomestic strategy is that value chain activities can more closely reflect local market conditions. A disadvantage of a multidomestic strategy is that with increased variety come increased costs. Therefore, an important task for managers is to try to determine the point at which differentiation increases an organization's costs more than the value it adds for the consumer. At this point differentiation fails to be appreciated by the consumer. In addition, a multidomestic strategy tends to impede learning across country boundaries as capabilities which reside within a given country are not automatically shared.

Wal-Mart entered the German market in 1998 with the acquisition of the Wertkauf and Interspar grocery chains. However, despite generating sales of $2.5 billion a year, it never posted a profit. Critics of the US giant said Wal-Mart failed to understand the different culture that exists in Germany. For example, an attempt to introduce 'greeters' in stores whose role was to smile at every customer is thought to have been particularly unpopular. In addition, a lawsuit by employees forced Wal-Mart to change part of an ethics manual which prevented romantic relationships between supervisors and employees. Although this practice was the norm in the US, German workers saw it as a violation of their personal rights. Added to this, Wal-Mart found that its position of being the cheapest retailer in its markets was already taken by Aldi (*Daily Telegraph* 2006).

> **For a further discussion of multidomestic strategies go to the Online Resource Centre and see the Key Work feature.**
> **www.oxfordtextbooks.co.uk/orc/henry2e/**

9.4.2 Global Strategy

With a global strategy the organization seeks to provide standardized products for its international markets. If a multidomestic strategy accepts cost increases as the price for local differentiation, a global strategy consciously embraces cost reductions as the benefit of manufacturing standardized products. An organization pursuing a global strategy will have their manufacturing, marketing, and R&D centralized in a few locations. A combination of standardization with centralized facilities and functions enables them to reap substantial economies of scale. Industry examples include aerospace, pharmaceuticals, consumer electronics, and semiconductors. Firms such as

Motorola, Sony, and Boeing have developed a global brand that crosses national borders. A disadvantage of a global strategy is that it may overestimate the extent to which tastes are converging and fail to respond to important local differences. For example, the US retailer Wal-Mart exited South Korea when it became clear its hypermarket formula did not appeal to local tastes.

9.4.3 International Strategy

An international strategy is based upon an organization exploiting its core competencies and distinctive capabilities in foreign markets. Local managers may be provided with some degree of autonomy in adapting products to suit local markets, but this is likely to be at the margin only. The core competencies and capabilities inherent within the organization will be centralized in the home country. For example, the sports shoe manufacturer Nike has core competencies in design and product development. These value chain activities are based in the US, while other activities, such as manufacturing, take place in Far Eastern countries like Thailand. A disadvantage of this strategy is that its concentration of some activities in one country can leave it open to threats from currency appreciations. Also, the geographical distance and different cultures often make it difficult to control production and quality. Finally, the lack of resources given to overseas subsidiaries can lead to a demotivation of local managers as their autonomy to make important decisions is eroded. Table 9.2 shows the organizational characteristics that relate to these three international strategies.

TABLE 9.2

Characteristics of multidomestic, global, and international companies.
Reprinted by permission of Harvard Business School Press. From C. Bartlett and S. Ghoshal (1998). *Managing Across Borders: The Transnational Solution* (2nd edn), p. 67. Copyright © 1989 by the Harvard Business School Publishing Corporation. All rights reserved.

Organizational characteristic	Multidomestic	Global	International
Configuration of assets and capabilities	Decentralized and nationally self-sufficient	Centralized and globally scaled	Sources of core competencies centralized, others decentralized
Role of overseas operations	Sensing and exploiting local opportunities	Implementing parent company strategies	Adapting and leveraging parent company competencies
Development and diffusion of knowledge	Knowledge developed and retained within each unit	Knowledge developed and retained at the centre	Knowledge developed at the centre and transferred to overseas units

9.4.4 Transnational Strategy[1]

Bartlett and Ghoshal (1989) argue that, until recently, most organizations in worldwide industries were faced with unidimensional strategic requirements. In any given

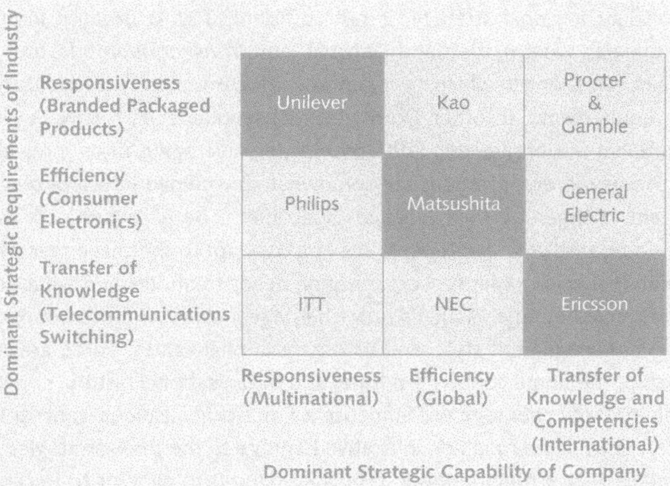

FIGURE 9.1

Industry requirements and company capabilities
Reprinted by permission of Harvard Business School Press. From C. Bartlett and S. Ghoshal (1998). *Managing Across Borders: The Transnational Solution* (2nd edn), p. 23. Copyright © 1998 by the Harvard Business School Publishing Corporation. All rights reserved.

industry, an organization could obtain success by matching its resources and capabilities to achieve efficiency, or responsiveness, or knowledge transfer required by that industry, that is, 'company performance was based primarily on the fit between the dominant strategic requirement of the business and the firm's dominant strategic capability' (Bartlett and Ghoshal 1989, p. 21).

Figure 9.1 shows nine leading organizations in three worldwide industries, and maps the strategic requirements of their industry against the strategic capability of the company. We can see from the diagram that Unilever, Matsushita, and Ericsson are successful examples of a multidomestic, a global, and an international company, respectively. The less successful companies include Kao, Japan's competitor to Procter & Gamble, and Unilever. Kao's dominant capability is global efficiency and standardization. However, it has failed to understand the differences between markets, and this lack of national responsiveness has prevented it becoming a global player. Interestingly, Bartlett and Ghoshal make the observation that Kao's lack of success informs us that Levitt's assertion of homogeneous consumers needs is not yet a reality. In contrast to Kao, the European company Unilever has been highly successful in this industry by recognizing the need for local product differentiation and strategic responses.

Today the search for a match between an organization's capabilities and a single set of environment forces no longer holds. This has been replaced by a more complex set of environment demands. Organizations operating in global industries have to reconcile diverse and often conflicting strategic needs. In the past companies could succeed with a unidimensional strategic capability that emphasized efficiency, or responsiveness, or transferring knowledge and core competencies, whereas now more and more industries are driven by the realization that a multidomestic, nor an international or a global strategy, is not sufficient. This is because industries are evolving towards what Bartlett and Ghoshal term *transnational industries*. A transnational industry is one in which an organization is confronted with multidimensional strategic requirements. In other words, it must simultaneously achieve global efficiency, national responsiveness, and a worldwide leveraging of its innovations and learning. However, organizations are somewhat constrained in responding to these environment changes by their internal capabilities. These, in turn, are contingent upon their *administrative heritage*. In seeking to adapt to the challenges of a changing international environment an organization needs to understand what determines its administrative heritage. Administrative heritage includes a firm's configuration of its assets, its management style, and its organizational values. These are influenced by leadership, the home country's culture, and organizational history.

The administrative heritage will influence a firm's organizational form as well as its capabilities. Thus, if we map administrative heritage to the three strategies discussed above we see that a multidomestic firm is structured to allow it to decentralize its assets and capabilities such that its foreign operations are able to respond to national differences between markets. An international firm is structured in a way that allows it to transfer knowledge and capabilities to foreign operations that are less developed. Its foreign operations possess some autonomy to adapt new products and strategies but they are more reliant on the parent company for these new products and ideas, which necessitates more coordination by the parent company than we see with a multidomestic firm. A global organization's structure allows for a centralization of its assets, resources, and responsibilities. The role of its foreign subsidiaries is to build global scale. Unlike the multidomestic or international organization, the global organization has less autonomy to adapt new products or strategies. A *transnational organization* seeks to maximize the trade-offs between efficiency and responsiveness to local need by redefining the problem. As Bartlett and Ghoshal (1989, p. 59) state:

> It seeks efficiency not for its own sake, but as a means to achieve global competitiveness. It acknowledges the importance of local responsiveness, but as a tool for achieving flexibility in international operations.

Therefore, a transnational strategy recognizes the benefits of efficiency that derive from the global company, the response to local needs of the multidomestic firm, and the transfer of knowledge and capabilities across countries by the international firm. However, where the transnational strategy differs from the other organizational forms is that it neither dogmatically centralizes nor decentralizes, but instead makes selective decisions, that is, it recognizes that some resources and capabilities are better centralized in the home country to achieve economies of scale and protect its core competencies. For example, R&D is a capability that most organizations agree is best kept in the home country. Other resources may be centralized but not in the home country. For example, a production plant for labour-intensive products which service global operations may be built in a low-wage economy such as Mexico. Access to a particular technology may require centralization of activities in a specific country like the US. In the same way other resources may best be decentralized to create flexibility and avoid reliance on a single facility.

The managers of a transnational organization will centralize some resources in the home country and some abroad, and distribute others between the organization's various national operations. This leads to a far more complex configuration of resources and capabilities that are distributed but also specialized. The dispersed resources are managed throughout the organization by creating interdependencies between the subsidiaries. This cannot be achieved through existing organizational forms but requires an *integrated network*. This integrated network emphasizes 'significant flows of components, products, resources, people, and information that must be managed in the transnational' (Bartlett and Ghoshal 1989, p. 61). In Figure 9.2 each of these four broad strategies are plotted according to the extent to which they reflect competitive pressures to reduce costs and the extent to which there exists a need to adapt to local market conditions.

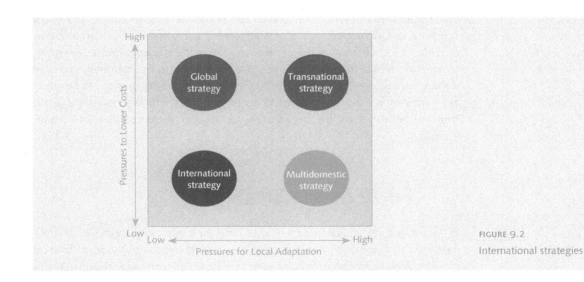

FIGURE 9.2
International strategies

For the transnational organization, each activity within the firm's value chain is undertaken in the location which provides for the lowest costs. Its resources and capabilities can be leveraged worldwide. However, accomplishment of this requires a move away from traditional organizational structures towards a different kind of corporate structure which allows the organization to manage these complex interactions through integrated networks. The discussion of the transnational organization, with its emphasis on internal resources and capabilities, has clear affinities with the resource-based view of competitive advantage that we discussed in **Chapter 5**. For the transnational organization, the key capability for success is not a choice among efficiency, responsiveness, or learning. It is the simultaneous attainment of all three that allows the organization to remain competitive.

GLOBAL STRATEGY

the organization seeks to provide standardized products for its international markets which are produced in a few centralized locations

MULTIDOMESTIC STRATEGY

is aimed at adapting a product or service for use in national markets and thereby responding more effectively to the changes in local demand conditions

INTERNATIONAL STRATEGY

is based upon an organization exploiting its core competencies and distinctive capabilities in foreign markets

TRANSNATIONAL STRATEGY

seeks to simultaneously achieve global efficiency, national responsiveness, and a worldwide leveraging of its innovations and learning

To summarize, a global strategy allows a multinational corporation to achieve low costs through economies of scale and a coordinated strategy, but at the expense of being responsive to the needs of local markets. The global organization is configured in a way which allows no slack resources for overseas subsidiaries. This effectively curtails its ability and, therefore, motivation to respond to local needs. This also prevents the global organization from accessing learning opportunities that exist outside its home country. A multidomestic strategy is the polar opposite of a global strategy. With a multidomestic strategy the organization responds effectively to local market conditions and customer preferences in different countries. However, this level of differentiation means it is unable to achieve greater efficiency through low costs. Any local innovations may simply be the result of managers trying to protect their turf rather than working towards the corporate good. An international strategy allows a parent company to transfer its knowledge and capabilities to other countries and the devolution of some autonomy to overseas managers, but less so than we find in a multidomestic strategy. It's configuration of assets make it less efficient than a global company, and less responsive than a multidomestic company. Lastly, an organization following a transnational strategy seeks to achieve the efficiency and local responsiveness inherent in the previous three strategies but also to leverage innovation and learning across countries. The idea is that its resources and capabilities can be leveraged worldwide. However, in order to accomplish this a different kind of corporate structure which allows the organization to manage these complex interactions is required.

9.5 Entry Mode Strategies

ENTRY MODE STRATEGIES

the different types of strategy that organizations can use to enter international markets

In Section 9.4 we evaluated a number of different international strategies that the multinational corporation can pursue in its search to reduce costs, adapt to local markets, and internalize across all markets the ability to learn and innovate. In this section we will address the different types of entry mode strategies that organizations can use to enter international markets. Brouthers (1995) states that in selecting an appropriate entry mode organizations need to answer two questions.

- What levels of resource commitment are they prepared to make?
- What level of control over their international operations do they require?

For instance, organizations may not be willing to commit resources in what they perceive to be high-risk countries. In contrast, where the perception of risk in countries is perceived to be low, organizations may want control over the operation. What is important is the organization's perception of international risk, which determines the answer to these two questions and drives the type of entry mode that an organization will choose.

According to Miller (1992), international risk can be seen to consist of three integrated parts: the general environment, industry, and firm-specific risks. Although these risks are also faced by firms which operate in the domestic environment, the difference is that for the international firm, some of these risks are far greater. General environmental risks refer to uncertainties which affect all industries within a given country in a similar way, such as political risk. Industry risks refer to input market uncertainties, such as labour or material supplies. Firm-specific risks include such things as uncertainties that arise as a result of employee disputes. These firm-specific uncertainties exist in the domestic market, but organizations operating abroad have the added responsibility of undertaking their activities in a different culture. Therefore, when considering an international entry mode strategy, managers need to be aware of the totality of risks since if they consider only one type of international risk, such as input market uncertainties, this may lead to adoption of an incorrect entry mode strategy. This is because the entry mode eventually adopted may result in unforeseen problems arising because the other international risk issues were not considered. We shall evaluate some of the different entry mode strategies in detail. These are exporting, licensing, franchising, joint ventures and strategic alliances, and wholly owned subsidiaries.[2]

9.5.1 Exporting

Organizations are naturally a little tentative about committing resources to new markets about which they have varying degrees of knowledge. Under these conditions an organization may initially want to limit its resource commitments abroad until it builds up more local knowledge and develops its capabilities. Exporting is where an organization makes goods and services in the home country and sells them in other countries. It is attractive in as much as it provides an opportunity for an organization to acquire international experience whilst minimizing its risk exposure and resource commitments. At the same time, it also allows an organization to gain economies of scale through increased sales. A disadvantage of exporting is that it relies on local distributors, some of whom may be less than committed to marketing and promoting the international firm's products.

Figure 9.3 shows each entry mode strategy drawn against the degree of perceived risk and the amount of control acquired. What is apparent is that the level of risk increases as the organization seeks to maintain more control over its activities. Thus, exporting provides little perceived risk but little control, whereas a wholly owned subsidiary produces total control but comes with substantial risk.

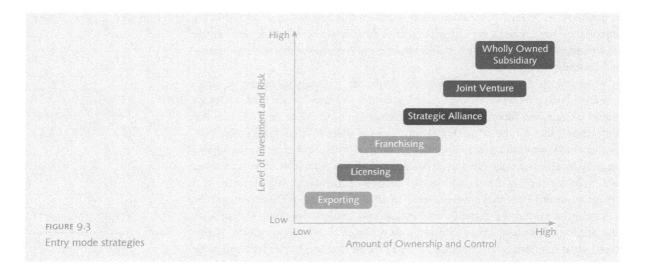

FIGURE 9.3
Entry mode strategies

9.5.2 Licensing

Licensing can be seen as another way of gaining entry into overseas markets without large resource commitments. In return for a fee, the organization grants the right to use its patent, trademark, or intellectual property. The advantages of licensing are that it requires little capital and offers a relatively quick access to overseas markets. The disadvantages of licensing are that it requires an appropriate licensee who may in time be able to imitate your product and become a competitor.

9.5.3 Franchising

Franchising is a form of licensing that is employed by many international companies such as McDonald's, Benetton, and Pizza Hut. Its popularity has grown considerably since 1970. It is a system largely pioneered by US companies. The franchiser agrees to transfer a package of products, systems, and services that it has developed to a franchisee for a fee. The franchisee provides local market knowledge and entre-preneurship. Unlike exporting, the host country may be more receptive to this form of market entry as it involves local ownership and employment. A disadvantage is that unless trust and understanding exist between both parties the franchise will underperform. To be successful franchising needs to be seen by both franchiser and franchisee as mutually beneficial.

9.5.4 Joint Ventures and Strategic Alliances

Joint ventures and strategic alliances were covered in detail in **Chapter 8** when we discussed how organizations implement growth strategies. We can briefly restate that a joint venture exists when two organizations form a separate independent company in which they own shares equally. It is often formed when organizations feel it may be beneficial to combine their resources and capabilities to develop new technologies or gain access to new markets. Strategic alliances take place when two or more separate organizations share some of their resources and capabilities but stop short of forming a separate organization. The idea is that each partner within the strategic alliance gains access to knowledge that it would not otherwise possess and that would be expensive to develop. A useful alliance will involve complementary resources and capabilities that allow both organizations to grow and develop according to their strategic objectives. The ultimate aim of strategic alliances is to learn from your partners. Both joint ventures and strategic alliances work well when each partner's objectives are clear and agreed, and when the working relationship is one based on trust. The disadvantage occurs when managerial differences exist as these must be resolved prior to entering into a strategic alliance. Such problems are compounded when there is the potential for state interference (see Strategy Focus: Joint Ventures in China).

STRATEGY FOCUS
Joint Ventures in China

When Danone, a French food giant, acquired a 51 per cent stake in Wahaha Beverage, a Chinese firm, in 1996, it considered it a coup. And in 2004 HSBC became the envy of rival banks when it acquired a 19.9 per cent stake in Bank of Communications, the smallest of China's national banks and the only one

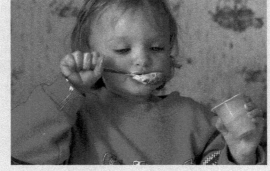

Yoghurt is one of Danone's core products.

that, by law, allowed for the possibility of full acquisition. In what has become a painfully familiar experience in China, however, both companies have since run into trouble. Danone's partnership with Wahaha has erupted into an acrimonious public dispute and the huge growth in Bank of Communications's assets has placed it within the small group of powerful banks that the Chinese government will not permit to be taken over.

Faced with a geographically vast but promising market obscured by a thicket of complex and contradictory rules, many foreign firms have entered China via joint ventures—and then been left grinding their teeth. In theory, the case for joint ventures was compelling. The foreign partner provided capital, knowledge, access to international markets, and jobs. The Chinese partner provided access to cheap labour, local regulatory knowledge, and access to what used to be a relatively unimportant domestic market. The Chinese government protected swathes of the economy from acquisitions, but provided land, tax breaks, and at least the appearance of a welcome to attract investment. In practice, these arrangements have collapsed for three reasons. Chinese companies were happy to receive money and technology, but did not want to be mere adjuncts to foreign firms; in many cases they have large, often global, ambitions of their own. Too often the allocation of profits and investments was unclear, leading to endless squabbling. But perhaps most importantly, China has now changed.

China has become far more open legally because of commitments made to the World Trade Organization as a condition of membership. But its hunger for foreign investors has been sated. The availability of labour and land has fallen, domestic capital is abundant, the local market is now understood to be among the most attractive in the world, and sentiment has become more nationalistic and self-satisfied. So there is less interest in providing access to foreign partners.

When Danone made its investment, Wahaha says it knew little about business and welcomed a partner. Now, alive to the opportunities, it is outraged that it must clear plans with a foreign majority owner which has its own alternative strategies in China through various other (though less important) joint ventures—and it is even more outraged that Danone wants full ownership. Danone says it believed things were going smoothly until 18 months ago, when it discovered Wahaha had started a parallel firm to market similar products. Better positioned are a small number of firms that were clever enough (unlike Danone) and allowed by law (unlike HSBC) to wrap up their original joint ventures amicably. Unilever has shut down more than a dozen and Coca-Cola and Starbucks have recently bought out their Chinese partners. 'For a joint venture to be successful,' says Jonathan Woetzel of McKinsey, 'you have to plan for it to die.'

Source: 'The lessons from Danone and HSBC's troubled partnerships in China' *Economist*, 19 April 2007.

9.5.5 Wholly Owned Subsidiaries

Where an organization seeks to have total control over its operations abroad, it will choose a wholly owned subsidiary as its market entry mode. There are two types: first, a *greenfield* site, in which the firm sets up a new operation. In the second type, the firm may acquire an existing organization abroad. Both types of entry involve the greatest commitment of resources and, therefore, the most risk. The advantage is that this type of entry strategy also generates the greatest returns. The downside is that there is no one with whom to defray the costs. This type of strategy is also referred to as foreign direct investment (FDI). Organizations which use a direct investment strategy include Nestlé, Procter & Gamble, and General Motors. Where an organization possesses unique resources and distinctive capabilities which provide for competitive advantage, it will be more inclined towards a wholly owned subsidiary. For example, Japanese auto makers like Toyota and Honda tend to set up wholly owned subsidiaries abroad. Further, FDI may attract support from the host government in the form of favourable financing, interest rate holidays, and help with local regulations in return for generating local employment. The disadvantages are the financial risk and exposure involved in undertaking a new venture abroad. This is compounded when the organization fails to adequately recruit managers who are familiar with local market conditions.

We have seen that exporting provides an organization with relatively low international risks but gives it little control over the marketing and distribution of its products. At the other extreme, a wholly owned subsidiary gives an organization total control over its operations and the ability to appropriate all its value but at the expense of incurring substantial risk. The strategic choice becomes one of more control and higher risks or low risk and low control. Licensing, franchising, joint ventures, and strategic alliances provide varying degrees of control and exposure to international risks. When the perceived risk is high, the organization may choose to manage this by entering into a joint venture or franchise agreement as a means of sharing the risk.

For a discussion of entry mode strategies go to the Online Resource Centre and see the Key Work feature.
www.oxfordtextbooks.co.uk/orc/henry2e/

9.6 Porter's Diamond of Competitive Advantage

Why do some nations achieve competitive advantage in some industries while other countries achieve a similar advantage in other industries? Porter (1990a,b) argues that a nation's competitiveness derives from the capacity of its industry to innovate and upgrade. Its organizations benefit from competing with strong domestic rivals, aggressive suppliers, and demanding local customers. A country's culture, national values, institutions, and economic structures all contribute to its competitive success. In this respect a nation's competitive advantage results from a localized process. As Porter (1990a, p. 74) states: 'nations succeed in particular industries because their home environment is the most forward looking, dynamic, and challenging'. In effect, organizations that thrive in this sort of competitive environment are better placed to compete abroad.

Organizations that achieve competitive advantage in international markets do this through innovation. Innovation in its broadest sense refers to both new technology and new ways of doing things. It may often involve small changes that build up over time rather than a major technological leap. It does not have to represent new ideas but can come about by pursuing established ideas more rigorously. Innovation does, however, involve investments in skills and knowledge. Sustainable competitive advantage in international markets requires an organization to engage in continuous improvements in its product offering. As competitors will eventually imitate any success, the key to sustainable competitive advantage is an ability to upgrade or continually increase the sophistication of product offerings.

Innovation is predicated on an ability to embrace change. However, as Miller (1990) points out in *The Icarus Paradox*, successful organizations have difficulties in seeing the need for change, let alone instituting change. When an organization is content to sit back and enjoy its current success, a change in its environment or a competitor will eventually overtake them. The British retailer Marks & Spencer, once the doyen of retailing, has taken the best part of half a decade to reconfigure its customer offerings to regain customer loyalty and once again begin adding value for its shareholders.

9.6.1 The Diamond of National Advantage

According to Porter (1990a), organizations are capable of consistent innovation because of four attributes that exist in their home market, which he refers to as the **diamond of national advantage**. These are *factor conditions*, *demand conditions*, *related and supporting industries*, and *firm strategy, structure, and rivalry*. Each point of the diamond contributes towards global success.

1. **Factor conditions.** Since the work of David Ricardo in the nineteenth century, it has been accepted that a country will tend to export goods which make the best use of the factors of production that it has in relative abundance. In other words, it will exploit its comparative advantage.[3] These factors of production include land, labour, and capital. For Porter, factor conditions refer to a country's use of its factors of production that enables it to compete in an industry, such as a skilled labour or a technological capability. In the modern world a country actively creates its most important factors of production, such as a skilled labour

PORTER'S DIAMOND OF NATIONAL ADVANTAGE

seeks to explain why nations achieve competitive advantage in their industries by using four attributes that exist in their home market. These are: factor conditions, demand conditions, related and supporting industries, and firm strategy, structure, and rivalry force for its industries. Therefore, in modern economies a nation's natural stock of factors is far less important as a determinant of international competitive advantage than it was in the past. Natural factors of production such as labour or local resources, however abundant, are insufficient to provide for competitive advantage. What are required are factors of production that are specialized to an industry's needs.

Today, much comparative advantage derives from human effort rather than natural conditions. Such factors will involve continuous investment to upgrade. For example, the concentration of computer companies around Silicon Valley resulted from Xerox's Palo Alto Research Centre, the proximity of Stanford University, and the work of two men, Hewlett and Packard. These dynamic factors could have occurred anywhere (Blinder 2006). Factors such as these that are developed within a country are scarce and difficult for competitors to imitate. Therefore, nations are successful in industries where they are especially good at factor creation (see Figure 9.4).

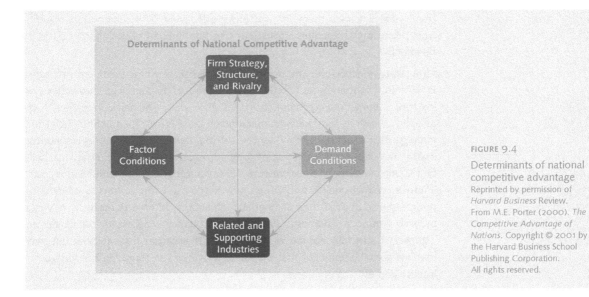

FIGURE 9.4

Determinants of national competitive advantage
Reprinted by permission of *Harvard Business* Review. From *M.E. Porter (2000). The Competitive Advantage of Nations.* Copyright © 2001 by the Harvard Business School Publishing Corporation. All rights reserved.

2. **Demand conditions.** Demand conditions that exist in the home country can have a positive impact on its industry and, therefore, on an organization's ability to compete abroad. This is particularly the case where consumers are both highly sophisticated and demanding. These consumers will be continuously pushing companies to innovate, and to improve and upgrade their products. A benefit of this is that the constant pressure to innovate and upgrade may provide an insight

into future global trends which the organization will be in a better position to exploit. It is in meeting the challenge of this robust consumer demand that organizations gain advantages over foreign competitors which contributes to their success abroad. For example, to benefit most Japanese consumers whose accommodation is small and tightly packed and who endure hot summers and high electrical costs, Japanese companies developed a small quiet air-conditioning unit utilizing energy-efficient rotary compressors.

3. **Related and supporting industries.** A third determinant of national advantage is the existence of related and supporting industries. For example, domestic suppliers that are capable of competing in international markets will be able to provide firms with the most cost-effective inputs. Firms which are located in close proximity to their suppliers can influence their technical efforts and thus increase their level of innovations. Close working relationships between related and supporting industries can produce mutually beneficial innovations. For example, a cluster of Italian footwear firms enables shoe producers to communicate readily with their leather suppliers and learn about new textures and colours which will help shape new styles. The suppliers benefit by receiving useful information about fashion trends which allows them to plan more effectively. This relationship benefits from proximity but requires a conscious effort on the part of both parties if it is to be effective.

4. **Firm strategy, structure, and rivalry.** The use of different management structures in different countries tends to reflect the dynamics of their particular industries. For instance, German management structures work well in technical industries, such as optics, which require precision manufacturing. This calls for a tightly disciplined management structure. The existence of strong domestic competitors is the most important factor for the creation of competitive advantage and international success. Domestic rivalry creates pressures for organizations to innovate, reduce costs, improve product quality, and design new products. It forces firms to continually update the sources of their competitive advantage. Intense domestic rivalry is a proving ground for domestic firms which acquire the necessary capabilities to compete successfully abroad. It is this rivalry that causes firms to seek out new markets abroad, confident that they have already been forged in the furnace of intense domestic competition.

In addition to these four country-specific determinants, there are also two external variables: *the role of chance* and *the role of government*.

1. **The role of chance.** This occurs as a result of unforeseen developments such as new inventions, political interventions by foreign governments, wars, major instabilities in financial markets, discontinuities in input costs such as the price of oil, and technological breakthroughs. These *discontinuities* or *tipping points* were addressed in **Chapter 2**, when we evaluated the role of macro-environmental tools in helping to determine market trends.

2. **The role of government.** Governments can influence all four aspects of the diamond through policies on subsidies, education and training, regulation of capital markets, establishment of local product standards, the purchase of goods and services, tax laws, and the regulation of competition.

9.6.2 Criticisms of Porter's Diamond

The main contention of Porter's diamond framework is that an organization builds on its home base to achieve international competitiveness. Competitive advantage for the organization depends upon four broad attributes which determine a nation's international competitiveness. An effective organization is able to leverage its resources, capabilities, and experience acquired through competing in a rigorous home country to compete successfully abroad. Rugman and D'Cruz (1993) agree that the single diamond framework works well for multinational enterprises based in the US, Japan, and the European Union (EU), the regional grouping referred to as the triad. However, they argue that it is less effective when determining successful global competition in smaller open economies such as Canada and New Zealand.[4] In fact, they state that in order to help improve the international competitiveness of Canada, Porter's framework needs to be substantially revised. Rugman and Verbeke (1993) also take issue with Porter's distinction between a country's home base which provides its firms with their source of competitive advantage, and other countries, which Porter argues can be selectively 'tapped into' but are much less important for competitive advantage than their home country. As Rugman and Verbeke (1993, p. 76) state:

> this viewpoint does not adequately address the complexities of real world global strategic management . . . small nations such as Canada and New Zealand . . . may come to rely on a particular large host nation . . . in such a way that the distinction between the home base and host nations as sources of global competitive advantage may become blurred.

According to Rugman (1992), if we look at Canada, the implication of this for Canadian-owned multinational enterprises is that their managers should treat the US diamond as their home market. This is because their competitive advantages derive from attributes that exist in the US diamond rather than the Canadian diamond. In effect, Canada and other smaller countries are simply too small to offer a basis for international competitive advantage on their own. Therefore, greater opportunities exist for small economies that treat a larger foreign diamond as their home diamond. To capture this, Rugman and D'Cruz (1991) suggest a *double diamond framework* in which managers of a Canadian multinational, for example, can address the determinants of competitiveness in Canada as well as in the US when formulating their strategies. Hodgetts (1993, p. 45) points out that the multinational enterprise Nestlé achieves around 95 per cent of its sales outside Switzerland.

Thus the Swiss diamond of competitive advantage is less relevant than that of foreign countries in shaping the contribution of Nestlé to the home economy. This is not only true for Switzerland but for 95 per cent of the world's nations.

When we look at smaller economies their home diamond may be important but it is the larger diamonds of major trading partners that are of *paramount* importance. Therefore, any assessment of competitive advantage must take account of the relationship between the organization and its home and foreign diamond. As Hodgetts (1993, p. 46) reminds us:

different diamonds need to be constructed and analyzed for different countries, and these diamonds often require integration and linkage with the diamonds of other economically stronger countries thus creating a double diamond paradigm.

9.7 The Myths of Global Strategy

Rangan (2000) argues that there are seven common myths about companies considering a global strategy.[5]

1. **Any company with money can go global.** The reality is that companies that succeed abroad possess valuable intangible assets that help them beat competitors in their own home market. This can include a superior value proposition such as that developed by the Swedish furniture retailer IKEA, and a well-know brand name (e.g. Coca-Cola). For example, if an organization's exports are growing, this is evidence that it can offer better value than local competitors. This explains why companies often export before seeking to commit assets aboard.

2. **Internationalization in services is different.** Service companies are no different from product companies. A service company can only internationalize successfully if it also possesses valuable intangible assets which can be replicated abroad.

3. **Distance and national borders don't matter any more.** An argument often put forward is that national cultures are converging, and distance is less important because of developments like the Internet. The reality is that transport costs may be small but they are still positive and increase with distance. Moreover, a country's culture shapes its institutions and its values. For example, US companies export to Canada first because of the common language. To be successful requires an organization to be local and global. For example, HSBC refers to itself as 'the world's local bank' and promotes its knowledge of local differences.

4. **Developing countries are where the action is.** There is a belief that large markets are in developing countries like China, India, and Mexico. However, despite the economic convergence of China, it is the Western economies that currently dominate world trade. The implication is that any organization seeking to go global cannot ignore Western economies.

5. **Manufacture where labour costs are cheapest.** Rangan argues, 'the only sounds that low wages should stir are loud yawns'. This is because, although important, labour costs are only part of the total delivered cost. An organization may find that low-wage economies impose tariffs and duties that increase the manufacturing cost. Furthermore, low wages may be associated with low productivity which actually increases unit costs.

6. **Globalization is here to stay.** The drivers of globalization are technological changes and economic convergence between nations. As countries experience similar per capita incomes, so their consumer tastes begin to converge. However, if we were to see a re-emergence of sustained unemployment that has characterized market economies in the past, this might force governments to take unilateral actions which reverse the trend towards globalization. The argument here is that corporations may have to accept a more socially active role if they require globalization to continue. Therefore, organizations need to 'explore issues such as unemployment, employee retraining and equality of opportunity . . . if business does not become more sensitive to this possibility . . . expect to see governments reasserting themselves' (Rangan 2000, p. 123).

7. **Governments don't matter any more.** Where organizations are believed to be pursuing their own self-interest, individuals will seek redress through their government. A global economy requires rules and these rules are set by governments. The implication for multinational corporations is that they need to work with governments to ensure an acceptable balance between the needs of companies and the needs of local people.

In discussing globalization and its drivers we have assumed, at least implicitly, that globalized companies exist. In fact, the idea of a globalized company may represent more wishful thinking than a state of reality. Rugman (2000) states that the largest 500 multinational enterprises (MNEs) account for around 90 per cent of foreign direct investment and about 50 per cent of world trade. These impressive figures reveal an even more interesting fact. Rugman and Verbeke (2004) argue that most of these firms are not global companies, if 'global' means that they operate across innumerable foreign markets. They are in fact 'regional', as the vast majority of their sales are in the home leg of their triad which comprises North America, the EU, and Asia. Thus, a US multinational enterprise would have the majority of its sales within the North American triad, a French multinational's sales would be predominantly in their home region, that is, the EU, and so forth. Therefore, what some refer to as globalization may more accurately be defined as regionalization (Ghemawat 2005).

9.8 The Challenge of Globalization

GLOBALLY INTEGRATED ENTERPRISE

integrates value chain activities such as procurement, research, and sales on a global basis in order to produce its goods and services more efficiently

In common with Bartlett and Ghoshal (1989), Palmisano (2006) asserts that the traditional multinational corporation is evolving into what he calls a globally integrated enterprise. The goal of this enterprise is the integration of products and value delivery worldwide. The focus of these corporations is *how* to make things rather than *what* to make, and *how* to deliver services rather than *which* services to deliver. The backdrop to these changes is the continuing economic liberalization and information technology which has standardized technologies worldwide. For example, we see financial institutions and software companies building R&D and service centres in India to support employees, customers, and production worldwide. American radiologists send X-rays to Australia for interpretation. As organizations share business and technology standards, so integration into global production systems is facilitated.

The increase in outsourcing encourages organizations to see themselves in terms of components or activities. The globally integrated enterprise integrates value chain activities such as procurement, research, and sales on a global basis in order to produce its goods and services for consumers. The choice for organizations is where they want the work for these activities to be done and whether they want them carried out in-house or outsourced. This should be seen as not merely a matter of outsourcing non-core activities but is 'about actively managing different operations, expertise, and capabilities so as to open the enterprise up... allowing it to connect more intimately with partners, suppliers, and customers' (Palmisano 2006, p. 131) (see Strategy Focus: IBM—A Globally Integrated Enterprise?).

STRATEGY FOCUS
IBM—A Globally Integrated Enterprise?

Last June IBM held its annual investors' day in the grounds of the Bangalore Palace... India's equivalent of Silicon Valley. Big Blue pulled out all the stops to impress the 50 or so investors and Wall Street analysts who turned up... to hear speeches by the president of India, the country's leading telecoms entrepreneur and IBM's own

The chairman and CEO of IBM, Samuel J. Palmisano, meeting employees at IBM in India.

Courtesy of International Business Machines Corporation.

boss, Sam Palmisano. By going to Bangalore, the technology giant was sending a strong message. With 53,000 employees, India is now at the core of IBM's strategy. With other big developing countries, including China, Brazil, and Russia, it is fast becoming the firm's centre of gravity.

Just three decades earlier, IBM had quit India, which was in the grip of corporatist and nationalistic industrial policies. Now, as Mr Palmisano pointed out . . . the domestic Indian market has become one of the fastest-growing in the world for IBM, with revenues rising by 40–50 per cent a year, albeit from a very small base. The firm now has more employees in India than in any other country except America. Mr Palmisano announced that IBM would invest a further $6 billion in India over the coming three years, up from $2 billion in the previous three. That sum does not include any acquisitions of Indian companies.

Rethinking the Multinational

In a speech last year at INSEAD business school in France, Mr Palmisano set IBM's Indian move in the context of the modern multinational company . . . the 'globally integrated enterprise'. Rather than have a parent with lots of Mini-Mes around the world, such a firm '. . . puts people and jobs anywhere in the world based on the right cost, the right skills and the right business environment. And it integrates those operations horizontally and globally'. In this approach, 'work flows to the places where it will be done best', that is, most efficiently and to the highest quality. The forces behind this 'are irresistible', he says.

IBM's big investment in India is not just about getting cheaper workers. IBM is doing cutting-edge research and development in India and writing valuable software, as well as running low-cost call centres. Places like India: the other message that Mr Palmisano was keen to get across was the part other emerging economies are playing in remaking IBM—which he admits will take many years. Thus, IBM's financing back office is in Rio De Janeiro. It has call centres round the world. Last April, when Bangalore was paralysed by rioting . . . IBM shifted data-centre operations to its facilities in Brazil and Colorado. IBM used to have separate supply chains in different markets, now it has one for the whole company. Reflecting the growing importance of China, John Paterson, IBM's chief procurement officer, moved to Shenzen in October. Asia already accounts for one-third of IBM's $40 billion purchasing budget. Mr Paterson felt he needed to raise the quality of IBM's purchasing staff in the region and to develop its base of suppliers.

Source: 'How India is changing IBM's world' *Economist*, 4 April 2007.

The globally integrated enterprise brings opportunities and a number of challenges. The opportunities include increases in living standards in developed and developing countries. Developing countries experience increased employment and prosperity as their workers become more integrated into global production systems. This is also helped by structural changes that allow small and medium-sized organizations in developing countries to participate in the global economy. However, there are difficult challenges. The globally integrated enterprise requires a supply of high-value skills which requires nations to invest in education and training. A key challenge in the global economy is how to prevent piracy of intellectual property rights without sacrificing collaboration. A possible solution is to shift the emphasis from protecting intellectual property, which limits its use, to maximizing intellectual capital based on shared ownership. How do firms maintain trust when their business models are dispersed globally? This will require shared values that transcend national borders. Finally, some of the changes that global corporate integration brings will require that capital markets and investors adjust their habits from short-term rewards to longer-term growth. Given the investment nature of Anglo-American economies, this is quite a challenge. Palmisano (2006, p. 136) concludes:

> *The shift from MNCs to globally integrated enterprises provides an opportunity to advance both business growth and societal progress. But it raises issues that are too big and too interconnected for business alone or government alone to solve.*

If we accept the model of the globally integrated enterprise as more optimal than the multinational corporation, there is a need to ensure that it evolves in a manner which benefits all members of society around the world. This issue will be addressed in greater detail in **Chapter 12** when we assess the role and impact of corporate governance.

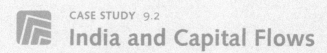

CASE STUDY 9.2
India and Capital Flows

THE world is divided into two, according to Shachindra Nath, chief operating officer of Religare Enterprises, an Indian financial firm. On one side of the divide is a world with 'cash but no opportunities'; on the other, a world with 'no money, just opportunities'. In October Religare announced its ambition to shepherd money across this divide, by creating an 'emerging-market investment bank'. The bank will be run from London by Martin Newson, a former head of global equities at Dresdner Kleinwort.

Religare will start small, attaching itself to growing companies and expanding with them. As India's companies go global, finding customers and buying companies abroad, they will want their banks to be global too, Mr Newson argues.

His bank may still lack manpower (it has about 80 bankers) and experience (last year, it completed only two deals in its home market), but Mr Newson applauds India's 'get-up-and-go, "let's attack" attitude'.

He would find a quite different mindset at the Reserve Bank of India (RBI), the country's central bank, which polices the flow of money across India's borders and keeps tabs on the foreign adventures of the country's financial firms. The RBI has a defensive approach to financial globalisation. The laws of economic gravity suggest capital should flow from where it is abundant to where it is scarce. But, the RBI fears, that flow can overwhelm an economy.

In 2007, for example, it tried to restrain a vigorous inflow of capital by making it harder for foreigners to play India's booming stockmarket and by tightening limits on corporate borrowing abroad. When capital flows abruptly reversed in 2008, it eased these limits. Now that foreigners are again flocking to India's stockmarket (see chart), capital inflows are once more playing on the RBI's mind. At the IMF's annual meetings in October, the RBI's governor worried that if he had to raise interest rates earlier than other economies, the gap in returns might attract more foreign money. At the RBI's latest meeting on October 27th, he kept rates on hold.

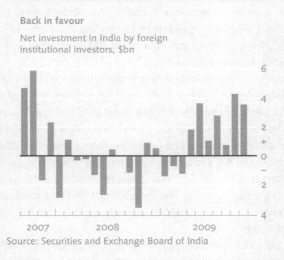

Back in favour

Net investment in India by foreign institutional investors, $bn

Source: Securities and Exchange Board of India

Despite these concerns, India is steadily becoming more financially stitched in to the rest of the world. Its foreign assets and liabilities add up to over 60% of GDP. In the 1990s that ratio was only about 40%. It has risen partly because India's own companies are eager to acquire foreign firms. In March 2009 India's stock of direct investment abroad was worth over $67 billion, more than twice the figure in March 2007.

As India's companies straddle borders, capital controls become harder to police. Foreign affiliates can transfer money into India disguised as a payment for services provided by their parent company. But if controls don't necessarily stop Indian multinationals raising money, they do stop India's financial system from meeting these firms' requirements. For example, India prohibits companies from listing their shares at home and on a foreign exchange. This ban was one reason, if hardly the only one, why Bharti Airtel, India's biggest mobile-phone company, was unable to merge in September with MTN of South Africa.

A 2007 report commissioned by the government to assess Mumbai's prospects of becoming an international financial centre argued that India has a comparative advantage in financial services, like the one it has in information technology. India, after all, has a common-law legal tradition and a stockmarket that is 130 years old. Many bankers working in London, Dubai and Singapore have their roots in India. Religare is hoping to hire a few of them.

It is not the only Indian financial firm with ambitions abroad. Indian banks have 141 foreign branches and 21 subsidiaries. Of the new private-sector banks, ICICI bank has the most foreign outposts. Its willingness to dabble beyond its borders marked it out for suspicion when crisis struck and doubts about its foreign exposures grew.

In November 2008 the RBI had to lend foreign currencies to Indian banks to help them meet the obligations of their foreign branches. It is now determined to monitor their activities more closely. Banks say 'We know how to manage our stuff, there are no government guarantees, so why are you bothered?' says Rakesh Mohan, a former deputy governor of the RBI. But 'When push comes to shove, you always have to be bothered.'

The RBI's prudence was justified by events. But it has its costs. By reining in its domestic banks, it prevents them from serving the global needs of India's companies. Tata Steel, for example, bought Corus with loans from banks in London, not Mumbai. The RBI worries about the foreign borrowing of Indian firms even as it makes it impossible for them to find necessary finance from domestic providers.

Mr Mohan thinks the RBI's approach is on the right side of history. He points out that the regulatory reforms the G20 now recommends are for the most part policies that the RBI was already pursuing. This includes its willingness to supervise the foreign subsidiaries of Indian banks. Was India ahead of the curve? 'Maybe accidentally,' he laughs.

But as more big Indian firms become multinational companies, it will be harder for politicians to resist the demands for a freer flow of finance. 'It's one thing for India to impose restrictions upon foreign multinationals like Enron or IBM,' says Ajay Shah of the National Institute of Public Finance and Policy, 'but it's harder for the Indian government to hobble its own multinationals. I think this is a qualitative change.' Indian companies are too ambitious to confine themselves to their borders. Likewise, India itself is too big a prize for foreign capitalists to ignore. Money has a way of finding opportunity.

Source: 'A world apart' *The Economist*, 29 October 2009.

Questions

1. What rationale is there for the Reserve Bank of India (RBI) to try to control capital flows across India's borders?
2. In a globalized economy what is the likely impact on any country which attempts to actively manage capital inflows?
3. What does the RBI's stance on capital inflows suggest about India's commitment to financial globalization?

Summary

We started this chapter with an evaluation of the views of Theodore Levitt on globalization. While globalization may indeed be increasing, the assertion that consumer preferences are *irrevocably homogenized* is considered by some to ignore the realities of important national differences. Douglas and Wind argue that while there exist global segments with similar needs, this is not a universal trend. This debate between globalization and localization is of crucial important as it goes to the heart of the type of international strategy an organization adopts. We saw that the motives for firms to expand internationally can be evaluated by looking at organizational and environmental factors. The organizational factors occur within the firm while the environmental factors are outside the firm's control.

A global framework for guiding managers is provided by Ghoshal who outlines three objectives for multinational corporations and the sources of competitive advantage open to them. In order to gain competitive advantage the organization will need to undertake actions that enable it to achieve these three goals. We assessed four basic types of international strategy that are a response to the globalization–localization debate: multidomestic, global, international, and transnational. The transnational organization, developed by Bartlett and Ghoshal, is a recognition that a search for a match between an organization's capabilities and a single set of environment forces no longer holds. Now industries are driven by the realization that neither a multidomestic nor an international nor a global strategy is sufficient. In other words, an organization must simultaneously achieve global efficiency, national responsiveness, and a worldwide leveraging of its innovations and learning. A constraint in responding to these environment changes is an organization's internal capabilities, what Bartlett and Ghoshal refer to as their *administrative heritage*.

In selecting an appropriate entry mode strategy organizations need to answer two questions: what levels of resource commitment are they prepared to make, and what level of control over their international operations do they require? The answer to these questions will be determined by an organization's perception of international risk. We saw that, according to Porter, firms are capable of consistent innovation because of four attributes that exist in their home market, which he refers to as the diamond of national advantage. These are factor conditions, demand conditions, related and supporting industries, and firm strategy, structure, and rivalry. Each point of the diamond contributes to global success. There are criticisms of Porter's diamond and some, such as Rugman and D'Cruz, argue that smaller nations' competitive advantage may actually derive from attributes that exist in their larger foreign diamond. To take account of this, Rugman suggests using a double diamond framework. Lastly, we addressed some of the myths of globalization, before looking at the globally integrated enterprise and the opportunities and challenges that globalization brings.

Review Questions

1. Examine the arguments for and against the increasing homogenization of consumer tastes.
2. Evaluate Porter's diamond of national advantage with reference to smaller trading nations such as New Zealand or Canada.

Discussion Question

There is no such thing as a global organization. Discuss.

Research Topic

Identify three well known companies which have adopted a different entry mode strategy to gain access to a foreign market. Examine the cost and benefit of each strategy, and its overall success.

Recommended Reading

For opposing perspectives on globalization see:

- Levitt, T. (1983). The globalization of markets. *Harvard Business Review*, **61**, 92–102.
- Douglas, S.P. and Wind, Y. (1987). The myth of globalization. *Columbia Journal of World Business*, **22**, 19–29.

For a proposal that a new organizational form, the transnational corporation, is needed to deal with today's dynamic business world, see:

- Bartlett, C.A. and Ghoshal, S. (1989). *Managing Across Borders: The Transnational Solution*. Harvard Business School Press, Cambridge, MA.

For an understanding of globalization and what it means to be a global company, see:

- Rugman, A.M. (2000). *The End of Globalization*. Random House, London.

www.oxfordtextbooks.co.uk/orc/henry2e/
Visit the Online Resource Centre that accompanies this book for activities and more information on international strategy and globalization.

online resource centre

Notes

1 The discussion of transnational strategy in Section 9.4.4 draws upon the work of Bartlett and Ghoshal (1989).
2 For a discussion of different entry modes see Mellahi *et al.* (2005), chapter 6.
3 Ricardo's work on comparative advantage is contained in *On the Principles of Political Economy and Taxation*, which was published in 1817.
4 For a discussion of the relevance of Porter's diamond for New Zealand, see Cartwright (1993).
5 See also Rangan and Lawrence (1999).

References

Bartlett, C. and **Ghoshal, S.** (1989). *Managing Across Borders: the Transnational Solution*. Harvard Business School Press, Boston, MA.
Blinder, A.S. (2006). Offshoring: the next industrial revolution. *Foreign Affairs*, **85**(2), 113–28.
Brouthers, K.D. (1995). The influence of international risk on entry mode strategy in the computer software industry. *Management International Review*, **35**(1), 7–28.
Cartwright, W.R. (1993). Multiple linked 'diamonds' and the international competitiveness of export-dependent industries: the New Zealand experience. *Management International Review*, **33**(2), 55–70.
Daily Telegraph (2006). Wal-Mart quits Germany but insists ASDA is safe. *Daily Telegraph*, 29 July 2006.
Douglas, S. and **Wind, Y.** (1987). The myth of globalization. *Columbia Journal of World Business*, **22**(4), 19–29.

Ghemawat, P. (2005). Regional strategies for global leadership. *Harvard Business Review*, **83**(12), 98–108.

Ghoshal, S. (1987). Global strategy: an organizing framework. *Strategic Management Journal*, **8**(5), 425–40.

Hodgetts, R.M. (1993). Porter's diamond framework in a Mexican context. *Management International Review*, **33**(2), 41–54.

Hofstede, G. (1991). *Cultures and Organizations: Software of the Mind*. McGraw-Hill, New York.

Hofstede, G. (1997). *Cultures and Organizations: Software of the Mind*. McGraw-Hill, New York.

Levitt, T. (1983). The globalization of markets. *Harvard Business Review*, **61**, 92–102.

Mellahi, K., Frynas, J.G., and **Finlay, P.** (2005). *Global Strategic Management*, Chapter 6. Oxford University Press, Oxford.

Miller, D. (1990). *The Icarus Paradox: How Excellent Companies Can Bring About Their Own Downfall*. Harper Business, New York.

Miller, K.D. (1992). A framework for integrated risk management in international business. *Journal of International Business Studies*, **23**(2), 311–31.

Palmisano, S.J. (2006). The globally integrated enterprise. *Foreign Affairs*, **85**(3), 127–36.

Porter, M.E. (1990a). The competitive advantage of nations. *Harvard Business Review*, **68**(2), 73–9.

Porter, M.E. (1990b). *The Competitive Advantage of Nations*, Chapter 3. Free Press, New York.

Rangan, S. (2000). The seven myths regarding global strategy. In *Mastering Strategy*. Prentice Hall, Harlow.

Rangan, S. and **Lawrence, R.Z.** (1999). *A Prism on Globalization*. Brookings Institute, Washington, DC.

Rugman, A. (1992). Porter takes the wrong turn. *Business Quarterly*, **56**(3), 59–64.

Rugman, A.M. (2000). *The End of Globalization*. Random House, London.

Rugman, A. and **D'Cruz, J.R.** (1991). *Fast Forward: Improving Canada's International Competitiveness*. Kodak Canada, Toronto.

Rugman, A. and **D'Cruz, J.R.** (1993). The 'double diamond' model of international competitiveness: the Canadian experience. *Management International Review*, **33**(2), 17–39.

Rugman, A. and **Verbeke, A.** (1993). Foreign subsidiaries and multinational strategic management: an extension and correction of Porter's single diamond framework. *Management International Review*, **33**(2), 71–84.

Rugman, A. and **Verbeke, A.** (2004). A perspective on regional and global strategies of multinational enterprise. *Journal of International Business Studies*, **35**(1), 3–18.

PART 3 CASE STUDY
Procter & Gamble—Corporate Parenting Skills

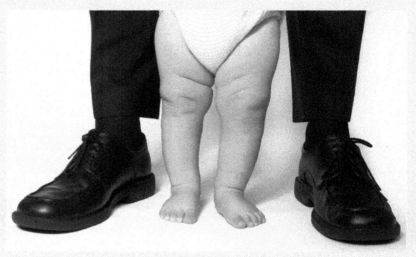

© iStockphoto.com/Sharon Dominick

What is the role of the corporate parent in adding value to the organization?

Three weeks ago A.G. Lafley, chairman and chief executive of Procter & Gamble, was shown 'a fascinating new material'. With a group of scientists from P&G alongside him, he was given 30 days to decide whether to take an option on the breakthrough—'No, I can't talk about (it)'—in case it eventually proved commercially viable. Mr Lafley recounts: 'We brainstormed a whole range of possible applications and said "OK, we're going to take a run at this thing." I just want to get a look. If we pass, and it becomes big, shame on us.'

His breezy yet calculated attitude to risk is not merely a sign of imagination at work. It points to how much has changed at the world's largest consumer products company since 2000 when the 28-year company veteran took the helm. It also offers a glimpse into the remarkable ease with which the once sclerotic company appears to be integrating its $57bn acquisition of Gillette, the razor blade and battery maker. After two consecutive profit warnings in the first half of 2000, P&G-watchers were preparing to write the obituary of an American corporate icon. Starting out as a supplier of candles to the Union army in the Civil War, it had become increasingly stifled by its own bureaucratic culture.

A restructuring began by predecessor Durk Jager has, under Mr Lafley, returned P&G to rude financial health. Total sales have grown 40 per cent to $57bn (£33bn, a48bn) since 2000. P&G has doubled its profits and generated over $30bn in free cash flow, with $11bn of that returned to shareholders. P&G's shares have almost doubled. His unassailable command of the company is reflected in his manner. The youthful-looking 58-year-old rarely pauses for breath as he lays out his vision for P&G during a 90-minute interview with the *Financial Times* in New York. In characteristically straightforward language, he describes the three key strategic choices he has made as 'Sesame Street simple'.

The first concerned its core laundry, baby-care, feminine-care, and hair-care businesses. He decided to expand them by incorporating existing technologies into other products. In the past year, for example, P&G has launched a variation of its Tide laundry detergent incorporating the odour-eliminating technology used in its Febreze line of sprays.

The second was to expand into beauty and healthcare—one of the most rapidly growing global businesses. 'The reasons were really simple,' says Mr Lafley. 'Demographics are driving those industries. Beauty alone is a huge industry— $150bn at least, worldwide.' In a sign of that approach, P&G last week linked with Dolce & Gabbana to produce luxury fragrances and beauty products under licence for the Italian fashion house.

The third choice was switching from concentrating on the 1bn most affluent consumers in the world—P&G's traditional turf—to figuring out how also to serve the remaining 5bn. For the low-income Chinese consumer, for example, P&G is testing a prototype disposable nappy made cheaply enough that it can be sold for the price of an egg.

It is not just the numbers that tell the story. P&G has also submitted to radical surgery on its corporate culture. Mr Lafley goes on: 'We were terribly internally focused. And that's still, honestly, an issue. It's an issue with any organization: the larger it is, the worse it is.' Units within P&G tended to compete with each other, with executives just 'as intra-murally competitive as (they were) externally competitive'.

'And frankly the people who were internally competitive were some of the ones I weeded out; they just couldn't get over it. I didn't care if the baby-care business was doing better than the coffee business—it was an irrelevant comparison. I cared whether the baby-care business was the best baby-care business in the world,' says Mr Lafley. He ruled in 2000 that half the company's ideas for new or enhanced products were to come from outside although he has set no deadline. The proportion stands at 35 per cent. And consumer research needed to improve. 'I wanted everybody in the company to understand that I wasn't the boss, that it was really this woman and family that we served, and I wanted to know more about her than she could articulate herself.' Mr Lafley says.

In addition, P&G's global operations have been restructured, doing away with 'fiefdoms' that had emerged in Europe and the US. 'In Europe we were too European and in the US we were too American. I brought up younger leaders who'd spent a lot more time outside of their home country, who had been on the ground in places where we didn't have leadership and who were, I thought, more open minded, more externally focused—more inspirational, frankly, to their peers.

Not the old fuddy-duddy style.' As a result the average age of the P&G leadership has fallen since 2000 by between 7–10 years.

This approach is already in evidence as P&G, a company of 110,000 employees, integrates Gillette, with 30,000. In contrast to its previous acquisitions—such as Wella and Clairol in hair care or the Iams pet food company—P&G is approaching Gillette as a mature global company with executives who may be better qualified than existing P&G staff for top jobs. The new head of the combined P&G/Gillette oral-care business—encompassing Crest toothpaste and Gillette's Oral B toothbrushes—will be a Gillette executive. 'It has been a little shocking on the P&G side because some P&G people are going and some plum jobs have gone to Gillette leaders. But that's the way it should be,' insists Mr Lafley. P&G says it has meanwhile been able to retain 80 per cent of the top Gillette managers to whom it has offered jobs. It helps that in the past decade, 40 per cent of P&G's total staff have joined the company as a result of acquisitions. 'At the (Gillette) leadership level we haven't lost a single business category or brand leader,' says Mr Lafley.

P&G is also being 'flexible' about the location of Gillette's operating units—most remaining where they were under previous ownership. Its willingness to learn lessons from Gillette underscores just how 'differently in virtually every way' the integration is being handled compared with previous acquisitions. P&G is studying the terms on which Gillette deals with retailers, distributors, and logistics. Instead of using different contractors according to whether the product is to be sold in big promotional sizes or in small packs, P&G plans in future to use one contractor as much as possible around the world—just as Gillette does.

'We looked at their trade promotion terms and trade incentive programmes and we looked at ours and we said, "You know, we like some things about their programme." They like some things about ours and we are in the process of putting them together and we will go to market with some combined "best of both" hybrid trade terms,' says Mr Lafley.

Last month P&G created a global consumer relations organization headed by three Gillette executives and two from P&G. It will combine Gillette's globally organized service—which operates with 800 phone lines—with that of P&G, which has long been organized on a regional basis. In spite of the apparently successful integration, analysts are on the alert given the tough competitive environment for consumer goods companies. Wendy Nicholson at Citigroup this month noted: 'We remain watchful of P&G's margins, as we fear that the competitive environment in many of its categories may intensify, such that P&G may need to invest more aggressively behind its businesses in order to meaningfully expand its market shares and drive sales growth.'

Still, Amy Low Chasen of Goldman Sachs says 'most impressive is that P&G is not simply integrating Gillette into its existing fold. Rather, it is looking across both companies for the best way to do business'.

For a combined P&G/Gillette, one of the biggest challenges will be how to deal not only with competitors such as Kimberly-Clark and Unilever but with private label manufacturers. In Europe, the spread of so-called hard discounters selling 'own-brand' or private-label products has forced some of the largest US consumer goods companies, such as Sara Lee, to start selling their best-selling brands in discount stores. In the US, private-label manufacturers pose a constant threat to consumer goods companies, which must maintain an appropriate gap between their branded products and the nearest cheaper-priced private-label product—or risk customer defection.

Mr Lafley does not see the relationship between a branded consumer company and a private-label supplier as antagonistic. 'We need each other. A private label or retailer brand cannot exist without the branded comparison. The manufacturers and brands that are in trouble are the ones that sell the number three to seventh, eighth, ninth, tenth-ranked [brands]. So we've had to rationalize our portfolio. When I was running the laundry business in the mid-eighties we sold 15 laundry brands in the United States. Today we basically sell four—and we sell the top four.'

For a combined P&G/Gillette, maintaining that edge will mean coming up with innovative products—what Mr Lafley frequently refers to as 'little gifts' for the consumer. Is the discovery of an innovation as revolutionary as the disposable nappy still possible? He says: 'I think it is, though not easy.' He suggests that fertile ground may be found in biotechnology or nanotechnology—even in 'nutraceuticals' and 'cosmeceuticals', the new crossover developments that link health with food and grooming. 'We're definitely poking around,' he says, explaining his interest in that mystery material he was shown. 'I have a corporate innovation fund and this is where we take our swings on totally new technologies . . . A lot of great invention comes on the boundaries. Do you look better because you feel better because you're eating better and you're really healthier? How does that all that stuff fit together? But you know, watch material science, and watch transferring technology from expected industries into unlikely and unexpected industries,' he adds. 'Every time some Korean scientist says he can microwave a shirt, we are there. There's a lot of stuff going on, right? We have to be all over that and experimenting. So if you meet some really interesting inventors and they have some cool stuff, send them our way.'

Source: 'Procter doctor: how Lafley's prescription is revitalizing a tired consumer titan' *Financial Times*, 22 December 2005.

◼ Questions

1. How has the chief executive, A.G. Lafley, managed to transform the organizational culture within Procter & Gamble?

2. What structural changes were necessary to achieve this, and why?

3. What does the case study tell you about the parenting skills of Procter & Gamble?

10 Organizational Systems and Strategic Change

10.1 Organizational Structures	10.2 Organizational Processes	10.3 Strategic Control Systems	10.4 Strategic Change
		Key Work Strategic control systems	**Key Work** Role of BHAGs in stimulating change
		Main Reference Goold, M. and Quinn, J.J. (1990). The paradox of strategic controls. *Strategic Management Journal*, 11(1), 43–57.	**Key Work** Benefits of understanding organizational culture when implementing strategic change

Learning Objectives

After completing this chapter you should be able to:

- Explain the trade-off between specialization and coordination
- Evaluate the role of different organizational structures
- Assess the impact of organizational processes on innovation and knowledge
- Evaluate strategic control systems
- Assess different approaches to strategic change
- Discuss the determinants of a visionary organization

Introduction

In Part 3 we assessed the role that strategy formulation plays in the achievement of competitive advantage. In this part we will turn our attention to strategy implementation. We might restate that although a linear approach aids the student of strategic management in getting to grips with the subject, in the fast moving corporate world organizations are often faced with implementing a strategy without the luxury of comprehensive analysis. That is not to say that analysis is unimportant, since organizations neglect strategic analysis at their peril. It is to recognize that decisions often need to be made quickly as competitors seldom wait for their rivals to undertake a complete analysis of the business environment.

It is often said that the best formulated strategy in the world will fail if it is poorly implemented. To implement strategies effectively requires the organization to be sufficiently flexible in its organizational design. Strategies need to be effectively communicated and properly resourced, and the reason for change needs to be understood and properly coordinated with stakeholders inside and outside the organization. In an age of collaboration, this may involve discussions with suppliers and partners. Although the leader of an organization will ultimately be responsible for a strategy's success or failure, their role should be to encourage and create an organizational culture that empowers managers to respond to opportunities. In this way each employee will be confident to try out new ideas and innovate without fear of reprisals. Appropriate reward mechanisms need to be in place which help to guide employee behaviour and signpost the important goals of the organization. The values of an organization will be important here in specifying what an organization stands for. There must also be sufficient control mechanisms in place that allow the strategy to be evaluated against its stated aims and if necessary, allow for changes.

Although systems, procedures, and policies may aid the implementation of a strategy, we should keep in mind that ultimately it is individuals who implement strategy. Unless key individuals and groups, within and outside the organization, accept the rationale for strategic change, any proposed implementation will be suboptimal at best. We will address the role that leadership plays in managing strategic change in greater detail in **Chapter 11**.

In this chapter we will address the impact of organizational structures, organizational processes, strategic control systems, and strategic change. The backdrop to the chapter is the role these play in providing an organization with competitive advantage.

- In Section 10.1 we start the chapter with a discussion of the trade-off between specialization and coordination and the impact of this on organizational structures. We consider the simple, functional, and divisional structures before moving on to more complex matrix and network structures.

- In Section 10.2 we move beyond structures to assess the impact of organizational processes in helping individuals to innovate and share knowledge across the organization.

- In Section 10.3 we evaluate strategic control systems and the tension inherent within them. This tension is a result of trying to ensure that managers are working towards a common goal while also allowing them to develop innovative business solutions without constraints.

- The chapter ends in Section 10.4 with a discussion of strategic change—the fit between an organization's resources and capabilities and its changing competitive environment. We evaluate different forms of integrative change and conclude with a discussion of strategic change in 'great' organizations.

10.1 Organizational Structures

Organizations exist because they are more efficient at undertaking economic activities than individuals are on their own. Therefore, organizations are a means by which human economic activity can be coordinated. Mintzberg (1993) argues that all organized human activity gives rise to two opposing forces: the need to divide labour into separate tasks, and the coordination of these tasks to accomplish some goal. Adam Smith first discussed specialization and the division of labour centuries earlier in 1776. Smith showed that if you specialize human activity such that individuals only undertake one or a few tasks, then they become proficient at that task. If each task is part of some larger activity, such as building a car, then we find that more cars can be built when each individual specializes than if an individual tried to build a car by himself. This is what made Henry Ford's Model T automobile so successful—the division of labour along a moving conveyor belt. Yet, as Mintzberg points out, greater specialization requires greater coordination.

The use of rules, policies, and procedures to coordinate employees will be appropriate for organizations that operate in relatively stable environment. This is especially the case where individuals have little autonomy and are not expected to make complex decisions. Where individuals are part of an organization that operates in a turbulent environment and are afforded far greater autonomy, the effort required by management to coordinate their activities will be greater. Nevertheless, these different activities must still be coordinated if the organization is to achieve economies of scale and synergy.

There is widespread acceptance that a change in strategy, other things being equal, will warrant a change in organizational structure to implement that strategy. Organizational structure is concerned with the division of labour into specialized tasks and coordination between these tasks. In 1962, Chandler wrote his famous dictum that 'structure follows strategy' (Chandler 1962). Chandler studied a number of large American corporations, including General Motors and DuPont, in the early part of the twentieth century. He found that as these organizations grew in size and complexity so this brought about a need to change their organizational structure. For instance, Chandler found that as DuPont increased its product lines so the ensuing complexity was too much for its centralized functional structure. An expansion of its activities produced 'new administrative needs' which required a new structure to meet these needs. In effect, the existing structure becomes suboptimal for supporting the strategic change which in turn necessitates a change of structure. The same was

10

ORGANIZATIONAL STRUCTURE

the division of labour into specialized tasks and coordination between these tasks true of General Motors. Therefore, DuPont decentralized its organization to what became known as a divisional structure. Under a divisional structure the head office retains control of overall strategic direction, but the divisional managers have autonomy as to how the strategy will be implemented. This is discussed in detail later.

For Chandler, it is the formulation of a new strategy which brings forth the need for a new structure. Hence his dictum 'structure follows strategy' (Figure 10.1). This is not to say that structure has no impact on strategy; for example, changes in the external environment may necessitate a change in an organization's structure. Therefore, there will be instances when Chandler's dictum may not hold, but as a general rule there is substantive support for this proposition. For example, a dynamic assessment of the contingent relationship between strategy and structure by Amburgey and Dacin (1994) found that a reciprocal relationship does exist. In other words, strategy affects structure but structure also affects strategy. However, they found that strategy was a more important determinant of structure than structure was of strategy. They conclude: 'our research supports the existence of a hierarchical relationship between strategy and structure', but note that 'a change in strategy is more likely to produce a change in structure than a change in structure is to produce a change in strategy' (Amburgey and Dacin 1994, p. 1446).

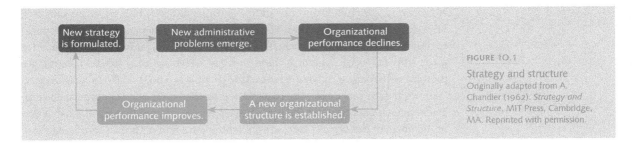

FIGURE 10.1

Strategy and structure
Originally adapted from A. Chandler (1962). *Strategy and Structure*, MIT Press, Cambridge, MA. Reprinted with permission.

In many respects, whether structure follows strategy or strategy follows structure may be a bit of a red herring. The real issue may be more about organizing complementary practices that fit together in a dynamic manner. For example, an organization introducing flexible technology will be unlikely to obtain increases in performance when it fails to change related working practices. Therefore, to ensure a better organizational fit it becomes necessary to go beyond a discussion of strategy and structure to include processes. This idea of complementarities is discussed in detail later in the chapter. We can now evaluate different types of organizational structures in terms of how well they meet the trade-off between specialization and coordination.

10.1.1 The Entrepreneurial Structure

The entrepreneurial or simple structure revolves around the founder of the firm. This is a centralized structure in which the founder or entrepreneur takes all the major decisions. This is not unexpected, especially where the founder possesses some technical expertise or specific knowledge that is the basis for the organization's existence. In these small organizations staff members will often be expected to be flexible in their work roles which may not be clearly drawn. The vision of the entrepreneur and flexible work patterns of staff are major strengths of this type of organization. As the organization grows, so the entrepreneur's ability to manage each facet of the business becomes stretched. Where the founder recognizes that his or her strength lies in formulating a strategic intent or purpose but not necessarily in trying to manage functions such as marketing or finance, he or she will recruit specialists to run these activities. Steve Jobs, the founder and hugely successful CEO of Apple, was initially believed to be a liability as the firm grew in size. He was eventually replaced, not by an individual who possessed his visionary zeal or technical expertise, but by John Sculley who was president of Pepsi, someone whom the financial markets believed could successfully manage a growing organization. In an ironic twist, Jobs once again heads the computer firm from which he was ousted.

10.1.2 The Functional Structure

A functional structure is appropriate for an organization which produces one or a few related products or services. Tasks are grouped together according to functional specialisms such as finance, marketing, and R&D. A manager will be responsible for a department which comprises these functions. The use of a functional structure promotes efficiency through the specialized division of labour. It allows individuals to learn from each other and may facilitate the development of distinctive capabilities. Under a functional structure, control systems, which are used to guide the behaviour of members of the organization, are straightforward and do not involve great complexity. There is a high degree of centralization with each functional manager reporting to the CEO and board of directors (Figure 10.2).

FIGURE 10.2
A functional structure

The functional structure has a number of disadvantages. Each functional or departmental manager may begin to focus exclusively on their departmental goals at the expense of the organizational goals. This can lead to the development of a departmental subculture whose values may not be fully congruent with those within the organization. As the organization grows and its range of products expands, co-ordination between functions becomes more difficult. This can lead to a decline in performance which, as Chandler argued, leads to a search for a new structure. This new structure will involve greater decentralization of decisionmaking to improve the efficiency of coordination.

STRATEGY FOCUS

Changing Structures— Hewlett-Packard

Hewlett-Packard recently acted to unscramble another part of the organizational structure put in place by Carly Fiorina, former chief executive, as the US computer maker announced it would scrap its stand-alone global operations division. The 5800-strong operations unit, which handles company-wide functions from purchasing and supply chain management to Internet marketing and customer relationship management, was created by Ms Fiorina after her controversial acquisition of Compaq. These functions will be handled directly by individual operating divisions, such as the imaging and printing group and the personal systems group, HP said.

HP Pavilion high-definition LCD television.

Courtesy of Hewlett-Packard

The creation of a separate operations unit was part of a plan by the company's former chief executive to split back-end from front-end activities, unifying group-wide support activities in central units while leaving product and customer control in the hands of HP's operating divisions. Since arriving at HP more than a year ago, Mark Hurd, chief executive, has reversed a number of Ms Fiorina's organizational moves. That has included separating the printing and PC divisions into different business units, as well as splitting IT into a stand-alone function again, under the control of a respected corporate IT veteran. HP said the remaining parts of the global operations unit had been split up to reduce costs, and to bring 'greater accountability and speed of operation' to its activities.

Source: 'HP to scrap Fiorina's global operations unit' *Financial Times*, 21 June 2006.

10

10.1.3 The Divisional Structure

As organizations grow and diversify into producing different products for different markets a more effective and efficient structure is required. The divisional structure comprises individual business units that include their own functional specialisms and have direct responsibility for their own performance (Figure 10.3). This decentralization of decision making is also necessary where the external environment is turbulent and exhibits some degree of uncertainty. It gives managers substantial autonomy to respond to local market conditions. A divisional structure may be organized according to *product*, *market*, or *geographic* areas. (See Strategy Focus: Changing Structures—Hewlett-Packard, which illustrates the difficulties of matching structures to business needs.) A structure based on product occurs when each product line is based in its own division with a manager responsible for profitability within that division. The divisional manager will have autonomy to set a business-level strategy based on his or her understanding of the product and markets. Organizations that have adopted a divisional structure by product include DuPont, General Motors, and Procter & Gamble. A structure based on market occurs when an organization is concerned to meet the needs of different customers groups. For example, HSBC and Barclays Bank are organized according to the markets they serve; corporate customers, small business customers, and retail customers. Each division has responsibility for its own profits and can see its contribution to corporate profitability. A geographic structure occurs when the divisions are categorized according to geographic location. Breaking the organization's structure down into geographic locations facilitates better management decisions by allowing managers to take decisions based upon the needs and attributes of consumers within different areas.

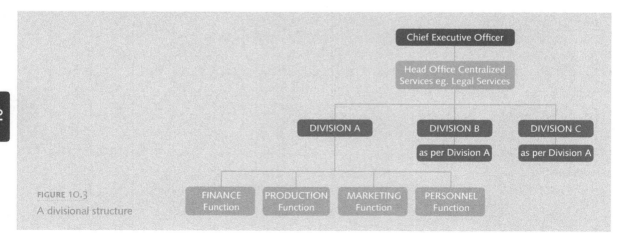

FIGURE 10.3
A divisional structure

The advantages of a divisional structure include the decentralized decision making which allows divisional managers to respond effectively to the needs of their business unit. There is a more clearly defined career path for individuals within the division rather than the limited specialisms that exist under a functional structure. This leads to higher levels of motivation and a commitment to innovation. Under a divisional structure, individuals are more likely to be aligned to the organization's objectives. A divisional structure allows head office to focus its attention on corporate strategy rather than being drawn into operational issues. In addition, the profit contribution of each division is transparent which helps the centre to make effective resource allocation decisions.

There are disadvantages with a divisional structure. Where the centre allocates resources to divisions according to their profit contribution, this presupposes that each division has an equal opportunity to make the same level of profits. Markets, products, and geographic regions will differ, and some mechanism which takes account of these differences and allocates resources fairly needs to be devised by head office. The emphasis on, for example, quarterly profit target may force the division to focus its attention on short-term issues rather than on key business-level strategies. The duplication of functions across many different divisions as well as at head office can be expensive and needs to be offset against improvements in performance. The use of divisional structures among large corporations is widespread, with many organizations adopting variations of the divisional form. Where organizations face greater uncertainty and more rapid change in their environment a different kind of organizational structure is required.

10.1.4 The Matrix Structure

A matrix structure is an attempt to increase organizational flexibility to meet the needs of a rapidly changing environment. It aims to simultaneously maximize the benefits from functional specialisms that occur from the division of labour while increasing the efficiency of coordination across these functions. It involves learning new roles and modes of behaviour. In a matrix structure an individual reports to two managers. This will include their functional head (for instance, the head of manufacturing) and also a project manager. Individuals are usually assigned to the project on a temporary basis (Figure 10.4). In theory, a matrix structure should increase the speed of decision making, facilitate innovation, and enhance responsiveness to the external environment. In reality, matrix structures can be complex and difficult to implement effectively. They violate a fundamental principle of management which is the unity of command.

To reiterate, under a matrix structure individuals are expected to report to two managers: their own functional manager and a project manager. However, unless both managers have the same expectations from individuals reporting to them this can create *role incompatibility* and *role ambiguity*. Role incompatibility occurs when the different expectations of managers make it highly unlikely that individuals can meet the expectations of both managers. Role ambiguity implies that individuals are unclear as to what their role and responsibilities are. The need to meet the expectations

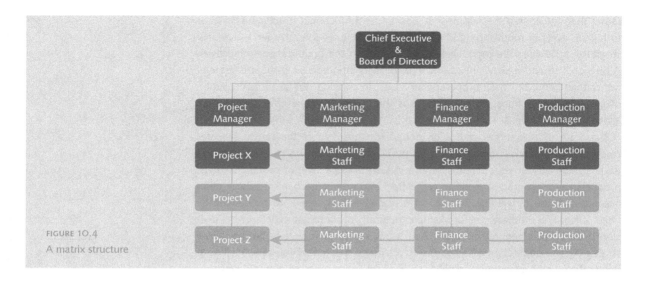

FIGURE 10.4

A matrix structure

of different managers may ultimately result in *role overload*, where an individual experiences difficulties in managing varied expectations. Bartlett and Ghoshal (1990) argue that concentrating on a matrix structure to manage complex and dynamic environments does little to change the other important elements that make up an organization. They distinguish between an organization's *anatomy*, that is, its structure, and its *physiology* and *psychology*. Its physiology includes the systems that allow information to circulate throughout the organization. Its psychology is the shared beliefs, norms, and values that permeate the organization. As they state, simply 'reconfiguring the formal structure is a blunt and sometimes brutal instrument of change' (Bartlett and Ghoshal 1990, p. 140). What is required is first to alter the organizational psychology—the beliefs and behaviours of individuals that pervade the organization. These changes can then be reinforced by improving the organizational physiology, which involves improvements in communication and decision making. Only then should senior managers realign the organizational anatomy by making changes to its formal structure.

10.1.5 The Network Structure

A network structure involves a configuration of outsourced activities that are controlled by a central hub. This is particularly useful in responding to fast-moving and unpredictable environments such as the fashion industry. The network structure allows the core competences of the organization to be retained at the centre while non-core activities are outsourced to specialist firms which allows for greater efficiency (Figure 10.5). The major advantage of the network structure is the flexibility it provides to organizations enabling them to respond quickly to changes in the marketplace. Organizations like Nike and Benetton both outsource manufacturing activities to specialist firms, while retaining tight control at the centre over their distinctive capabilities.

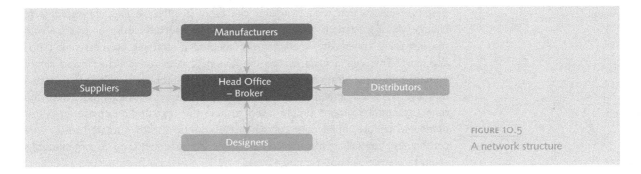

FIGURE 10.5
A network structure

Where an organization operates across many countries a *transnational structure* may be more effective in helping a multinational corporation to respond to the needs of local markets and achieve efficiencies from globalization. The transnational structure differs from the other organizational forms in that it neither dogmatically centralizes nor decentralizes, but instead makes selective decisions. The transnational corporation was discussed in detail when we looked at international strategies in **Chapter 9**.

In recognition of the complex and fraught nature of organization design Goold and Campbell (2002) propose a framework to guide executive management. Their *nine tests* of organization design are based on their observations of different size companies. The framework is an attempt to help top management to evaluate their existing structure or, indeed, a new structure objectively. The first four tests help executives to assess alternative structures by seeing whether a proposed structure can support the strategy being pursued. The remaining five tests are used to adjust potential organization designs by tackling problem areas, such as the problem of effective control that results from increased decentralization. This framework is not a panacea, and Goold and Campbell acknowledge this. Rather, it is an attempt to de-politicize and depersonalize the process of organization design.

10.2 Organizational Processes

The division of labour allows organizational activities to be separated out and common activities grouped together. However, this creates a dilemma. While the level of coordination improves within a homogeneous group, the level of coordination across different groups may decline. What is required is organizational integration which allows coordination to occur effectively across an organization's activities. This is not

10

an easy task given that each specialized group will have a tendency to seek its own goals and adopt behaviour to support this. One answer may be to concentrate more on horizontal processes rather than organizational structure. Ghoshal and Bartlett (1995) argue that top management has continued to focus on structural solutions despite evidence that such structures can become inflexible and unresponsive to change. As organizations grew and their divisional structure struggled to cope with the increased complexity, management adopted a strategic business unit (SBU) approach. This was a variation on the divisional structure which allowed senior managers to concentrate on specific businesses. The problem was that this created business silos which impeded coordination across different business units. These and other structural solutions simply failed to help the organization create an entrepreneurial culture, build core competences, and to discard outdated ideas. The consequence of failing hierarchical structures led to downsizing as organizations sought to remove nonperforming layers.

Ghoshal and Bartlett studied twenty organizations in the US, Europe, and Japan which understood the importance of processes over structures. They identified three distinct processes: *entrepreneurial process*, *competence-building process*, and *renewal process*. Together they constitute what Ghoshal and Bartlett refer to as a firm's 'core organizational processes'.

1. **The entrepreneurial process.** seeks to motivate employees to manage their operations as if they belonged to them. This requires a change in the current role of managers as simply implementers of strategy with only the most senior managers having the authority to initiate new ideas. To institute an entrepreneurial process requires a culture that recognizes the capabilities of individuals in the organization. Top management needs to understand that individuals perform more effectively when they are trusted to work, utilizing their own self-discipline rather than a formal control system. A self-disciplined approach requires that top management adopts a supportive role. This does not mean that no control systems exist. For example, 3M use small project teams to foster creativity and entrepreneurship. These project teams include someone with an innovative idea, and a few individuals who want to support it. If the idea takes off, the project team may eventually grow into a department or division. However, this entrepreneurial activity is set within the context of clear corporate targets, such as contributing to a 25 per cent return on equity.

2. **Competence-building process.** Large organizations need to be able to exploit the vast amount of employee knowledge that exists in their different businesses. This requires a competence-building process which coordinates the distinctive capabilities or core competencies across those businesses. The employees within the individual businesses need to be given the task of creating these competencies. This recognizes their closeness to the customer and hence greater ability to exploit local opportunities. As with the entrepreneurial process, the role of senior management is to ensure that the competencies are coordinated across different

business units. Senior managers must also ensure that their control systems are fair and transparent to encourage risk-taking. Individual employees need to adopt the organization's values and goals to help build a sense of community. This type of culture can only exist if it is nurtured by top management. For example, throughout the Japanese organization Kao there are open meeting areas. This entitles every employee who has an interest in a subject being discussed to sit in on a meeting and contribute their ideas.

3. **The renewal process.** This process 'is designed to challenge a company's strategies and the assumptions behind them'. This requires senior management to proactively shake up the organization's status quo. Their role is then to mediate the resulting conflict that will inevitably arise. Intel's move away from memory chips and towards microprocessors represents a renewal process. The organization was founded on memory chips. The decision by co-founder Andy Grove to re-base the organization on microprocessors directly cut across entrenched views of what Intel stood for. A result of emphasizing process over structure is to create an organization in which individual employees are willing and able to innovate. They will share new ideas and knowledge, and work towards common organization-wide goals. This occurs without the constant intrusion of managerial control systems.

10.3 Strategic Control Systems

The design of all organizations must include control and reward systems which ensure that members of an organization are actively working to achieve the corporate goals. Control systems are necessary for senior managers to be able to assess the performance of individual business units. A control system will include agreed objectives between senior managers and managers of business units, and a mechanism for monitoring performance based on these objectives and for providing feedback to managers. It will also include a system of rewards and sanctions that motivate managers and make them aware of the consequences of not meeting agreed targets. Most organizations use budgetary controls which measure and monitor financial performance. However, as we saw in **Chapter 6**, financial controls need to be used with broader strategic controls (Kaplan and Norton 1996) if important competitive information is not to be overlooked.

A well-designed reward system can be instrumental in successful strategy implementation. That said, a great deal of contention has arisen over rewarding executives for achieving lacklustre results and revising performance targets downwards to enable them to be more easily met. A reward system should recognize an individual's or group's achievement and motivate them to work towards the organization's goals. Where individuals are already highly paid, a reward system has to move beyond merely pecuniary factors to keep them motivated. A tension exists between the short-term quarterly targets on which managerial rewards are commonly based, and getting managers to adopt longer time horizons which more effectively exploit opportunities in their competitive environment. We saw in **Chapter 6** that the use of a balanced scorecard is helpful in moving managerial attention away from purely financial concerns to consider other issues that impact upon the business, such as customer retention.

Strategic control systems include similar elements to budgetary control systems but they involve longer-term objectives. This can create difficulties because, other things being equal, managers will be more inclined to invest their time in achieving short-term targets than targets that are many years off. To overcome this, strategic control systems can include a series of short-term milestones that need to be achieved if a strategy is to be implemented. In this way the management reward systems can be aligned with the implementation of the strategy. Goold and Quinn (1990) suggest three reasons for establishing control systems.

- First, a strategic control system should help coordinate the activities of members of an organization. Where the nature of strategic change is emergent (Mintzberg and Waters 1985) and incremental rather than planned and precise, strategic control systems need to be designed to reflect this. On the one hand, strategic control systems must be loose enough to deal with dynamic environments such as the software industry. On the other hand, they must be rigorous enough to allow effective control to take place.

- A second reason for strategic control systems is to motivate managers to achieve their agreed objectives. Research has shown that clearly defined goals result in improved performance. These goals should be objectively measured and involve a challenge for individuals. They should not be perceived as too easy or insurmountable. Similarly, participation in setting objectives for complex tasks also helps improve performance. When addressing the goals of business unit managers the strategic controls can focus on a few results-orientated goals which help guide behaviour. These should be financial and non-financial (Kaplan and Norton 1996). However, this approach is less helpful in circumstances where the business output is difficult to measure and what constitutes *results* is unclear. In such a case organizations may choose not to use strategic control systems but instead adopt what Ouchi (1980) calls *clan controls*. This is where individual members of a clan have shared values which ensure that they pursue organizational goals without the overt need for a system of control. New members joining the organization are socialized into the values of the clan.

- A third reason for a strategic control system is to help senior managers to know when to intervene in the decisions of their unit managers. In theory, a useful strategic control system needs to be able to assess continually the assumptions on which a strategy is based as well as monitor management objectives. In reality, rather than undertake this kind of in-depth analysis, senior managers prefer to use their intuition and business experience to help them decide when to intervene in businesses. However a control system is designed, we might bear in mind that all control systems stand or fall according to the level of trust they embody. Trust is the key ingredient in all effective control systems.

Goold and Quinn suggest that managers may need to adapt strategic control systems to different business conditions. They point out that while in theory there are benefits to be derived from a strategic control system, in reality there are difficulties in trying to devise one.

> Such difficulties are likely to be more pronounced in certain sorts of businesses, and strategic control processes may need to be designed to take account of the specific circumstances faced by each business. (Goold and Quinn 1990, p. 54)

Their solution is a framework for a contingency theory of strategic control, high-lighting the conditions under which strategic control systems might be useful for an organization (Figure 10.6). It compares environmental turbulence with the ability of senior managers to state and measure strategic objectives.

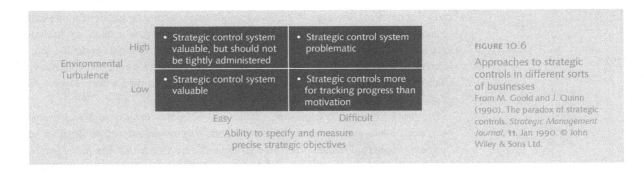

FIGURE 10.6
Approaches to strategic controls in different sorts of businesses
From M. Goold and J. Quinn (1990). The paradox of strategic controls. *Strategic Management Journal*, **11**. Jan 1990. © John Wiley & Sons Ltd.

The ideal use of strategic controls is when the environment faced by the organization exhibits low turbulence and it is easy to state and measure precise objectives. In this type of organization a formal strategic control system can be designed which will help monitor strategy implementation. In addition, because strategic objectives can be stated and readily measured, the strategic control system can be used to set goals and motivate managers. This is shown in the lower left-hand quadrant of Figure 10.6. In organizations where the environmental turbulence is high but the ability to specify objectives is high, a strategic control system may still be of benefit but needs to be more loosely exercised. This reflects the dynamic nature of the environment in which the organization operates.

Where the organization faces an environment in which turbulence is low but there is difficulty in specifying and measuring objectives, strategic controls can act as a means of monitoring strategy. This might be done through the use of milestones or signposts. Finally, in organizations which exhibit high turbulence and a difficulty in measuring objectives, strategic control systems pose a real problem. The difficulty in measuring objectives precludes their use as a motivational vehicle for managers. In this case, a looser arrangement is required that emphasizes informal relationships between senior managers and unit managers. Therefore, a strategic control system may be best thought of as contingent upon the business environment the organization faces.

For a further discussion of strategic control systems go to the Online Resource Centre and see the Key Work feature.
www.oxfordtextbooks.co.uk/orc/henry2e/

In addressing control systems, Argyris (1977) makes the point that organizations need to move beyond what he calls *single-loop* learning. This occurs when firm performance is measured against agreed goals. Feedback is obtained only after seeing if the goals have been met at the end of a specified period (e.g. a quarter). Until this time has elapsed, no action to change strategy or goals is taken. In a stable and relatively predictable environment a single-loop control system would not be a cause for concern. However, in an environment characterized by greater change and uncertainty, single-loop learning is inappropriate. Argyris argues instead for *double-loop* learning in which learning becomes a continuous process. As part of double-loop learning the assumptions on which strategies and goals are based are continually challenged and monitored. This allows the organization to detect and respond to changes in its environment more readily.

The more formal an organization's structure, the more constrained are its members, particularly in networking across functions to provide innovative solutions to business problems. The less prescribed an organization's structure, the more autonomy and flexibility its members have to cross boundary lines in pursuit of knowledge and capabilities. Therefore, the more likely it is that an innovative culture can be encouraged. However, a conflict arises as to how 'loose' an organization's structure should be before this impacts negatively on individual members' roles. One solution is a loose–tight structure: *tight*, in that there is an unflinching pursuit of the organization's objectives; *loose*, in that there is flexibility as to how these will be achieved.

The chairman and CEO of Internet giant Google, Eric Schmidt, argues that as Google grows older so its capacity to innovate quickly may start to suffer. This is because there is a natural tendency to become more conservative as an organization grows older leading to it becoming more risk averse; taking small steps instead of big strides. Schmidt argues 'true innovation comes from doing things differently, often radically different, and that involves risk.' Google have what they call 20 per cent time which allows its engineers to spend around one day a week working on things they find interesting. To date this has produced innovations such as Google Chrome. The Case Study: Organizational Systems at WL Gore highlights the counter-intuitive approach of leading a company without traditional organizational structures and strategic control systems.

Organizational Systems at WL Gore

In most companies, turning down the founder and chief executive's request to look after a pet project would be a career-stopper for a young engineer on her first assignment. But WL Gore and Associates is not most companies. And Terri Kelly, the engineer in question who became its president and chief executive in 2005—only the fourth in the company's 50-year history—tells that story to illustrate a couple of Gore's most singular characteristics.

At Gore—a $2.4bn, hi-tech materials company that most people know best for the Gore-Tex fabric that waterproofs their anoraks and walking boots—no one can tell any of the company's 8,500 associates what to do. Although there is a structure (divisions, business units and so on) there is no organisation chart, no hierarchy and therefore no bosses. Kelly is one of the few with a title.

As she acknowledges, that makes her job rather different from that of most CEOs. Bill Gore, who set up the company with his wife Vieve (short for Genevieve) in the family garage in 1958, wanted to build a firm that was truly innovative. So there were no rule books or bureaucracy. He strongly believed that people come to work to do well and do the right thing. Trust, peer pressure and the desire to invent great products—market-leading guitar strings, dental floss, fuel cells, cardiovascular and surgical applications and all kinds of specialised fabrics—would be the glue holding the company together, rather than the official procedures other companies rely on.

Traditionalists looking at Gore wonder how it works. Kelly laughs—as she does frequently—and counters that it works just fine, particularly in chaotic times like these. The financial crisis is also a management crisis and the symptom, she believes, of a wider issue: a deficit of trust. Gore, however, has 'focused on generating value through trust—with our associates [the privately-held company is co-owned by the Gore family and the workforce], suppliers and customers'. Counter-intuitively, the best governance, especially in troubled periods, is the absence of external rules: Gore would rather rely on fiercely motivated people who, having internalised true north, have no fear of challenging leaders to justify decisions, and leaders who know they can't rely on power or status to get themselves out of a fix.

In Gore's self-regulating system, all the normal management rules are reversed. In this back-to-front world, leaders aren't appointed: they emerge when they accumulate enough followers to qualify as such. So when the previous group CEO retired three years ago, there was no shortlist of preferred candidates. Alongside board discussions, a wide range of associates were invited to nominate to the post someone they would be willing to follow. 'We weren't given a list of names—we were free to choose anyone in the company,' Kelly says. 'To my surprise, it was me.'

10

Similarly, Gore doesn't have budgets in the sense that most companies do. 'When I joined we didn't have a planning process—budgeting wasn't in the vocabulary,' she says. Gore now does a better job of planning investment and forecasting, she maintains, but it still tries to avoid the games-playing and inflexibility of the traditional budget.

'Budgets hinder associates from reacting in real time to changing circumstances,' she says. Most of Gore's investment will only have an impact years ahead: 'We don't want folks making short-term decisions that are not in the best interest of the long term. The planning and investment horizons have to match.'

Gore also seems to reverse the usual notions of economies of scale. Kelly cites Bill Gore's counter-intuitive belief in the need 'to divide so that you can multiply'. When Gore units grow to around 200 people, they are usually split up. These small plants are organised in clusters or campuses, ideally with a dozen or so sites in close enough proximity to permit knowledge synergies, but still intimate and separate enough to encourage ownership and identity. An accountant might complain that creates duplication of costs; Gore believes those are more than offset by the benefits smallness brings.

A Gore lifer, Kelly joined the company as a process engineer in 1983 after graduating with distinction from the University of Delaware with a degree in mechanical engineering. (It's perhaps no coincidence that, like leaders in many of the most interesting of today's companies, she has no formal business education—and no regrets at having missed out.) She cut her teeth as a product specialist with the military fabrics business—a unit she eventually led—before moving to head the global fabrics division. Here she helped set up a fabrics manufacturing plant in Shenzhen, China, Gore's first fabrics plant in Asia, now at the centre of one of the company's fastest growing operations. While leading the fabrics division, Kelly also served on the enterprise team overseeing Gore's strategic direction.

Is lack of experience outside the company a disadvantage, or an essential qualification for running Gore? It is hard to imagine an outsider being able to understand, let alone manage, a distinctive culture such as this. Kelly argues that the ability to develop its own ways of doing things is crucial to the company's success. Proof of the importance of the 'Gore factor' is the company's consistently high ranking in 'good places to work' surveys—the UK arm, with units in Livingston and Dundee, headed the Sunday Times Best Companies to Work For list four years in a row.

Most companies find safety in numbers, ending up broadly resembling their industry counterparts in strategy, products and management processes. For the consequences, look no further than the credit crunch, which has overwhelmed the copycats in the financial sector.

Kelly, on the other hand, spends most of her time on emphasising difference and preventing people from reverting to the conventional wisdom that in other firms would be the norm. This is a fine line to tread. Protecting the core heritage is one thing; not allowing anything to change is another. Where Gore has tripped up in the past, she says, has been in confusing the core values, which don't change, with the practices for getting things done, which do. So in the late 1980s there was a furious argument over whether 'structure' was bureaucracy and therefore bad and counter-cultural. 'We didn't pay enough attention to accountability and decision making and who was actually leading. It was a good exercise for us to understand the need to distinguish between practices, which change with time, and who we really are, which doesn't. Otherwise you're paralysed.'

Although at present, Gore is being prudent with investment plans, cutting back on hiring in areas most exposed to the downturn, Kelly is not rowing back from the promise that the company will double in size over the next few years. As a private company, Gore doesn't release detailed figures, but it is no secret that the balance sheet is strong and the company has been in the black every year in its history. It doesn't lack opportunities, whether geographical or technical, nor is it constrained by ability to invest.

Growth, then, will largely be dictated by its ability to assimilate new people. 'It's all about how we bring new folks in, get them to understand our values and focus leadership on fitting it all together,' Kelly says. 'For our associates to know we aren't constrained by markets or finance, just by our own culture—that's a good problem to have. It's all in our own hands.'

Source: 'Gore-Tex gets made without managers' *The Observer*, 2 November 2008.

Questions

1. Assess the role of WL Gore's core values in helping the company to compete successfully without adopting a traditional organizational structure.

2. How does WL Gore achieve *organizational integration* across its highly decentralized plants?

3. In the absence of strategic control systems how is the behaviour of Gore's associates motivated and guided?

10

It is often said by leaders of organizations that people are their most valuable assets. It is a truism that without the actions of individual members of an organization a strategy cannot be effectively implemented. The question thus arises: How much support do organizations provide to their employees? And what impact does an organization's commitment to its employees have on organizational performance? Lee and Miller (1999) suggest that an organization's commitment to its employees can be seen in the way that it cares for employee welfare and satisfaction, the fairness of its rewards, and the investment it makes in their development and compensation. Their study of the competitive strategies of Korean firms found that, other things being equal, an organization's commitment to its employees provides only a small financial benefit to the organization. However, when an organization's commitment to its employees is aligned to a dedicated positioning strategy, its potential for achieving a sustainable competitive advantage substantially improves. Therefore, a 'strategy appears to be necessary to channel effort to achieve the maximum benefit', in this case the positioning strategies developed by Porter which include *cost leadership*, *differentiation*, and *focus* (see **Chapter 7**).

This suggests that a loyal and committed workforce implementing a dedicated strategy may be a basis for improved profitability. This is because a dedicated positioning strategy is implemented more effectively by an organization which shows a commitment to its employees. While an organization's commitment to its employees has a positive impact on its return on assets in the context of an intensive positioning strategy, this study also suggests that the resource-based view and positioning approach to strategy both have their part to play. An asset-specific resource, such as a motivated workforce, can help in the implementation of a positioning strategy, while a positioning strategy is clearly necessary to channel the efforts of employees. However, a sense of trust that emanates from an organization's commitment to its employees and their commitment to the organization's success takes time to establish.

10.4 Strategic Change

Strategic change is about changing the way in which an organization interacts with its external environment. It is about creating new and innovative ways of doing business. It involves changing an organization's systems in order to adapt to external changes. Organizational systems may be divided into three elements: structure, processes, and culture. Organizational structure is concerned with the division of labour into specialized tasks and coordination between these tasks. Organizational processes deal with the control systems to manage employees and guide their behaviour to ensure that the firm achieves its goals. This will include such things as budgeting and formal planning. Organizational culture can be thought of as the shared norms and values adopted by the members of an organization. In the absence of formal control mechanisms values and culture can be a powerful force in motivating and guiding behaviour (Ouchi 1980).

Strategic change is necessary for an organization to ensure a fit between its internal resources and capabilities and the requirements of a changing environment. However, the organization should not be seen as passive, simply responding to changes in its environment. An organization may instead seek to actively influence its competitive environment. It may seek to drive the changes taking place in its industry. For example, Gillette is constantly redefining the *rules of the game* by actively destabilizing existing competitive advantages in its industry. In implementing strategic change, organizations need to consider the *size* of any change and the *speed* with which that will be undertaken. In a classic article, Greiner (1972) argued that as organizations grow they go through five distinct phases of development. These phases are characterized by relatively calm periods of growth that end in a management crisis. The extent to which these crises can be anticipated will depend upon how well management knows its own organizational history. This is because each phase is influenced by the preceding phase. As an organization grows, it proceeds through evolutionary change and revolutionary change. How management tackles each revolutionary change will determine whether or not the organization will proceed to the next evolutionary change.[1]

Revolutionary change describes 'those periods of substantial turmoil in organizational life' (Greiner 1972, p. 38). It involves a break with existing business practices which occurs over a short period of time. It is usually a response to changes in the external environment, such as a shift in the use of certain technologies. It may also occur as a result of internal changes in the organization. For instance, a new CEO often has a window of opportunity in which he or she can push through fundamental changes in the way the organization delivers its products or services. When this window closes organizational inertia often precludes radical change.

REVOLUTIONARY CHANGE

periods of substantial turmoil in organizational life

In contrast, evolutionary change describes 'prolonged periods of growth where no major upheaval occurs in organizational practices' (Greiner 1972, p. 38). It involves a series of small gradual changes. However, the end result may be the same as for revolutionary change. This is because the accumulated effect of many small changes is similar to making one large change. The main difference is the timescale it requires to undertake the changes. The rationale for evolutionary change is best seen by addressing how individuals learn. Most individuals learn incrementally over a period of time. By definition an organization, which is fundamentally a collection of individuals, learns in the same way. If individuals are to internalize change for the benefit of organizations they need time to learn.

EVOLUTIONARY CHANGE

prolonged periods of growth where no major upheaval occurs in organizational practices

According to Greiner, how an organization develops is determined by the interactions between its age, its size, its stages of evolutionary and revolutionary change, and the growth rate of its industry. The task of management during each revolutionary change is to develop a new set of practices that will help them to manage in the next evolutionary growth period. However, each new management practice will eventually become obsolete for managing change in the next growth period. As Greiner states: 'managers experience the irony of seeing a major solution in one period become a major problem in a later period' (Greiner 1972, p. 40). The five phases of growth identified by Greiner are *creativity*, *direction*, *delegation*, *coordination*, and *collaboration* (Figure 10.7).

- **Phase 1—Creativity** is characterized by product development and market growth. Communication between individuals in the organization is informal, and tasks are less clearly defined. The founders of the organization spend their time on the product or service and neglect managerial functions. As the organization grows the

10

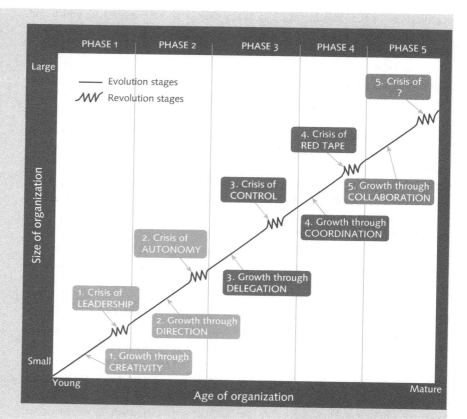

FIGURE 10.7

The five phases of growth
Reprinted by permission of
Harvard Business Review.
Exhibit II: The five phases of
growth, in L.E. Greiner (1972)
Growing Organizations, *Harvard
Business Review*, 50(4).
Copyright © 1972 by the Harvard
Business School Publishing
Corporation. All rights reserved.

founders are unable to keep pace with the increased managerial functions, such as
finance, marketing, and manufacturing. At this point a *crisis of leadership* occurs,
which is the basis for the first revolutionary change. A manager is needed to lead
the business who has knowledge and experience of managing these different functions. Success in Phase 1 leads the company to Phase 2.

- In **Phase 2—Direction** the evolutionary growth phase is characterized by the
  implementation of a functional structure with clear lines of responsibility and
  authority. Communication becomes more formal. Organizational hierarchy becomes
  prevalent, reinforced by control systems. As the organization continues to grow, so
  these existing structures become increasing cumbersome. The growing complexity
  of the environment requires individual employees to exercise their discretion in
  making decisions. A *crisis of autonomy* results in a second revolution which is born
  out of the conflict between autonomy and tight control systems.

- **Phase 3—Delegation** is epitomized by a decentralized structure. In fact, in an
  update to this classic article, Greiner (1998) suggests that decentralization sums up
  more clearly than delegation what is occurring in this phase. Managers experience

greater autonomy and responsibility. Motivation is achieved through a bonus structure that rewards business goals. In time, however, top managers at the centre perceive a tendency for business managers to subordinate the overall corporate goals in favour of their own business goals. This leads to a *crisis of control*, in which top management seek to assert their control.

- In **Phase 4—Coordination** top management institutes formal control systems to help them coordinate these diverse businesses. These decentralized business units may be reconfigured into product groups. The allocation of resources is far more carefully evaluated and controlled at the centre. The return on capital employed is used by the centre as a criterion for justifying their allocation decisions. In time this leads to a *crisis of red tape* in which business unit managers come to resent decisions from the centre which are seen as remote and lacking an understanding of local market conditions. The organization becomes too big and complex to be efficiently managed by formal systems—the next revolution begins.

- In **Phase 5—Collaboration** self-discipline and working towards agreed organizational objectives replace formal control systems. Teamwork, flexible working, and networking are common practices characterizing this evolutionary growth phase. The question for leaders of organizations is what kind of revolution change will supplant this evolutionary growth phase. A real difficulty for leaders is to understand where they are in this development process and consciously act to learn from, rather than replicate, the past. Although the rate of change has accelerated since Greiner first introduced his model, it does provide an outline of the broad challenges that managers of growing organizations face (Greiner 1998).

Those who advocate revolutionary change accept that all firms need periods of relative stability but argue that this can breed rigidities. Organizational rigidity is an inability and unwillingness to change even when your competitive environment dictates that change is required. In addressing strategic change, tools such as *business process re-engineering* can help managers to see that change must be integrative across the organization's systems rather than be conducted in isolation (see Section 10.4.1). A challenge for managers of revolutionary change is to avoid the organization sinking back into old rigidities after the change. As we saw in **Chapters 3** and **7**, companies that compete in turbulent environments are forced to innovate constantly. This leaves little room for complacency and resting on former successes. For an understanding of some of the difficulties that executive managers face in trying to implement strategic change and change the organizational culture, see Case Study: Managing Strategic Change at ITV.

ORGANIZATIONAL RIGIDITY

an inability and unwillingness to change even when your competitive environment dictates that change is required

10

CASE STUDY 10.2
Managing Strategic Change at ITV

At 10.30am on Thursday every member of staff at ITV received an email from Archie Norman, the new chairman who arrived at the beginning of the year.

In it Norman encouraged anybody and everybody to email him direct with thoughts on ITV's strategic review. 'I promise you will get a response from me and often from a member of the strategy team as well,' Norman said, attaching his personal email address. It was a very 'just call me Archie' moment. Archie Norman, former chief executive of ASDA, former chairman of telecommunications company, Energis, and former leading Conservative politician, is at the start of a journey at ITV. He has never worked in broadcasting and many eyebrows were raised when his name was announced last autumn.

Archie Norman wants to make the most of ITV's assets.

Next month, Adam Crozier, the former chief executive of Royal Mail, arrives as the new chief executive. He hasn't any experience in broadcasting either.

Those who have watched Norman, 55, immerse himself in the business over the past few weeks say it has become eminently clear that the lack of television experience matters little. 'He's absolutely forensic,' said one. 'He immediately understood the huge challenges here.'

Analysts were cooing with pleasure after Norman's much-praised performance at ITV's annual results announcement earlier this month. The broadcaster revealed better-than-expected advertising revenue, that its cost-cutting programme had overshot its target and the pensions deficit had been cut by more than £200m to £436m. Nick Bertolotti, analyst at Credit Suisse, summed up the mood when he said: 'His grasp of the issues is phenomenal.'

Although Norman is keen to stress that strategy and its execution will be a matter for Crozier and not for him as non-executive chairman, many wonder how much room Norman will leave the Man from the Mail when he arrives on April 26.

Norman knows that, although speed will be vital, ITV is coming out of a year of crisis and he needs to tread carefully. Most of last year was taken up with the board's forlorn attempt to find a chief executive after Michael Grade, the executive chairman, announced his intention to move on. Fought out on the front pages of the business media, ITV was left embarrassed when Tony Ball, the former head of Sky, eventually turned down a deal worth £42m over five years.

As he gives his first interview since taking up the post, Norman faces a series of significant challenges. Should ITV sell its production arm? Will the free-to-air broadcaster commit to pay television? Will it need to find more cost savings to reduce its net debt of £612m? Will the advertising upturn continue or crash and burn? How dangerous is the BBC to commercial broadcasting and to ITV? What can he learn from Susan Boyle, the Britain's Got Talent singing phenomenon who become a YouTube sensation? The questions go on and on.

And, before all that, what about the announcement on Thursday that Grade had received a £1.2m payment following his resignation and that Crozier will enjoy a starting salary of £775,000, a £620,000 cash-and-shares award on joining and the possibility of a 4.1m shares option over the next three years which, at today's prices, is worth more than £2.2m? Including bonuses, pension contributions and share options, the whole package could be worth £11m by 2013. One newspaper helpfully described Crozier as 'Fat Cat One'.

'People will fuss over the bits they will fuss over,' Norman said about the slew of negative headlines. 'Michael Grade's departure package was nothing to do with me and was pre-decided as part of last year's manoeuvres around who was going to be chairman and chief executive. It was an entirely contractual agreement so it is water under the bridge now.

'Adam's got the same bonus entitlement as the rest of the executives which are based on targets we set annually which are rather more stretching than those in the past, I may say. Then he gets what are effectively deferred shares which become exercisable in four years' time but only if we outperform a basket of European media companies, the UK FTSE index, and then the incentives for strategic change in the business.'

Although remuneration packages receive a lot of attention, Norman knows ITV shareholders will want to see substantial improvement in performance for a broadcaster that often appears stuck somewhere in the 1970s.

'Looking at it today, this is a business which is financially 100 per cent dependent on free-to-air, is structured around an old-fashioned broadcasting model and is culturally bound to it.

'And that is why ITV has found change very challenging. The world has changed and we have to start monetising our content on different platforms. We've got to start being an owner of property and rights.

'It is not just that people [here] are bound into habits—which they are—but we are not organised to do that. I would like to think that under Adam's leadership in a year's time ITV is seen as one of Britain's most rapidly changing companies. We should not underestimate the extent of change, not necessarily in economic superstructure but in the way people work here.

'For people in ITV you either see that as a slightly scary message or an exciting message. The way we want to organise it is to give everyone a sense that they are part of the journey, that involving style of management is very important for ITV because we are a talent company, we depend on our people.' Hence the need for that email to all staff.

'In five years' time we need a platform of sustainable and profitable growth because today we are looking at a platform of continued long-term decline and that is not acceptable.

'We will go through a phase of very substantial change. It will mean having a thriving content business, a broadcasting business and a growing international presence with capacity to buy and sell content around the world. A lot of the decisions about the form these will take is for Adam and his team; my role is to set the agenda for change.'

Norman, who has previously admitted that ITV 'trails the competition' when it comes to online, uses the example of Susan Boyle to make his point about the broadcaster's somewhat clog-footed approach to the digital world.

'The famous clip of Susan Boyle which played out on YouTube, nobody made any money out of that,' he says. 'That was probably one of the most famous clips globally and was not successfully monetised.

'Why did ITV not say, "Let's agree on the clip rights. How can we do this in everybody's interests, in Simon Cowell's interest, in Susan Boyle's interest?" Well, because it didn't occur to people that this could happen. 'Until it got 18m hits in four days nobody thought that an episode of Britain's Got Talent could become a global brand.

'All these things are very instructive. Our market is changing so fast. We've got programmes now where already 30 per cent of the viewing is video on demand, most of that by young people on computers. Now, video on demand total share of market is tiny but that is a glimpse of the future.' Later, at the end of the interview, Norman says with a shake of the head, 'We don't even have a clips sales department.' The conclusion is obvious—a lot of people will have to change their jobs. And ITV will not be a simple vanilla free-to-air broadcaster by 2015 and pay will play an increasing role in a mixed free and pay environment.

'I think it is very likely [we will use some elements of pay-TV] because one of the things that is going to happen as people consume their television off different platforms—such as internet-enabled TV, off your laptop, off your iPad as you commute to work—for some parts of the content that ITV own or others own, people will pay.

'They will maybe pay per view, maybe subscription or maybe a more conventional pay-TV arrangement as Sky do. We don't know.

'That is the way television is going to be consumed tomorrow. For properties that don't require huge audiences, that are not mass market but have very strong specialist interest, content owners will say "I need to be paid every time somebody watches this".'

'It wouldn't apply to Coronation Street or the X-Factor. Those are mega-brands, they create a national conversation and they need huge audiences and the advertisers need huge audiences and that is a different part of the market from what might be pay or subscription.'

Investors will exhale a pent-up sigh of relief that Norman is looking at new revenue streams. With high levels of debt, admittedly falling, a large pensions deficit and advertising revenue volatile and a victim of the cyclical vagaries of the economy, ITV needs to be on a firmer income footing. There are glimmers of hope, some snowdrops pushing through the snow, as one report described the healthier numbers announced a fortnight ago. Norman, though, is not impressed.

'We didn't announce good numbers,' he says, rapping his finger on the table for emphasis. 'We announced numbers which were good in the context of the worst advertising recession for a century. But ITV can't pay a dividend today, that is not a happy situation.

'We're starting from a position where the team here did a remarkable job in steering the ship through the icebergs. ITV had a life-threatening challenge at the beginning of last year and we had to make painful cuts, not just in people but in programmes.

'We have seen the biggest reduction in programming in recent history, which has meant the biggest reduction in new content commissioning, not just us, but also at Channel Five and Channel 4.

'My absolute rule here is that the genesis of any recovery is recognising where you are—the unvarnished truth is sacrosanct. I'm not interested in the good-news brigade, I'm not here to tell people we're doing very well really. There are great things about ITV but we are facing formidable challenges.'

He admits that the programme of cuts and efficiencies will continue and says that ITV is not exactly 'lean and mean' in everything it does. The advertising upturn, though, must be heartening for a company that relies on the breaks in the programmes as much as it relies on the programmes themselves.

'You have to look at the long-term trend—next month [in advertising] is just another wave on the big sea. The disconcerting thing about this market is that it is highly volatile, which obviously puts you in a risky position. Yes, we're seeing a recovery. Last year it was down 20pc; this year it could be up 20pc; in two years we could be about where we started. On a 10-year basis we're below where it was in 1999. Three of the last five years have seen a decline and this is before the real development of video on demand and internet television.

'So it is reasonable to think that on a five-to-10-year basis, television advertising is going to be a declining market. Now, we can be the tallest poppy, we need to claim our market share, we need to perform fantastically well to even grow our advertising revenue. But, as a business, it is important to be realistic about what is happening and say that we need to compete in the new marketplace as well as the old.'

With so many major challenges, and some with costs attached, many suggest that the hunt for revenue streams could mean another return to the market for cash. 'The strategic review will define the investment requirements for the business and therefore will have implications for funding,' Norman says. 'As it stands today, although we have a reasonably stretched balanced sheet, I am comfortable we can operate within our means. We are in reasonably robust form, the upturn in the advertising markets, which may be very short term, is helpful.'

The other elephant in the room is ITV's production arm, something that would be a valuable business if it was separated out and sold. When Luke Johnson, the former Channel 4 chairman, suggested that ITV should divest itself of the business in an interview in the *Sunday Telegraph*, there were mutterings of irritation from the direction of Norman's open-plan office on the 20th floor of London Television Centre.

'In this world, to not have the capacity to create your own brilliant content would be to shoot ourselves in the foot,' he says.

'It's not just that ITV Studios has historically produced some fabulous properties—maybe not so much recently, we know we have a job to do—it is also clear that, in tomorrow's world, being able to produce content that you own 100 per cent is a huge competitive advantage.'

The elephant not so much in the room as towering over the whole ITV building is the BBC. At least when Norman ran ASDA he did not have a publicly-funded supplier next door giving away its cabbages for free.

Norman treads carefully, saying that he hugely respects the public broadcaster. I ask him about the recent announcement from Mark Thompson, the BBC's director general, who said that the BBC could save £600m by cutting back its internet sites and cutting radio stations such as 6 Music and the Asian Network. Didn't that show, despite the fact that the BBC would keep the money rather than return it to the public purse, that Thompson understood the need for the BBC to clip its considerable wingspan?

'As a presentational manoeuvre it was very impressive,' he says, his eyes betraying nothing of the archness of the comment. 'If it is true, as they assert, that they can save £600m from cutting back peripheral activities that they believe have no great value like Asian radio, then the question you have to ask is why they need £600m in the licence fee in the first place and why the licence fee is going up 2.5 per cent this year.

'I don't think you can ever get around the point that if the BBC needs to be, as Mark Thompson says and I agree with him, focused on quality and being distinctive, then, in order to ensure that, you need to be making hard choices born of the fact that you don't have unlimited funding.

'£600m is a phenomenal amount of money. It is 70 per cent of the total ITV programming budget. People are entitled to ask how on earth the BBC managed to spend that amount of money on things they no longer value. I think there is a real question which must be in the forefront of Mark Thompson's and Michael Lyons's [the BBC Trust chairman] minds and that is an incoming government—at a time when the country is likely to enter a period of austerity and cut back public services—is bound to ask what contribution the BBC is going to make to the cut-backs. Should they receive less money from the public purse? To me, that is the unavoidable conclusion of their strategy review.'

A job like ITV, Norman knows, is as much about politics as it is about business. Investors want to see robust returns, the public wants to see well-made and popular programmes and the government keeps a beady eye on how the whole sector is regulated.

The Conservatives have already signalled a much more liberal approach to media companies if they win the next election. Norman certainly agrees, saying the current regulatory regime is only fit for the past. Of course, if there is any group Norman knows well—as a former Tory shadow minister who cut his teeth at McKinsey's with one William Hague—it is the Conservatives. ASDA, Energis, the Tories—all organisations that need a turnaround specialist to plot a new way forward. ITV is no different.

Source: 'ITV: the beginning of the future' *The Telegraph*, 20 March 2010.

◉ Questions

1. Outline the key strategic issues facing ITV's chairman, Archie Norman, as the company struggles to compete in a changing market.

2. Using Greiner's model explain which of 'the five phases of growth' you believe ITV occupies.

3. Real and lasting strategic change requires a change in an organization's culture. How likely is it that Archie Norman and chief executive Adam Crozier can change ITV's existing business model to take account of the market realities they face?

Those who advocate evolutionary change see revolutionary change as perpetual; another similar-size change will eventually be required after the firm sinks back to its old ways. They also point out that such revolutionary change is difficult to sustain and simply awaits another business issue to grab the organization's attention. In contrast, evolutionary change focuses on the organization's long-term goals and moves towards this. Individuals are still expected to learn, share ideas, and engage in innovation. In common with Japanese companies, evolutionary change should embrace all members of an organization. The role of management is to support and facilitate this learning and continuous improvement.

10.4.1 Integrative Change

Information technology is often introduced by organizations seeking to address deteriorating business performance. The work of Hammer (1990) on business process re-engineering warns against naively using new technology with outdated business practices to boost performance. Instead of seeing technology as a panacea, it should be viewed as a tool to help radically redesign business processes. As he states:

Reengineering strives to break away from the old rules about how we organize
and conduct business . . . reengineering cannot be planned meticulously and
accomplished in small and cautious steps. It's an all-or-nothing proposition.
(Hammer 1990, pp. 104–5)

Hammer argues for a revolutionary approach to change in which management are prepared to embrace an uncertain future. Re-engineering calls for senior management to question the assumptions of their existing business processes and change outdated rules. We have seen that specialization in organizations tends to lead to a subculture in which organizational goals are replaced by their department goals. In re-engineering the fundamental processes of the firm needs to be addressed from a cross-functional perspective, that is, any attempt to change a poorly performing department in isolation will be prone to failure. What is required is an understanding of the interactions and interdependencies between departments. This requires a change management team that is drawn from the units involved in the process being re-engineered, as well as the units that depend on them, in order to assess which processes add value. Re-engineering involves a shift in thinking about organizational structure in which the people who undertake the work make the decisions. These individuals would then become self-managing and self-controlling, which allows for management layers to be depleted. It also changes the management role from one of control to one of support and facilitation. Given the disruption and discontinuity of this sort of revolutionary change, re-engineering requires leaders who possess vision. Such leaders are not afraid to adopt audacious goals and possess the drive and ability to see them to completion.

Brynjolfsson *et al.* (1997) argue that effective change requires an understanding of complements that exists between strategy, technology, and business practice. They suggest management would benefit from adopting a *matrix of change* approach to help them understand the complicated interrelationships that surround change. Their framework draws upon the work of Milgrom and Roberts (1993) on complements. This suggests that in implementing complex change, management needs to take account of the interactions that exist, for example, between business practices, rather than trying to implement change in a disaggregated fashion. The matrix allows managers to think through the following change issues before attempting implementation: (a) *feasibility*—the coherence and stability of any proposed change; (b) *sequence*—the order in which change should take place; (c) *pace*—the speed with which change should be undertaken and the magnitude of change; and (d) *location*—whether a proposed change should take place at an existing or a new site.

The drivers of organizational change, which include information technology and increasing competition, have brought about new organizational forms. Where these forms constitute a discontinuity or break with old practices, the benefits to organizations can be considerable. For example, Hallmark, which produces greeting cards, gift wrappings, and other personal expression products, was able to reduce the time it takes to introduce new products by 75 per cent. This was achieved by changing their practice of sequential product development to one involving a cross-functional team. A difficulty arises, as we saw earlier, when organizations introduce technology without thinking through the contingent changes in working practices. This is one reason why US firms have failed to obtain the same benefits from introducing technology that comparable Japanese firms achieve.

A matrix of change system involves three matrices: (1) an organization's current practices, (2) its proposed or target practices, and (3) a transitional state that helps an organization move from matrix (1) to matrix (2). In addition, the matrix system includes stakeholder evaluations which provide employees with a forum to state the importance of the practices to their jobs. The matrix of change helps managers to be aware of the assumptions that underlie how their organization works. Its value is in identifying complementary and competing practices. Complementary practices are reinforcing. This means that undertaking more of one complement increases the return to the other complement. In contrast, doing less of a competing practice actually increases the return to other competing practices. In making complementary and competing practices explicit, managers can immediately see where there is likely to be reinforcement or interference between existing and target practices. This allows managers to select the practices which will be most effective in meeting organizational goals.

Therefore, to achieve superior performance we require an understanding of change that takes into account a complete and coherent system of practices. However, we need to recognize that organizational performance may experience a decline as new complements disrupt the old ways of doing things. In this respect putting together a coherent set of complements may take a number of years. This is not to say that change must always be evolutionary, since a powerful leader with a strong vision may introduce rapid system-wide change. This occurred when Percy Barnevik merged the Swiss company Brown Boveri with the Swedish company ASEA to create ABB in 1988. Barnevik's strategy was to reconcile a global organization and a local presence, and a decentralized structure with centralized reporting and control. In effect, ABB is a global organization which responds to national differences (see **Chapter 9** for a discussion of international strategy). To do this, Barnevik organized ABB's activities in a matrix structure consisting of about 1300 separate companies and a substantially reduced head office staff. The context of this change may account for its revolutionary nature. Barnevik's successor Goran Lindahl has built on Barnevik's changes and continues globalization in a decentralized structure albeit in an evolutionary manner.

10.4.2 Visionary Organizations

What is it that makes an organization the best in its industry and widely admired by its peers? Where does the resilience that allows some companies to overcome adversity come from? Why do some companies make a lasting impact on the world around them? The answers to these questions are part of what determines a visionary organization. Research by Collins and Porras (1994) suggests that visionary organizations are particularly adept at simultaneously managing continuity and embracing change. Using responses from CEOs they identified eighteen visionary companies, those with superior long-term performance who have made an impact on society. These were then compared with a control group of companies that had similar products, services, and markets when they were founded. In common with the visionary organizations, the comparison companies were also identified by the CEOs that Collins and Porras surveyed. The difference is that these companies were mentioned less often by CEOs when identifying who they considered to be great companies. The comparison companies had an average founding date of 1892, compared with 1897 for the visionary organizations.

The idea was to identify the factors that distinguish visionary from non-visionary companies. We might add that although the comparison companies did not attain the same performance heights as the visionary companies, nonetheless they outperformed the stock market. The difference is that, whereas the comparison companies outperformed the stock market by a factor of more than two, the visionary companies outperformed it by a factor of more than fifteen. Collins and Porras found that the visionary companies, which include Sony (the only non-American firm in the study), the Walt Disney Company, Merck, 3M, Hewlett-Packard, and Ford,[2] have a *core ideology* that comprises their *core values* and *purpose*. The core values can be thought of as the principles on which the firm was founded. An organization's purpose is the reason why it exists, which transcends merely making money. The core values of an organization do not change; they are the bedrock of the organization. Similarly, visionary organizations pursue their purpose knowing that this is ongoing and will never be fully achieved. John Young, former CEO of Hewlett-Packard, neatly sums up the thinking of visionary companies.

> *Our basic principles have endured intact since our founders conceived them. We distinguish between core values and practices; the core values don't change, but the practices might. We've also remained clear that profit—as important as it is—is not why the Hewlett-Packard Company exists; it exists for more fundamental reasons. (Collins and Porras 1994, p. 46)*

Core values and purpose are important for visionary organizations in that they help to guide continuity but also provide a stimulus for change. In **Chapter 1** we mentioned the importance of Johnson & Johnson's credo, a set of core values that guides all members of that organization. The credo was applied in helping Johnson & Johnson to overcome the Tylenol scares of 1982 and 1989. Visionary companies are prepared to change everything, except their fundamental core values. Their strategy, structure, practices, resources and capabilities, and systems all need to change at some point to ensure forward momentum or progress. For visionary companies this drive for change comes from within—a constant dissatisfaction with the status quo—rather than a reaction to the external environment. How do such organizations stimulate change? The answer is that they institute BHAGs—big hairy audacious goals. These are clear stretching goals that can be easily communicated to everyone in the organization. For example, Henry Ford wanted 'to democratize the auto-mobile' by giving the majority of individuals the freedom to buy a car. This was in 1907 when Ford was not the dominant player in the industry. The irony is that Ford failed to replace this BHAG with another to continue to stimulate progress and lost its market dominance to General Motors. Therefore, BHAGs need to be continually updated to avoid organizational complacency.

BHAGs

big hairy audacious goals: goals that stretch the organization and are readily communicated to all its members

> For information on the role of BHAGs in stimulating change go to the Online Resource Centre and see the Key Work feature.
> **www.oxfordtextbooks.co.uk/orc/henry2e/**

Hamel and Prahalad (1989) make a similar point using the concept of *strategic intent*. As with BHAGs, strategic intent is more than mere rhetoric. It requires a major level of commitment from the organization to pursue these over-arching goals. Although these goals will invariably involve a longer-term time horizon, BHAGs and strategic intent help provide some consistency to short-term actions. Boeing's decision to build the jumbo jet, the 747, when failure would have meant bankruptcy, represents a most audacious goal. Its rival, McDonnell Douglas, tended to adopt a more cautious wait-and-see approach. In short, BHAGs fall outside an organization's comfort zone. They are consistent with its core ideology, and help stimulate progress by maintaining forward momentum.

Visionary companies embrace what Collins and Porras refer to as the genius of the 'AND' rather than succumb to the tyranny of the 'OR'. In other words, where rival corporations see paradoxes and conflict, visionary companies succeed in achieving synthesis. For example, visionary companies actively pursue their ideology and profit. Being idealistic is not a reason for them to sacrifice the pursuit of profits. Although much is often made of the role of charismatic leaders in shaping organizations, it was found that this was not the case in visionary companies. At various times throughout their history organizations such as 3M, Procter & Gamble, Merck, and Sony have had CEOs who made significant changes but were not what might be understood as high-profile charismatic leaders. In fact, by setting BHAGs that are independent of management style the succession of charismatic leaders proves far less of a problem.

In addition, Collins and Porras also found a *cult-like culture* in visionary organ-izations. This cult-like culture is built around the core values of the organization. It constantly reinforces the core ideology of the organization through socialization. It indoctrinates the employees in the ways of the company and thereby influences their

10

ORGANIZATIONAL CULTURE

the values and beliefs that members of an organization hold in common

attitude and behaviour. This is manifest in organizations like Walt Disney, Procter & Gamble, and Wal-Mart. Organizational culture can be defined as 'the pattern of basic assumptions that a given group has invented, discovered, or developed in learning to cope with its problems of external adaptation and internal integration' (Schein 1984). It can be thought of as the values and beliefs that members of an organization hold in common. The outward manifestations of organizational culture can include such things as dress code, employee inductions, symbols, and office layout. However, to gain a deeper understanding of culture it becomes necessary to investigate the assumptions that guide how members of an organization perceive, think, and feel. A strong sense of culture or shared values, such as exists at Procter & Gamble, can help to coordinate, motivate, and guide individual behaviour. This invariably precludes the need for formal control systems to manage employee behaviour. There are similarities with the *Theory Z* Japanese style of management (Ouchi 1981). A Theory Z type organization is based on trust. Therefore, it requires a less hierarchical structure which in turn helps to engender greater employee involvement. A key characteristic of a Theory Z organization is its informal control systems reinforced by formal measures.

An organization's culture can be a force for change and innovation but it may also be an impediment to change. For example, the culture that exists within 3M encourages managers to experiment, to take risks, to try out new ideas, and not be afraid of failure. Within 3M, there is an expectation that managers will spend around 10 per cent of their time on projects of their own choosing. These projects are subject to the scrutiny of their peers which provides constructive feedback. Even when an idea seems to fail there is latitude for employees to enlist the support of like-minded managers (or *product champions*) in an attempt to foster creativity and a breakthrough. The product champion can be thought of as a change agent, someone who takes responsibility for ensuring that change takes place. Without such a culture the world may never have had Post-It Notes. Its inventor, Art Fry, had been working on developing a strong adhesive for 3M but failed to achieve this. What he did develop was a weak adhesive which allows paper to be stuck down but also easily removed. This resulted in the creation of Post-It Notes (see Strategy Focus: Culture at 3M). It is important for organizations like 3M that they also have appropriate reward systems in place if employees are to produce these steady streams of innovations.

For a discussion of the benefits of understanding organisational culture when implementing strategic change go to the Online Resource Centre and see the Key Work feature.
www.oxfordtextbooks.co.uk/orc/henry2e/

STRATEGY FOCUS

Culture at 3M

© iStockphoto.com

Post-It Notes were the result of a 3M researcher looking to attach page marks in his hymnal—now they are worth hundreds of millions of dollars a year to the company.

The diversified manufacturer makes products ranging from telecommunications connectors to Post-It Notes to flexible circuits for inkjet printers to pharmaceuticals to auto supplies. It has a well-known brand and products that are repeat purchases on most continents.

The roughly 50 000 3M products have their roots from one seedling—sandpaper. Its expansion into tape followed after it had gained knowledge of adhesives from affixing sand to paper. From this simple process, 3M went on to create some of its most famous—indeed ubiquitous—products: Scotch masking tape in 1925, Scotch tape in 1930, and Post-It Notes in 1980.

Invention stories are part of 3M's history, culture, and business model. It spent $1bn on research last year and built its reputation by letting its scientists loose and then figuring a way to make money from their inventions. Masking tape was invented after company officials went to talk to paint shop workers using their sandpaper before painting cars. According to company legend, a painter talked of the need for something that could be easily and safely affixed to cover or protect areas of the car not being painted. From this advice, masking tape was born.

Post-It Notes were the result of a researcher looking to attach page marks in his hymnal. He remembered that a co-worker had made a loosely sticky adhesive, and had painted it on some paper squares—now everything is covered with them. 3M reaps hundreds of millions of dollars per year from them. 'It is widely believed to be one of the most creative companies in the world . . . Its integrated approach and philosophy seeking any good invention are deeply ingrained in an egalitarian corporate culture.'

Source: 'Challenge to an integrated approach: 3M' *Financial Times*, 15 December 2000.

10

In subsequent research Collins (2001) seeks to answer the question: What turns a company from being 'good' into being 'great?' Or, put another way, what strategic change occurs within organizations that allows them to leap from being good to being great? To do this Collins and his research team identified organizations that had fifteen-year cumulative stock returns at or below the general stock market. The companies then experienced a transition point before going on to achieve cumulative returns at least three times the market over the next fifteen years. The timescale of fifteen years allows the research to filter out those spectacular companies that achieve great results but which cannot sustain them. The choice of returns three times the stock market means that such companies would have to beat the returns achieved by recognized great companies such as Coca-Cola, Motorola, and Intel.

The research team identified eleven companies[3] which met their criteria for great organizations. For comparison they made use of companies that were in the same industry and which had the same opportunities and similar resources at the time of transition, but did not make the transition from good to great, and companies that temporarily went from good to great but were unable to sustain their performance. A key finding for companies that make the transition from good to great is their use of the *hedgehog* concept. The hedgehog concept is drawn from Isaiah Berlin's story 'The Hedgehog and the Fox'. In this story the hedgehog and the fox are adversaries. The fox is very clever and knows many things. In contrast, the hedgehog knows only one big thing. In their duels, the hedgehog always rolls up into a spiky ball and therefore always beats the fox. Collins draws an analogy between the hedgehog and the leaders of good to great companies. Like the hedgehog, these leaders know and pursue one thing. Their rivals meanwhile are trying many different approaches to match the complexity of their world, while the hedgehog-like leaders construct the world into a simple unifying concept, as shown in Collins's book *Good to Great*, and reproduced here as Figure 10.8.

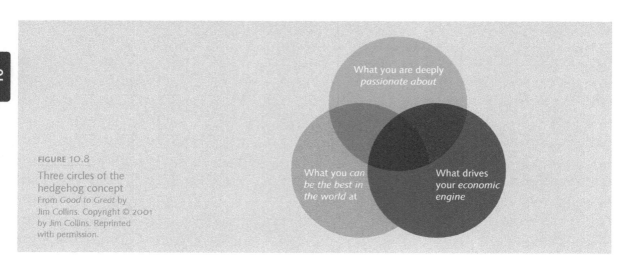

FIGURE 10.8

Three circles of the hedgehog concept
From *Good to Great* by Jim Collins. Copyright © 2001 by Jim Collins. Reprinted with permission.

According to Collins, a route to greatness is defined by an understanding of three issues.

- 'What you can be the best in the world at'. Collins sees this as going beyond the resource-based view of core competencies, arguing that possessing a core competence does not mean you are the best in the world at it. One might argue that this depends on how you define core competence, since for many organizations their core competence does make them the best in the world at what they do (e.g. Toyota's production system).
- 'What drives your economic engine'. This helps managers to understand the single performance measurement that has the greatest impact on their business. For instance, for the American pharmacy Walgreen's it was profit per customer visit.
- 'What you are deeply passionate about'. What is it that makes you passionate about the business you are in?

The good to great companies developed their strategies based on an understanding of these three issues. This understanding was then translated into a simple concept—a hedgehog concept. The point for leaders is not to try to be the best but to understand where you can be the best. We will say more on leadership in the next chapter.

 ## Summary

The chapter started with a discussion of the trade-off between specialization and coordination and the impact of this on organizational structures. We evaluated the simple functional and divisional structures before moving on to more complex matrix and network structures. The matrix structure, which initially held promise for managing complex and dynamic environments, has been found wanting. Its violation of the unity of command and complex interactions has proved costly and burdensome. In response to this Ghoshal and Bartlett have argued for a focus on organizational processes and a more integrative approach. This approach goes beyond the limitations inherent in merely making structural changes.

Goold and Quinn provide three reasons for establishing a strategic control system. They produce a contingency framework highlighting different conditions when strategic control systems might be useful for an organization. This compares environmental turbulence with the ability of senior managers to state and measure strategic objectives. We assessed strategic change looking at evolutionary changes and revolutionary changes, and Greiner's model showing some of the challenges facing managers of growing organizations. We also addressed integrative change by showing that change needs be part of a coherent and stable system that recognizes the role of complements. We ended the chapter with a discussion of visionary organizations and the use of BHAGs to guide their onward progress, before looking at how 'great' companies deal with strategic change.

10

In **Chapter 11**, we will discuss the role of leadership and assess its impact on strategic change.

Review Questions

1. Examine the relationship between an organization's structure and its performance.
2. Evaluate the role of strategic control systems in helping organizations to achieve and measure strategic objectives.

Discussion Question

Without a vision an organization will fail. Discuss.

Research Topic

Research organizations which change their structure as their strategy changes and those which change their strategy as their organizational structure changes. On the whole does the evidence support or refute Chandler's famous dictum that structure follows strategy?

Recommended Reading

For perspectives on the debate between strategy and structure see:

- **Amburgey, T.L.** and **Dacin, T.** (1994). As the left foot follows the right? The dynamics of strategic and structural change. *Academy of Management Journal*, **37**(6), 1427–52.
- **Mintzberg, H.** (1990). The design school: reconsidering the basic premises of strategic management. *Strategic Management Journal*, **11**(3), 171–95.

For a discussion of how organizations grow and evolve, see:

- **Greiner, L.E.** (1972). Evolution and revolution as organizations grow. *Harvard Business Review*, **50**(4), 37–46.

For a discussion of strategic control systems and the disadvantages of focusing merely on organizational structure, see:

- **Goold, M.** and **Quinn, J.J.** (1990). The paradox of strategic controls. *Strategic Management Journal*, **11**(1), 43–57.

- **Ghoshal, S.** and **Bartlett, C.A.** (1995). Changing the role of top management: beyond structure to processes. *Harvard Business Review*, **73**(1), 86–96.

For an insightful discussion of visionary organizations, see:

- **Collins, J.C.** and **Porras, J.I.** (1994). *Built to Last: Successful Habit of Visionary Companies*. Random House, London.

---

www.oxfordtextbooks.co.uk/orc/henry2e/
Visit the Online Resource Centre that accompanies this book for activities and more information on organizational systems and strategic change.

online resource centre

📖 Notes

1. A useful discussion of revolutionary and evolutionary change is given by De Wit and Meyer (2004).
2. The eighteen visionary companies identified by Collins and Porras were 3M, American Express, Boeing, Citicorp, Ford, General Electric, Hewlett-Packard, IBM, Johnson & Johnson, Marriott, Merck, Motorola, Nordstrom, Philip Morris, Procter & Gamble, Sony, Wal-Mart, and Walt Disney.
3. The eleven 'good to great' companies were Abbott, Circuit City, Fannie Mae, Gillette, Kimberly-Clark, Kroger, Nucor, Philip Morris, Pitney Bowes, Walgreen's, and Wells Fargo (see Collins 2001, p. 8 for a list of comparison companies).

📖 References

Amburgey, T.L. and **Dacin, T.** (1994). As the left foot follows the right? The dynamics of strategic and structural change. *Academy of Management Journal*, **37**(6), 1427–52.

Argyris, C. (1977). Double-loop learning in organizations. *Harvard Business Review*, **55**(5), 115–25.

Bartlett, A. and **Ghoshal, S.** (1990). Matrix management: not a structure, a frame of mind. *Harvard Business Review*, **68**(4), 138–45.

Brynjolfsson, E., Renshaw, A.A., and **Van Alstyne, M.** (1997). The matrix of change. *Sloan Management Review*, **38**(2), 37–54.

Chandler, A.D. (1962). *Strategy and Structure: Chapters in the History of the American Industrial Enterprise*. MIT Press, Cambridge, MA.

Collins, J.C. (2001). *Good to Great*. Random House, London.

Collins, J.C. and **Porras, J.I.** (1994). *Built to Last: Successful Habit of Visionary Companies*. Harper, New York.

De Wit, B. and **Meyer, R.** (2004). *Strategy: Process, Content, Context*, Chapter 4. Thomson, London.

Ghoshal, S. and **Bartlett, C.A.** (1995). Changing the role of top management: beyond structure to processes. *Harvard Business Review*, **73**(1), 86–96.

Goold, M. and **Campbell, A.** (2002). Do you have a well designed organization? *Harvard Business Review*, **80**(3), 117–24.

Goold, M. and **Quinn, J.J.** (1990). The paradox of strategic controls. *Strategic Management Journal*, **11**(1), 43–57.

Greiner, L.E. (1972). Evolution and revolution as organizations grow. *Harvard Business Review*, **50**(4), 37–46.

Greiner, L.E. (1998). Evolution and revolution as organizations grow. *Harvard Business Review*, **76**(3), 55–63 (his 1972 classic article revisited).

Hamel, G. and **Prahalad, C.K.** (1989). Strategic intent. *Harvard Business Review*, **67**(3), 63–76.

Hammer, M. (1990). Reengineering work: don't automate, obliterate. *Harvard Business Review*, **68**(4), 104–11.

Kaplan, R.S. and **Norton, D.P.** (1996). Using the balanced scorecard as a strategic management system. *Harvard Business Review*, **74**(1), 75–85.

Lee, J. and **Miller, D.** (1999). People matter: commitment to employees, strategy and performance in Korean firms. *Strategic Management Journal*, **20**(6), 579–93.

Milgrom, P. and **Roberts, J.** (1993). Complementarities and fit: strategy, structure, and organizational change in manufacturing. *Journal of Accounting and Economics*, **19**(2), 179–208.

Mintzberg, H. (1993). *Structures in Fives: Designing Effective Organizations*. Prentice Hall, Englewood Cliffs, NJ.

Mintzberg, H. and **Waters, J.A.** (1985). Of strategies: deliberate and emergent. *Strategic Management Journal*, **6**(3), 257–72.

Ouchi, W.G. (1980). Markets, bureaucracies, and clans. *Administrative Science Quarterly*, **25**(1), 129–42.

Ouchi, W.G. (1981). *Theory Z: How American Businesses Can Meet the Japanese Challenge*. Addison-Wesley, Reading, MA.

Schein, E.H. (1984). Coming to a new awareness of organizational culture. *Sloan Management Review*, **25**(2), 3–16.

11 Strategic Leadership

11.1 Leadership and Management

11.2 The Learning Organization

11.3 Emotional Intelligence and Leadership Performance

Main Reference
Goleman, D. (1998).
What makes a leader?
Harvard Business Review,
76(6), 93–102.

11.4 Narcissistic Leaders and Leadership Capabilities

Key Work
Narcissistic leaders and their importance

11.5 The Impact of Leadership on Vision, Values, and Culture

Key Work
Impact of culture on organizations

11.6 Leading Strategic Change

Key Work
Difficulties faced when implementing strategic change

11.7 The Impact of Chaos on Leadership

Learning Objectives

After completing this chapter you should be able to:

- Explain the difference between leadership and management
- Discuss the role of leaders in creating a learning organization
- Evaluate the impact of emotional intelligence on effective leadership
- Assess the benefits and dangers of a narcissistic personality trait
- Discuss the role of leaders in developing a shared vision and shaping the values of an organization
- Assess the effects of different national cultures on leadership
- Assess the leadership skills necessary for directing strategic change
- Discuss the impact of chaos on innovation and strategic direction

Introduction

A key factor in effective *strategy implementation* is the quality of strategic leadership at the top of the organization. The ability of leaders to communicate organizational goals clearly and guide employees to focus their attention on achieving these goals is crucial to success. This leadership ability is equally relevant in public, private, and not-for-profit sectors. This is not to imply that individuals lower down in the organization cannot exercise a leadership role. Rather, it is to recognize that without effective leadership at the top of the organization, individuals throughout the organization will be less likely to be empowered and, therefore, less likely to develop their own leadership skills.

We noted in the introduction to **Chapter 10** that the best formulated strategy in the world will fail if it is poorly implemented. Also, although the leader of an organization is ultimately responsible for a strategy's success or failure, their role should be to encourage and create an organizational culture that empowers individuals to respond to opportunities. We saw in the previous chapter how appropriate reward and control mechanisms help to guide employee behaviour and signpost the important goals of the organization. We might reiterate that systems, procedures, and policies may aid the implementation of a strategy but ultimately it is individuals who implement strategy. Therefore, it is individuals and groups, within and outside the organization, who must accept the rationale for strategic change.

In this chapter we address the role that *leadership* plays in strategy implementation. We start the chapter with a discussion of the differences between leadership and management, and note the role of leadership in directing change. We discuss the role of leaders in creating a learning organization. This recognizes that the speed with which organizations learn may be a source of sustainable competitive advantage (Stalk 1988). A challenge for leaders then is to create organizations in which people continually learn. We evaluate the impact of emotional intelligence on effective leadership and the links between emotional intelligence and company performance. We next assess the advantages and the dangers of narcissistic leaders, noting that this personality type may actually be beneficial in turbulent markets. We discuss the role of leaders in developing a shared vision and shaping the values of an organization and how this helps guide employee behaviour. The effects of national culture on people's beliefs and behaviour will be assessed, and the importance of this for different leadership approaches will be noted. Given the complexity and uncertainty that surrounds most organizations we assess the role leadership plays in directing strategic change, and look at some of the leadership skills necessary to achieve change. We end with a discussion of chaos theory and its impact on innovation and strategic direction.

- In Section 11.1 we start the chapter with a discussion of the difference between management and leadership.

- In Section 11.2 we discuss the role of leaders in creating a learning organization.

- In Section 11.3 we explain emotional intelligence and assess the impact of emotional intelligence on effective leadership. We look at the links between emotional intelligence and business performance.

- Section 11.4 assesses the effects of a narcissistic personality trait on leadership. This section also evaluates whether leadership capabilities can transpose from one organizational setting to another.

- In Section 11.5 we discuss the role of leaders in developing an organization's shared vision, its values, and its culture. We assess the importance of national cultures and how an understanding of culture can benefit leaders of multinational corporations.

- Section 11.6 assesses the role of leadership in directing strategic change. We look at some of the obstacles to implementing change effectively and the leadership skills necessary to overcome them.

- The chapter ends in Section 11.7 with a discussion of chaos theory and how an understanding of chaos may help leaders bring about innovation and strategic direction.

11.1 Leadership and Management

A great deal of early work on leadership was taken up with discussions on nature and nurture. That is, are leaders born or can leadership abilities be learned? We will eschew this debate and focus instead on the role of leadership in helping organizations develop a sustainable competitive advantage. We might start by addressing the question: what is leadership and how does it differ from management? We should make it clear that some scholars in the field of strategic management use the term 'management' when it might be more appropriate to refer to 'leadership'. Some refer to *goals* meaning a short-term budgetary process, while others use the term *goals* to imply a longer-term horizon. Therefore, readers should be mindful of this as they work through the chapter.

MANAGEMENT

is about coping with complexity to produce orderly and consistent results

LEADERSHIP

is concerned with creating a shared vision of where the organization is trying to get to, and formulating strategies to bring about the changes needed to achieve this vision

In distinguishing between leadership and management Kotter (1990) argues that management is all about coping with complexity, whereas leadership is about dealing with change. The complexity arises out of the proliferation of large corporations that occurred in the twentieth century. In order to operate effectively within these corporations managers use a range of practices and procedures (see **Chapter 10** for a discussion of strategic control systems). According to Kotter, a key function of management which helps it to deal with complexity is planning and budgeting, that is, the setting of targets or goals for the next quarter or year, designing detailed steps for achieving those goals, and allocating resources as they are needed. The purpose of planning then is to produce *orderly results*, not change.

In contrast, leadership is concerned with setting the direction for organizational change. It is about producing a vision and developing strategies to realize that vision. The vision does not need to be overly complex or innovative; in fact, it should be clear and readily understood by all within the organization. In their research into visionary organization, Collins and Porras (1994) found that successful organizations use BHAGs—big hairy audacious goals—to motivate and inspire individuals, thereby creating a *unifying focal point of effort*. BHAGs also have the benefit of providing continued momentum within an organization after the leader has gone (see **Chapter 10**,

Section 10.4.2 on visionary organizations). A key point for any vision is how well it serves the organization's stakeholders and how easy it is to translate into a competitive strategy. The planning of management and the direction setting of leadership works best when they are used to complement rather than substitute for each other, that is, a vision can be used to guide the planning process by providing a direction for its efforts and placing boundaries on its activities. Porter (1996) argues that the leader's role is to develop strategy and make choices and trade-offs within the organization clear, and to teach others about strategy and help them to acquire the discipline to make choices in their day-to-day activities. This need to make choices reflects the fact that not all activities an individual may pursue will fit with the organization's strategy (see Strategy Focus: Leadership—World Economic Forum).

STRATEGY FOCUS
Leadership—World Economic Forum

It was billed as Taking Responsibility for Tough Choices. But tough choices were thin on the ground at the World Economic Forum in Davos, the world's foremost gathering of business and political leaders, last week. Once lambasted for its harsh neo-liberal thinking, this year's forum was mostly motherhood and apple pie. There was little discussion of the hard

© Pascal Lauener/Reuters/Corbis

Participants in the G8 and Africa session stand on stage at the World Economic Forum (WEF) in Davos: (left to right) former US President Bill Clinton, Bill Gates, Chairman of Microsoft Corporation, Thabo Mbeki, President of South Africa, Britain's Prime Minister Tony Blair, singer Bono, and Olusegun Obasanjo, President of Nigeria.

trade-offs business and political leaders need to make. This is of more than parochial interest, because leadership is about making tough choices, and there is not enough leadership around.

Back in the 1990s the World Economic Forum epitomized the triumph of the Washington consensus. Talk was all about business and the onward march of markets. This time poverty and climate change were top of the agenda. Small wonder that the rival anti-globalization gathering at the World Social Forum in Porto Alegre is in danger of going out of business. The non-governmental organizations are not only inside the tent, they are dictating the agenda.

This is not to say that poverty and climate change do not belong on the agenda for business leaders. They are probably the world's most pressing public policy

11

problems, and business cannot escape responsibility for being part of the solution. But a balance needs to be struck. Business should not be apologetic about its principal contribution to society: providing goods and services people want, jobs they need, and innovation for the future.

Moreover, both business and political leaders need to engage directly in the difficult trade-offs that lie at the heart of decision making. This was sadly absent. Climate change was discussed mostly as a win–win situation in which business could profit from new technologies—and not, for instance, in terms of regulatory costs. There was no focused debate as to whether nuclear power is the answer.

Source: 'Davos's poverty of leadership: hard trade-offs need to be made in business and politics' *Financial Times*, 31 January 2005.

In modern organizations, as we saw in the previous chapter, organizational systems are interdependent. These include such things as structure, reward and control mechanisms, and processes. Therefore, trying to adjust one part of the system in isolation can have no effect, or worse, a negative effect on the organization (Brynjolfsson *et al*. 1997). A role of management is to develop coherent systems which will allow plans to be efficiently implemented. This means communicating plans to individuals within the organization, making sure that the right people are in place to carry it forward, and providing appropriate incentives. As part of this organizing function, management must also have systems in place to monitor the outcomes of human action. This allows corrective action to be taken to ensure that plans are properly implemented.

The respective leadership role is one of *aligning*. The aim is to get key stakeholders inside and outside the organization to move in the same direction. Alignment can be thought of as an orchestral ensemble which includes everyone who can help implement the leader's vision or who may be able to impede it. Members of the organization, suppliers, customers, and regulatory bodies are a few of the cast members who might need to be aligned if change is to occur successfully. It includes communicating the vision clearly as well as getting individuals to accept the vision. The trust and integrity of the leader are paramount here, as is the perception that a leader's actions reflect his words. This helps to empower people in the organization as they can use their initiative to take decisions that reflect the communicated vision without fear of reprisals.

In addition to planning and budgeting, and organizing systems, management is also involved in *controlling and problem-solving*. The purpose of control mechanisms is to ensure that people's behaviour conforms to the needs of the plan and that any variance can be quickly identified and correctly. This means that management is about pushing people in a given direction. As Kotter (1990, p. 107) states:

the whole purpose of systems and structures is to help normal people who
behave in normal ways to complete routine jobs successfully, day after day.
It's not exciting or glamorous. But that's management.

In contrast, leadership is about change, and change requires an adjustment in people's behaviour. Unlike the control mechanisms of management, leadership motivates by satisfying our human needs for achievement, recognition, and a sense of belonging. An effective leader will ensure that the organization's vision is in line with its employees' own value system. As such, employees will derive intrinsic satisfaction from working towards its achievement. This satisfaction is likely to increase where individuals are also actively involved in discussions of how the vision can be achieved and are rewarded for their efforts. Table 11.1 provides a summary of leadership and management activities.

Leadership activities	Management activities
Dealing with change	Coping with organizational complexity
Developing a vision and setting a direction for the organization	Planning and budgeting
Formulating strategy	Implementing strategy
Aligning stakeholders with the organization's vision	Organizing and staffing to achieve strategy
Motivating and inspiring employees	Controlling behaviour and problem-solving to ensure strategy is implemented
Recognizing and rewarding success	

TABLE 11.1
Leadership and
management activities

Whereas management involves dealing with organizational complexity, leadership involves dealing with change. Such change includes the deregulation of markets, faster technological change, and shifting social trends. The role of leadership is to create a shared vision of where the organization is trying to get to, and to formulate strategies to bring about the changes needed to achieve the vision. Effective leaders encourage leadership throughout the organization by empowering participants to make decisions without fear of reprisals. This dissemination of leadership allows organizations to deal effectively with increasing change in their competitive environments. A challenge is to blend the distinct actions of leadership and management so that they complement each other within the organization.

There is general agreement that management and leadership involve different functions. For example, Cyert (1990) states that most people in leadership positions would be better characterized as managers rather than leaders. He argues that leaders perform three broad functions: (1) an *organizational function*, (2) an *interpersonal*

11

function, and (3) a *decision function*. The organizational function involves the leader in trying to get participants in the organization to behave in a way that he or she feels is desirable. A leader can do this by influencing the process for setting goals in an organization. This is because what will be desirable for a leader will be the achievement of agreed goals which in turn will derive from the leader's vision. According to Cyert, the leader's role is to steer the organization by setting a vision and being actively involved in the goal structure. The interpersonal function involves the leader in ensuring that the morale of participants is maintained. This is more of an empathetic role which requires the leader to be aware of the concerns of members of the organization. The third function—the decision function—involves the leader taking decisions to allow the organization to achieve its goals.

However, we should not forget that organizations are collections of individuals. Regardless of the strategies that are put forward to achieve a vision, it is these individuals who will ultimately determine whether the strategy succeeds or fails. The question then arises as to how leaders ensure that participants in an organization behave in a way that they would like. For Cyert, leaders accomplish this by controlling the *allocation of attention* of members of an organization. The attention of individuals in an organization will be drawn to many different things. The leader's role will be to focus their attention on the achievement of the vision. Organizations operate in dynamic environments. Therefore, if a vision is modified, the leader must ensure that participants' attention, and therefore their behaviour, is also changed to reflect these changing issues. In the same way a leader must ensure that all participants buy into a single goal structure such that any goal conflicts between different parts of the organization are quickly resolved. This ensures that everyone in the organization is working towards the same outcome.

All leaders seek to improve the performance of their organization. A solution is often thought to be a change in the organizational structure. However, as we have seen, the key point to bear in mind is whether this change in structure will have an impact on the attention focus of participants. Any change in organizational structure should only be undertaken with a view to its impact on the attention focus of participants. As Cyert states, 'attention focus is central to the organizational function of leadership'. Similarly, if we look at the interpersonal function, the style adopted by a leader in his interaction with members of the organization is also important. However, the issue is not one of whether the leader's style is open or friendly *per se*, but rather whether the style allows members to focus their attention on issues that the leader feels are important. The same is true for the third function of leadership, the decision function. A leader takes decisions with a view to making the priorities for participants' attention clear. In this way leadership decisions guide and modify individuals' behaviour by focusing on the areas where they want individuals to apply their attention. This presupposes that the leader possesses sufficient organization or industry-specific knowledge to allow him or her to identify and translate changes in their competitive environment into the correct attention focus for participants of the organization.

11.2 The Learning Organization

It is said that the only sustainable competitive advantage is the speed and ability of an organization to learn. In the past there were great leaders who 'thought' and 'learned' for the organization. These included Thomas J. Watson of IBM, Alfred Sloan of General Motors, and the eponymous Henry Ford and Walt Disney. The role of everyone else within the organization was assumed to be to carry out the leader's vision and earn their approval. The traditional hierarchical structures that ensure the command and control of individuals are no longer conducive to competing in more dynamic environments or for generating organizational learning. The shift is away from the leader as panacea and towards a solution that requires all levels of the organization to participate actively. Senge (1990a, p. 7; 1990b) argues that 'the old model, the top thinks and the local acts, must now give way to integrating thinking and acting at all levels'. Senge sees the learning organization as comprising both adaptive and generative learning. Adaptive learning is the ability to cope with changes in one's environment, while generative learning is about creating change by being prepared to question the way we look at the world.

A transition from adaptive learning to generative learning can be seen in the total quality movement (TQM) in Japan. Initially the focus was on making consumer products that were fit for purpose. That is, the product would perform according to its specification. This evolved into understanding and reliably meeting customer needs. Now the focus has shifted to creating what customers want but may not have yet realized. This requires organizations to be prepared to view the competitive environment differently. A major reason for the success of Japanese automobile companies such as Toyota and Honda is their ability to view issues in manufacture in a systemic way. They adopt a way of thinking that does not focus on one aspect of manufacture as *the problem* but see any problem as part of an integrated system. As such they avoid being stuck in a cycle of adaptive learning.

11.2.1 Building the Learning Organization

The leadership role in a learning organization is one of *designer*, *teacher*, and *steward*. These new roles require the leader to develop a shared vision of where the organization wants to be—to make explicit and challenge the assumptions on which decisions are made. In other words, to challenge the mental models of how we view the world and to encourage a more systemic pattern of thinking. For Senge, the leader's role is to help bring about learning in the organization. This requires the leader to develop a vision of where the organization wants to be and to juxtapose this with the current reality of where the organization actually is. The difference between the two positions generates what Senge calls a 'creative tension'. It is the leader's role to make explicit a vision of the organization which galvanizes people to want to create change. This is different from problem-solving which seeks to get away from an undesirable current position. Creative tension uses the difference between current reality and the vision to generate change, but it is not the undesirability of the current situation itself that generates the creative tension. The disadvantage with an approach based on problem-solving is that as soon as the problem is resolved or reduced, the momentum for change decelerates. With creative change, as we saw with visionary companies in **Chapter 10**, the motivation for change is intrinsic not extrinsic.

11.2.2 Leadership Roles

We can address the three distinct leadership roles that Senge identifies. These are *the leader as designer*, *the leader as teacher*, and *the leader as steward*.

The Leader as Designer

The leader's role as designer can be seen in the building of the core values and purpose of the organization. This is the quiet behind the scenes work of leadership which will have an enduring impact into the future. This includes the credo of Johnson & Johnson that guided the behaviour of people in the company during the tampering with Tylenol in 1982 and 1989. It includes the decision of Merck to give away a drug to cure river blindness, which was guided by their core values and purpose. The other aspects of the leader as designer include developing the strategies and structures that help to convert organizational values and purposes into business decisions.

The Leader as Teacher

The leader as teacher involves helping individuals in the organization to be aware of their mental models and the assumptions on which these are based. This allows people to continually challenge their view of reality such that they can see beyond merely superficial issues and discern the underlying causes of problems. Leaders in learning organizations influence individuals' perceptions of reality at three levels: *events*, *patterns of behaviour*, and *systemic structure*. As we saw with Cyert's work on leadership, if we want to engender change it is important to focus attention on what really matters. Events are primarily short term and often dramatic, for example an increase in interest rates as a result of a rise in inflation. Patterns of behaviour see current events in the light of historical changes which may have an impact in bringing them about, such as extrapolation or trend analysis. It is only systemic structural explanations that deal with the underlying causes of behaviour. Therefore, the leader's focus is predominately on systemic change. The example the leader sets will be more likely to be replicated in the focused attention of organizational members. Therefore, it is crucial that a leader's behaviour matches his rhetoric.

The Leader as Steward

The concerns of the leader as steward involve stewardship for all the people in the organization that he directs. It also involves stewardship for the purpose and core values on which the organization is based. A leader in a learning organization actively seeks to change how the competitive environment works to create a more successful organization with more satisfied workers than would be achieved in a traditional organization. Along with these three leadership roles comes the development of new leadership skills.

11.2.3 Leadership Skills

These leadership skills need to be disseminated throughout the entire organization; they are not the preserve of a few key individuals. They are *building a shared vision*, *surfacing and testing mental models*, and *systems thinking*.

Building a Shared Vision

Creating a shared vision is an ongoing process which involves the leader sharing his vision with members of the organization to ensure that it accords with their own personal values. In this way the shared vision is more likely to be accepted by everyone. Strong leaders can create a vision which allows themselves and others in the organization to see clearly the steps to take, building on their present capabilities to get there (Kanter 1983). It is recognizing that developing a vision is a continuous process.

Surfacing and Testing Mental Models

If the leader is to attract new and innovative ideas, another leadership skill which needs to be disseminated throughout the organization is surfacing and testing mental models. The leader needs to ensure that members of an organization can differentiate between generalizations and the observable facts on which they are based. In challenging our mental models we need to be aware of when we are generalizing and when what we say is actually based on fact.

Systems Thinking

To engage in systems thinking leaders need to move beyond a blame culture. They need to discern the interrelationships between actions. They should recognize that small well-focused actions can have magnified results, if they occur in the right places (Brynjolfsson *et al*. 1997). A visionary leader who deals only in *events* or *patterns of behaviour* will disseminate a reactive or responsive culture rather than a generative one.

11

11.3 Emotional Intelligence and Leadership Performance

A great deal of research has been undertaken to ascertain if there are certain attributes or capabilities that can distinguish effective leaders. Some of the most interesting research is by Goleman (1998) into large global companies to determine the personal capabilities that drive outstanding performance. Goleman grouped capabilities into three categories: (1) purely technical skills, such as accounting and business planning, (2) cognitive abilities, such as analytical reasoning, and (3) emotional intelligence, which manifests itself in an ability to work with others. His findings suggest that an organization's success is linked to the emotional intelligence of its leaders. Emotional intelligence proved to be not only the key ingredient for outstanding leaders; it was also linked to better performance in organizations.

Traditional attributes of leaders have usually included such factors as technical skills and IQ. Goleman does not dismiss these attributes but argues that they can be seen as threshold capabilities or entry-level requirements for executive positions. They may be necessary for senior positions but they are not a sufficient criteria for effective performance in leaders. As Goleman (1998, p. 94) states: 'When I calculated the ratio of technical skills, IQ, and emotional intelligence as ingredients of excellent performance, emotional intelligence proved to be twice as important as the others for jobs at all levels.'

This shows that great leaders require more than an analytical mind or a stream of good ideas, they need emotional intelligence. The components of emotional intelligence are *self-awareness*, *self-regulation*, *motivation*, *empathy*, and *social skills*. We can assess each of these components of emotional intelligence in more detail.

11.3.1 Self-awareness

Self-awareness is the first component of emotional intelligence. Individuals who possess a degree of self-awareness are capable of speaking candidly about their own emotions and the impact of their emotions on their work. Self-aware people can also be recognized by their self-confidence. According to Goleman, they play to their strengths, are aware of their limitations, and are not afraid to ask for help if it is needed. It is this emotional capability of self-awareness that also allows these leaders to honestly assess the organization they work for.

11.3.2 Self-regulation

Self-regulation is a recognition that as human beings we are driven by our emotions, but we can also manage them and channel them for productive purposes. Leaders who are in control of their feelings and emotions can create an environment

EMOTIONAL INTELLIGENCE

an ability to recognize your own emotions and the emotions of others. Emotional intelligence is manifest in self-awareness, self-regulation, motivation, empathy, and social skills

SELF-AWARENESS

an ability to speak candidly about one's own emotions and the impact they have on one's work as well as their effect on others

SELF-REGULATION

recognition that as human beings we are driven by our emotions but we can also manage them and channel them for productive purposes characterized by trust and fairness. Self-regulation is helpful in dealing with change in the competitive environment as such individuals can consciously listen to new ideas and approaches rather than immediately reacting to what is being said. They are comfortable with change and ambiguity, and are not easily panicked by a change in the competitive landscape. Goleman goes further and argues that self-regulation enhances integrity. That is, abuse of corporate power may have a tendency to occur where individuals have low impulse control. We should perhaps be a little of wary of the argument that self-regulation enhances integrity because in some instances the self-regulation of one's emotions may derive more from a fear of the consequences or being 'found out' than integrity.

11.3.3 Motivation

A trait found in almost all effective leaders is motivation—a desire to achieve for the sake of achievement. People who are motivated will be passionate about their work and actively seek ways to improve what they are doing. They constantly seek to measure their individual performance and that of their organization. They are committed to their organization and will not be readily swayed to move for mere financial gain. In seeking to stretch themselves, such individuals will also be looking to improve their organization.

> MOTIVATION
>
> is a desire to achieve for the sake of achievement

11.3.4 Empathy

Empathy implies that leaders will consciously consider employees' feelings as well as other factors when they are making decisions. For example, when leading a team a leader must be capable of sensing and understanding the different points of view that each individual in the team holds. In a globalized economy the need for empathy is required to interpret accurately what people from different regions and cultures may be saying. For example, being empathetic allows a leader to read accurately the body language of an individual as well as listening to their spoken words. Empathy is also important for leaders in the knowledge economy who wish to retain people with important tacit knowledge.

> EMPATHY
>
> a willingness to consider the feelings of others when discussing and making decisions

11.3.5 Social skills

Whereas self-awareness, self-regulation, and motivation are emotional capabilities that we self-manage, empathy and social skills concern our abilities for managing relationships with others. Social skills involve moving people in a desired direction. Cyert (1990) refers to this as an organizational function of leadership—getting participants in the organization to behave in a way that the leader feels is desirable.

> SOCIAL SKILLS
>
> are the culmination of self-awareness, self-regulation, motivation, and empathy (emotional intelligence capabilities)

11

Social skills are the culmination of the other emotional intelligence capabilities. That is, people will be socially skilled when they have honesty in evaluating their abilities, have mastered their own emotions, are motivated, and can empathize with others. Therefore, social skills will manifest themselves through the working out of any of the previous four capabilities. It is social skills that enable leaders to put their emotional intelligence to work.

Thus, the question arises: Can emotional intelligence be learned? Goleman believes that it can, and furthermore that one's emotional intelligence increases with age. That said, emotional intelligence is not automatic. It requires clearly directed effort and resources if individuals are to learn to enhance their emotional intelligence. The pay-off is more effective leaders throughout the organization and improved company performance.

11.4 Narcissistic Leaders and Leadership Capabilities

We have seen that leaders who possess emotional intelligence are more effective and capable of managing change in organizations. In contrast with these leaders, Maccoby (2000) identifies a different type of leader who is equally effective in dealing with dynamic change but also has the potential for creating destruction. Today's leaders who are transforming industries are different from their predecessors, and Maccoby attributes this to a change in their personality. Today's leaders, he argues, exhibit a personality type which Freud termed *narcissistic*. Freud identified three main personality types: *erotic*, *obsessive*, and *narcissistic*. Erotic personality types should not be confused with a sexual personality, but rather one for whom loving and being loved are important. Typically these are teachers, nurses, and social workers. Obsessive personalities are self-reliant and conscientious. They are always looking for ways to help people listen better and find win–win situations. Narcissists are independent, aggressive, and innovative; they want to be admired.

Narcissistic leaders have always existed in the past and tend to emerge in times of political and social upheaval. As business began to dominate the social agenda, so narcissistic leaders such as Henry Ford and John D. Rockefeller emerged. The problem is that the very leaders who may be required for certain epochs can become obsessed with their own grandiose ideas, emotionally isolated, and distrustful of alternative viewpoints. In many respects a narcissistic leader represents the antithesis of a leader who possesses emotional intelligence. Thus, the key is to differentiate between productive and unproductive narcissism. Productive narcissistic leaders, such as Jack Welch of GE, are risk-takers who are capable of seeing the big picture. They possess vision and an ability to communicate this vision through oratory. They have a desire to leave a legacy behind. They are able to attract followers through their skilled oratory and charisma, and generate enthusiasm throughout their organization, which helps galvanize change. However, narcissistic leaders need adulation and the affirmation provided by their followers. And herein lies a danger—the very adulation that a narcissist demands brings self-assurance but also allows him to ignore those who disagree with his views. Narcissistic leaders can become destructive when they lack self-knowledge and restraint, and pursue unrealistic and grandiose dreams.

The weaknesses of a narcissistic leader can be seen as they become more successful. They are over-sensitive to criticism and become increasingly poor listeners. They cannot handle dissent and will tend to be hard on employees who question their views. They do not want to change, and their success simply reinforces the need not to. For example, Jan Carlzon, the former CEO of the Scandinavian airline SAS, originally turned around the airline's fortunes and garnered for himself much public adulation. In the 1990s he continued to expand the business with expensive acquisitions while paying too little attention to spiralling costs. As the organization expanded and losses increased, this brilliant narcissist was eventually fired.

CASE STUDY 11.1

Leadership at Microsoft

Reprinted with permission from the Microsoft Corporation.

Leaders of Microsoft: (right) Steve Ballmer, CEO, and (left) Bill Gates, Chairman: 'The relationship between us is about as complicated as it is between most husbands and wives.'

Steve Ballmer is a very big man. And the chief executive of Microsoft, who is now Bill Gates's boss, no less, is having quite a big day, even by his own standards. We meet in Microsoft City, just outside Seattle, where Microsoft is formally announcing a range of products aimed at small and medium-sized companies, complete with the 12th version of its ubiquitous Office software.

Analysts, hacks, and customers have gathered to see the gods of the geek world do their stuff. The dress code is 'business casual': chinos, not jeans; open-neck shirts, not T-shirts. The atmosphere is ruthlessly conformist. Sheepish smokers

11

huddle outside. Inside, coffee, muffins, cheese snacks, and salty nut mixes are in limitless supply as the conference hall monitors flick into life.

Our appointment is scheduled for early afternoon, after a morning's hard networking. The crisp late-summer sun makes the buildings seem like cut-outs against a huge blue sky. This is the kind of gorgeously bleak cityscape that would have appealed to the painter Edward Hopper.

But that famous sense of isolation and meaninglessness doesn't come from figures trapped in their environment. That ambience has been created by the dehumanizing language of the conference sessions. Gates, a grown man visibly upset that people in offices still use Post-It Notes, intones: 'The word "dynamics" speaks to some very specific architectural capabilities'—this seems to be a claim that new software works quite well.

Ballmer is also a geek. But Ballmer is a sales-orientated geek—or part red-blooded, broad-shouldered, all-American sales director. In public and private, Ballmer has mastered the art of amiable shouting. The volume is always set to maximum, and the message delivered by the deep-set blue eyes is intense. He is a leader of geeks, and has a somewhat military air—which is fitting for a business that has a history of wiping its competitors from the face of the earth.

The issue of its competitive tactics is a hot one because only a week ago Ballmer was the subject of some embarrassing publicity that speaks of the depth of rivalry between Microsoft and Google, the Internet search engine giant. According to a sworn statement, Ballmer picked up a chair and threw it across the room when a former Microsoft engineer met him in November to discuss his intention to defect to Google. So did he really throw a chair? He's clearly powerful enough. Ballmer insists: 'I've never thrown a chair in my life.' So what about the colourful language?

Suddenly the body language is that of a chastened schoolboy. In the morning session, Ballmer was making points about Microsoft's persistence and tenacity at maximum decibels ('If we didn't get it right we'd keep working it and working it and working it') while punching the air. That animation has gone now: 'Did I want to keep that fellow at the company? Yes. Did I say I wanted to compete with Google? I don't know what words . . . Did he write down the exact words? I don't know. By and large I made a commitment nine years ago that I was not going to curse. I know I've had one or two transgressions in nine years, but I made that commitment to myself. Is that one of them? I don't recall.' It's hardly a denial. But you get the sense that Ballmer is more upset about this than anyone else.

He inspires immense loyalty from his team and he effervesces energy. But there is the occasional concern raised among the army of analysts who follow Microsoft that all that charisma and dashing leadership would benefit from some checks and balances. As Ballmer himself says: 'In jobs like this you get very little feedback from anybody else. People might tell you whether things are good or bad, but really, how are you doing in aggregate? I get a little help from my board of directors once a year. It's mostly me.'

So perhaps a little pressure from the media and the markets isn't such a bad thing. But what about Bill Gates? Isn't he the founder, the daddy of all in the 60,000-strong family of Microsoft, and therefore mentor-in-chief?

Well, yes, and no. The relationship is an interesting and obviously complex one. There's a hint of defensiveness when this even more famous name is dropped into the conversation. And there's also a flurry of apparently contradictory assertions: '[Gates is] chief software officer. The relationship between us is about as complicated as it is between most husbands and wives. I'm his boss. He's my boss. We're friends. He used to be my boss and I was not his boss. We changed that five years ago—because he wanted to, which was an odd thing in itself.'

'I get gratification in our friendship, I get gratification in our partnership. It's always gratifying to hear "good job" from Bill.' But clearly he sees himself as the natural leader of the pack: 'I think my range as a leader has changed a lot. Ask anybody round here 10 years ago they'd have said I was a leader by decree and energy. Decree on its own sounds authoritarian. But I'd be—"whoo, whoo, let's go, let's go, let's go"—direction, and a lot of energy.'

The grammar may not be perfect, but there's a classic pant-hoot from an alpha primate at the end of that passage that leaves you in no doubt as to how he used to get things done. Now, as the organization has grown, Ballmer has a more measured style: 'I'm not less energetic than I used to be, but I spend a whole lot more time to some degree building consensus and to some degree supporting the people who work for me with my energy.'

As one of the original three top men at Microsoft (he joined in 1980 from Procter & Gamble, having met Gates at Harvard—there were 30 in the company then) you have to admire Ballmer's drive. He is worth more than $12bn (£6.5bn), and claims that he doesn't mind the inevitable criticisms of Windows, which attracts attacks from all sides, including consumers and hackers. 'I think it's cool that people expect that much of us. That's what [drives] us to be at the top level. I feel energized and challenged by that.' Fierce, driven, proud, he still does it for the love of the game—even if it can all sound a bit corny: 'At Microsoft we have [engaged] and will continue to genuinely engage in making the world a better place. We can change the world; our products change the world; our industry changes the world.'

Source: 'I've never thrown a chair in my life' *Sunday Telegraph*, 11 September 2005.

■ Questions

1. Why has CEO Steve Ballmer's style of leadership changed as Microsoft has grown in size and complexity?

2. Identify which of the leadership roles identified by Senge you believe Steve Ballmer possesses.

3. Evaluate the extent to which Steve Ballmer possesses emotional intelligence and a narcissistic personality.

For a discussion of narcissistic leaders and their importance to organizations go to the Online Resource Centre and see the Key Work feature.
www.oxfordtextbooks.co.uk/orc/henry2e/

A narcissistic leader can avoid potentially self-destructive behaviour by forming a close partnership with someone he trusts. Bill Gates is able to engage in blue-sky thinking because he has Steve Ballmer as chief executive, who ensures everything works as it should (see Case Study: Leadership at Microsoft, which provides insights into the leadership style of Steve Ballmer, chief executive of Microsoft). Another approach is to indoctrinate the organization with your views. Jack Welch did this when he articulated his views that GE become number one or two in its markets or exit them. Those who disagreed with Welch's approach and the culture it engendered did not last long in GE. The dilemma is that a dynamic environment characterized by discontinuities needs narcissistic leaders—people like Steve Jobs who possess intellect, phenomenal vision, flair, and innovation, and who can *create* the future. The challenge is to get such luminaries to listen to, respect, and internalize the ideas that other members of the organization can contribute.

11.4.1 Leadership Capabilities

We have seen that effective leadership is associated with emotional intelligence and a narcissistic personality, particularly in turbulent times. We might expect leaders who exhibit these qualities, especially emotional intelligence, to be equally effective in different industry environments. Groysberg *et al.* (2006) studied twenty former GE executives who became chairman, CEO, or CEO designate at different companies between 1989 and 2001. Their choice of GE reflects its wide recognition as the premiere training ground for top executives. Groysberg and colleagues wanted to see if the skills these leaders possess are portable, that is, does the fact that such leaders performed well at GE mean that they can also perform as well at another organization? We might also infer that as these executives were successful leaders at GE, they possessed a fair degree of emotional intelligence.

A massive seventeen of the twenty appointments all saw an increase in the market capitalization of the companies they were moving to. This represents a belief by the stock market that such individuals possess skills that can easily transfer to different settings. For instance, in 2000 when James McNerney and Robert Nardelli were passed over to replace Jack Welch, they moved to 3M and Home Depot, respectively. The value of 3M increased to more than $6.5 billion and Home Depot to almost $10 billion. However, it is not perception but leadership skills that deliver results. Groysberg and colleagues found that what is important is *context*, or the fit between the executives' strategic skills and the needs and the strategy of the organization. A given executive will possess general management skills such as the ability to develop a vision, motivate employees, and monitor performance. These skills are readily transferable to new environments. Other management skills, such as know-ledge of a particular company's processes and management systems, do not transfer as well. Therefore, the reaction of the stock market is simply a signal that it believes these GE executives have transferable general management skills.

Groysberg *et al.*'s research found that company-specific skills may also be valuable in a new job. Furthermore, they found that other skills and experience which shape performance in one job can have an impact when transferred to a new job. These skills include *strategic human capital*, which manifests itself in an individual's exper-tise in cost-cutting and pursuing growth; *industry human capital*, such as technical or regulatory knowledge of a specific industry; and *relationship human capital*, which involves an executive's effectiveness as a result of the relationships he or she develops from working as part of a team. The outcome of their research is that human capital can be thought of as part of a portfolio of skills. At one end of the portfolio are skills likely to be portable, while at the other end are skills which are less portable. Thus, at one extreme we find *general management human capital*, which is highly portable. At the other extreme is *company-specific human capital*, which is rarely portable. In between these two fall the three skills mentioned above, that is, *strategic human capital*, *industry human capital*, and *relationship human capital*, with strategic human capital being the most portable and relationship human capital the least portable of the three.

This research tells us that the companies that hired these twenty GE executives performed well relative to the stock market *depending* on whether there existed a good fit between the executives' human capital and the needs of the companies they went to. If not, they performed poorly against the market. Therefore, the more closely the match between an executive's new and old environment, the more likely it is that they will succeed in their new role. When executives enter a new industry, their existing industry human capital will not transfer to the new industry. Their company-specific skills will also not be relevant to a new job and will need to be unlearned. What this research means for companies thinking of hiring such high-profile star executives is that where they come from should not be the deciding factor in hiring them. The deciding factor should be an understanding of the portfolio of human capital that each CEO candidate possesses and whether their skills will transfer and meet the needs of the organization's strategy and new situation. This is particularly important when we remember that such high-profile executives come at a premium.

11.5 The Impact of Leadership on Vision, Values, and Culture

In addition to the capabilities and personality traits that make for an effective leader, we need to address the role of leaders in relation to an organization's shared vision, its values, and its culture. We will also assess the effect of national cultures on the beliefs and behaviour of individuals within organizations. An understanding of national cultures and their impact on behaviour is particularly important for leaders of multinational corporations.

11.5.1 Leadership, Vision, and Values

The characteristics of visionary organizations were covered in detail in **Chapter 10**, Section 10.4.2. We discussed the research of Collins and Porras (1994) which suggests that visionary organizations are particularly adept at simultaneously managing continuity and embracing change. Visionary companies have a *core ideology* which comprises their *core values* and *purpose*. The core values can be thought of as the principles on which the firm was founded. An organization's purpose is the reason why it exists; this transcends merely making money. The core values of an organization do not change. Visionary organizations pursue their purpose knowing that this is a continuous process and will never be fully achieved. Core values and purpose are important for visionary organizations because they help to guide continuity and provide a stimulus for change.

In looking at how executives spend their time, Peters (1979) noted that although their time and attention are fragmented this can work to their advantage. For example, when assessing work, top executives tend to be given a single option to review rather than competing options. Their decision on this single option does not say anything about the proposal's optimality but rather sends a clear signal back to organizational members as to whether the organization is moving in the desired direction or not. Their input is a check on the vision of the organization. It also signals to middle managers, for example, what the next proposal should look like. If senior executives had more time, they would not be inclined to fine-tune proposals but would be engaged in a more fundamental overhaul. The downside to this fragmentation of time is that the constant flow of information multiplies the opportunity for inconsistent signals to the organization.

Peters's approach portrays top executives as coping with the reality of disorder and non-linear events (this resonates with Mintzberg's (1987) approach to strategic management in which leaders craft strategy rather than deliberately planning it). Amidst this relative chaos what leaders can do is shape their organization's values and lead by example. In this untidy world 'the effective leader...is primarily an expert in the promotion and protection of values', and dealing with 'the shaping of... values...becomes pre-eminently the mission of the chief executive' (Peters 1979, p. 170). The leader's role is to build consensus throughout the organization. Their actions, over time, are part of a 'guiding, directing and signalling process that are necessary to shape values in the near chaos of day-to-day operations' (Peters 1979, p. 171). How a leader behaves is crucial for sending the right signals to the rest of the organization.

11.5.2 Leadership and Culture

Hofstede (1997) studied the culturally determined values of people in over fifty countries. They all worked in the local subsidiaries of a large multinational corporation (IBM). The benefit of looking at people who work for a multinational corporation is that they are similar in all respects except their nationality. Hofstede was initially able to devise a model of culture based on four separate dimensions. A dimension is simply an aspect of culture which can be measured in relation to other cultures. The four dimensions are *power distance*, *collectivism versus individualism*, *femininity versus masculinity*, and *uncertainty avoidance*. The model is a way of measuring differences between national cultures. A country will attain a score on each of the dimensions according to its nearness to each dimension. Over time a fifth dimension was identified: the extent to which society has a *long-term orientation* to life in contrast to a *short-term orientation*. Interestingly, Hofstede attributes the fact that this dimension was not identified before to the bias that exist in the minds of researchers studying culture. That is, even researchers studying culture have their own mental models determined by *their* national cultural frames of reference.

Courtesy of International Business Machines Corporation.

IBM Chairman, President, and CEO Samuel J. Palmisano and India President A.P.J. Abdul Kalam at a ceremonial Indian lamp lighting ceremony. An understanding of national cultures is clearly important for leaders who manage multinational organizations.

11

Although the use of a dimension is not without its methodological limitations, it does have the benefit of allowing clusters of countries with similar scores to emerge. We might also note that research into national cultures and their dimensions provides only part of the picture of our understanding of corporate culture. We can evaluate each of the five dimensions to determine, to some extent, their impact on organizational behaviour.

Power Distance Index (PDI)

Power distance is defined as the extent to which the less powerful members of institutions and organizations within a country expect and accept that power is distributed unequally (Hofstede 1997, p. 28). What it shows us is the extent to which employees in IBM's subsidiary in one country answer the same questions differently from IBM employees in another country. Or, put another way, it helps to explain the impact of national cultures on leadership styles. The study showed a high power distance for Latin American countries such as Mexico and Guatemala, and for India, France, and Hong Kong. Lower power distances exist in the UK, the US, and Scandinavian countries such as Finland, Norway, and Sweden. This informs us about dependence relationships in a country. What it tells us is that, other things being equal, employees in high power distance countries have a preference for leadership that involves an autocratic style. There is likely to be much more dependence of subordinate employees on their leaders. In contrast, employees in low power distance countries prefer leadership that involves consultation and much less dependence on their leaders. This helps to explain why certain Western leadership styles which bring success in the UK or US flounder when used in Mexico, for example.

Individualism versus Collectivism

Individualism refers to societies in which there are fewer ties between individuals and where everyone is expected to look after themselves and their own immediate family. At the other end of the spectrum is collectivism; these are societies where people are integrated into strong cohesive groups, and the interests of the individual are sub-ordinate to those of the group.

The extent to which countries scored as individualistic or collectivist was based on respondents' answer to questions about what they would consider as their ideal job. Individualistic employees believe that a job which leaves quality personal time for family is important. In contrast, collectivist individuals saw training opportunities to improve learning as more important. The USA, Australia, and the UK scored top on this index as the most individualistic nations, and Guatemala, Ecuador, and Panama were the most collectivist. Individualism, such as the pursuit of personal time, emphasizes the individual's freedom from the organization. Training and development, in contrast, is something the organization does for the employees. The extent of a nation's individualism versus collectivism may also go some way to explaining why Japanese leadership practices seem to experience difficulties when transported verbatim to the US.

Western organizations competing abroad would do well to remember that in collectivist societies, such as Saudi Arabia, the personal relationship between individuals takes precedence over any task and needs to be established first. This takes time and patience.

Masculinity and Femininity

This concerns *the desirability of assertive behaviour against the desirability of modest behaviour*; Hofstede refers to the former as masculinity, and to the latter as femininity. Masculinity refers to societies in which gender roles are clearly defined: men are expected to be assertive and tough. Femininity refers to societies in which gender roles are less clearly defined: both men and women are expected to be modest and caring. This was the only dimension in which male and female IBM employees scored consistently differently. It shows that, among other things, men attach greater importance to earnings and job recognition, whereas women attach more importance to good working relationships with their immediate supervisor and their colleagues. The former is associated with masculine competitive roles, and the latter with more caring feminine roles. Japan, Austria, and Venezuela scored highest as the most masculine countries, with clearly defined roles for men and women, while Sweden, Norway, and the Netherlands scored highest as the most feminine countries. Therefore, we can deduce that Japan's masculine culture and work practices, which invariably translate into few, if any, female management positions, would be difficult to implement in Scandinavian countries.

Uncertainty Avoidance

Uncertainty avoidance is the extent to which people feel threatened by uncertain or unknown situations. This manifests itself in the need for predictability, and clearly defined rules. Countries which experience high uncertainty avoidance are seeking to reduce ambiguity. People from these countries are looking for structure and stability. Greece, Portugal, and Guatemala scored highest on this index with Belgium and Japan not far behind. Denmark, Singapore, and Jamaica scored lowest on uncertainty avoidance, closely followed by the UK and the US. We should be careful not to confuse uncertainty avoidance with risk avoidance. A country which experiences high uncertainty avoidance is still able to take risks.

Long-Term Orientation

This fifth dimension, as noted, did not originate with Hofstede but from subsequent research. We can 'map' a long-term orientation for different countries. China, Hong Kong, Taiwan, and South Korea scored highest in having a long-term orientation, while Pakistan, Nigeria, and the Philippines scored lowest, followed by Canada, the UK, and the US; nations with a long-term orientation value thrift (careful with resources), persistence, and hard work. In contrast, nations with a short-term orientation tend to be less persistent and expect quick results. An understanding of national cultures is clearly important for leaders who manage multinational organizations. The benefits of an appreciation of national cultures, for instance by leaders involved in international mergers and take-overs, should not be underestimated. An understanding of culture and its effect on employees' behaviour will, amongst other things, help leaders to develop appropriate reward and control systems. An appreciation of cultures can also help in implementing strategic change and avoid wasting resources through avoidable cultural errors.

This said, the needs of the competitive environment may force counter-cultural changes. For example, the Japanese investment bank Nomura bought the collapsed Lehman Brothers' European, Middle Eastern, and Asian businesses in order to expand internationally. The former Lehman traders working for Nomura in Japan now face Nomura executives who are much more hands on than the executives in their former firm. More importantly, Nomura expects that by hiring former Lehman employees this may help facilitate a change in the corporate culture in its Japanese operation. For instance, Nomura now offers employees in Japan the prospect of higher pay and bonuses in return for accepting that they can be fired more easily if they fail to meet performance targets. This change links remuneration to personal and departmental performance, largely anathema to Japanese employees, rather than organizational performance which has always been the norm.

For more information on the impact of culture on organizations go to the Online Resource Centre and see the Key Work feature.
www.oxfordtextbooks.co.uk/orc/henry2e/

11.6 Leading Strategic Change

In **Chapter 10** we looked in detail at how organizations can undertake strategic change. Here we will address the specific role of business leaders in directing strategic change. We will assess the links between the acceptance of ideas for change and an organization's existing culture. We will also look at some of the leadership skills necessary to implement change effectively and the barriers that need to be overcome.

The values of an organization will inevitably manifest themselves in its core or dominant culture. The culture may have existed for generations and will take time to change in a desired direction. Therefore, an organization's culture is a powerful instrument for exhibiting or inhibiting change. Even good ideas that conflict with the existing culture may be difficult to implement. Schneider (2000) argues that good ideas will fail unless they are aligned with the organization's business strategy, leadership, and dominant culture. Indeed, for an organization to be effective alignment must occur between its strategy, culture, and leadership. Schneider suggests four reasons why good management ideas may not be adopted within the organization.

1. **All organizations are living social organisms.** All organizations have their own idiosyncratic culture. They are communities of people and not machines, although they may have some machine-like characteristics. All living systems grow and develop from the inside out. They start from their core and develop outwards. We can draw a parallel between biological systems and organizations. In the same way, people, organizations, and societies exist in relation to each other. They have their unique patterns, which are non-linear, but their development occurs from the core to the periphery. The point is that for any ideas to work they must be based on the non-linear nature of the organization.

2. **Culture is more powerful than anything else in the organization.** An organization can have a brilliant strategy, but if it does not align with the organization's culture it will inevitably fail. To succeed any change must align with one of four different types of culture. These are *control*, *collaboration*, *competence*, and *cultivation*. Therefore, regardless of the validity of any given idea, it must also fit with the particular type of culture prevalent in an organization if it is to succeed.

3. **System-focused interventions work while component-focused interventions do not.** We have seen in the previous chapter that a systems approach that emphasizes alignment between different parts of the organization is more likely to succeed in implementing change. This is simply a recognition that *one size fits all* does not apply.

4. **Interventions that are clearly linked to an organization's business strategy work.** It is strategy that adds value to an organization. Therefore, all management ideas have to be clearly aligned with the organization's strategy otherwise there is a danger of pushing the organization off course. Here, as we have reiterated before, it is the alignment of new ideas with an organization's value-creating strategy that is important in trying to instigate change.

The paradox of strategic change is that all organizations compete in changing environments, but the individuals who make up these organizations are resistant to change. Organizations face pressures for change from competitors, suppliers, and customers, as well as internally from poor leadership, high labour turnover, and other such factors. These factors will eventually begin to coalesce into an urgency to do something. However, it is often as the need for change becomes increasingly apparent that employees' resistance to change becomes greatest. If the nature of individuals is to avoid change, then the first challenge for leaders is to manage employee resistance. According to Manfred Kets de Vries (1998) this requires an effective change agent, ideally the CEO, who has power and authority to drive change initiatives.

11

The change agent will be a visionary who combines charismatic qualities with an architectural role. For example, in an effort to restore Sony to profitability its first non-Japanese chief executive, Sir Howard Stringer, implemented an efficiency drive that closed 20 per cent of the consumer electronics company's manufacturing and shed 20,000 jobs. In an effort to gain a creative momentum he has persuaded Sony's engineers, amidst much resistance, to embrace the networked era. Stringer's approach is most usual in Japanese corporations but as he says, 'these kinds of measures are part of business life . . . I think people recognise it is good to be constantly competitive. It doesn't make life easy, but it is ultimately good' (Lewis 2010).

CHARISMATIC LEADERS

individuals who are dissatisfied with the status quo and who can articulate a vision that captures the imagination of their followers

Charismatic leaders can be effective change agents because they seek to change the status quo and are gifted at building alliances and making individuals feel valued. This is important because if people are inspired and empowered to act they will produce greater efforts and take risks in pursuit of a shared vision. However, as we saw in **Chapter 10**, trust, rewards, and communication are essential if individuals are to engage in change (Lee and Miller 1999; Kotter 1990).

Kets de Vries interviewed two leaders who epitomize the ability to sustain change and innovation in their organization. Richard Branson, of the Virgin Group, and Percy Barnevik, previously CEO of ABB, both combine charismatic leadership with architectural skills to bring about change in their organizations. Richard Branson's Virgin Group is famous for taking on established industries. The Virgin Group's core businesses include megastore retail outlets, hotels, communications, and an airline. The company's business maxim is similar to the credo of Johnson & Johnson, although where Johnson & Johnson put customers first, Branson has staff first, customers second, and shareholders third. Branson clearly believes that looking after his people comes first. It is this commitment to staff which helps facilitate change. In addition to charismatic qualities, Richard Branson's architectural skill allows him to design the Virgin Group's structure in a way which encourages a creative entrepreneurial atmosphere.

His divested record company provides a blueprint. When his record company grew to around fifty employees, Branson recalls that he would go and see the deputy managing director, the deputy sales manager, and the deputy marketing manager and say: 'You are now the managing director, the sales manager, and the marketing manager' . . . and put them into a new building . . . when that company got to a certain size, say 50 people, I would do the same thing again' (Kets de Vries 1998, p. 10). The culture that Branson has created is one of speed of decision making, devoid of formal board meetings and committees. He is accessible to anyone who wants to discuss an idea, but prefers that they just go ahead and do it. His passion is for shaking things up, remoulding established industries. Indeed, his legacy to the Virgin Group will no doubt be this.

Percy Barnevik merged ASEA, a Swedish engineering group, with Brown Boveri, a Swiss competitor, in 1987 to create ABB. ABB competes in global markets for electric power generation and transmission equipment, robotics, high-speed trains, and environmental control systems. Barnevik's vision was one of exploiting the organization's core competences and global economies of scale while maintaining and encouraging a local market presence. Barnevik's architecture involved the introduction of a matrix structure which simultaneously allows managers around the globe to make decisions about product strategy without having to think about their impact on national markets. At the same time, national companies within the group have the freedom to remain focused on their local markets. As Barnevik stated:

What I have tried to do is recreate small company dynamism and creativity by building 5000 profit centres . . . fewer layers means bigger spans of control and fewer jobs to which one can be promoted. But the advantages lie in communication and feedback . . . an environment where you can have creative, entrepreneurial people . . . (Kets de Vries 1998, p. 13)

Barnevik recognized that to get the best out of people requires more than architecture; it requires tapping into the values of employees and aligning the organizational vision with those values. The vision needs to be audacious and engaging (a BHAG), inspiring people and bringing out the best in them. The mission statement should make people feel proud of what the organization is trying to achieve. Importantly, the leader must live up to the values he or she sets for the organization. Like Branson, Barnevik was passionate about change, breaking into new industries, and galvanizing employees to break new ground.

The charismatic and architectural skill of Richard Branson and Percy Barnevik is not simply building organizational structures but creating an environment in which employees feel free to make decisions, take risks, and even fail. This requires a focus on the customer as the driving force for change. A key success factor for the Virgin Group is its ability to move fast. As Branson says: 'I can have an idea in the morning in the bath tub, and have it implemented in the evening' (Kets de Vries 1998, p. 19). The need for strategic control systems is reduced when employees internalize shared corporate values. These values go beyond an increase in the bottom line—which fails to motivate anyone. In directing change both Branson and Barnevik (during his time at ABB) motivate their employees to embrace the dynamic of change and actively promote environments which mitigate the inherent resistance to change. Unlike the narcissistic leader, there is a confidence and security that employees can try ideas which have not emanated from the CEO. There is also a clear recognition that people need more than financial rewards and financial targets to motivate them. As Branson puts it: 'I think fun should be a motivator for all businesses' (Kets de Vries 1998, p. 20).

In contrast with Kets De Vries, Collins and Porras (1994) argue that a little too much is often made of the role of charismatic leaders in shaping organizations. Their research (discussed in **Chapter 10**) suggests that charismatic leaders are not of paramount importance in visionary companies. They cite organizations such as 3M, Procter & Gamble, Merck, and Sony who have at various times throughout their history had leaders who made significant changes but were not what might be understood as high-profile charismatic leaders. Instead Collins and Porras argue for the setting of BHAGs that are independent of management style, thereby ensuring that the succession of a charismatic leader becomes less of a problem.

THEORY E

assumes that organizational
change should be based on
enhancing shareholder value

THEORY O

assumes that change should help
develop corporate culture and
improve organizational
capabilities

Beer and Nohria (2000) suggest two archetypes or theories of change which are based on different assumptions about why and how change should be made. These are Theory E and Theory O. A Theory E change strategy is based on achieving economic value for shareholders and is characterized by downsizing and restructuring. This type of change is frequently found in the US, particularly in turnaround situations. Theory O adopts a *softer* approach which recognizes that if change is to be constructive and endure, it must affect the corporate culture and the way in which employees work. This type of theory is more likely to be found in European and Asian businesses. Both theories are useful for organizations, but both have their costs. The challenge is how to build sustainable competitive advantage while managing the inherent tensions between Theory E and Theory O.

To do this, leaders must engage in corporate transformations which do not simply institute Theory E and Theory O strategies in sequence, that is, one after the other, but rather combine the two strategies in a more holistic manner. Jack Welch, when CEO of GE, used a sequenced approach to change. He started with a Theory E type strategy by setting a goal for managers to be the first or second in their industry, or else exit. It was only once the *hard* issues of widespread redundancies and restructuring had taken place that Welch turned his attention to organizational changes which affected the culture within GE. The problem with sequencing is the time it takes; at GE the timescale was almost twenty years. Also, unlike Welch, once a leader engages in a Theory E approach he loses the trust and confidence of employees necessary to change the corporate culture. Few employees would be willing to listen attentively to a CEO who wields a corporate axe in one instance, and then wants to talk about trust and commitment. However, the research by Beer and Nohria suggests that it is possible to increase economic value quickly while also nurturing a trusting corporate culture. This was done by the UK retailer ASDA under the stewardship of Archie Norman and his deputy CEO, Allan Leighton. When Archie Norman took over as CEO of ASDA in 1991, he and Allan Leighton successfully improved economic value and were widely credited with bringing about a change in the behaviour and attitudes of employees. (See Strategy Focus: Complementary Leadership—NTL and Virgin Mobile, which describes some benefits of different leadership styles that can work together to achieve a common goal.)

STRATEGY FOCUS

Complementary Leadership— NTL and Virgin Mobile

Simon Duffy, chief executive of NTL, the cable company that is merging with its rival Telewest in a £3.8bn agreement, and Sir Richard Branson go back a long way. When he joined EMI, the music group, one of the first jobs for Mr Duffy—who went on to be EMI's finance director—was to integrate Virgin Records, which EMI had bought, into the larger group. On paper, the two men, who will have to work together if the Virgin/NTL agreement comes off, appear very different.

Mr Duffy is conventional in dress and demeanour and comes across in presentations to analysts as 'a details' man. Perhaps because of his unflashy style, not everyone had predicted that he would emerge as the chief executive of the enlarged NTL, at the announcement of its merger with Telewest. By contrast, Sir Richard is one of the world's most high-profile business figures and his globe-trotting style and love of publicity stunts, including the occasional foray into cross-dressing, are well known. However, according to people who know both men, their personalities could be said to complement each other.

Courtesy of Virgin Media

Sir Richard Branson is one of the world's highest-profile business figures and his globe-trotting style and love of publicity stunts are well-known.

Mr Duffy is also a no-nonsense operational man who is good at analysis and strategy, while Sir Richard is an entrepreneur, with nous for brand building, who is not scared of bold deals. And while Mr Duffy has worked at several listed firms including EMI, Orange, and now NTL, Sir Richard's relations with the Stock Exchange have not always been easy. 'Sir Richard is a very good deal maker and is very straightforward. He does not get confused by the advice he is given,' says one businessman who has worked with Sir Richard in the past.

Mr Duffy and Sir Richard have come together following the creation of Virgin Net, a broadband joint venture between NTL and Virgin. NTL bought out Virgin's half of the stake last year, but furthering the relationship between the two groups had been on Mr Duffy's mind.

'This has very much been Simon's deal. He introduced it to [the NTL board] a year ago,' says an NTL non-executive director. 'He has nursed the idea and has nursed the relationship with Richard. Richard does things on a personal relationship basis although he would not be doing this deal if it didn't work in business terms,' he adds. Others have noted that 'They do trust and respect one another.'

Source: 'Contrasting characters set to make for a complementary business in Virgin territory' *Financial Times*, 6 December 2005.

11

Beer and Nohria argue that all corporate transformations can be compared according to six dimensions of change. These are *goals*, *leadership*, *focus*, *process*, *reward system*, and *the use of consultants*. Given the different assumptions on which the two theories are based, they will manage change on these six dimensions differently. If we look at each of these in turn we can see how Norman and Leighton successfully combined the Theory E and Theory O approaches to bring about effective change.

1. **Goals—Confront the tension between Theory E and Theory O.** Archie Norman made it clear at the outset that he would be applying E and O strategies of change. He said: 'Our number one objective is to secure value for shareholders,' but went on to say that 'I intend to spend the next few weeks listening . . . we need a culture built around common ideas and goals that include listening, learning, and speed of response' (Beer and Nohria 2000, p. 139). In effect, he was saying that without an increase in shareholder value ASDA will fail to exist over the long term, but also that he wants all employees to participate and be emotionally committed to improving ASDA's performance.

2. **Leadership—Set the direction from the top and engage people below.** Although Norman was clearly the architect of ASDA's strategy, he set up programmes such as 'Tell Archie' to encourage employee participation. We saw earlier that a narcissistic leader can often benefit from having a trusted significant other. The same is true for a leader pursuing a strategy of change that involves Theory E. Archie Norman recognized the benefit of employing an opposing leadership style, hence the early recruitment of Allan Leighton who adopted a more employee-focused approach which contrasted with Norman's analytical style.

3. **Focus—Address the hard and soft sides of the organization at the same time.** Norman removed unproductive senior management layers and instigated a wage freeze which affected everyone in the organization—Theory E. At the same time, he was committed to making ASDA an enjoyable place to work by removing hierarchies, and making it fairer and more transparent.

4. **Process—Plan for spontaneity.** Stores managers were encouraged to experiment with their store layout, change employee roles, change the product ranges, and generally use their initiative to make changes that they believed would benefit the consumer. ASDA set up some experimental stores to help develop a learning environment. The culture within these experimental stores was one of 'risk-free', that is, no negative sanctions were applied for trying things that failed.

5. **Reward system—Incentives should reinforce change, not drive it.** ASDA has a share-ownership plan which covers all employees. Financial incentives, an E-type incentive, were used to reward employees who were already motivated and committed to change.

6. **Use of consultants—As expert resources who empower employees.** Consultancy firms were used by ASDA but their role was deliberately cut short by Archie Norman to avoid building up a dependency on their expertise. Consultants were used to reinforce what Norman and Leighton were already planning to do.

ASDA is an example of an organization which successfully combined Theory E and Theory O change patterns through its willingness to develop and change in the long term without sacrificing the need to generate acceptable shareholder returns. In 1999 ASDA was bought by Wal-Mart, and Archie Norman stepped down as CEO, having accomplished the changes he set out to achieve.

The Case Study: Leading Strategic Change at Severn Trent illustrates the difficulties in trying to implement change in a UK public utility organization which has powerful external stakeholders who require convincing if they are to endorse a change in the industry business model.

CASE STUDY 11.3

Leading Strategic Change at Severn Trent

Striding into the utility giant's modest London office near St James's Park, the water boss dives straight into the difficult topic of his company's chequered past under previous management. Severn Trent's forthright head has now had two years to re-invent the company's image after the Serious Fraud Office and industry regulator fined it a record £40m for misreporting leakage data to Ofwat—making it the first utility to be convicted of a criminal fraud.

Wray's arrival in the role coincided with a scandalous time for the industry in general. Thames Water was fined £9.7m for accidentally giving wrong data to the regulator and Southern Water was hit with a £20.5m fine for deliberately misreporting customer service data. He then had to deal with the fallout of catastrophic floods in Gloucestershire, including £40m for residents whose water stopped flowing from their taps for up to a week.

Since taking over in October 2007, Wray hasn't given a big interview, preferring to concentrate on improving the company's conduct. But now—happy that his £2.7bn company is no longer referred to as 'the disgraced water giant'—he wants to become known as the visionary player in the industry. Analysts expect Severn Trent to reveal revenue roughly flat at £1.66bn and pre-tax profits substantially higher than the previous year at £312.5m this week.

Wray doesn't believe water companies have seen the last of the recession, with consumer bad debt still too high and sector leverage at a record high. But he doesn't think economic uncertainty should distract the industry from tackling its long-term problems: the threat of water shortages, rising bills and financing challenges. The goal is to push the traditionally staid sector, populated by Britain's last regulated monopolies, down the path to more deregulation. 'I do think now is the time to be known as a company with interesting things to say, even if it means my photo appearing on the front of *Utility Week* for my children to use as a dartboard,' he said. 'But honestly, the Serious Fraud Office issues all get mentioned a whole lot less. We learnt the consequences of poor behaviour and the value of good behaviour, making Severn Trent a more demanding place to work.'

His preferred time frame for persuading the industry and the government of the crucial need for change is five years. Deregulating the gas market took just three, he says. 'We're two years into the regulatory cycle and if something doesn't start happening within the next 12 months, that's not a good sign,' he says.

The idea that there ought to be more competition among water companies—the last sector dominated by regional monopolies—has been knocking around since 2002 when Tony Blair commissioned the Cave Review. It was published in March 2009, but since then, little progress has been made towards its aims—reducing bills for customers and ultimately giving them the power to choose their supplier, as with gas and electricity.

This spring, Wray, decided to commission Severn Trent's own report, warning that lack of action could leave water companies struggling to raise enough finance for improvements. The burgeoning debt of the water giants, which has topped £33bn, could almost double during the next 10 years. 'We've done our mathematics and economics and figured out a way of having a more sustainable regime,' he says. 'We could reduce the capital bill for the sector by about £10bn and the carbon footprint by about 13 per cent.'

The review also suggested that there should be consolidation among Britain's 22 water companies to create economies of scale—which is almost impossible under strict merger and competition laws. Severn Trent—seemingly keen to snap up smaller rivals—could be a major beneficiary of such a policy. 'It wouldn't be at any price,' Wray says, inserting a careful caveat. 'But yes, some of the infrastructure investments needed are too huge for the small companies. There needs to be consolidation and we would look at that.' He argues that such changes are not optional, but imperative if the UK is to avoid shortages and unaffordable bills in future. Water is relatively cheap, he warns, but it won't be for much longer under the current system.

'The obvious thing to do straight away is water trading,' he says, betraying frustration that this step should have been taken years ago. 'We would like to see upstream competition to secure long-term security of supply, with water flowing from north to south and east to west. It hasn't happened before because water has been relatively cheap compared with other bills at around 84p per day. Now they are going up.' He points to the madness of one water company building a desalination plant in one part of the country when another business is swimming in excess supply. Transferring water from the wet north and west to the starved south and east would be done via pipelines, and companies would naturally become more efficient with the incentive to save water to sell on, he says. Traditionally, water companies have liked pouring concrete into the ground. The more they build, the more their investors have the chance of steady returns over a long period of time—justifying rises in consumer bills with the regulator.

'Regulators have been very supportive of the £84bn of investment in water quality since privatisation, but it has come at a cost,' he says. 'Bills are rising at a rate greater than inflation, there's the indebtedness of the sector and there's still more to come on both fronts. Carbon footprints are much higher. Our view is that this doesn't have to be the way going forward.'

Another problem is climate change causing the mismatch in water supply between the North West and South East. Although the UK's looming shortage of energy by 2015 is now acknowledged as a problem by government and on the public radar, fewer people are aware that the UK is facing a degree of water scarcity in the next decade.

'It's happening already,' Wray says. 'You can see climate change right now in the floods that happened in Gloucester, then Hull, then Sheffield, then Cumbria and Northumbria. There have been hosepipe bans in some areas for years. Now Southern is going to start charging different rates for water in the summer and winter. And Folkestone is moving to 100 per cent water metering to help householders save more. It seems wrong to me that people are paying more than others for their water just because of where they live.'

The UK could use Australia as a model for water trading, he says. Cap-and-trade systems in Australia between regions have been in place since 1983, but now an increasing number of trades take place through electronic exchanges, with lawyers, conveyancers and brokers all taking part in the system. Their water trade is now worth A$2.7bn (£1.55bn). Proponents of these schemes say water—now increasingly precious—needs to be properly priced by the market as a commodity.

But critics of Severn Trent's enthusiasm for ferrying water about the country have pointed out that customers will ultimately have to pay for all the extra capital expenditure on improving the pipe network. 'We could build less by spreading risks more effectively,' he says. 'We don't need a massive national grid. Most of the infrastructure is there. It would value water more accurately and make the costs of running a network clearer.'

Wray dismisses critics who suspect that his fervour for the scheme is because his company would dominate the centre of the network. As one of the team to deregulate telecoms in Northern Ireland and the UK gas markets, he believes that deregulation will benefit everyone. There are no insurmountable obstacles, he claims. 'It's no different from energy and I've done it in those markets. People say water's really important—you can't do that with it. But what do they think happened with electricity? The lights didn't go out but bills did go down. All these models for utilities have found a way of trading.' Deregulation of the industry should not stop there, he argues.

'We're only 20 years into a 40-year journey that's going to transform the sector.'

Source: 'Severn Trent CEO Tony Wray reveals his radical plans for change' The *Telegraph*, 22 May 2010.

Questions

1. What are the key strategic changes facing Severn Trent?

2. How will consolidation of the water industry help and what likely impact will this have on the water sector's leverage?

3. Deregulation was fervently propounded by Kenneth Lay, disgraced former chairman of US utility Enron, the biggest corporate collapse in US history. What is the likely impact for water companies and UK consumers of deregulating the water industry?

4. Who are the key stakeholders for Severn Trent?

For examples of the difficulties faced by leaders when implementing strategic change in organizations go to the Online Resource Centre and see the Key Work feature.
www.oxfordtextbooks.co.uk/orc/henry2e/

11.7 The Impact of Chaos on Leadership

In a rational world in which events in the external environment are repetitive or subject to some form of knowable pattern strategic management as espoused so far has a key role to play. However, if the world is also non-rational and periods of stability sit alongside periods of instability, then this may require leaders to adopt a different mental model when developing strategy. When we see an organization as part of a dynamic system we are concerned with how it changes over time and the patterns of change that subsequently develop. We want to know whether these patterns display properties that are stable or unstable, predictable or unpredictable.

CHAOS

an irregular pattern of behaviour generated by well-defined non-linear feedback rules commonly found in nature and human society

Stacey (1993, 2003) argues that **chaos** is an irregular pattern of behaviour generated by well-defined non-linear feedback rules commonly found in nature and human society. As systems move away from their equilibrium state they are prone to small changes in their environment which can cause major changes in the behaviour of the system itself. In the business world a leader may attach great importance to small differences in customer requirements and develop hugely differentiated products. Under conditions of chaos the long-term future of an organization is assumed to be unknowable. If leaders cannot know what the future holds, then chaos theory holds little place for long-term plans and visions of future states.

However, this may be slightly overstating the case since the future may be unpredictable at a specific level but at a general level there are recognizable patterns. For example, no one can predict the shape of individual snowflakes as they fall to the ground, but we can still recognize them as snowflakes. It is this ability to recognize patterns at a general level that allows leaders to cope with chaos. Indeed, we might argue that this gift is much more highly developed in some than in others. For example, although Bill Gates and Steve Jobs were unable to state specifics, they did correctly envision in the early 1980s that a time would come when we would all have computers in the home. It is these boundaries around instability that allow us to make sense of our world. The use of reasoning, intuition, and experience helps us to cope with change and, therefore, chaos.

11.7.1 Chaos and Innovation

Stacey suggests eight steps to help leaders encourage innovation and create a new strategic direction.

1. **Develop new perspectives on the meaning of control.** Innovation may be more likely to come about if leaders allow self-organizing processes and learning groups to develop. This means rethinking their traditional ideas about control of individuals' behaviour and letting the group itself exercise that function.

2. **Design the use of power.** The group dynamic that is conducive to complex learning occurs when the leader's power is used to create an environment in which the assumptions that are the basis for decisions can be challenged, and there is open questioning of the status quo. In contrast, when power is wielded through force and authority, the group dynamic will be one of submission, rebellion, or suspension of critical faculties. In these cases complex learning among individual members of the group will not take place.

3. **Encourage self-organizing groups.** In common with networks, which we discussed in **Chapter 10**, a self-organizing group is free to make decisions within the context of the boundaries of its work together. A self-organizing group works best if it is allowed to form spontaneously and set its own aims and objectives. The output may conflict with the views of senior management, but this is to be expected when ideas are allowed free reign.

4. **Provoke multiple cultures.** This allows new perspectives to proliferate across the organization by moving people from different business units and functions to create a more culturally diverse organization.

5. **Present ambiguous challenges instead of clear long-term objectives or visions.** Top management can encourage individuals to think about new ways of doing things by giving them ambiguous challenges and partially developed issues to consider. Senior management should also be open to having their own ideas challenged by subordinates.

6. **Expose the business to challenging situations.** Leaders should not be afraid to expose their organization to demanding situations. We saw in **Chapter 9** (Section 9.6 on Porter's diamond of competitive advantage) how organizations in home markets which have the world's most challenging customers and innovative competitors will learn far more than other organizations, and therefore will be more likely to build a sustainable competitive advantage (Porter 1990a,b).

7. **Devote explicit attention to improving group learning skills.** Senior managers encourage new strategic directions to emerge when they allow the dominant mental models that are held within the organization to be challenged. We saw this when we looked at Senge's work on the learning organization. This is a prime role for leaders if learning is to take place.

8. **Create resource slack.** New strategic directions and innovations in the organization will only occur when top management invests sufficient time, effort, and organizational resources.

Chaos theory, then, sees that a traditional planning approach to strategic management may benefit the organization over the short term. Over time, however, the lack of a causal link between organizational actions and outputs means that the role of leadership should be to shun visions and long-term plans and create instead an environment characterized by spontaneity and self-organization. Chaos theory does not make traditional approaches to strategic management obsolete; rather it places them in a much more constrained time horizon. As we have seen in preceding chapters, the choice is seldom *either/or*, but more one of *and*.

 # Summary

We started the chapter with a discussion of the differences between management and leadership in order to distinguish their different roles. We noted that *management* is about coping with complexity, whereas *leadership* is about dealing with change. We discussed the role of leaders in building a learning organization, and looked at the leadership skills and roles within a learning organization. We noted the importance of allowing individuals to challenge mental models that exist within the organization if we desire complex learning to take place. We then assessed the impact of emotional intelligence on effective leadership and company performance. We noted that emotional intelligence is a better predictor of the success of a leader than either IQ or technical skills.

The benefits and dangers of narcissistic leaders were evaluated and suggestions put forward to help narcissists remain productive. We then discussed the impact of leaders on an organization's vision, value, and culture, noting that a great deal had already been said about research into visionary companies in **Chapter 10**. The impact of national cultures on domestic organizations was also discussed. We assessed the leadership skills necessary for directing strategic change and looked at some of the obstacles to change. Theory E and Theory O strategic changes were introduced as we discussed the importance of successfully combining them to simultaneously achieve lasting change and an increase in shareholder value. The chapter ended with a discussion of chaos theory and its implication for long-term plans and visions.

In **Chapter 12**, we will evaluate corporate governance by looking at its development and its impact upon organizations.

Review Questions

1. Under what conditions might a narcissistic leader be good for company performance?
2. In seeking to appoint a new leader from outside the organization what factors should be borne in mind?
3. Explain why both Theory E and Theory O are important for organizational change.

Discussion Question

Learning organizations do not exist in reality because individuals simply do not want to change. Discuss.

Research Topic

Consider the following. Andy Grove, former CEO of Intel, Bill Gates of Microsoft, Sir Richard Branson of the Virgin Group, and Sir Terry Leahy, former CEO of Tesco: to what extent are each of these individuals narcissistic leaders? Justify your answers with reference to interviews, decisions, and remarks that each has made.

Recommended Reading

For a discussion of the respective roles of management and leadership see:

- **Kotter, J.P.** (1990). What leaders really do. *Harvard Business Review*, **68**(3), 103–11.
- **Cyert, R.M.** (1990). Defining leadership and explicating the process. Reprinted in *Strategy: Process, Content, Context* (2004) (eds B. De Wit and R. Meyer), pp. 496–9. Thomson, London.

The learning organization is comprehensively covered in:

- **Senge, P.M.** (1990). *The Fifth Discipline*. Century, London.
- **Senge, P.M.** (1990). The leader's new work: building learning organizations. *Sloan Management Review*, **32**(1), 7–23.

For an assessment of emotional intelligence on company performance see:

- **Goleman, D.** (1998). What makes a leader? *Harvard Business Review*, **76**(6), 93–102.

For research on whether leadership skills can readily translate from one industry to another, see:

- **Groysberg, B., McLean, A.N.,** and **Nohria, N.** (2006). Are leaders portable? *Harvard Business Review*, **84**(5), 92–100.

online
resource
centre

www.oxfordtextbooks.co.uk/orc/henry2e/
Visit the Online Resource Centre that accompanies this book for activities and more information on strategic leadership.

References

Beer, M. and **Nohria, N.** (2000). Cracking the code of change. *Harvard Business Review*, **78**(3), 133–41.

Brynjolfsson, E., Renshaw, A.A., and **Van Alstyne, M.** (1997). The matrix of change. *Sloan Management Review*, **38**(2), 37–54.

Collins, J.C. and **Porras, J.I.** (1994). *Built to Last: Successful Habit of Visionary Companies*. Harper, New York.

Cyert, R.M. (1990). Defining leadership and explicating the process. Reprinted in *Strategy: Process, Content, Context* (2004) (eds B. De Wit and R. Meyer), pp. 496–9. Thomson, London.

Goleman, D. (1998). What makes a leader? *Harvard Business Review*, **76**(6), 93–102.

Groysberg, B., McLean, A.N., and **Nohria, N.** (2006). Are Leaders Portable? *Harvard Business Review*, **84**(5), 92–100.

Hofstede, G. (1997). *Cultures and Organizations: Software of the Mind*. McGraw-Hill, New York.

Kanter, R.M. (1983). *The Change Masters*. Simon & Schuster, New York.

Kets de Vries, M.F.R. (1998). Charisma in action: the transformational abilities of Virgin's Richard Branson and ABB's Percy Barnevik. *Organizational Dynamics*, **26**(3), 7–21.

Kotter, J.P. (1990). What leaders really do. *Harvard Business Review*, **68**(3), 103–11.

Lee, J. and **Miller, D.** (1999). People matter: commitment to employees, strategy and performance in Korean firms. *Strategic Management Journal*, **20**(6), 579–93.

Lewis, L. (2010). Stringer gives up song and dance act as Sony pulls itself together *The Times*, 5 February (online). Available at: http://business.timesonline.co.uk/tol/business/industry_sectors/consumer_goods/article7015575.ece

Maccoby, M. (2000). Narcissistic leaders: incredible pros, and inevitable cons. *Harvard Business Review*, **78**(1), 69–77.

Mintzberg, H. (1987). Crafting strategy. *Harvard Business Review*, **65**(4), 66–75.

Peters, T.J. (1979). Leadership: sad facts and silver linings. *Harvard Business Review*, **57**(6), 164–72.

Porter, M.E. (1990a). The competitive advantage of nations. *Harvard Business Review*, **68**(2), 73–9.

Porter, M.E. (1990b). *The Competitive Advantage of Nations*, Chapter 3. Free Press, New York.

Porter, M.E. (1996). What is strategy? *Harvard Business Review*, **74**(6), 61–78.

Schneider, W.E. (2000). Why good management ideas fail. *Strategy and Leadership*, **28**(1), 24–9.

Senge, P.M. (1990a). The leader's new work: building learning organizations. *Sloan Management Review*, **32**(1), 7–23.

Senge, P.M. (1990b). *The Fifth Discipline*. Century, London.

Stacey, R. (1993). Strategy as order emerging from chaos. *Long Range Planning*, **26**(1), 23.

Stacey, R.D. (2003). *Strategic Management and Organizational Dynamics: The Challenge of Complexity*, 4th edn. Prentice Hall, Harlow.

Stalk, G. (1988). Time—the next source of competitive advantage. *Harvard Business Review*, **66**(4), 41–51.

12 Corporate Governance

Key Work
Importance of corporate social responsibility

Main Reference
Cadbury, A. (1992). Report of the Committee on the Financial Aspects of Corporate Governance (Cadbury Report). Gee, London.

Key Work
Controversy surrounding executive remuneration

Key Work
Financial crisis and solutions

Learning Objectives

After completing this chapter you should be able to:

- Explain what is meant by corporate governance
- Discuss the origins of corporate governance and explain the growth of modern corporations
- Discuss the purpose of corporations
- Evaluate shareholder and stakeholder theories of corporate governance
- Discuss corporate collapses and corporate governance failures
- Assess the impact of the Sarbanes–Oxley Act on corporations
- Evaluate excessive executive pay
- Discuss corporate governance reform

Introduction

In assessing organizational performance in **Chapter 6** we started by evaluating the role and purpose of business. We can expand on this issue and show that approaches to corporate governance, and indeed business ethics, reflect how we define business. That is, if the purpose of business is defined as maximizing the long-term value of owners or shareholders, then the role of corporate governance will be relatively narrow. If, however, the purpose of business is defined as congruent with all its stakeholders, such as customers, suppliers, and the local community, then we might expect the role of corporate governance to be somewhat wider. We should stress that although we evaluate corporate governance in this chapter, it may be more properly thought of as permeating all business decisions and, therefore, affects all aspects of what we have discussed so far. As such, corporate governance requires a change in the attitudes of leaders in the boardroom and needs to be an integral part of the strategy of organizations.

Corporate governance is inextricably bound up with one's views of the purpose of corporations and, indeed, how one defines a corporation or business. Although different definitions of corporate governance exist, these only really make sense when we place them in the context of the purpose of corporations. We start our evaluation of corporate governance with a review of the origins of corporate governance and a discussion of the corporate form. We explain the reasons for the growth of modern corporations which in turn has led to an increase in the separation of ownership and control. We then evaluate the different perspectives that exist on the role of corporations. This is important because a divide exists between those who advocate a shareholder approach to corporate governance and those who adopt a stakeholder approach. The collapse of major corporations more than anything else has put corporate governance on the boardroom agenda. We evaluate corporate collapses and subsequent corporate governance codes to see whether they have helped lessen the likelihood of further failures. Key players in ensuring that executive board members behave in a responsible manner are non-executive directors (NEDs). We discuss the collapse of the American multinational corporation Enron and assess the role of non-executive directors. The collapse of Enron led to the enactment of the Sarbanes–Oxley Act. We assess the impact of the Sarbanes–Oxley Act on corporations. In addition to the collapse of corporations, another facet that has occupied much time and attention is the perennial issue of excessive executive pay. We discuss whether executive pay should represent some multiple of the average worker's salary. We end the chapter with a discussion of corporate governance reform, noting that this debate is far from over.

- In Section 12.1 we start the chapter with a discussion of the different definitions of corporate governance.

- In Section 12.2 we discuss the origins of corporate governance and the corporate form, noting that the fear of large corporations subjugating the rights of individuals is not a recent phenomenon.

- Section 12.3 explains the growth and acceptance of modern corporations as a result of four key factors: the limited liability of investors; free transferability of investor interest; legal personality; and centralized management.

- In Section 12.4 we evaluate two different perspectives on the role of corporations; these are shareholder and stakeholder approaches.

- In Section 12.5 we evaluate corporate collapses and corporate governance codes. This section also deals with the collapse of the US multinational corporation Enron and the role of non-executive directors, the enactment of the Sarbanes–Oxley Act, and excessive executive pay.

- Lastly, in Section 12.6 we discuss different perspectives on corporate governance reform.

12.1 **What is Corporate Governance?**

CORPORATE GOVERNANCE

two definitions are provided: (1) the way in which organizations are directed and controlled, or (2) the process by which corporations are made responsive to the rights and wishes of stakeholders

The use of the term corporate governance gained prominence in the UK following the publication of the *Report of the Committee on the Financial Aspects of Corporate Governance* in 1992, commonly referred to as the Cadbury Report (Cadbury 1992). The collapse of major corporations in the UK, such as Polly Peck, Coloroll, Bank of Credit and Commerce International (BCCI), and the Mirror Group, highlighted a rift between the annual report and accounts of these corporations and reality. For example, Polly Peck went from a market capitalization of £1.75 billion to a deficit of almost £400 million in under four weeks (Cadbury 2002). Their annual report and accounts, signed off by external auditors, showed little signs of their true financial state. At the same time there was growing controversy over directors' pay which effectively widened the initial remit of the Cadbury Report. Since then we have had much more substantial failures as global corporations such as Enron and WorldCom have collapsed, threatening instability across global stock markets.

Corporate governance has been around since companies began to take their present form. Cadbury (2002, p. 3) argues that governance issues are about 'power and accountability. They involve where power lies in the corporate system and what degree of accountability there is for its exercise'. Shleifer and Vishny (1997) state that corporate governance 'deals with the way in which suppliers of finance to corporations assure themselves of getting a return on their investment'. In other words, corporate governance is concerned with ensuring that the suppliers of finance (investors) receive something back from the managers to whom they entrust their funds.

In 2004 the Organization for Economic Cooperation and Development (OECD) produced a set of revised guidelines entitled *OECD Principles of Corporate Governance*. It states that corporate governance 'involves a set of relationships between a company's management, board, shareholders and other stakeholders'. It goes on to say that corporate governance 'should provide proper incentives for the board and management to pursue objectives that are in the interests of the company and shareholders' (OECD 2004). Thus, corporate governance provides a structure through which an organization sets its objectives and its performance is monitored. In common with Shleifer and Vishny, the OECD sees the main governance problems as arising from the separation of ownership and control. However, it does recognize that a corporation needs to be aware of the interests of communities in which it competes if it is not to damage its reputation and long-term success.

Others also see the emphasis on setting and achieving strategic objectives, but argue that accountability is to an organization's stakeholders. Demb and Neubauer (1992) define corporate governance as 'the process by which corporations are made responsive to the rights and wishes of stakeholders' (cited by Cadbury 2002). According to Baukol (2002), the fundamental basis of corporate governance and responsibility is the value system of the organization. In contrast to others, Baukol argues that corporate governance is necessary to counteract a tendency for corporations to be selfish and myopic. He suggests that the role of corporate governance is to guide corporations to achieve corporate and societal responsibilities. There are some who would vehemently disagree with this.

The emphasis on agency theory, prevalent in the US, in which one party, the principal, provides capital to another party, the agent, to employ on his behalf, tends to obscure the role of corporations being managed in the interest of stakeholders. Instead, the focus is on the return on investment of owners (Shleifer and Vishny 1997). The Cadbury Committee stated that a country's economy depends on the drive and efficiency of its companies. Thus, the effectiveness with which their boards discharge their responsibilities determines a country's competitive position. For Cadbury, boards of directors must be free to drive their companies forward but must exercise that freedom within a framework of effective accountability (Cadbury 1992). There is general agreement that publicly quoted companies, which are a country's main engine for growth, also carry with them great responsibility for the people who are affected by their actions (or inaction). In the US 'publicly listed corporations constitute barely 1 per cent of all business organizations. Yet in 1997, they produced more than half of the United States' economic output' (Gregg 2001, cited by Zandstra 2002).

Does corporate governance enhance corporate performance or, by placing an added burden on corporations, stifle enterprise and initiative? In the UK, the Hampel Committee (1998) stated that the benefit of corporate governance 'lies in its contribution both to business prosperity and to accountability. In the UK the latter has preoccupied much public debate...We would wish to see the balance corrected' (Hampel 1998, p. 7). However, good corporate governance should not imply an *either/or* scenario. The pursuit of best practice for accountability should enhance an organization's performance and not reduce it. Indeed, Clarke (1998) sees the two as mutually compatible: 'The spirit of enterprise must work within a sound framework of accountability, and the balance between them is critical'. He is not alone; as Charkham (1998) points out, 'good governance means a proper balance between enterprise and accountability' (cited by Spira 2001).

12

The Institute of Chartered Accountants in England and Wales (ICAEW) argue that there are two fundamentals to corporate governance. The first is that shareholders have primacy over all other stakeholder groups because it is their money at stake. The second draws upon the Cadbury Report in stating that the foundations of corporate governance are based on the way in which companies are directed and controlled. Clearly there is an explicit expectation that where stakeholders are included the role of shareholder remains one of primacy. The Higgs Committee (2003) in the UK stated that corporate governance 'provides an architecture of accountability—the structures and processes to ensure companies are managed in the interests of their owners', although it went on to acknowledge that architecture in itself does not deliver good outcomes (Higgs 2003). Although a definition of corporate governance that is acceptable to all parties is difficult to find, we do know that following the collapse of Enron in 2001, policy makers around the globe continue to debate corporate governance and how to ensure those in positions of trust behave responsibly and morally. Terms such as ethics, morals, and right and wron g that have arguably been implicit in boardrooms now have a more explicit resonance.

12.2 The Origins of Corporate Governance[1]

The origins of corporate governance date back at least as far as 1600, when a Royal Charter was granted to The Company of Merchants of London trading into the East Indies. The governance structure of the East India Company consisted of a Court of Proprietors and a Court of Directors. The Court of Proprietors comprised individuals with voting rights, which they received as result of contributing a sum of money of around £200. The Court of Proprietors seldom met because it comprised hundreds of individuals, but it had ultimate authority. Its authority was required to raise funds and to appoint directors. The Court of Directors was the executive body which was responsible for the running of the company, appointing a chief executive, and setting the strategy direction, although each policy decision required agreement by the Court of Proprietors. The Court of Directors consisted of a governor, a deputy-governor, and 24 directors who met frequently.

The structure of the East India Company has clear antecedents with modern companies today. The Court of Proprietors were the shareholders, the Court of Directors was the board, and the Royal Charter laid down the framework in which the company operated. Similarly, the issues faced by their board will resonate with modern companies. Some investors adopted a short-term horizon, requesting a return on their money after each sea voyage, while others adopted a longer view. The Court of Directors had the added problem of controlling appointees such as sea captains for the voyage to the East Indies. These individuals were acting not only for the company but also often for themselves in faraway places without communication for long periods of time. Cadbury argues that corporate governance issues are rooted in the development of the corporation. They are about power and accountability. In shareholder-owned corporations, the balance of power between shareholders, boards of directors, and managers is continually shifting.

The corporate structure has continued to develop in response to needs that were not being met by earlier corporate forms. In 1932, US Supreme Court Justice Louis Brandeis argued 'the privilege of engaging in such commerce in corporate form is one in which the state may confer or may withhold as it sees fit' (cited in Monks and Minow 2004, p. 10). It is interesting to reflect that, for Brandeis, the conferring of corporate status went hand in hand with the needs of public policy and welfare. His concern was that a corporation was used to benefit the public. He went on to state that even when the value of the corporation in commence and industry was fully recognized, 'incorporation for business was commonly denied long after it had been freely granted for religious, educational, and charitable purposes' (cited in Monks and Minow 2004, p. 11).

For Brandeis, incorporation for business was denied because of a fear that the corporation may use its power to subvert the needs of employees to the needs of investors. With great insight he noted that there was:

> a sense of some insidious menace inherent in large aggregation of capital, particularly when held by corporations.

As a result:

> The corporate privilege was granted sparingly; and only when the grant seemed necessary to procure for the community some specific benefit otherwise unattainable. The later enactment of general corporation laws does not signify that the apprehension of corporate domination had been overcome. (cited in Monks and Minow 2004, p. 10)

While few would deny the enormous benefits and affluence that modern corporations have brought, Brandeis, like the economist John Kenneth Galbraith after him, was wary of the influence of overarching powerful corporations.

12.3 The Growth of Modern Corporations

The spread and acceptance of the modern corporation are owed to four characteristics: limited liability of investors, free transferability of investor interest, legal personality, and centralized management (Clark 1986). We can look at each of these in turn.

CORPORATION

an organization owned by its shareholders but managed by agents on their behalf

- **Limited liability.** This entails a separation between the corporation and its owners and employees. This ensures that what is owed to the corporation is not owed to the individuals in the group that make up the corporation; and whatever debts the corporation owes are not owed by individuals that make it up. Importantly, if a corporation becomes bankrupt and is pursued by its creditors for recovery of debts, the individual members of the corporation are not individually liable. The corporate form provides certainty for investors as to the extent of their loss; it will only ever be the amount of capital they have invested in the corporation. However, limited liability is accompanied by limited authority to influence the direction of the corporation. It is the shareholders' low level of risk derived from having limited liability that makes their low level of control acceptable.

- **Transferability.** An ability to transfer one's holdings freely also provides the shareholder with an acceptable level of risk. A shareholder who is concerned that their shares may be losing value can sell almost immediately. However, this does imply some timely information that would prevent the shareholder incurring further losses. Often by the time this information is disseminated to individual shareholders their holdings may have substantially fallen in value. Transferability is a function of limited authority. The shareholders agree to put their capital at risk. They have little authority to control the corporation but they have the assurance that they can have some control over their risk by selling their shares when they want to.

- **Legal personality.** Whereas a partnership dissolves with the death of its partners, a corporation lives for as long as it has capital. A legal personality ensures that actions that would result in a negative sanction for an individual have no such consequences when the individual commits them as part of a corporation. Recently, in the UK, corporate manslaughter has been invoked in an attempt to hold negligent corporate directors to account. Because corporations are defined as legal persons, they may own property, including copyrights. The bestowing of a legal personality allows a corporation to act, own, and continue beyond the lifespan of any individual or group.

- **Centralized management.** The board of directors determines the setting of a company's aims and objectives, and therefore its strategy, and managers control its day-to-day operational issues. For the board to drive the company purposefully into the future, it needs to be aware of the opportunities that exist in the marketplace and how best to exploit these. Cadbury argues that it is insufficient for the board simply to determine aims and objectives without also considering the manner of their achievement. Thus, although the board is responsible for devising strategy, it needs to undertake these decisions in consultation with management who have the task of achieving the results. As corporations grew in size and age, their ownership became more dispersed and markets developed to provide for far greater liquidity. At the same time, the law tried to develop a standard of performance for directors acting on behalf of shareholders that would hopefully encourage the same sense of duty and care that they exercise with their own affairs.

12.4 The Purpose of Corporations

The purpose of the corporation is far from unambiguous. Theoretical perspectives abound that are rooted in ideology and dogma. Growing concern within corporations for the needs of stakeholders and society has had the effect of polarizing these perspectives. To understand corporate governance, corporate social responsibility, and business ethics, we need to address the fundamental question: Why do businesses exist?[2] Before we do so we can define what we mean by a corporation. Monks and Minow (2004, pp. 8–9) remind us that definitions of the term *corporation* invariably reflect the perspectives and biases of those writing the definition. They state: 'a corporation is a mechanism established to allow different parties to contribute capital, expertise, and labour, for the maximum benefit of all of them'. They argue that a corporation has to relate to a wide variety of constituents including directors, managers, employees, shareholders, customers, and suppliers, as well as society and the government, and that each of these relationships has the ability to affect the direction and focus of the corporation. Therefore, we can take *corporation* to mean an organization owned by its shareholders but managed by agents on their behalf.

Baukol (2002) contends that a better understanding of corporate governance and corporate social responsibility derives from an understanding of the role of the corporation in modern society or fundamentally answering the question: Why does a corporation exist? O'Sullivan (2003) makes the same point, asserting that an understanding of corporate governance needs to first address what the objectives of the corporation are or what a company is in business to do. Once the objectives are established, discussions of corporate governance focus on the mechanisms that will ensure goal achievement. If a firm wishes to maximize shareholder value, the relevant governance mechanisms are those influencing the relationship between shareholders and corporate managers.

Sternberg (2000) argues that it is necessary to first understand what business is (and is not) by disaggregating it from other forms of activity. Sternberg argues that the defining purpose of business (a corporation) is 'maximizing owner value over the long term by selling goods and services'. For Baukol, corporations exist because, unlike other institutions, which include government, the corporation provides economic sustainability. The corporation is unique in allowing individuals to practise their skills in a group setting that creates employment and value which others are prepared to pay for. The corporation generates wealth for society and for its own members. Few would argue with Baukol's assertion that the corporate entity is the major institution for wealth creation. The arguments surround the role and responsibilities of corporations. As Brandeis noted, the corporation will not necessarily pursue the interests of the society of which it is a part.

If we take corporations, there is an assumption that these organizations are in business to create value and that the profit they produce is to be distributed among the owners of the business, the shareholders. We saw in **Chapter 6** that there is a

12

presumption that the objective of corporations is to maximize profits. This is standard neoclassical economic theory. In the 1930s, Berle and Means (1932) cast doubt on profit-maximizing theories. They were not proposing a shift away from profit maximizing but rather questioning whether this actually occurs. Indeed, in an article in the *Harvard Law Review*, Berle (1932) states, 'you cannot abandon emphasis on the view that business corporations exist for the sole purpose of making profits for their shareholders until . . . you are prepared to offer a clear and reasonably enforceable scheme of responsibilities to someone else'.

ASYMMETRY OF INFORMATION

exists when the agents (managers) running a corporation have greater access to information than the principal (shareholders) by virtue of their position

Their concerns were around the principal–agent problem. The principal–agent problem refers to the separation of ownership from control within corporations, where the owners are the principal but the control of the organization is by salaried managers who act as the agent. There is a tendency for an asymmetry of information to exist when managers are running companies which are owned by numerous dispersed shareholders. This asymmetry of information between the principal (owners) and the agent (managers) occurs when managers have access to corporate information that the owners do not. The dispersal of shareholders is related to the legal framework that exists within countries (La Porta *et al.* 1998). However, the profit-maximizing assumption is contested by behavioural psychologists who claim that organizations consist of shifting coalitions and how they behave is dependent on the interests and beliefs of the dominant coalition(s) (Cyert and March 1963).

It is apparent that the purpose of corporations is by no means clear. Many of the arguments are rooted in ideology. With this in mind we can evaluate the two main perspectives based on shareholders and stakeholders.

12.4.1 The Purpose of Corporations is to Maximize Shareholder Value

SHAREHOLDER THEORY

a view of corporations that sees shareholder interests as paramount

In the US and UK there exists a predominate belief that the role of corporations is to serve the owners of the business, that is, the shareholders. In a much quoted passage, Friedman (1962, p. 133) argues, 'there is one and only one social responsibility of business—to use its resources and engage in activities designed to increase its profits so long as it stays within the rules of the game, which is to say, engages in open and free competition without deception or fraud'.

Friedman's contention is that corporate executives act as agents and, therefore, to engage in forms of corporate social responsibility is using their position to spend someone else's money for a general social interest (Friedman 1970). The effect of this is to impose a tax on the owners by ensuring that they receive lower returns from their investment than they otherwise would. If the effect of such actions by corporate executives is to raise prices to consumers, then this places a tax on consumers, and likewise if the effect of such actions lowers the payments of some employees, they are effectively taxed. Indeed, Sternberg (2000, p. 41) would argue that in the case of corporations (i.e. organizations owned by shareholders) the use of an organization's resources by managers for anything other than business purposes is tantamount to theft! The fact that managers may be involved in the pursuit of socially responsible aims does not mitigate their actions and still amounts to embezzling shareholders' wealth.

Friedman (1970) does not recognize a social role for the corporations that would encompass the needs of stakeholders apart from the immediate shareholders. However, he does argue against the violation of accepted legal business practices. In this respect Friedman would have perceived the fraudulent use of corporate funds as a gross misallocation of resources which ultimately leads to suboptimal decision making for shareholders. Friedman asserts a role for the corporation that is rooted in the ideology of the market mechanism.

> *In a free enterprise, private property system, a corporate executive is an employee of the owners of the business. He has direct responsibility to his employers. That responsibility is to conduct the business in accordance with their desires, which generally will be to make as much money as possible. (Friedman 1970, p. 1)*

Friedman's concern was that the blurring of corporate executives' boundaries of responsibilities resulting from intrusions into social responsibilities would ultimately lead to an erosion of free enterprise and the onset of a socialist state. The very act of executives being involved in decisions that are in the domain of the political arena and not the business arena turns such executives into public employees and civil servants, although they remain employees of a private enterprise. And if they are public servants they must be elected through a political process and not chosen by shareholders. Friedman does concede that actions he terms 'social responsibility' may be in a corporation's self-interest and, therefore, justified to some limited extent.

There is growing evidence that corporations in the UK and the US are beginning to see their corporate purpose more widely than simply the pursuit of profit. The consensus in the scientific community on global warming is challenging corporations to include the needs of society more actively in their strategic decision making. However, this does not mean that the dominance of shareholder primacy is waning. For example, Hermes is one of the largest fund managers in the UK. In 2005 it had approximately £58 billion under management and manages assets of two of the four largest UK pension funds. It invests funds on behalf of around 200 clients, including pension funds, insurance companies, government entities, and financial institutions, as well as charities and endowments. As an institutional investor with an interest in corporate governance, Hermes believes that a company should be run in the long-term interest of its shareholders.[3] This approach is typical of the vast majority of listed companies in the UK and the US. It goes on to state that a company run in the long-term interest of its shareholders will have to manage the relationships with its employees, suppliers, and customers effectively.[4]

In contrast, Anita Roddick, the founder of The Body Shop, openly advocated the pursuit of social causes as a legitimate business practice (Roddick 2000). Given the

12

values of its founder, which clearly permeated the organization, it was somewhat surprising to see The Body Shop acquired by the French multinational L'Oréal in 2006. The former Chairman of Cadbury Schweppes, Adrian Cadbury, argues that the fact that some companies such as The Body Shop pursue wider objectives demonstrates that not all shareholders are concerned with maximizing profits (Cadbury 2002). For Cadbury, the issue for shareholders is not whether an organization is pursuing social objectives *per se* but, rather, that this is transparent and allows shareholders to make informed decisions about whether to invest in these companies.

12.4.2 The Agency Problem

The principal–agent framework has occupied economists since the time of the Scottish economist Adam Smith. In the eighteen century, Smith documented what is now known as the agency problem. The agency problem arises because of the separation between ownership of an organization and its control. It is inherent in the relationship between the providers of capital, referred to as the principal, and those who employ that capital, referred to as the agent.

AGENCY PROBLEM

this is inherent in the relationship between the providers of capital, referred to as the principal, and those who employ that capital on their behalf, referred to as the agent (see principal–agent problem)

> *The directors of such companies however being the managers rather of other people's money than of their own, it cannot well be expected that they should watch over it with the same anxious vigilance which the partners in private copartnery frequently watch over their own . . . Negligence and profusion, therefore, must always prevail. (Adam Smith, *The Wealth of Nations, 1776, quoted in Cadbury 2002, p. 4)*

Jensen and Meckling (1976) argue that an agency relationship exists when one party, the principal, contracts work from another party, the agent, to perform on their behalf (Fama and Jensen 1983). However, this agency relationship can give rise to a number of agency problems. These occur because no contract, however precisely drawn, can possibly take account of every conceivable action that an agent may engage in. The question arises as to how to ensure that the agent will always act in the best interest of the principal. The spread of modern corporations has brought about a separation between the owners of corporations and those who manage those corporations on their behalf. Agency costs occur when there is a divergence between these interests. Thus, agency costs can be seen to be the costs associated with monitoring agents to prevent them acting in their own interests.

AGENCY COSTS

the costs resulting from managers abusing their position as agent, and the associated costs of monitoring them to try to prevent this abuse

There is increasing pressure on institutional shareholders to take a more active role in the corporations in which they invest. This has been driven by corporate scandals which revealed a lack of non-executive director effectiveness, and a tendency, widely reported in the media, for boards of directors to be remunerated for poor performance. This has prompted a call for greater transparency and disclosure in an attempt to rebalance the information asymmetry and provide investors with more timely information about their company's activities. The agency problem continues to be important in governance terms because it has an influence on the structure and composition of boards, the requirements for disclosure, and the balance of power between shareholders and directors (Cadbury 2002).

Berle and Means argued that the separation of ownership from management has resulted in shareholders being unable to exercise any form of effective control over boards of directors. However, Cadbury argues that issues of accountability did not arise simply because ownership was divorced from management but more so because ownership was increasingly dispersed. As he states: 'It was the fragmentation of ownership that neutered the power of shareholders' (Cadbury 2002, p. 4). This dispersal of ownership is a double-edged sword. The fact that many holdings are small means that shareholders have no difficulty in selling their shares if they lose confidence in the management of their corporation. However, when the majority of shareholdings are small, shareholders are less able to hold the board of directors to account. However, as we shall see, small shareholdings in the UK and US have since given rise to majority holdings by powerful institutional investors.

Stakeholder theorists argue that this focus on the owners of corporations fails to take account of the needs of other individuals and groups, for example employees who have invested in the corporation's pension funds. The actions of those at the helm of the corporation have a direct impact on these individuals. (See Strategy Focus: Business and Morality at Farepak, which highlights the case of Farepak, a British savings club, which collapsed leaving its savers, many of them poor, without money they had been setting aside for a special occasion.) In this respect, a narrow definition of shareholder supremacy quickly comes into conflict with the realities of corporate responsibility. Institutional shareholders, they argue, are starting to recognize the value of an inclusive and motivated workforce and the external value of reputation. Similarly, the adoption of business ethics by corporations is increasingly seen as crucial to business sustainability (Fombrun and Foss 2004). We can address these issues in detail with an evaluation of stakeholder theory.

STAKEHOLDER THEORY

a view of corporations which argues that corporations should be run in the interests of all stakeholders

CASE STUDY 12.1

Business and Morality at Farepak

British families that have lost as much as £40m in the collapse of Farepak, a savings club, face a grim Christmas. Bankers, government, and regulators have all been blamed. But those who have the most serious questions to answer are the managers and directors of the business. Savers paid Farepak a few pounds a week in return for vouchers at the end of the year to spend on Christmas presents. About 25,000 self-employed agents collected contributions from about 150,000 savers. But on 13 October [2006], Farepak and its parent, a listed company called European Home Retail (EHR), called in the administrators. The immediate cause was inability to

The collapse of Farepak left more than 100,000 people without their expected Christmas hampers and savings.

secure further credit from their banker, HBOS. But bad business decisions were made over a long period.

Caveat emptor, some will say. But this was a saving scheme aimed at poor people who nevertheless wanted to save rather than borrow for Christmas. They were most unlikely to know that EHR was diversifying into online retail and television shopping, that it had made losses on an acquisition that went wrong, or that its liabilities exceeded its assets for the past two years.

The government regulates banks for precisely this reason. But it did not regulate Farepak because Farepak was not providing a financial service: all it offered was a way to pay for goods in advance. That is hard to regulate without limiting things such as magazine subscriptions or the deposit on a new flat as well. But the government must find ways to protect the vulnerable in whatever way they save their money. Sir Clive Thompson, the chairman of EHR, says that HBOS pulled the plug too soon. But EHR's accounts suggest it was struggling as early as 2003. HBOS could reasonably be expected to support Farepak for as long as possible, but at some point it had to stop extending funds.

Those who come out of the affair with the least credit are EHR's managers, directors, and family shareholders. They should have realized the business was in trouble some years ago. But rather than consolidate and cut back they tried to trade their way out of trouble by making acquisitions. Several dividends were paid out. That makes them morally responsible for what happened. They have no legal obligation to make recompense: there is no suggestion of lawbreaking. But their moral obligation is overwhelming. Any business involves taking risks. But these risks have turned out to be unwise and the losers are some of the least protected in society.

In Charles Dickens's *A Christmas Carol*, Scrooge is described as 'a squeezing, wrenching, grasping, scraping, clutching, covetous old sinner'. Those who have the means, and feel that they share in the blame, should give to those who have lost money. Those who do not, deserve a visit from all of the ghosts of Christmas past.

Source: 'Farepak and the Ghost of Christmas Present' *Financial Times*, 17 November 2006.

■ Questions

1. If *caveat emptor*—let the buyer beware—applies, the directors of Farepak should bear no responsibility for Farepak's collapse. Discuss.
2. Outline the extent to which you believe the executive management of Farepak have a responsibility to all their stakeholders, which includes their customers.
3. What role might regulation play in protecting the most vulnerable members of society from such financial collapses?

12.4.3 The Purpose of Corporations is to Meet the Needs of Stakeholders

We have seen that where the focus is on shareholders there is a presumption that shareholder value is the dominant objective of the organization. An alternative approach, which is seen to have acquired greater legitimacy following Enron and other major financial scandals, is a view of the organization that serves the interest of stakeholders. According to Freeman (1984, p. 46), stakeholders are those individuals or groups which affect or are affected by the achievement of an organization's objectives. They may include customers, suppliers, employees, government, competitors, the local community, and, of course, shareholders. The primary role of corporations as a vehicle to create shareholder value is contested by those who advocate a stakeholder model.

Stakeholders may be separated into internal and external stakeholders. Internal stakeholders are those whose impact is felt inside the organization, such as employees; external stakeholders have their impact outside the organization, such as shareholders. This distinction is somewhat arbitrary since some stakeholders, for example employees, may also be shareholders and, therefore, occupy both internal and external categories. Those who suggest that the corporation should serve stakeholders accept that shareholders are the owners of the organization but reject the notion that this somehow makes them of greater importance in the organization's decisions. In fact, they would argue that without the involvement of employees, suppliers, and customers there would be no business activity. Of course, the same argument can be said of shareholders as the providers of finance—without which there would be no organization.

Stakeholder theorists argue that many different stakeholders are affected by an organization's decisions and, therefore, the role of management is to balance the needs of each stakeholder rather than focus upon shareholders only. For example, the collapse of the Enron Corporation in the US was felt far beyond the capital loss to shareholders. Many employees associated with the organization found themselves out of work, suppliers suffered the loss of major contracts, and national and international economies experienced instability. The sheer size of some corporations requires an explicit recognition by board executives that their actions have effects way beyond their borders because of the linkages between the organization and the outside world through the globalized economy.

The problem is that stakeholders may exhibit conflicting needs, which makes the task of management in balancing these different interests very difficult. In an ideal world it would be great if managers first considered the impact of their strategic decisions upon different stakeholder groups. In reality this is seldom possible. This is precisely because stakeholders themselves may have different objectives, which means that managers are faced with trying to achieve multiple objectives. One way of trying to prioritize the different interest of stakeholders is to assess the influence they exert on an organization's objectives. For example, governments may have a benign interest in the activities of organizations but be forced to exercise their legislative powers when organizations behave in an unacceptable manner.

An example of government intervention was apparent during BP's disastrous oil rig explosion which resulted in eleven deaths and unleashed oil from a well head one mile down into the Gulf of Mexico in 2010. This unprecedented threat to marine life and coastal livelihoods led to a personal reprimand of BP's chief executive Tony Hayward and his company by US President, Barack Obama. As well as the tens of billions of pounds wiped off BP's share price during the incident the organization faced a major loss to its corporate reputation. As events unfolded the British CEO's position became increasingly untenable and he was replaced by an American. In the UK there is a reliance on the self-regulation of corporations.

A former Chancellor of the Exchequer, Nigel Lawson, stated emphatically, 'the business of government is not the government of business'. This was a signal to financial markets and the business community that the Conservative government, of which he was a member, did not expect to regulate the business community. It was assumed that self-regulation would ensure that organizations behaved responsibly. In the US, the enactment of Sarbanes–Oxley has signalled a move away from reliance solely on self-regulation, and marks a recognition of the responsibilities of corporations in the globalized economy.

When Nike's operations abroad did not conform to US health and safety standards for their overseas workers, including minimum age restrictions on employees, this caused an outcry and was reported worldwide. Although the decision to employ workers abroad was to enhance profitability, the result was a damaged reputation and an initial fall in sales. This shows that even where an organization's priority is to create value for its shareholders, it cannot afford to do so without some understanding of the expectations of stakeholders and society. Those who adopt a stakeholder perspective expect that organizations will actively pursue measures which result in a net welfare gain to the environment and society. As such, their criteria for successful performance will differ markedly from shareholder maximization. In the modern age an organization cannot afford to ignore the expectations of stakeholders, and many firms have started to move away from simply paying lip service to important environment issues. The oil industry, arguably one of the worst polluters, has begun to engage stakeholders in debate about renewable sources of energy. This is not altruism but a realization that their interests are inextricably tied to the interests of their wider stakeholders. Table 12.1 summarizes the key elements of agency and stakeholder theory.

	Agency theory	Stakeholder theory
Main players	Principal (owners/shareholders), agent (manager)	Employees, customers, suppliers, shareholders, local community, government
Key objectives	Value maximization, i.e. maximize shareholders' interests	Multiple objectives to try to benefit all stakeholders
Strengths	Clear and achievable	Recognizes that long-term success of the organization depends on the participation of all stakeholders
Weakness	Maximizing shareholder wealth fails to motivate employees	Pursuit of multiple objectives is deemed unrealistic and too difficult for managers to achieve
Key protagonists	Milton Friedman (1962, 1970)	R.E. Freeman (1984)

TABLE 12.1
A comparison of agency and stakeholder theory

The Japanese concept of *kyosei*, loosely translated as 'living and working for the common good' has become a philosophy of doing business for some Japanese corporations (Baukol 2002). From the perspective of *kyosei*, a corporation is not a self-sufficient organism set apart from society but is outward looking, aware of its duty to people outside its organization such as customers, suppliers, and the community. By taking account of this wider network of relationships, the corporation can be profitable and sustainable over the long run. Baukol argues that business leadership is not just about financial success, but that business leaders should also be working to improve their societies, ensuring social, economic, and environmental sustainability.

From this perspective the proper course of corporate governance is to manage the relationship of the corporation with its stakeholders. Although Baukol acknowledges that corporations will continue to create much of the wealth of society he sees that this is only possible because a corporation is a set of relationships among stakeholders,

12

each of whom plays a role in the success of the corporation. See Strategy Focus: Corporate Social Responsibility at Time Warner, which illustrates how a global media corporation meets the needs of shareholders whilst also pursuing standards of business conduct based on a clear, codified set of ethical values. These standards of business conduct are endorsed by Time Warner's chairman and chief executive. Corporate social responsibility occurs when an organization takes into account the impact of its strategic decisions on society. Increasingly corporations are moving towards the position espoused by Time Warner that the success of the organization and corporate social responsibility are simply two sides of the same coin. In 2007, the British retailer Marks & Spencer announced a £200 million five-year plan to make the company carbon neutral. As part of a planned reduction in its air freight Marks & Spencer will look to source its food from the UK and the Republic of Ireland where it can. Its CEO at the time, Stuart Rose, said, 'we believe responsible business can be profitable business'.

STRATEGY FOCUS
Corporate Social Responsibility at Time Warner

Dear Time Warner Colleagues:

I'm pleased to share with you Time Warner's Standards of Business Conduct (SBC). The SBC was updated this year to make it easier for employees to use and to address some of the business issues that we currently face. As always, the SBC reflects our commitment to maintaining the highest level of integrity and ethics in the way we operate our businesses. This brochure should serve as your guide on how to interact with our key stakeholders, including competitors, partners, government agencies and fellow employees.

The responsibility for upholding the highest standards of conduct at Time Warner belongs to each and every one of us. If we fail to hold ourselves and each other accountable for doing the right thing, we're putting the future success of our Company and the reputation of our businesses—which are recognized and trusted throughout the world—at great risk. We understand that the SBC doesn't provide answers to all of the complex business situations you may face on a daily basis. That's why it's so important to ask questions if you're just not sure about the right thing to do. The Ethics & Compliance Office is here to help.

Sincerely,
Jeff Bewkes, Chairman & CEO

We must act with integrity at all times in doing our jobs. We are committed to promoting a culture throughout the Company of integrity, honesty, incorruptibility and fair dealing in everything we do. This means that we must all stand by the following principles:

- We do not tolerate acts of fraud. Fraud, whether large or small, harms our Company, our employees and our stockholders. We must also protect Company assets from theft, waste and misuse.

- We will be truthful and honest in all statements made in performing our jobs. When we prepare Company reports and documents of any kind (such as time sheets, personal leave sheets, expense reports and corporate financial statements), we should do so honestly and with care. False statements, particularly those made to the government and regulatory agencies, not only are contrary to this standard, but also may be illegal and carry severe consequences for both the Company and the individual employee.

- We do not seek competitive advantages through illegal or unethical business practices. Each of us should deal fairly and ethically with our customers, service providers, suppliers, competitors, colleagues and government officials and agencies. Examples of unfair and unethical dealings that are not tolerated by the Company include:

  ◦ Making false or deceptive statements to influence someone to enter into a contract or take any action.

  ◦ Committing industrial espionage to acquire competitors' trade secrets.

  ◦ Soliciting or offering bribes or kickbacks to get or award business.

  ◦ Making false or misleading comments about competitors' products or services.

  ◦ Making false or misleading claims about Time Warner, its divisions or our products.

Source: *Time Warner Standards of Business Conduct*, 29 April 2010 at www.timewarner.com

For further discussion on the importance of corporate social responsibility for organizations go to the Online Resource Centre and see the Key Work feature. www.oxfordtextbooks.co.uk/orc/henry2e/

12

In this era of corporate collapse an organization that actively pursues a socially responsible attitude can enhance its corporate reputation, which may help it achieve a sustainable competitive advantage.

We can see that without each stakeholder the corporation cannot function efficiently or cannot function at all. Therefore, without capital and shareholders there is no corporate entity. Without banks and other debt investors, the corporation cannot maximize its ability to earn a return on its capital. But without customers there will be no business for the corporation to do. Similarly, without employees, the corporation will be unable to do business. And, if the community loses confidence in a corporation, it may quickly lose its business legitimacy, resulting in collapse. It is only by aligning and attending to the needs of different stakeholders that the corporation fulfils its duty to society—to promote prosperity in a sustainable manner. Given that a corporation has duties and responsibilities to different stakeholders, this may cause conflict about how a corporation should decide what to do. Baukol (2002) asserts this is the role of corporate governance: 'Corporate governance is the mechanism by which the values, principles, management policies, and procedures of a corporation are made manifest in the real world.' Therefore, it follows that the fundamental basis of corporate governance and responsibility is the value system of the corporation. This might include principles such as respect and dignity for all, or the use of transparent accounting, or a concern for the environment, among others.

Those who argue that within business the owners' needs are paramount see problems with the stakeholder approach. Sternberg (1997) argues that trying to balance stakeholder needs or benefits is unworkable. This is because using Freeman's definition of stakeholders leads to an infinite number of stakeholder needs. Stakeholder analysis, she believes, cannot offer guidance as to which stakeholders should be selected. And if it could, it does not explain what counts as a bona fide benefit. Importantly, no guidance is provided as to what weighting each stakeholder group should have *vis-à-vis* other stakeholders. For Sternberg, corporate governance is quite simply corporate actions that ensure that the objectives of the shareholders are adhered to. Can the divide between shareholder value maximization and stakeholder theory be bridged? Jensen (2005) proposes *enlightened value maximization* as a way in which organizations can achieve a trade-off between the competing needs of stakeholders. This is accomplished by accepting the maximization of the long-run value of the organization as the criterion for trade-offs between competing stakeholders. This single long-term objective, it is argued, solves the dilemmas managers are faced with when they try to achieve the multiple objectives inherent in stakeholder theory. It is arguable whether proponents of stakeholder theory would accept this as a dispassionate assessment of the corporation's activities or simply another way of saying that shareholders' needs predominate, albeit over *the long-term*.

However business is defined, it is clear that the role of corporations is changing. Cadbury (2002, p. 217) states: 'society's expectations of the role of companies in the community are changing and . . . Companies need to engage with those groups which can affect their ability to conduct their businesses'. He goes on to say that 'companies should stand their ground for what they believe to be in their and society's interests, even if this may lead at times to confrontation'.

12

12.5 Corporate Collapse and Corporate Governance Codes

There is a presumption that corporate managers can be left to act in the best interests of shareholders. This thinking is based on the belief that a poorly performing corporation will be the subject of takeovers, the very threat of which is sufficient to discipline managers to act in the shareholders' interests. However, the reality does not always bear this out. Instead of this threat galvanizing boards of directors to improve their performance, it often leads to them erecting myriad defences.

> We have assessed that the market for corporate control is not a very effective way to discipline management. If target shareholders win, bidder shareholders break even or lose, and furthermore efficiency gains are quite low (Gugler 2001, cited by Cadbury 2002, p. 9)

In this respect, takeovers are a costly and inefficient way to change the board of directors. A more efficient way to encourage better corporate performance might be for institutional investors to engage in dialogue with boards of directors. According to the Department of Trade and Industry (DTI), institutions now hold around 75 per cent of the shares of UK companies. Cadbury suggests that this change in the pattern of share ownership in favour of investing institutions has encouraged the institutions to use their influence with boards. Therefore, rather than simply selling their shareholdings, *exit* is giving way to *voice*, as shareholders seek to improve their returns.

Corporate governance came to prominence following a number of high-profile corporate collapses. At the same time there was growing controversy over what was seen as excessive directors' pay and rewarding of poorly performing directors. Over the past years the UK has initiated a series of investigations into ways to improve the corporate governance of UK listed companies. These investigations have been high profile, led by experienced individuals who have given their names to the final reports. They include the Cadbury Report (1992), the Greenbury Report (1995), the Hampel Report (1998), and the Higgs Report (2003). In addition, there have been specialist reviews such as those led by Paul Myners (DTI 1996; HM Treasury 2001) into institutional investment. The UK government completed a long-running investigation associated with Company Law Review (DTI 2001). We can address the response to these corporate failures by looking at the Cadbury Committee Report and subsequent Hampel Committee Report. In assessing the collapse of Enron we will also draw attention to the Higgs Report (2003) on the role of non-executive directors.

12

12.5.1 The Cadbury Committee (1992)

The Committee on the Financial Aspects of Corporate Governance, commonly referred to as the Cadbury Committee, was instituted in 1991 and reported its findings in 1992. It was appointed in the aftermath of the collapse of prominent UK listed companies such as Polly Peck, Bank of Credit and Commerce International, and Maxwell Communications Corporation. The Committee's sponsors were concerned that the lack of public confidence in financial reporting and the ability of auditors to provide the safeguards sought and expected by users of company reports would undermine London as a major financial centre (Cadbury 2002). The voluntary codes of conduct contained in the report have since gained international currency, although they are not without their critics. Some argue that the focus on the control and reporting functions of boards and the role of auditors is narrow, omitting as it does a substantive role for stakeholders.

The Committee's recommendations are focused on the control and reporting functions of boards of directors and on the role of auditors, although it recognized that it also has a contribution to make to the promotion of good corporate governance (Cadbury 1992). At the heart of the Committee's recommendations is a Code of Best Practice designed to achieve the necessary high standards of corporate behaviour. All listed companies registered in the UK must state whether they are complying with the Code and give reasons for any areas for non-compliance. This allows shareholders to make a more informed decision about the companies in which they may want to invest.

The Committee acknowledged that 'no system of control can eliminate risk of fraud without so shackling companies as to impede their ability to compete in the marketplace' (Cadbury 1992). The belief that self-regulation, based on compliance with a voluntary code coupled with disclosure, will prove more effective than a statutory code is rooted in a belief in the merits of the market mechanism. Nevertheless, the Report contained a veiled threat which implied that if companies were to fail to adopt its Code then legislation was a real possibility: 'We recognize, however, that if companies do not back our recommendations, it is probable that legislation and external regulation will be sought to deal with some of the underlying problems which the report identifies' (Cadbury 1992, para. 1.10).

Some of the main recommendations of the Cadbury Report are as follows:[5]

- The board of directors should meet regularly, retain full and effective control over the company, and monitor the executive management.

- A division of responsibilities at the head of the company to ensure that no one individual has unfettered powers of decision.

- Directors' contracts should not exceed three years without shareholders' approval.

- The majority of non-executive directors should be independent of management and other business matters that might affect their judgement.

- Directors' pay should be subject to the recommendations of a remuneration committee made up of non-executive directors.
- Non-executive directors should be selected through a formal process and by the whole board.

These recommendations were seen as a route to ensuring greater transparency and accountability of board members. For example, the proposal of *a division of respon-sibilities at the head of the company* was an attempt to separate the positions of CEO and chairman such that no one individual had *unfettered powers* of decision making. It was also a recognition that the roles of the chairman and the CEO are distinct. Therefore, unless the corporation has a good reason for keeping them combined, they should be separated. A higher profile was given to non-executive directors. Greater emphasis was placed on their independence of judgement from executive board members. Their selection was to be transparent and fair, undertaken through a formal process. The Cadbury Report also recommended that their fee be tied to the amount of time they devoted to the company.

All listed companies had to 'comply' or 'explain'. That is, they either comply with the code or explain in their annual report and accounts *why* they are unable to do so. This puts the emphasis on the board of directors and gives shareholders an oppor-tunity to see which corporations are adhering to the code.

12.5.2 The Hampel Committee (1998)

The Committee on Corporate Governance was established by the chairman of the Financial Reporting Council and chaired by Sir Ronald Hampel to promote high standards of corporate governance (Hampel 1998). In its review of the Cadbury Report and the Greenbury Report on directors' remuneration, the Hampel Com-mittee agreed that the importance of corporate governance lies in its contribution to business prosperity and to accountability. However, it argued that in the UK the latter had preoccupied the public debate and it was time to correct this imbalance.

> *Public companies are now among the most accountable organizations in society. . . . We strongly endorse this accountability and we recognize the contribution of the Cadbury and Greenbury Committees. But the emphasis on accountability has tended to obscure a board's first responsibility—to enhance the prosperity of the business over time. (Hampel 1998, p. 7)*

The Committee's concern was that a focus on rules and regulations implied a formula for success, and therefore prosperity, whereas corporate governance is not a matter of prescribing rules but instead applying broad principles flexibly according to the different circumstances facing companies. The Hampel Committee saw no inconsis-tency in not following some Cadbury Report guidelines, such as the separation of

12

the roles of chairman and chief executive officer, arguing that guidelines will be appropriate in most cases but not all. Indeed, the Cadbury Report allows for companies to explain circumstances in which they may feel that it is not in their interest to follow the guidelines. In such cases, the Hampel Committee argued, it would be damaging to a company's reputation if its explanation for non-compliance were rejected out of hand.

The Hampel Report confirmed the enhancement over time of shareholder investment as the overriding objective of companies, but it did so iterating that business prosperity involved many economic actors working together. Thus, directors can meet their obligations to shareholders and obtain long-term shareholder value only by developing and sustaining stakeholder relationships. Good governance ensures that stakeholders with a relevant interest in the company's business are fully taken into account (Hampel 1998). For the Hampel Committee, companies need to be mindful of their responsibilities but this needs to be couched within structures and principles that allow businesses to grow and prosper. The Hampel Report argued that previous reports (including Cadbury) had placed too great a burden on what it referred to as 'box-ticking' at the expense of wealth creation, thereby placing an unwelcome burden on corporations. In assessing the impact of the Cadbury Report, the Hampel Report does concede, 'it is generally accepted that implementation of the code's provisions has led to higher standards of governance and greater awareness of their importance' (Hampel 1998, p. 9).

It is widely accepted that of all the codes addressing corporate governance issues, the Cadbury Report has had the greatest impact on corporate governance development around the world. Many corporate governance reports, including the King Reports I and II of South Africa, acknowledge their debt to Cadbury. These and other reports tend to use the Cadbury Report as a blueprint, but tailor the specifics to suit their individual country's needs.

12.5.3 The Role of Non-Executive Directors

The collapse of Enron, a former energy trading giant, was felt far beyond the owners of the corporation. It wiped out shareholders' investments and employees' retirement savings, and led to 21,000 people losing their employment. Enron, once the seventh-largest company in the US, filed for bankruptcy in December 2001 with debts of £18 billion. It had hidden these mounting debts through a series of complex financial dealings. Its collapse wiped out more than $60 billion in market value. It took sixteen years for Enron to go from $10 billion of assets to $65 billion of assets; it took twenty-four days to go bankrupt. At the time Enron was praised by analysts as a new business model. The CEO's use of market-to-market accounting allowed Enron to book potential future profits on the day a deal was signed irrespective of how much money was actually realized. For example, Enron lost $1 billion on a power plant in India but the company executives were paid multi-million dollar bonuses on

Enron management give evidence at the trial. Jeffrey Skilling (left), the former chief executive of Enron, and company founder, Kenneth Lay (not pictured), were found guilty of defrauding investors by using off-balance-sheet deals to hide debts and inflate profits.

© Martin H. Simon/Corbis

the basis of profits which never materialized. In 2000, Fortune 500 voted Enron as America's most admired, innovative company. It is clear that the demise of Enron owed much to inadequate checks by its external auditors Arthur Andersen and weak controls within the company. In 2001 Andersen were paid $1 million a week by Enron. Andersen was taken over when its corporate status became untenable. This followed the shredding of documents relating to Enron's collapse by Andersen employees. Amanda Martin-Brock, a former Enron executive, has said that the fatal flaw at Enron was 'pride, then arrogance, intolerance and greed.'

In September 2006, Andrew Fastow, the former chief financial officer credited with the financial schemes that brought Enron down, was jailed for six years. Fastow pleaded guilty in 2004 and cooperated with prosecutors during the trial. His evidence helped prosecutors gain a conviction against Enron founder Kenneth Lay and CEO Jeffrey Skilling. In May 2006, Skilling and Lay were found guilty of defrauding investors by using off-balance-sheet deals to hide debts and inflate profits. In October 2006 Jeffrey Skilling received a jail sentence of twenty-four years and four months. Both Skilling and Lay had tried to argue that the crisis of confidence that undid Enron was caused by a few rogue employees, primarily Andrew Fastow. In fact, Andrew Fastow artificially maintained the share price through 'structured finance'. He devised hundreds of special companies to bury Enron's debt where investors could not see it. To outside investors it appeared that cash was coming into the company while at the same time Fastow used his special companies to perform a magic trick—prop up Enron's share price by making its debt disappear. The most important special company set up by Fastow was called LJM. Skilling, Lay, and the Enron board had all signed off on Fastow's LJM funds. Following his subsequent death, the courts have

12

ruled that the conviction against Kenneth Lay cannot stand. This is because his death effectively rules out the possibility of an appeal which his legal team were planning to mount. These lengthy jail terms are evidence that the US authorities are not prepared to countenance such damaging white-collar crimes. To date, the longest sentence has been given to Bernard Ebbers, the founder of WorldCom, who received a twenty-five year sentence. The former Tyco chairman Dennis Kozlowski received an eight to twenty-five year sentence. In the Enron case, the prosecution had pushed for a lengthy jail sentence for the former CEO arguing that the corporation's collapse had far-reaching repercussions. For one the integrity of the market was damaged by what occurred at Enron as individuals lost their confidence in the market economy. It is arguably this attack on the integrity of the market that has prompted reforms in the way companies report their finances.

The collapse of Enron is particularly disturbing given the wealth of experience of non-executive directors that sat on the board. These included a British former cabinet minister and Energy Secretary, Lord Wakeham. The implosion of Enron and WorldCom suggested to the US government that the self-regulatory regime in the US was not working properly. It was quite apparent that it proved incapable of dealing with the largesse of corporate greed. Corporations like Enron, Arthur Andersen, and WorldCom, which were widely admired, would be remembered as being led by individuals who put personal gain above the needs of the corporations' owners. The role of non-executive directors at Enron is interesting. Their high salaries (each was paid a minimum of $350,000), long tenures (they had an average of seventeen years service), and lack of a nominating committee to ensure transparency should have raised concerns earlier (Monks and Minow 2004). Fast forward less than a decade and we have the collapse of a major US investment bank, Lehman Brothers, as a result of the same arrogance and greed which brought down Enron. We might ask where were the lessons learned from Enron and the checks and balances in the system to prevent such a collapse.

In the UK this lack of accountability of non-executive directors led to the Higgs Report which was undertaken to look at *the role and effectiveness of non-executive directors* (Higgs 2003). A decade earlier the Cadbury Committee had said that non-executive directors required independence of judgement if they were to perform their role effectively. The collapse of Enron cast doubt on the model of effective non-executive directors challenging the decisions of executive board directors. Too often non-executive directors were seen as merely *rubber-stamping* decisions taken by executive directors. The recommendations of the Higgs Report included the following:

• Non-executive directors should meet as a group at least once a year without executive directors being present.

• The board should inform shareholders why they believe an individual should be appointed as a non-executive director and how they meet the requirements of the role.

- A full-time executive director should not hold more than one non-executive direc-
  torship or become chairman of a major corporation.

These and other recommendations sought to tighten the role of non-executive
directors in their accountability to shareholders. Although the UK stopped short of
legislation, the US was less reticent; it enacted sweeping legislation in the form of the
Sarbanes–Oxley Act.

12.5.4 The Sarbanes–Oxley Act 2002

The Sarbanes–Oxley Act has been called a number of things—a knee-jerk reaction, a
piece of poorly drafted legislation, perhaps even tick-boxing *ad infinitum*. A deeper
question that Sarbanes–Oxley does not address is whether we can (or indeed should)
legislate for human greed. Sarbanes–Oxley was enacted in July 2002 by the US
Congress. It was proposed by Republican Congressman Michael G. Oxley and
Democratic Senator Paul Sarbanes. It seeks to correct market imperfections by introducing financial disclosure rules and enhancements to statutory enforcements. It is
perhaps too early to measure the impact of Sarbanes–Oxley, but anecdotal evidence suggests that many American corporations are struggling with the procedures
necessary to adhere to this law. Harder evidence comes from stock market flotations.
In 2000, nine out of every ten dollars in the world's initial public offerings were
raised *in* America. In 2005, nine out of every ten dollars were raised *outside* America.
This loss of initial offerings, primarily to the London Stock Exchange's Alternative
Investment Market, is blamed on America's costly Sarbanes–Oxley Act (*Economist*
2006). The main recommendations of Sarbanes–Oxley include the following:

- Chief executives now have to attest personally for the accuracy of company
  accounts; this is a concern for corporations wishing to list in New York and may
  explain the flight of funds to London.
- A higher standard for board members who sit on the audit committee.
- The prevention of loans to executives.
- Further criminal and civil penalties for securities violations.

In November 2006, the then US Treasury Secretary Henry Paulson stated that the
Sarbanes–Oxley Act did not need to change. However, he did go on to say that
the government should look at how the rules were being enforced. He pointed to the
need for 'high standards of integrity and accountability' in corporate governance
alongside the need for 'innovation, growth, and competitiveness'. Also, if America's
capital markets are not to be disadvantaged, its regulatory regime must be more
responsive to changes in the marketplace. The concern of US corporations is that
they are now embroiled in far too much regulation. This echoes comments made
by the Hampel Committee almost a decade earlier with respect to UK corporations
after publication of the Cadbury Report. However, the financial crisis that started in

12

2007–08 from the collapse of major financial institutions may actually suggest that financial institutions require more robust regulation.

12.5.5 Excessive Executive Pay

A concern with excessive executive pay is always topical. In the UK the Greenbury Report reported on investor concerns over excessive directors' pay (Greenbury 1995). This followed the huge pay increases awarded to the heads of the recently privatized public utilities. We should be clear that the issue is not one of high salaries *per se* but the difference between fair and excessive compensation. Institutional investors are becoming increasingly vocal about what is seen as compensation for poor performance and the setting of easy bonus targets. In 2003, angry shareholders voted against the pay package of Jean-Pierre Garnier, the boss of GlaxoSmithKline (GSK), because it would reward him handsomely even if he were to fail.[6] In 2006, the board of the US retailer Home Depot launched a review of its executive compensation package following criticisms of the pay awarded to its CEO, Bob Nardelli.[7] He received over $124 million in less than six years. Over the same period Home Depot's share price fell 15 per cent. The board of Home Depot were content to award these sums because they said the CEO met the targets set for him (see Strategy Focus: Home Depot).

For more discussion on the controversy surrounding executive remuneration go to the Online Resource Centre and see the Key Work feature. www.oxfordtextbooks.co.uk/orc/henry2e/

 STRATEGY FOCUS
Home Depot

Home Depot's board has launched a review of its executive compensation policies following criticism of the soaring pay awarded to Bob Nardelli, chief executive. Bonnie Hill, head of the retailer's compensation committee, said directors were consulting with investors and outside experts to make sure that executive pay was aligned with shareholders' interests.

Mr Nardelli is at the centre of a growing campaign by activist shareholders against excessive executive compensation, having received more than $124m since joining the company nearly six years ago. Over the same period, Home Depot's share price has fallen by 15 per cent. 'We've been working with consultants and experts that are helping us sort through this issue and we've sat down with shareholder groups to listen to their concerns,' Ms Hill said. She added that it was too soon to say whether any changes would be made to how Mr Nardelli's pay is determined. A decision is expected before the end of the year.

Investor anger against Home Depot came to a head at the company's annual meeting in May, when Mr Nardelli refused to answer questions about his salary and more than 30 per cent of voting shareholders withheld support for his re-election to the board. Ms Hill said directors were sensitive to investor frustration about the sagging stock price but argued that the company's underlying performance was strong. 'Bob has met all of the performance metrics that have been set for him,' she said.

Source: 'Home Depot to review pay policy' *Financial Times*, 19 September 2006.

A recent study of 367 big American firms by the Institute for Policy Studies found that in 2004 the ratio of chief executives' compensation to the pay of the average production worker increased to 431 to 1, from 301 to 1 in 2003. In 1990 the ratio was 107 to 1, and in 1982 it was 42 to 1.[8] In the UK in 2005, the top FTSE 100 chief executives earned ninety-eight times more than the typical employee; in 2000 it was thirty-nine times more than the average employee. The average total earnings of a chief executive were almost £2.9 million in the year to July 2006.[9]

STRATEGY FOCUS
Multiple Pay

Jeffrey Immelt, chairman and chief executive of General Electric, has urged company leaders in the US to ensure their pay does not dramatically outstrip that of their senior managers and to limit the influence of compensation consultants. Mr Immelt's intervention in the debate over executive pay—featured in a video interview with the *Financial Times*—underlines the growing importance of the issue for shareholders and executives of America's largest companies. 'These are public jobs, there were so many abuses in the late 90s and in the early part of this century and that created concerns,' he said.

Mr Immelt argued that chief executives should not have multi-year contracts, which could lead to large pay-offs if they were dismissed, and the bulk of their compensation should be linked to performance. Yesterday, the FT revealed that a group of leading public pension funds had urged the top 25 companies in the US, including GE, to ban pay consultants from advising the board and working on other company matters.

Mr Immelt, who took over the leadership of the industrial conglomerate five years ago from Jack Welch, did not mention the letter but said the board should be the final judge of executive pay. 'I think it should be based on the good judgment of the compensation committees, the board and the CEO,' he said. 'I don't think consultants should be involved.'

In a separate conversation with the FT, he said that, to motivate staff and avoid excesses, chief executives' pay should remain within a small multiple of the pay of their 25 most senior managers. The key relationship is the one between the CEO and the top 25 managers in the company because that is the key team. Should the CEO make five times, three times, or twice what this group make? That is debatable, but 20 times is lunacy,' he said. Mr Immelt, who last year received $3.2m in salary and no cash bonus, added that his pay was within the 2–3 times range.

Source: 'Immelt wades into debate over pay' *Financial Times*, 3 November 2006.

At the forefront of changes to executives' pay are chief executives like Jeffrey Immelt (see Strategy Focus: Multiple Pay). The CEO and chairman of GE has been urging business leaders to make sure that their pay does not substantially outstrip that of their senior managers.[10] He believes that if staff are to remain motivated and excess remuneration avoided, then chief executives' pay should be a small multiple of that of their twenty-five most senior managers. He argues that a multiple that represents up to five times what senior mangers make is up for discussion. However, a multiple of twenty times he regards as madness. His own pay is in the range of two to three times that of his top twenty managers. The issue of excessive executive pay is discussed in the Case Study: Excessive Executive Remuneration—Fat Cats, which looks at the issues surrounding fair and excessive compensation, and whether chief executives' pay should represent some multiple of the average worker's pay within the organization.

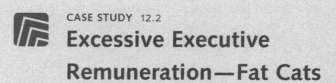

CASE STUDY 12.2
Excessive Executive Remuneration—Fat Cats

I can today report an exciting new development concerning the future employment prospects of my 19-month-old daughter—a theme that, attentive readers may recall, has occupied this column in the past. She has now perfected the art of calling for more food, even as her mouth is being filled with another spoonful. A successful career as a chief executive (CEO) can be only a matter of months away. A cheap shot? Perhaps. If so, it is the only cheap thing about the endless debate on 'fat cat' pay. Kevin Murphy, a professor at the University of Southern California's Marshall School of Business, estimates that average CEO pay at S&P 500 companies stands at $10.5m, taking account of options and bonus payments. That figure is four times what it was in 1993.

In the UK, Incomes Data Services reports that the average pay of a FTSE100 company boss went up by 43 per cent last year while average earnings rose only 3.7 per cent. The average overall pay of top UK chief executives now stands at £2.9m—86 times what a typical employee receives. In the US, Prof Murphy suggests that average CEO pay is an amazing 369 times as large as an ordinary worker's salary. Legislators and activists of all kinds have been unable to halt the executive pay bandwagon. And so much for the power of the press! Chief executives and remuneration committees seem to have decided that a day or two's bad publicity is a price well worth paying for the riches that are now available to business leaders. Well-intentioned interventions have proved counter-productive.

In the US in the early 1990s, Congress removed tax breaks on executive pay exceeding $1m. This both encouraged the growth in alternative forms of payment, such as options, that were to be abused so extensively in the following years, and also served as an unofficial floor below which no self-respecting CEO, of however modest an enterprise, wanted to allow his salary to fall. Greater transparency has made it easier for company bosses to compare their respective pay levels, leading to increased jockeying for bigger packages. Not everybody's pay can be in the upper quartile at the same time, of course, but that may not stop people from trying to get there. Something has happened as far as attitudes to immense wealth are concerned.

The triumphant march of capitalism, which began stutteringly with the fall of communism in 1989, is now reaching top speed in spite of corporate scandals and the volatility of equity and commodity markets. Its victory was saluted enthusiastically by Lester Thurow, a professor at the Sloan School of Management at MIT, in his 1999 book, *Building Wealth*. Here he accurately described the underlying ethos that has made possible the monster pay packages of today. 'Wealth ultimately is the way the score is kept in capitalism,' he wrote. 'Wealth has always been important in the personal pecking order but it has become increasingly the only dimension by which personal worth is measured. It is the only game to play if you want to prove your mettle. It is the big leagues. If you do not play there, by definition you are second rate.'

© iStockphoto.com/Nicholas Monu

12

Are vast CEO salaries simply a question of supply and demand? Boards and shareholders want the best available person to lead the organization and, perhaps, hardly anyone will be up to the job. Those who are can command a high price. In a fascinating recent podcast, Wayne Guay, a professor at the Wharton School of the University of Pennsylvania, explains why CEO pay has reached such extraordinary levels. He is unimpressed by the data that reveal the gap between CEO pay and that of ordinary employees—like comparing 'a carpenter to a computer programmer', he says. (Remind me, what did that nice young carpenter from Nazareth say about the rich and the Kingdom of Heaven?)

Supercharged salaries seem to be the product of a self-perpetuating system. Pay consultants advise their clients on the latest schemes to reward performance, headhunters push up the asking price for 'talent', while non-executive directors sit on each other's pay review boards. It all looks a bit cosy. But this is merely the logical outcome of a world where, as Prof. Thurow explains, anyone with any sense is trying to earn as much as possible as quickly as possible.

Income inequality is beginning to worry people on all points of the political spectrum. Pay for ordinary workers in the developed world seems to be standing still while their leaders continue to make hay. But can one executive really claim so much credit, and be so disproportionately rewarded, for the results achieved by a huge multinational corporation? That is doubtful at best. The problem cannot be regulated away. Instead, what John Kay calls the 'disciplined pluralism' of markets may be our best bet, a world where people's behaviour is regulated by values and not by rules. But there is little evidence at the moment of the sense of shame needed to inhibit the spread of excessive pay.

We should ask the super-rich CEO the same searing question that was put to Senator Joe McCarthy by special counsel Joseph Welch at the Army–McCarthy hearings of 1954: 'Have you no sense of decency, sir, at long last? Have you left no sense of decency?' Picture the CEO who answers 'no' to that question. He may look a bit like a certain 19-month-old of my acquaintance, the one with half-chewed lumps of food still dribbling down her face.

Source: 'Fat cat pay packages show no signs of causing indigestion' *Financial Times*, 31 October 2006.

▪ Questions

1. To what extent is chief executive pay simply a matter of demand and supply?
2. As the gap between CEO pay and the salary of the average worker in the same organization continues to widen, what does this say about the role of stakeholders in these corporations?
3. Comment on whether you believe CEO pay reflects their superior performance, improving market conditions largely outside their control, corporate largesse, or some combination of all three.

12.6 Corporate Governance Reform

We can identify three different perspectives on corporate governance reform (O'Sullivan 2003). The first is that the existing system of corporate governance may need some revision, but only around the edges. Second, the system of corporate governance that assumes shareholder primacy needs to be changed, albeit leaving shareholders at the centre. Third, the primacy of shareholders is itself open to question. The proponents of minor revisions to the existing system argue that a debate about the purpose of the corporation is not required. They see the proper role of the corporations as being the maximization of shareholder value (Friedman 1970). From this perspective corporate governance in the real world is not without faults but corporate failures such as Enron, WorldCom, and Tyco are presented as statistical outliers rather than a systemic problem. The second perspective argues that reforms need to be more radical. Whilst these reformers apportion some blame to the auditors and regulators, they point out that it was the governance mechanisms themselves which failed. This perspective does not, however, question shareholder primacy. A third perspective asks whose interest corporations should be run in. It does not take it as self-evident that corporations should be run in shareholders' interest.

For Baukol (2002) corporate governance should satisfy the needs of different stakeholders while contributing to the sustainable growth of the organization, and making a contribution to society. The outworking of this means that its reputation is enhanced, its employees are efficient, and shareholders receive an acceptable return on their investment. From this perspective corporate governance exists to counteract the tendency to be selfish and short-sighted. In essence, corporate governance aligns the interests of management, shareholders, and other stakeholders. It is based on the corporation's values but is the responsibility of all members of the corporation.

In the UK and the US discussions of corporate governance have invariably put shareholders above stakeholders, such as employees. Armour *et al.* (2003) note that both the Sarbanes–Oxley Act in the US and the Higgs Report in the UK completely ignore stakeholder claims in favour of further entrenching accountability to shareholders. They undertook a study of corporate governance institutions in the UK and found that 'certain core institutions—takeover regulations, corporate governance codes and the law relating to directors' fiduciary duties are indeed highly shareholder orientated' (Armour *et al.* 2003, p. 531). On the basis of their analyses of UK institutions, Armour *et al.* reject the claim made by some writers (Hansmann and Kraakman 2001) that the fundamental issues of corporate ownership have been settled in favour of the shareholder value model. They point out that the institutions which support the shareholder model, such as the City Code on Takeover and Mergers, and the corporate governance codes in the UK are of recent origin.

Those who adopt the stakeholder model of corporate governance recognize a central role for the corporation in wealth creation but see this in the wider context of meeting differing stakeholders' needs. Whilst accepting the corporation as a force

12

for economic prosperity and social well-being, they argue that this wealth creation requires all stakeholders to actively participate, and all stakeholders, including society, must be taken account of in the corporation's strategic decisions, including its distribution of the wealth that stakeholders have helped generate.

Those who adopt a model of corporate governance that enshrines the primacy of shareholders believe that corporations are the main engines for growth in industrialized societies but that a focus on stakeholders, many of which have conflicting needs, leads to a misallocation of resources and ultimately less help for those members of society who may need it most. The outcome of this might be to raise prices for consumers and/or lower the returns that shareholders could have earned (Friedman 1970; Shleifer and Vishny 1997; Hansmann and Kraakman 2001).

The scandals that rocked the UK in the 1980s and 1990s led to a need to restore public and investor confidence in the role of corporations to behave in a morally responsible manner. Faced with a threat of legislation, corporations have largely welcomed the code of conduct proposed by the Cadbury Committee (1992). However, following the findings of the Hampel Committee (1998) which itself was part review of the Cadbury Committee, there is a move away from what is seen by some as intrusive accountability towards the more familiar self-regulatory regime. Corporations, it is argued, need to be left alone to pursue their primary goal of business prosperity.

In 2008 the UK government was forced to use tax payers' money to take stakes in British banks, the Royal Bank of Scotland and Lloyds Banking Group to prevent their financial collapse. In 2010 the tax payer owned 43.4 per cent of Lloyds, acquired at an average price of 124.5p, and 70.3 per cent of RBS, bought at 51.2p. In common with the US investment bank Lehman Brothers, the Royal Bank of Scotland, and other financial institutions exemplified management arrogance by engaging in activities that were peripheral to their core activities. It is argued that it is not bad regulation of these institutions that caused the financial crisis but 'greedy and inept bank executives who failed to control activities which they did not understand' (Kay 2009).

The argument that banks cannot be allowed to remain 'too big to fail' has found support from the Governor of the Bank of England, Mervyn King. He argues there is merit in dividing retail and investment banking operations into separate, smaller businesses. That way, problems that arise in these individual elements do not jeopardize the whole. As such he would favour retail banks hiving off their riskier activities such as proprietary trading. In 2010 he argued that 'the system cannot be allowed to revert to its former ways as if nothing had happened. We must seize the opportunity for reform'.

Others have argued that what is required is better regulation that is fully coordinated across international boundaries to prevent such failures in the future. This coordination will protect consumers and the financial economy, preventing the need for government assistance. However, this approach is seen by some to be little more than wishful thinking. What is needed if we are to safeguard the economy and protect public finances is to ensure that the financial services needed by individuals and businesses are regulated while simultaneously refusing to underwrite risk-taking.

As long as banking groups know their activities will be underwritten by an implicit government guarantee, for them it becomes 'business as usual' (Kay 2009).

Kakabadse and Kakabadse (2001) in evaluating different corporate governance models argue that the pursuit of shareholders' interests leads to ever widening social inequalities. They suggest instead that:

> the governance debate needs to be pursued more at the societal/political level, rather than the enterprise level, as burning issues surrounding governance are ones of social inequality and not of transparency in reporting economic performance for the purpose of greater enterprise economic gain. (Kakabadse and Kakabadse 2001, p. xiv)

They argue that building and promoting positive community values in conjunction with the creation of wealth are the prime governance challenge in an age of globalization.

For a further discussion of the financial crisis and solutions that have been proposed go to the Online Resource Centre and see the Key Work feature. www.oxfordtextbooks.co.uk/orc/henry2e/

Summary

Corporate governance as a discipline is in a state of flux. A main debate within corporate governance concerns whether corporations should be run for the benefit of shareholders or stakeholders. Those who argue that corporations should be run for shareholders cite the fact that shareholders are the owners of the corporation and it is their money that is at stake. Those who argue the case for stakeholders are not convinced that stakeholders are simply a means to an end. They argue that suppliers, customers, employees, and, yes, shareholders must all be able to participate in determining the strategic direction of the corporation.

Following the collapse of major organizations, a number of codes of conduct have been implemented in the UK; these all seek to tighten accountability to shareholders. Sarbanes–Oxley has been implemented in the US following the collapse of the energy trading multinational corporation Enron. The collapse of Enron had repercussions for stock markets around the globe, and the fall-out left thousands of employees without work. The near collapse of the Royal Bank of Scotland and Lloyds Banking Group in the UK, Citigroup in the US, and the actual collapse of Lehman Brothers spread unrest in global financial markets. One could be forgiven for expecting that this cycle will simply repeat itself if nothing is done. The thinking that major banks are *too big to fail* and must be propped up by state intervention fails to factor in that this encourages unsustainable risk-taking. It will be interesting to watch corporate governance develop and monitor the direction that corporations take. It will also be interesting to see whether legislation and codes of conduct can ever be effective against corporate greed which stems from human nature.

Review Questions

1. Evaluate stakeholder and shareholder perspectives of corporations.
2. What is corporate social responsibility (CSR) and how have organizations sought to embrace it?

Discussion Question

Corporations should be run for the benefit of stakeholders. Discuss.

Research Topic

Identify the issues that led to the collapse of Lehman Brothers. Why were the corporate governance arrangements and the existing market regulation unable to prevent this collapse?

Recommended Reading

For a practical discussion of corporate governance see:

- **Cadbury, A.** (2002). *Corporate Governance and Chairmanship: A Personal View*. Oxford University Press, Oxford.
- **Monks, R.A.G.** and **Minow, N.** (2004). *Corporate Governance*, 3rd edn. Blackwell, Boston, MA.

A robust defence of shareholder primacy is provided by:

- **Friedman, M.** (1970). The social responsibility of business is to increase its profits. *New York Times Magazine*, 13 September 1970.
- **Sternberg, E.** (2000). *Just Business: Business Ethics in Action*, 2nd edn. Oxford University Press, Oxford.

The case for stakeholder theory is made by:

- **Freeman, R.E.** (1984). *Strategic Management: A Stakeholder Approach*. Pitman, Boston, MA.

For a discussion of agency theory see:

- **Jensen, M.C.** and **Meckling, W.H.** (1976). The theory of the firm: managerial behaviour, agency costs and ownership structure. *Journal of Financial Economics*, **3**(3), 305–60.
- **Fama, E.F.** and **Jensen, M.C.** (1983). The separation of ownership and control. *Journal of Law and Economics*, **88**(2), 301–25.

www.oxfordtextbooks.co.uk/orc/henry2e/
Visit the Online Resource Centre that accompanies this book for activities and more information on corporate governance.

online resource centre

Notes

1. Section 12.2 draws upon Cadbury (2002, Chapter 1).
2. These fundamental questions are discussed by the Caux Round Table, an organization of business leaders who seek to include moral responsibility within business decisions (www.cauxroundtable.org); see also Sternberg (2000) for an agency theory perspective.
3. Hermes believes that companies with active and informed investors will achieve superior returns over the long term. For more information on Hermes's approach to corporate governance, visit their website (www.hermes.co.uk).
4. Hermes Investment Management, Statement on Corporate Governance and Voting Policy, July 1998 (quoted in Cadbury 2002).
5. For an expanded version of the Cadbury Committee recommendations, see Cadbury (1992).
6. *Economist* (2004). Glaxo's big challenge. *Economist*, 13 May 2004.
7. *Financial Times* (2006a). Home Depot to review pay policy. *Financial Times*, 19 September 2006.
8. *Economist* (2005). Too many turkeys. *Economist*, 25 November 2005.
9. *Financial Times* (2006b). Escalating pay gap is socially divisive and economically harmful. *Financial Times*, 6 November 2006.
10. *Financial Times* (2006c). Immelt wades into debate over pay. *Financial Times*, 3 November 2006.

References

Armour, J., Deakin, S., and **Konzelmann, S.J.** (2003). Shareholder primacy and the trajectory of UK corporate governance. *British Journal of Industrial Relations*, **41**(3), 531–55.

12

Bank of England Annual Report (2010).

Baukol, R. (2002). Corporate governance and social responsibility. Available online at: www.cauxroundtable.org.

Berle, A.A. (1932). For whom are corporate managers trustees? *Harvard Law Review*, **45**, 1365–7.

Berle, A.A. and **Means, G.C.** (1932). *The Modern Corporation and Private Property*. Macmillan, New York.

Cadbury, A. (1992). *Report of the Committee on the Financial Aspects of Corporate Governance* (Cadbury Report). Gee, London.

Cadbury, A. (2002). *Corporate Governance and Chairmanship: A Personal View*. Oxford University Press, Oxford.

Charkham, J. (1998). Corporate governance: overcoded? Has Hampel meant progress? *European Business Journal*, **10**(4), 179–83.

Clark, R.C. (1986). *Corporate Law*. Little, Brown, Boston, MA.

Clarke, T. (1998). The contribution of non-executive directors to the effectiveness of corporate governance. *Career Development International*, **3**(3), 118–24.

Cyert, R.M. and **March, J.G.** (1963). *A Behavioural Theory of the Firm*. Prentice-Hall, Englewood Cliffs, NJ.

Demb, A. and **Neubauer, F.F.** (1992). *The Corporate Board: Confronting the Paradoxes*. Oxford University Press, New York.

Economist (2004). Glaxo's big challenge. *Economist*, 13 May 2004.

Economist (2005). Too many turkeys. *Economist*, 25 November 2005.

Economist (2006). Battle of the bourses. *Economist*, 25 May 2006.

Fama, E.F. and **Jensen, M.C.** (1983). The separation of ownership and control. *Journal of Law and Economics*, **88**(2), 301–25.

Financial Times (2006a). Home Depot to review pay policy. *Financial Times*, 19 September 2006.

Financial Times (2006b). Escalating pay gap is socially divisive and economically harmful. *Financial Times*, 6 November 2006.

Financial Times (2006c). Immelt wades into debate over pay. *Financial Times*, 3 November 2006.

Fombrun, C. and **Foss, C.** (2004). Business ethics: corporate responses to scandal. *Corporate Reputation Review*, **7**(3), 284–8.

Freeman, R.E. (1984). *Strategic Management: A Stakeholder Approach*. Pitman, Boston, MA.

Friedman, M. (1962). *Capitalism and Freedom*. University of Chicago Press, Chicago.

Friedman, M. (1970). The social responsibility of business is to increase its profits. *New York Times Magazine*, 13 September 1970.

Greenbury, R. (1995). *Directors' Remuneration* (Greenbury Report). Gee, London.

Gregg, S. (2001). *Corporations and Corporate Governance: A Return to First Principles*. Centre for Independent Studies, Sydney.

Gugler, K. (ed.) (2001). *Corporate Governance and Economic Performance*. Oxford University Press, Oxford.

12

Hampel, R. (1998). *Final Report: Committee on Corporate Governance* (Hampel Report). Gee, London.

Hansmann, H. and **Kraakman, R.H.** (2001). The end of history for corporate law. *Georgetown Law Journal*, **89**, 439.

Higgs, D. (2003). *Review of the Role and Effectiveness of Non-Executive Directors* (Higgs Report). Department of Trade and Industry, London.

Jensen, M. (2005). Value maximization, stakeholder theory and the corporate objective function. In *Corporate Governance at the Crossroads: A Book of Readings* (eds D.H. Chew and S.L. Gillan). McGraw-Hill Irwin, New York.

Jensen, M.C. and **Meckling, W.H.** (1976). The theory of the firm: managerial behaviour, agency costs and ownership structure. *Journal of Financial Economics*, **3**(3), 305–60.

Kakabadse, A. and **Kakabadse, N.** (2001). *The Geopolitics of Governance: The Impact of Contrasting Philosophies*. Palgrave, Basingstoke.

Kay, J. (2009) 'Too big to fail' is too dumb an idea to keep. *The Financial Times*, 28 October (online). Available at http://www.johnkay.com/2009/10/28/%E2%80%98too-big-to-fail%E2%80%99-is-too-dumb-an-idea-to-keep/

La Porta, R., Lopez-de-Silanes, F., Shleifer, A., and **Vishny, R.** (1998). Law and finance. *Journal of Political Economy*, **106**(6), 1113–55.

McLean, B. and **Elkind, P.** (2004). *The Smartest Guys in the Room*. Penguin, London.

Monks, R.A.G. and **Minow, N.** (2004). *Corporate Governance*, 3rd edn. Blackwell, Boston, MA.

O'Sullivan, M. (2003). Corporate governance: scandals, scoundrels, scapegoats and systems. *INSEAD Quarterly*, **4**, 6–8.

OECD (2004). *OECD Principles of Corporate Governance*. OECD Publications, Paris.

Roddick, A. (2000). *Business as Unusual*. Thorsons, London.

Shleifer, A. and **Vishny, R.** (1997). A survey of corporate governance. *Journal of Finance*, **52**(2), 737–83.

Spira, L.F. (2001). Enterprise and accountability: striking a balance. *Management Decision*, **39**(9), 739–47.

Sternberg, E. (1997). The defects of stakeholder theory. *Corporate Governance: International Review*, **5**(1), 3–10.

Sternberg, E. (2000). *Just Business: Business Ethics in Action*, 2nd edn. Oxford University Press, Oxford.

Time Warner Standards of Business Conduct (2010) Available at http://www.timewarner.com/corp/corp_governance/pdf/SBC_External_042910.pdf

Zandstra, G. (2002). Enron: board governance and moral failings. *Corporate Governance*, **2**(2), 16–19.

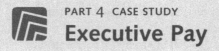

PART 4 CASE STUDY
Executive Pay

© David Simonds

Headlines about fat cats and executive snouts in troughs have been rare of late. But this week Cable & Wireless, an ailing British telecommunications company, revealed a plan to pay its top managers up to £220m ($415m). Just two months earlier, the firm had announced the loss of 3000 jobs. Cable & Wireless's bonus scheme sparked controversy because of its egregious size. But there are subtler shifts in the way bosses are rewarded elsewhere in corporate Britain that in many ways are more disturbing.

When the chief executives of Royal Bank of Scotland and Lloyds TSB, two of Britain's largest banks, missed out on bonus payments last year, members of the banks' compensation committees should have celebrated. It proved that pay had been successfully linked to performance. But instead of rejoicing, the pay committees of the two companies threw out their incentive plans and replaced them with new ones that look suspiciously as if they are designed to give managers an easier path to the trough.

Take Royal Bank of Scotland. In 2001 it presented shareholders with what was, for its time, a model incentive scheme. The plan, based on the premise that only exceptional performance should attract exceptional rewards, was designed to pay out only if two separate targets were met. First, earnings per share had to increase by 3 per cent above the rate of inflation each year. Second, the bank's share price and dividends had to rise by more than the median average of ten of its competitors.

Royal Bank's new share plan, introduced this year, splits the performance measures. Instead of having to hit both targets to earn any payment at all, executives can take a shot at either. Hitting one pays out half, hitting both pays in full. 'It gives them two bites at the cherry,' says Alan MacDougall of PIRC, a research and consulting firm that advises shareholders. Royal Bank of Scotland is not alone. Lloyds TSB has also introduced a split award, as has Barclays, another British bank.

Overall, just 37 per cent of new pay plans introduced in the past year by Britain's 350 biggest companies used shareholder return as the main measure of performance, down from 47 per cent a year earlier, according to Deloitte Touche Tohmatsu, an accounting firm. That is a sharp reversal of a trend. Over the preceding three years, the yardstick of relative performance grew in popularity; by 2004, it was the most commonly used measure, according to PIRC. So what accounted for the rise of this measure and what explains the abrupt demise of payment schemes based on it?

Relative measures of performance blossomed in the early years of this decade. A rash of accounting scandals, such as that at Enron, put a premium on corporate governance and the protection of shareholders' interests. Stock options, which were blamed for encouraging a culture of greed in America, became less fashionable. There was greed before stock options, but they are a deeply flawed method of rewarding executives. Because their value depends only on share prices, they reward bad bosses when markets are buoyant and punish good ones when markets fall.

But the fact that stock options fell from favour had as much to do with the market as it did with corporate scandals. With equity markets ailing, smart executives were quite happy to accept the new yardsticks. Relative performance measures, unlike options, can still pay out even when share prices are generally falling.

The bursting of the Internet bubble also gave investors the upper hand for a while. Large numbers of eager unemployed executives made it a buyers' market for shareholders, who began to dictate more onerous employment terms. That was reflected not just in the structure of incentive plans, but in pay inflation too. By last year, the rate of pay inflation for all executives in Britain's biggest companies was 7 per cent. That is much lower than it had been a few years earlier, points out Independent Remuneration Solutions, a consulting firm. In America, too, companies moved from stock options to incentives based on longer-term measures of performance.

But pay moderation among British executives may now be coming to an end. Hedge funds and private-equity deals are proliferating, bringing with them rewards that make the offerings from public companies look stingy. So remuneration committees are approving more generous schemes to retain their best executives.

Transplanting pay plans from private-equity firms to public companies is dangerous, not least because doing so confuses two quite separate issues: how much executives ought to be paid and what their incentives should be. Managers involved in buy-outs are usually expected to put some of their own money at risk. And it is far easier to fire an executive in a private company than in a public one. Big rewards in private-equity firms are in part supposed to compensate for bigger risk. But more important, private-equity investors typically have direct control of the companies they manage and are able to set targets and structure incentives that align managers' interests with their own.

Royal Bank of Scotland, Lloyds TSB, and Barclays say they decided to move away from relative performance measures because they can reward and punish executives for things beyond their control (such as the collapse of an incompetent or crooked rival). This is true, but it is also true that the new performance regimes tend to be less challenging than the ones they replaced. If executives miss one target there is a good chance they will be able to hit another. And, by moving from performance measures tested in tandem to solitary targets, companies make it easier for executives to manipulate performance to meet the target. An ill-advised acquisition, for instance, may boost earnings per share even as it causes the share price to fall.

Lastly, moving from measuring a company's performance against its rivals to using an absolute yardstick breaks the link between exceptional performance and exceptional reward. Because relative tests ask if executives are doing better than their rivals, they reduce the frequency of payments. Indeed, if all companies used them, only half of all bosses would get a payout in any given year.

On the other hand, when absolute performance tests are used executives simply have to clear a bar, and if it is set low enough they can all scamper over it. And that seems to be a rather frequent occurrence. Lloyds TSB, for example, asks only that its executives increase earnings per share by 3–6 per cent above inflation, which means they may collect at least a portion of their bonus for growing just a little faster than the economy as a whole.

The move from relative measures of performance to absolute ones is worrying for another reason. Whereas relative performance is easily understood, some of the measures replacing it are not. Already, targets are proliferating. Phone companies are choosing to target sales growth and water companies are aiming at customer satisfaction, say pay consultants. All may be worthy targets in their own right, but the net effect of such proliferation is to force shareholders to rely on the judgments and impartiality of board remuneration committees. If only they could. A survey by PIRC found that only 46 per cent of these committees are 'fully independent'. Snouts up, everybody.

Source: 'Lowering the bar' *Economist*, 18 May 2006.

▣ Questions

1. Why should a move from relative to absolute measures of performance be a cause for concern?

2. Board remuneration committees are there to ensure that directors receive an appropriate remuneration package. If they are doing their job why is there always such a furore about CEO pay?

3. Why might stakeholders be concerned that the remuneration of senior executives bears some relationship to the pay of an average employee in the organization?

Glossary

Accounting profit—measures the difference between the total revenue generated by the organization and its total cost. (Page 159)

Acquisition—when one organization seeks to acquire another, often smaller, organization. (Page 236)

Agency costs—the costs resulting from managers abusing their position as agent, and the associated costs of monitoring them to try to prevent this abuse. (Page 400)

Agency problem—this is inherent in the relationship between the providers of capital, referred to as the principal, and those who employ that capital on their behalf, referred to as the agent (see principal–agent problem). (Page 400)

Asymmetry of information—exists when the agents (managers) running a corporation have greater access to information than the principal (shareholders) by virtue of their position. (Page 398)

Balanced scorecard—provides managers with a more comprehensive assessment of the state of their organization. It enables managers to provide consistency between the aims of the organization and the strategies undertaken to achieve those aims. (Page 170)

Benchmarking—a continuous process of measuring products, services and business practices against those companies recognized as industry leaders. (Page 176)

BHAGs—big hairy audacious goals: goals that stretch the organization and are readily communicated to all its members. (Page 343)

Blue oceans—comprise untapped market space, demand creation, and the possibility of highly profitable growth. (Page 210)

Business strategy—deals with how an organization is going to compete within a particular industry or market. (Page 18)

Cash cow—a business which has a high market share in low-growth or mature industries. (Page 247)

Causal ambiguity—exists when the link between the resources controlled by an organization and its sustainable competitive advantage is not understood or only partially understood. (Page 146)

Chaos—an irregular pattern of behaviour generated by well-defined non-linear feedback rules commonly found in nature and human society. (Page 384)

Charismatic leaders—individuals who are dissatisfied with the status quo and who can articulate a vision that captures the imagination of their followers. (Page 376)

Competencies—can be defined as the attributes that firms require in order to be able to compete in the marketplace. (Page 132)

Competitive strategy—is concerned with the basis on which an organization will compete in its chosen markets. (Page 191)

Complementor—a player is a complementor if customers value your product more when they have that player's product than when they have your product alone. (Page 84)

Co-opetition—competitive behaviour that combines competition and cooperation. (Page 86)

Core competence or strategic capability—can be thought of as a cluster of attributes that an organization possesses which in turn allow it to achieve competitive advantage. (Page 133)

Core ideology—this is made up of core values and purpose. (Page 9)

Core values—an organization's essential and enduring tenets which will not be compromised for financial expediency and short-term gains. (Page 9)

Corporate governance—two definitions are provided: (1) the way in which organizations are directed and controlled, or (2) the process by which corporations are made responsive to the rights and wishes of stakeholders. (Page 392)

Corporate parent—refers to all those levels of management that are not part of customer-facing and profit-run business units in multi-business companies. (Page 226)

Corporate parenting—concerned with how a parent company adds value across the businesses that make up the organization. (Page 226)

Corporate social responsibility—is a recognition that organizations need to take account of the social and ethical impact of their business decisions on the wider environment in which they compete. (Page 50)

Corporate strategy—is concerned with what industries the organization wants to compete in. (Page 18)

Corporation—an organization owned by its shareholders but managed by agents on their behalf. (Page 395)

Cost-leadership strategy—is where an organization seeks to achieve the lowest-cost position in the industry without sacrificing its product quality. (Page 194)

Critical success factors—the factors in an industry that are necessary for a business to gain competitive advantage. (Page 254)

Differential firm performance—refers to the observation that firms which possess similar resources and operate within the same industry experience different levels of profitability. (Page 105)

Differentiation strategy—involves the organization competing on the basis of a unique or different product which is sufficiently valued by consumers for them to pay a premium price. (Page 197)

Discontinuities—threats faced by organizations that have the potential to undermine the way they do business. (Page 40)

Distinctive capabilities—are important in providing an organization with competitive advantage. They derive from three areas: an organization's *architecture*, *innovation*, and *reputation*. (Page 133)

Diversification—occurs when an organization seeks to broaden its scope of activities by moving into new products and new markets. (Page 229)

Dog—a business which has a low market share within a low-growth industry. (Page 247)

Durability—refers to the rate at which an organization's resources and capabilities depreciate or become obsolete. (Page 207)

Economic rent or economic profit—the surplus left over when the inputs to a productive process, which include the cost of capital being employed, have been covered. (Page 159)

Economic value added (EVA)—an attempt for organizations to include a more realistic profit figure. It is worked out by taking the difference between a company's operating profit after tax and its annual cost of capital, and discounting this to find out its present value. (Page 159)

Emergent strategy—where managers use their experience and learning to develop a strategy that meets the needs of the external environment. (Page 21)

Emotional intelligence—an ability to recognize your own emotions and the emotions of others. Emotional intelligence is manifest in self-awareness, self-regulation, motivation, empathy, and social skills. (Page 362)

Empathy—a willingness to consider the feelings of others when discussing and making decisions. (Page 363)

Entry mode strategies—the different types of strategy that organizations can use to enter international markets. (Page 284)

Evolutionary change—prolonged periods of growth where no major upheaval occurs in organizational practices. (Page 331)

First-mover advantages—refers to organizations which benefit from the learning and experience they acquire as a result of being first in the marketplace. (Page 133)

Five forces framework—tool of analysis to assess the attractiveness of an industry based on the strengths of five competitive forces. (Page 67)

Focus strategy—occurs when an organization undertakes either a cost or differentiation strategy but within only a narrow segment of the market. (Page 198)

Global strategy—the organization seeks to provide standardized products for its international markets which are produced in a few centralized locations. (Page 284)

Globalization—refers to the linkages between markets that exist across national borders. This implies that what happens in one country has an impact on occurrences in other countries. (Page 268)

Globally integrated enterprise—integrates value chain activities such as procurement, research, and sales on a global basis in order to produce its goods and services more efficiently. (Page 296)

Horizontal integration—occurs when an organization takes over a competitor or offers complementary products at the same stage within its value chain. (Page 230)

Hybrid strategy—this is where an organization is able to combine being a low cost producer with some form of differentiation. (Page 205)

Hypercompetition—where organizations aggressively position themselves against each other and create new competitive advantages which make opponents' advantages obsolete. (Page 97)

Industry—is determined by supply conditions and based on production technology. (Page 190)

Industry life cycle—suggests that industries go through four stages of development which include: introduction, growth, maturity, and decline. (Page 213)

Intangible resources—may be embedded in routines and practices that have developed over time within the organization. These include an organization's reputation, culture, knowledge, and brands. (Page 132)

Intended strategy—the strategy that the organization has deliberately chosen to pursue. (Page 21)

Internal development—sometimes referred to as organic growth. This involves the organization using its own resources and developing the capabilities it believes will be necessary to compete in the future. (Page 241)

International strategy—is based upon an organization exploiting its core competencies and distinctive capabilities in foreign markets. (Page 284)

Joint venture—when two organizations form a separate independent company in which they own shares equally. (Page 242)

Key success factors—elements in the industry that keep customers loyal and allow the organization to compete successfully. (Page 6)

Knowledge-based economy—the tacit knowledge and specialist skills of employees which constitute an intangible resource that is difficult for competitors to imitate. (Page 131)

Knowledge management—processes and practices through which organizations generate value from knowledge. (Page 150)

Leadership—is concerned with creating a shared vision of where the organization is trying to get to, and formulating strategies to bring about the changes needed to achieve this vision. (Page 354)

Linkages—the relationships between the way one value activity is performed and the cost or performance of another activity. (Page 112)

Locational advantages—The activities that go to make up an organization's value chain may be located in different countries to take account of differential costs and other locational advantages that a country may possess. (Page 274)

Management—is about coping with complexity to produce orderly and consistent results. (Page 354)

Market—is defined by demand conditions and based on an organization's customers and potential customers. (Page 190)

Market development—entering new markets with your existing products. (Page 229)

Market penetration—increase market share in your existing markets using your existing products. (Page 228)

Marketing mix—is a set of marketing tools commonly referred to as the 4Ps: product, price, place, and promotion. (Page 214)

Merger—occurs when two organizations join together to share their combined resources. (Page 236)

Mission—seeks to answer the question why an organization exists. (Page 9)

Mobility barriers—factors that prevent the movement of organizations from one strategic group to another. (Page 89)

Motivation—a desire to achieve for the sake of achievement. (Page 363)

Multidomestic strategy—is aimed at adapting a product or service for use in national markets and thereby responding more effectively to the changes in local demand conditions. (Page 284)

Organizational culture—the values and beliefs that members of an organization hold in common. (Page 344)

Organizational rigidity—an inability and unwillingness to change even when your competitive environment dictates that change is required. (Page 333)

Organizational routines—are regular, predictable and sequential patterns of work activity undertaken by members of an organization. (Page 207)

Organizational structure—the division of labour into specialized tasks and coordination between these tasks. (Page 314)

Parenting advantage—occurs when an organization creates more value than any of its competitors could if they owned the same businesses. (Page 250)

Path dependency—is a way of describing the unique experiences a firm has acquired to date as a result of its tenure in business. (Page 145)

Porter's diamond of national advantage—seeks to explain why nations achieve competitive advantage in their industries by using four attributes that exist in their home market. These are factor conditions, demand conditions, related and supporting industries, and firm strategy, structure, and rivalry. (Page 290)

Positioning—a view that strategy is about how an organization positions itself to mitigate the prevailing industry structure (five forces) that exists. (Page 67)

Primary activities—activities which are directly involved in the creation of a product or service. (Page 109)

Principal–agent problem—refers to the separation of ownership from control within corporations, where the owners (shareholders) are the principal but the control of the organization is by salaried managers who act as the agent. The problem is how to ensure that the agent acts in the best interest of the principal. (Page 158)

Product development—developing new products to sell in your existing markets. (Page 228)

Product life cycle—is a concept which states that products follow a pattern during which they are introduced to the market, grow, reach a maturity stage, and eventually decline. (Page 214)

Purpose—the reasons an organization exists beyond making a profit. (Page 12)

Question mark—(also known as 'problem child') a business which competes in high-growth industries but has low market share. (Page 247)

Realized strategy—the strategy that the organization actually carries out. (Page 21)

Related diversification—movement into an industry in which there are some links with the organization's value chain. (Page 230)

Replicability—is the use of internal investments to copy the resources and capabilities of competitors. (Page 208)

Resource-based view—emphasizes the internal capabilities of the organization in formulating strategy to achieve a sustainable competitive advantage in its markets and industries. (Page 130)

Resources—can be thought of as inputs that enable an organization to carry out its activities. They can be classified as tangible or intangible. (Page 131)

Revolutionary change—periods of substantial turmoil in organizational life. (Page 331)

Scenario—challenging, plausible, and internally consistent view of what the future might turn out to be. (Page 42)

Self-awareness—an ability to speak candidly about one's own emotions and the impact they have on one's work as well as their effect on others. (Page 362)

Self-regulation—recognition that as human beings we are driven by our emotions but we can also manage them and channel them for productive purposes. (Page 362)

Shareholder theory—a view of corporations that see shareholder interests as paramount. (Page 398)

Shareholders—individuals or groups who have invested their capital within an organization, and are therefore deemed to be the owners. (Page 158)

Social complexity—an organization's resources may be difficult to imitate because they may be based on complex social interactions. These may exist between managers in the organization, a firm's culture, and a firm's reputation with its suppliers and customers. (Page 146)

Social skills—the culmination of self-awareness, self-regulation, motivation, and empathy (emotional intelligence capabilities). (Page 363)

Stakeholder theory—a view of corporations which argues that corporations should be run in the interests of all stakeholders. (Page 401)

Stakeholders—are these individuals or groups which affect or are affected by the achievement of an organization's objectives. (Page 162)

Star—a business unit that is characterized by high growth and high market share. (Page 247)

Strategic alliances—when two or more separate organizations share some of their resources and capabilities but stop short of forming a separate organization. (Page 245)

Strategic business unit—is a distinct part of an organization which focuses upon a particular market or markets for its products and services. (Page 191)

Strategic change—the fit between an organization's resources and capabilities and its changing competitive environment. (Page 330)

Strategic group—a group of firms in an industry following the same or a similar strategy. (Page 88)

Structural uncertainties—where no probable pattern of outcomes can be derived from previous experience. (Page 42)

Substitutability—implies that there must be no strategically equivalent valuable resources that are themselves not rare or can be imitated. Two valuable firm resources (or bundles of resources) are strategically equivalent when they can be exploited separately to implement the same strategies. (Page 146)

Support activities—activities which ensure that the primary activities are carried out efficiently *and* effectively. (Page 109)

Sustained competitive advantage—occurs when an organization is implementing a value-creating strategy that is not being implemented by competitors *and* when these competitors are unable to duplicate the benefits of this strategy. (Page 144)

Synergy—occurs when the total output from combining businesses is greater than the output of the businesses operating individually. It is often described mathematically as $2 + 2 = 5$. (Page 227)

Tangible resources—refer to the physical assets that an organization possesses and include plant and machinery, finance, and human capital. (Page 131)

Theory E—assumes that organizational change should be based on enhancing shareholder value. (Page 378)

Theory O—assumes that change should help develop corporate culture and improve organizational capabilities. (Page 378)

Theory of the business—the assumptions that affect an organization's behaviour, the decisions about what and what not to do, and determine what an organization thinks are meaningful results. (Page 14)

Tipping point—an unexpected and unpredictable event that has a major impact on an organization's environment. (Page 42)

Transferability—refers to the ease with which a competitor can access the resources and capabilities necessary to duplicate an incumbent's strategy. (Page 207)

Transnational strategy—seeks to simultaneously achieve global efficiency, national responsiveness, and a worldwide leveraging of its innovations and learning. (Page 284)

Transparency—is the ease with which a competitor can identify the capabilities which underpin a rival's competitive advantage. (Page 207)

Unrelated diversification—a situation where an organization moves into a totally unrelated industry. (Page 232)

Valuable and rare resources—provide a means of competitive advantage. However, if the organization is to achieve sustainable competitive advantage, it is necessary that competing organizations cannot copy these resources. (Page 144)

Value chain—the activities within an organization that go to make up a product or service. (Page 107)

Value chain analysis—allows an organization to ascertain the costs and value that emanate from each of its value activities. (Page 107)

Value chain system—the relationship between the value chain activities of the organization and its suppliers, distributors, and consumers. (Page 107)

Value net—a map of the competitive game, the players in the game, and their relationship to each other. (Page 84)

Value or margin—the difference between the total value received by the firm from the consumer for its product or service and the total cost of creating the product or service. (Page 107)

Vertical integration—occurs when an organization goes upstream, i.e. moves towards its inputs, or downstream, i.e. moves closer to its ultimate consumer. (Page 230)

Vision—is often associated with the founder of an organization and represents a desired state that the organization aspires to achieve in the future. (Page 8)

Weak signals—barely perceptible changes in the external environment whose impact has yet to be felt. (Page 40)

Index